D0926502

Praise for *The Philanthropic Planning Companion*

"Brian and Robert have their finger on the pulse of not only how our donors are evolving, but what needs to be done to engage them to make meaningful transformative gifts for the future. We have adjusted our phone center and certain annual appeals to meet the needs of Leading Boomers, Younger Boomers, Gen X and Millennials, resulting in greater participation from younger donors. If you are a fundraiser in any area of development, I'd highly recommend reading this book."

—Gregory G. Dugard, Senior Director,
Office of Gift Planning, University of Notre Dame

"Advisors of all professions need to take the authors' comments about working together to heart. In 'Chapter 5: The Role of Professional Advisors,' the authors adroitly describe the non-adversarial role advisors should embrace. As an Investment Manager and Financial Planner, I believe in employing the full power of the team approach and my clients have certainly benefited. The authors describe the different types of potential philanthropists and their unique perspectives on giving to charity. This enlightening insight will definitely help me more carefully craft my approach to philanthropy when working with these different types of individuals."

—Douglas Lyons, CFA, CFP®, President, Trident Wealth Advisors

"Includes analysis and insight from two respected philanthropy professionals, plus the facts and figures to back them up. This is real-world, practical knowledge that no serious fundraiser can afford to ignore."

—Viken Mikaelian, founder and CEO of PlannedGiving.com

"*The Philanthropic Planning Companion* delves into the heart and soul of 'philanthropic planning' and lays out the essential elements for achieving success in reaching major and principal donors while maximizing the impact of their philanthropy through a donor-centric approach. This is not another technical manual describing the twists and turns of various charitable gift vehicles under the federal tax code—rather it is a comprehensive and well-documented guide that describes best practices for an integrated approach to working with philanthropists (and would-be philanthropists!)"

—Chris Yates, Associate Senior Vice President for
Major and Planned Gifts, University of Southern California

"*The Philanthropic Planning Companion* is a must-have resource for fundraisers. Not-for-profit organizations rely for their very survival on the information provided in *The Philanthropic Planning Companion*. Now you can get expert tips from two of the nation's top fundraisers, Brian Sagrestano and Robert Wahlers."

—Gail L. Freeman, President & founder,
Freeman Philanthropic Services, L.L.C., Retained
Executive Recruitment for the Not-for-Profit Sector

"*The Philanthropic Planning Companion* is terrific. A real asset to anybody seeking to build or enhance their gift planning program and a very timely addition to our professional resources."

—David L. Unruh, Senior Vice President,
Institutional Advancement, Temple University

"The Partnership for Philanthropic Planning evolved to emphasize that philanthropic planning is about helping donors make the most meaningful charitable gifts. Philanthropic planning can never be limited by tools, but also must use processes, assets, collaborations, and partnerships, to help donors be most effective in accomplishing their philanthropic goals. Sagrestano and Wahlers not only explain the case for this 'donor-centered, values-based' model, but give charitable planners and professional advisors practical advice for their own professional evolution. I'm glad these gentlemen have created such a wonderful resource."

—Michael Kateman, 2012 Chair, Board of Directors,
Partnership for Philanthropic Planning; Executive Director,
Development, Alumni and Public Relations, Columbia College

"With *The Philanthropic Planning Companion* Brian Sagrestano and Robert Wahlers share planned gift strategies that work with today's donors using contemporary techniques and tools. They have given our field the 'go-to guide' that brings philanthropic planning into the 21st century. I cannot recommend this book highly enough."

—John W. Hicks, CFRE, President and CEO, J.C. Geever, Inc.

The Philanthropic
Planning Companion

The AFP Fund Development Series

The AFP Fund Development Series is intended to provide fund development professionals and volunteers, including board members (and others interested in the nonprofit sector), with top-quality publications that help advance philanthropy as voluntary action for the public good. Our goal is to provide practical, timely guidance and information on fundraising, charitable giving, and related subjects. The Association of Fundraising Professionals (AFP) and John Wiley & Sons, Inc. each bring to this innovative collaboration unique and important resources that result in a whole greater than the sum of its parts. For information on other books in the series, please visit:

Association of
Fundraising Professionals

http://www.afpnet.org

The Association of Fundraising Professionals

The Association of Fundraising Professionals (AFP) represents over 30,000 members in more than 207 chapters throughout the United States, Canada, Mexico, and China, working to advance philanthropy through advocacy, research, education, and certification programs.

The association fosters development and growth of fundraising professionals and promotes high ethical standards in the fundraising profession. For more information or to join the world's largest association of fundraising professionals, visit www.afpnet.org.

2011-2012 AFP Publishing Advisory Committee

Benjamin T. Mohler, CFRE
Director of Development, UNC Charlotte
Robert J. Mueller, CFRE
Vice President, Gift Planning, Hospice Foundation of Louisville
Maria-Elena Noriega
Director, Noriega Malo y Asociados. S.C.
Timothy J. Willard, Ph.D., CFRE
Vice President of Development, Ranken Technical College

AFP Staff:
Rhonda Starr
Vice President, Education and Training
Reed Stockman
AFP Staff Support
Chris Griffin
Professional Advancement Coordinator
Jacklyn P. Boice
Editor-in-Chief, Advancing Philanthropy

John Wiley & Sons, Inc.:
Susan McDermott
Senior Editor (Professional/Trade Division)

The Philanthropic Planning Companion

The Fundraisers' and
Professional Advisors'
Guide to Charitable
Gift Planning

BRIAN M. SAGRESTANO, JD, CFRE

AND

ROBERT E. WAHLERS, MS, CFRE

WILEY

John Wiley & Sons, Inc.

Published by John Wiley & Sons, Inc., Hoboken, New Jersey.

Published simultaneously in Canada.

For general information on our other products and services or for technical support, please contact our Customer Care Department within the United States at (800) 762-2974, outside the United States at (317) 572-3993, or fax (317) 572-4002.

Wiley also publishes its books in a variety of electronic formats. Some content that appears in print may not be available in electronic books. For more information about Wiley products, visit our web site at www.wiley.com.

Library of Congress Cataloging-in-Publication Data:

Sagrestano, Brian M., 1969-
   The philanthropic planning companion : the fundraisers' and professional advisors' guide to charitable gift planning / Brian M. Sagrestano and Robert E. Wahlers.
        p. cm. – (The AFP Fund Development series)
      Includes bibliographical references and index.
   ISBN 978-1-118-00454-8 (hardback); ISBN 978-1-118-22184-6 (ebk);
   ISBN 978-1-118-23549-2 (ebk); ISBN 978-1-118-26033-3 (ebk)
  1. Fund raising. 2. Nonprofit organizations–Finance. 3. Charities. 4. Endowments.
  I. Wahlers, Robert E., 1965- II. Title.
  HV41.2.S24 2012
  658.15'224–dc23

                                                                        2012008097

Printed in the United States of America

10 9 8 7 6 5 4 3 2

To Christine, my partner in life—and in all things.
—Brian

To Denise, my friend and love, you continue to
support all that I do as we plan our lives together.
To Willow and Brock, my children, you
make me proud and constantly remind me
why energy and effort are important to success.
—Robert

Contents

Foreword

In the wonderful world of fundraising, organizations that take their universe of current and potential givers and focus their energies on the "top" tier of people come out winners every time. Not only is this the most logical approach, history has proven time and time again that the top people who are engaged, active, and thrilled to be attached to a charity will make large and often transformational gifts.

In *The Philanthropic Planning Companion,* Robert and Brian have taken an Etch A Sketch® to the traditional approach of raising planned gifts and have improved upon the winning major gift fundraising formula. Through their extensive analysis of the psychology and giving patterns of people who have made or have the potential to make gifts over each generation, coupled with the inclusion and involvement of professional advisors, the leadership of the organization, and all areas of the nonprofit's development program, this book is the new *reality forecaster* to raising gifts while meeting the needs of donors through philanthropic planning. Whether you are a fundraiser or professional advisor, the *Companion* will enlighten you about a collaborative process that leads to an integrated solution for your donor or client.

Over the years I have worked with and watched many nonprofits that were extremely happy and proud to have a solid bequest program, as well as the systems in place to capture large charitable trusts, annuities, and insurance policies. These were wonderful experiences and yes, for some, milestones to be celebrated. This book, for me, changed the paradigm and put gift planning on a whole new plateau, building on the past successes and now poised to be what the authors refer to as a first-time-ever "donor-centered philanthropic planning" approach.

I would take that concept a step further and say that this book *is* your "companion" to approach and focus with laser vision on the select group of individuals who can and want to give charities the "unbelievable and incredible" gifts that take organizations to new heights for years to come. These philanthropists are everywhere, and now you—as a fundraiser or advisor—will know exactly the right way to unleash the power and impact of their amazing and phenomenal gifts through philanthropic planning.

Laura Fredricks, JD
International Philanthropic Advisor
Author of *The ASK: How to Ask for Your*
Nonprofit Cause, Creative Project, or Business Venture

Preface

Humanity has always measured itself against time. As we evolved from hunter-gatherers toward a more stable existence where we developed agriculture and began to harmonize with nature, we used the shadows of the sun to mark the passage of our days. But to just react to what we stumbled upon was not wise. Instead we learned that planning yielded the best crops and outcomes. We could wish for good fortune, but if we could follow a planting calendar and use proven steps to success, our results could be assured. Time and planning could be used to our advantage.

On a visit to Monticello, the magnificent home of Thomas Jefferson that was a thriving agrarian estate in the late eighteenth and early nineteenth centuries, I was most amazed by the fact that at a time when nearly everyone told time by the position of the sun, Jefferson had a clock in the foyer of his home that was accurate to the second. As an educated man of many talents, he knew the value of planning and precision.

Performance and precision are the hallmarks of exceptional timepieces. Like the gears on our cover, every detail has its purpose, its function. This technical exactness is expressed through pure lines, perfect proportions, and timeless elegance along with precise craftsmanship of every part. While the arrow of a compass may only point north to orient you to your location, a precise watch can measure your most valuable commodity—time.

Knowledge grows over time, and wealth is built over time while passion can blossom over time. Just like the master watchmakers of Geneva, Switzerland, can design, develop, assemble, and create the ultimate tools for time through their craftsmanship, an astute team of professionals can design, develop, assemble, and create a plan for a family that will offer the precision of financial, estate, and philanthropic planning.

Like the complex and precise mechanism of an exceptional watch, a plan that is calibrated to match the wishes of a donor/client will run true. Knowledge, wealth, and passion for personal causes can come together to meet the needs of the individual and family to serve multiple generations over time. Philanthropic planning can be the tool to align those needs and wishes.

THE ROLE OF PHILANTHROPIC PLANNING

Philanthropic planning is a powerful way for individuals to give to the charities they believe in and care about to ensure the charity's long-term future, while also meeting personal planning objectives. It is an integrated solution meeting the needs of both the family and the charity for today and tomorrow, which makes charitable giving most meaningful.

Donor-centered philanthropic planning is an emerging model for raising funds. Instead of asking what individuals can do for particular charities, it asks what philanthropists need to accomplish for themselves, their families, and their futures. It seeks out what is really important to them in their lives. It then asks how charity can be integrated into their tax, estate, and financial planning to help meet these goals. The people and tools of philanthropic planning provide donors with the ability to meet both their personal planning objectives and their philanthropic goals to leave a more meaningful and lasting legacy.

OUR APPROACH

Using our combined experience in financial, estate, tax, and gift planning, we will explore the new donor-centered, values-based model of philanthropic planning. Paying respect to the traditional approach that has brought the sector this far, we will explain the need for the next step in the evolution of gift planning and help nonprofit and for-profit practitioners to meet the needs of the next generations of donors, who we refer to as the New Philanthropists.

Gift planning is a young and quickly evolving field. In its short history, it has also been known as deferred giving, planned giving, legacy giving, future giving, and philanthropic planning. Originally focused on obtaining gifts from the elderly and wealthy, it now focuses on those engaged by the mission of the charity, commonly referred to as loyals and assisting them in creating gifts that meet the long-term needs of charities. As the field has evolved, a broad range of practitioners working in both the nonprofit and for-profit sectors has become involved in helping philanthropists create legacies. At the same time, it has become clear that charitable mission is the true motivator of charitable gifts, not the tools, gift vehicles, or tax benefits of making these gifts.

The turbulent economic circumstances of recent years and changes in the generational makeup of the donor population have substantially altered the gift planning landscape. The National Committee on Planned Giving recently adopted a new name, the Partnership for Philanthropic Planning, to reflect the fundamental changes in the industry. Unfortunately, there is limited literature explaining the implications of these changes, and most of the writings on planned giving are out of date, based upon a decades-old model. We will illustrate how a donor-centered, philanthropic planning approach is required in order to meet the needs of the New Philanthropists.

Over the last 20 or so years, we have both worked closely with professional advisors and fundraisers. We have had both successes and failures, learned from our mistakes, and honed our skills in the field. Our formal education has served us well while our experience has allowed us to amass an understanding of the many different perspectives that look upon philanthropy. We have met and nurtured relationships with donors and advisors and have become accustomed to the differing personalities and the varying motivations that shape the discussions around philanthropic planning.

We have written this book with two audiences in mind—nonprofit fundraisers (particularly those dedicated to gift planning or philanthropic planning) and professional advisors.

For fundraisers, we hope to raise the sightline for their work to a level that would encourage a higher plane of activity for those 10 percent of philanthropists who give 90 percent of all individual gifts. This concept has become the foundation of activity for principal and major gift officers who have found greater success in dealing with fewer donors in a more meaningful way. Strategies that foster personalized attention to philanthropists with a budding passion for their favorite organizations can bloom into a bouquet of giving that is exciting for both the philanthropist and organization alike.

For professional advisors, we know that there are some who have embraced the comprehensive approach that encompasses the multiple facets of a client's situation and portfolio. Many of you have joined Advisors in Philanthropy and sought out the Chartered Advisor in Philanthropy or Certified Wealth Consultant designations.

If you are one of the fortunate few who manage your client's entire list of assets, then you are perhaps already working with them in all areas of their planning, but as we have found, most advisors have only come to know their clients through one piece of their puzzle. Perhaps it was through their retirement planning or through their estate planning. Perhaps it was a broader approach through financial planning or it came as a result of a risk assessment related to life insurance or it could have been due to their need for tax planning. Whatever the point of entry, an opportunity to work with your client from a comprehensive planning approach would not only help your client to consider gaps or other areas that may need attention, but it also may lead to additional business and greater assets under management.

USING THE COMPANION

Throughout its chapters, the *Companion* will disseminate and analyze the latest research focused on donor behavior and discuss the need for novel approaches to charitable gift planning. We like to use lists so you'll see that we often employ them to convey information quickly and efficiently. We will offer a perspective from our experience that you can put into practice right away to increase your success.

The book is divided into four sections:

- *The Emergence of Philanthropic Planning*
- *Working with Philanthropists*
- *Marketing to Prospects and Those Interested in the Mission*
- *Program Infrastructure*

In *The Emergence of Philanthropic Planning*, we present the evolution of the gift planning field over its history. We define the New Philanthropists and introduce the Philanthropic Planning Pyramid of donors, illustrating the four tiers of prospects and how each should be approached. We explain how fundraisers, professional advisors, board members, and volunteers need to work collaboratively with the New Philanthropists in a philanthropic planning model.

The second part of the book, *Working with Philanthropists,* outlines how an integrated, donor-centered, values-based, philanthropic planning approach can be implemented among charities, professional advisors, and philanthropists to meet the charitable and personal planning objectives of the top 10 percent of all philanthropists, what have commonly been referred to as principal (tier one) and major gift (tier two) donors. For most fundraisers and professional advisors, the philanthropic planning methodology represents a fundamental shift in approach to this group, but one that should produce larger and more meaningful gifts, as well as enhanced estate and financial plans, for the philanthropists involved.

The terms philanthropist, donor, client, donor/client, and prospect are used interchangeably throughout the fundraising and planning industry. To provide clarity, we will mainly use the term philanthropist to describe those donors/clients who are engaged in the process of philanthropic planning. At other times, when referring to donors or prospects, we are speaking of the other 90 percent who make gifts to their favorite charities, and when referencing clients, we are speaking of those people that are working with professional advisors who have yet to come to know about philanthropic planning and its comprehensive approach.

The third part of the book, *Marketing to Prospects and Those Interested in the Mission,* suggests how charities should approach tiers three and four of the Philanthropic Planning Pyramid. This donor-centered, moves management system of gift planning outreach to the loyal donors and those with an interest in the mission allows fundraisers to continue to build their pipeline of prospects without the same intensity of personal visits and relationship building utilized for the top two tiers in the philanthropic planning process. It is a program designed for the 90 percent of prospects that contribute to the success of charities, but who are not able or are unwilling to make more significant gifts.

Part Three also introduces our seven touches philosophy, detailing how to reach this broad audience and engage them and their families in the mission of the charity now and in the future. We discuss the impact of changing technology and social media, suggesting methods to adapt this technology to reach Generation X and Millennials. For professional advisors, we highlight charitable methods that fundraisers will be using to help donors/clients meet personal planning objectives such as *increasing income in retirement* or *crafting a meaningful legacy* while also being charitable, allowing them to see the potential in all of their clients who have charitable intent.

The final section, *Program Infrastructure* provides the architecture to charities for building a donor-centered gift planning component as an integrated part of their fundraising effort. Too often gift planning has been separated out from the rest of the fundraising operation and is seen as the purview of experts. To be effective, donor-centered gift planning is the responsibility of all of the players involved—donors, professional advisors, volunteers, board members, and professional fundraisers. Successful fundraising programs have an effective infrastructure to support this fundraising approach. The tools in this section will ensure charities can sustain their philanthropic planning and gift planning efforts long term.

*   *   *

As time passes and the New Philanthropists become dominant, a new, donor-centered, philanthropic planning paradigm will emerge from the traditional field of gift planning. Professional advisors and fundraisers need a companion to help all philanthropists, and particularly the New Philanthropists, create the same type of precision plans found in a quality time piece. *The Philanthropic Planning Companion* provides this guidance, demonstrating how a donor-centered, values-based philanthropic planning philosophy is created, maintained, and utilized and how it will enhance and sustain the mission of the charities supported as well as meet the personal planning objectives of the philanthropists involved.

Acknowledgments

W hen you write your first book, there are so many people who have helped you along the way in your career that it is impossible to name them all. We have had the privilege to know and work with some of the finest gift planners and professional advisors in the industry and thank each and every one of you. These acknowledgements are not complete without an expression of gratitude to our past and current donors, employers, and clients. Their faith and trust in us has been humbling and provided us with opportunities we never thought possible. Their gift planning programs have been the source of many of the stories found throughout this book, and we feel their successes and challenges as our own. It is through our work together that many of the ideas herein were refined and honed. This book belongs as much to you as it does to us.

FROM BRIAN M. SAGRESTANO

My career in charitable gift planning almost seemed predestined. I started working with my parents, Loretta and Montoro Sagrestano, at our family CPA practice when I was just a little boy and learned a great deal about both taxes and hard work. Dad was the first one from his family to go to college, and he went for free to City College (now Baruch) in New York City and then finished at Rutgers University. It was the power of that experience that led me to become a charitable gift planner, in the hopes that I could help educational institutions raise enough endowment dollars so that higher education could be available to all those who sought it, regardless of their ability to pay. It is perhaps fitting that since starting my consulting practice, I have had the opportunity to help both of those institutions with their gift planning programs.

My love of tax and estate planning was cemented at the University of Notre Dame Law School by Professors Matthew Barrett and Carol Ann Mooney, now president of St. Mary's College in Notre Dame, Indiana. They taught me that a tax and estate planning practice was about more than the Internal Revenue Code—it was about people. They also taught me that doing the right thing always trumped the easy or convenient thing. Morals and ethics are a part of everything we do for our clients and donors.

My very first legal job was as the law clerk to the Hon. Marilyn Rhyne Herr, JSC, a judge, lawyer, and friend. Together we worked with Hunterdon County, New Jersey, Surrogate Susan J. Hoffman. We saw many estates, most of them unplanned. We saw families in conflict because information had not been shared. We saw potential unfulfilled.

Diane McConnell, JD, was the first estate planner to truly take me under her wing. Working for Diane I found my passion for non-profit work, helping administer an estate which would ultimately benefit the Nature Conservancy. It tied together my education and values into a career I could believe in.

When I first considered the transition to a career in charitable gift planning, Ben Madonia, director of planned giving at Hamilton College, served as my guide and mentor, sharing a lifetime of experiences. Brian Sischo, then director of major gifts at Clarkson University and now associate vice president at Syracuse University, gave me my first job.

The initial opportunity I had to shape my own program was at Middlebury College, a wonderful liberal arts college in Vermont. I worked with some exceptional people who kept the focus on donors rather than the tools of gift planning, most notably Ann Jones-Weinstock, Ann Crumb, Kelly Kerner, and Terry Mayo. Ann was the first to introduce me to the idea of donor-centered fundraising, where the needs of the donor came first.

The impetus for many of the stories and strategies found in this book were from my time running the gift planning program for the University of Pennsylvania. I worked for two gentlemen, John Zeller and Tom Farrell, who provided the support and resources that allowed me to take Penn's gift planning program in entirely new directions. It was at Penn that the idea for a donor-centered, moves management-based gift planning marketing program, which provides the basis for much of the second part of this book, was created and tested with my colleague Colleen Elisii. It was also working with Penn donors that I had the opportunity to experiment with many of the ideas for working with principal and major donors using a philanthropic planning approach, which are found in the first part of this book. I would be remiss not to thank the other members of my team at Penn, including Pat Wiseley, Lorleen Maxwell, Tamra Dunston, Rebecca Cordner, J. Michael Washburn, Meaghan Hogan, Deb Layton, Lynn Malzone Ierardi, Greg Johnson, Frank Barr, and Janine Eshani, for their help and dedication building that program, for which I am forever grateful.

When I left Penn to start Gift Planning Development, LLC, I had the good fortune to get help and advice from some of the best in the industry, my dear departed friend Deb Blackmore Abrams, Kathryn Miree, Viken Mikaelian, Sam Caldwell, and Caleb and Trish Rick. They provided me with excellent suggestions and direction which have allowed me to serve the charitable community.

Over my career, I have had the opportunity to serve on a wide range of volunteer committees and boards for the Partnership for Philanthropic Planning, the Partnership for Philanthropic Planning of Greater Philadelphia, the Gift Planning Council of New Jersey, the Journal of Gift Planning and Planned Giving Mentor, among others. I learned a great deal from each of those experiences and each of those with whom I served. While there are too many to name, you know who you are and I appreciate the opportunity to have worked with and learned from you.

To my friend, colleague, and co-author Robert E. Wahlers, CFRE, this book would not exist without your suggestion that we do it together and your dedication to the project. I am fortunate to have met you many years ago and to have worked with you on this project. Thank you for thinking of me.

Finally, to my wife Christine and my four children, Katherine, Sophia, Holly, and Luke, to whom I owe so much: You have tolerated the many nights when I have been away to work with charities, the weekends when I am holed up in my office writing when we should be swimming at camp, playing outside, or just spending time together. When you bring me fresh-baked cookies or just stop by for a hug on your way from one activity to the next, you remind me of why the work I do is important and of the sacrifices you make so that I can do it. Know that you inspire me and I love you with all my heart.

FROM ROBERT E. WAHLERS

My career in the financial services industry was where I learned the value of planning. I am grateful to Frank Congilose, CFP, CLU, ChFC, who first showed me that doing what's right for your client is worth doing. He and my colleagues at Congilose & Associates regularly discussed and debated strategies around financial and estate planning. Frank taught us that a comprehensive approach can be beneficial to our clients in that it allows them to consider the total sum of their situation when making a decision and not just a product to fit a part. Frank also encouraged giving back in the community and Scouting was one of the places that I volunteered. It reminded me that service can be a wonderful outlet in your life. I'm indebted to my Mom and Dad who taught me by example. Mom through her service to my school and our community, and Dad through his tremendous work ethic.

I thoroughly enjoyed my time in Scouting with the Jersey Shore Council, BSA. As I reflected on my situation and being an Eagle Scout, I felt a real calling to work for the benefit of a higher goal and Scouting offered me that opportunity. Jere Williams, CFRE, Bill Davis, and Rick Garland were early fundraising mentors as they showed me how character and integrity are important ingredients in soliciting funds for a cause. Jere and Bill encouraged my first annual and major gift asks and taught me much about nonprofit administration. Jere also allowed me to take on the responsibility of planned giving and endowment support that was a perfect transition from my training and experience in financial services. He also introduced me to Ron Carroll and Robert Sharpe, Jr. With all that the Boy Scouts of America has developed, I learned to follow the plan and it taught me the basics. Steve Simmonds, JD, recognized my talents and involved me in training others in fundraising conferences and the first National Endowment Seminar where I could collaborate with fellow Certified BSA Fundraising Executives to advance what was being developed. John Kline, CFRE, and I had great discussions about what was working for him in Baltimore while I built the program at Jersey Shore.

Karen Radwin and RandE Chase, CFRE, then gave me an opportunity to work for the American Cancer Society where I could shape the program of planned giving for New Jersey. I worked with several colleagues including Frank Mascia, Roseann Weber, Lynne Jones, CFRE, and Michael

Baker, CFRE, who were tremendous supporters as we worked to bring in gifts for ACS. Together we developed several exciting gifts in a collaborative effort. I also met Peter Witherell, who along with the National Planned Giving Marketing Workgroup at American Cancer Society, helped to shape my ideas around marketing to planned giving donors and professional advisors. Peter led the design and implementation of the National Professional Advisors Network that was one of the best tools I had seen to cultivate and develop relationships with professional advisors. I used it extensively to open doors in New Jersey and New York City and when I left ACS was proud to have met with more than 571 professional advisors. Thank you Peter for your friendship, professionalism, and leadership of our work for ACS.

I am also grateful to Paul Hansen, CFP, CLU, CSPG, CAP, who showed me the value of collaboration with professional advisors. As I'll explain at a later point in the book, I met Paul with my approach to advisors and he has impressed me ever since with his knowledge of gift planning and his commitment to the nonprofit sector in his work as a financial expert. Paul has introduced me to so many outstanding individuals and continues to be a friend to philanthropy.

My journey has given me the great pleasure to meet and work with many colleagues through both the Association of Fundraising Professionals in New Jersey and at the national level—Steve Ryan, CFRE; Hilary Brown Kruchowy, CFRE; Kimberly Armenti; Kwi Nam Brennan, CFRE; Michael Baker, CFRE; John Carno, CFRE; Anthony Alonzo; Michael Rosen; John Hicks, CFRE; Laura Fredricks, JD; Bill Sturtevant; Andrea Nierenberg; Rhonda Starr; John Joslin, CFRE; and Andrew Watt—and with the Gift Planning Council of New Jersey—including Tim Throckmorton, JD; James Dawson, JD; and Andrew Grumet, JD—and the Partnership for Philanthropic Planning where I have had the pleasure to be associated with and learn from Bryan Clontz, CFP; Jon Ackerman, Esq., Erik Dryburgh, Esq.; Jay Steenhuysen; and Bill Samers, JD. And more recently, I have enjoyed working with Stephen Levy, CFRE through our work on the faculty at Columbia University in the Masters of Fundraising Management Program. I greatly appreciate all these relationships along with many others that I have not mentioned.

Through AFP, I also came to know David Flood, who offered me an opportunity to join him at Meridian Health to build the gift planning program that Brian had started years earlier. David has revitalized my perspective on relationship building and doing for others. He along with Carrie Boardwick, CFRE, and the rest of the staff have all shown me what it is to be a team. And Board leaders Mollie Giamanco, Tom Kononowitz, Peter Cancro, Phil Perricone, Scott Ferguson, and Karen Goldblatt have reminded me how much fun it can be to fundraise for a meaningful cause. I am also grateful for my budding relationship with Fred Schoenbrodt, Jr., Esq. and Brian Appel who Co-Chair the Meridian Philanthropic Planning Council. Together we have put many of the ideas in this book into practice as we work with philanthropists, donors/clients, and professional advisors.

To my friend and co-author Brian M. Sagrestano, JD, CFRE, who shared the vision for this book as someone who knows the importance of philanthropic planning and has had great success in building Gift Planning Development, LLC, around the principle of donor-centered gift planning, my thanks for your friendship and professional support and for joining me in this worthwhile project.

My greatest appreciation goes to my wife Denise and my two children, Willow and Brock, who have endured the many nights and weekends of my writing when they would rather have had me helping with homework, attending soccer games, or playing a game, and just being a husband and dad. Thank you for the coffee milkshakes and hugs. You all have sacrificed for me to follow my calling of working in the nonprofit sector. All my love and thanks for your unending support.

* * *

There have been many who contributed ideas and materials to this book. We have done our best to call each of them out in the section of the book where their thoughts, creativity, and original ideas are noted. If we missed any, we are truly sorry, as a book is really just a collection of ideas from the authors and from those who influenced our thinking, and we thank you for it.

We hope that by writing the *Companion*, we have brought together all of those great ideas in a single place and in a format that is useful to fundraisers and professional advisors alike.

PART ONE

The Emergence of Philanthropic Planning

Philanthropy is defined by Webster's as "works or endeavor, as charitable aid or endowments, intended to increase the well-being of humanity."[1] The etymology literally translates to "loving mankind." Throughout its history, the United States has fostered a sense, or a culture, of philanthropy. Rather than rely upon the government to meet the needs of others, those who could afford to make a gift provided for the common good. This approach contrasts sharply with Europe, where the government has a much more significant role in providing for the poor, funding research, providing social supports, and more.

The basic idea that people should help and support one another is a core tenet of philanthropy in the United States. While that culture has always existed, it has evolved over time from a very basic, simple idea of those with more supporting those with less, to a complex system of laws and charitable giving incentives which allow those who are so inclined to make charitable gifts which meet their own needs while also supporting the charities about which they are passionate.

The first part of the *Companion* reviews how from the time of Benjamin Franklin to today the fundraising marketplace has evolved. It starts in Chapter 1 with a short history of fundraising and how different donor views, shaped by generational cohorts, impact how Americans view philanthropy. Chapter 2 discusses the living generational cohorts and how the events occurring during their formative years have shaped their world view and their views on philanthropy. It identifies the "New Philanthropists," those born since 1946, whose giving behavior is proving to be motivated by different factors than the generations which came before them. Building on donor behavior, Chapter 3 outlines how charities should identify the best prospects within these cohorts, using the Philanthropic Planning Pyramid and donor loyalty to create a fundraising matrix which can be used to determine the best prospects to approach and the sequence to approach them. Addressing the role of the Board of Trustees and volunteers, Chapter 4 discusses the critical need to engage leadership in the philanthropic planning process. New Philanthropists will not give to charities unless they have a firm belief in the mission and can readily identify the dedication of the Board for carrying out that mission. The final chapter in Part I outlines the role of professional advisors in the philanthropic planning process. It suggests ways that advisors and fundraisers need to work together in the philanthropic planning process to ensure the personal planning and charitable goals of the prospect are met.

CHAPTER 1

The Changing Fundraising Marketplace

There has been significant evolution in the fundraising marketplace over the last 250 years. When Benjamin Franklin, considered by many to be the father of fundraising in the United States, started his first *subscriptions* (the precursor of the *capital campaign*), he noted that people give because they want to achieve a goal. He warned against asking just those who the charity believes will give, and reminded charities not to "over-solicit". He understood that donors made gifts because they wanted to create impact or achieve a long-term outcome.[2]

The Great Depression brought with it great demands on the charitable sector. With such a range of needs, donors learned to trust charities to put gifts to work where the need was greatest. The Traditionalists (people born pre-1946), made up of the Depression Cohort, the World War II Cohort, and the Post-War Cohort, grew up in this culture and it shaped giving over their lifetimes. In the 1960s, when the Older and Younger Baby Boomers were in their formative years, they developed an inherent distrust for the establishment, including charitable causes. This distrust grew with Generation X and the Millennials who followed them. Chapter 2 will provide detailed information about these generational cohorts and their behaviors.

In the approach to retirement, as the Older Boomers have sought for more meaning in their lives, they have engaged with charities in dramatic ways. This involvement though, has been fundamentally different than that of the Traditionalists. Because the Older Boomers still distrust charities, they demand accountability. They limit their unrestricted giving compared to the Traditionalists and they have returned to Franklin-era values by

demanding to see the impact and long-term outcomes of their philanthropy and asking for both accountability and verifiability. They also seek
to integrate their philanthropy into their overall tax, estate, and financial
planning.

Most fundraising programs today were built during the height of giving
from the Traditionalists. Their methodology and systems were built around
the needs of the charity rather than focusing on the goals and objectives of
the donors. As the Older and Younger Boomer Cohorts have reached their
peak earning and giving years with a fundamentally different approach to
philanthropy, charities have been slow to adapt their methodology and
systems to meet the needs of these generational cohorts, attempting to fit
them into a giving model designed for the Traditionalists.

For charities that want to continue to ignore this change in donor motivation, the news only gets worse. Generation X and the Millennials not
only want to see the impact and outcomes from their philanthropy, they
also want to be meaningfully engaged in shaping the programs they
support. Those charities which cannot adapt will find that they have been
left behind or passed by charities which meet the needs of their donors
using a donor-centered, philanthropic planning approach.

THE EVOLUTION FROM DEFERRED GIVING TO PHILANTHROPIC PLANNING

From the advent of the first fundraising programs, donors were asked to
include the charity as a will beneficiary. These deferred giving programs
were focused heavily on meeting the needs of the charity without a great
deal of concern for the donor. As early as the seventeenth century, the
Reformed Church offered the first charitable gift annuity as a means for
donors to make a gift and receive income back, largely as an enticement to
get the gift in the door.

When an income tax was passed in 1917, it permitted individuals to
deduct charitable contributions, but this incentive mainly encouraged
annual giving. Its purpose was to avoid individuals paying income tax on
monies that they were voluntarily giving to charity and for which they
would get no benefit themselves.

When Congress passed the Tax Reform Act of 1969, it codified
deferred giving options beyond the charitable bequest and charitable gift

annuity, such as the charitable remainder trust. The focus of deferred giving programs moved from the needs of the charity to the selection of the right charitable giving vehicle or tool and the tax benefit of the particular gift form. Robert E. Sharpe, Sr. coined the term *planned giving* for the industry, highlighting the change in approach from gifts that would mature in the future to gifts which required an element of tax planning. A common definition for planned giving has been the integration of sound personal, financial, and estate planning concepts with the individual donor's plans for lifetime or testamentary giving. As a complimentary fundraising activity, it helped individuals with charitable intent to make the largest gift possible with the right asset, in the most advantageous form, and at the most appropriate time. At least that was the idea.

The 1990s saw the advent of the *gift planning* program. Gift planning programs put the focus on meeting the needs of the donor in a *donor-centered* approach, rather than pursuing the needs of the charity first or the gift vehicle involved. The Partnership for Philanthropic Planning (PPP, formerly the National Committee on Planned Giving or NCPG) defined *charitable gift planning* as the process of cultivating, designing, facilitating, and stewarding gifts to charitable organizations. The PPP definition states that charitable gift planning:

- Uses a variety of financial tools and techniques for giving.
- Requires the assistance of one or more qualified specialists.
- Utilizes tax incentives that encourage charitable giving, when appropriate.
- Covers the full spectrum of generosity by individuals and institutions, and is based on powerful traditions of giving in the United States.[3]

FROM STRUCTURE TO PLANNING

The charitable gift planning model incorporates the very best of the deferred giving and planned giving programs of the past while meeting the needs of the donor using a donor-centered approach. In May 2007, the NCPG Strategic Directions Task Force issued a report on the needs of the gift planning industry going forward. The task force, led by Chris Yates, then of Stanford University (now at the University of Southern

(continued)

California), found that "Sophisticated planned giving officers have changed their emphasis from structure of the gift to impact, becoming more donor-centered and holistic in their approach. Planned giving is being incorporated in a "cycle" of philanthropy."[4]

While a few sophisticated charities today utilize this model, many more traditional non-profits still use the older planned giving and deferred giving models. Regrettably, these three terms are often used interchangeably in the industry, so prospects and professional advisors have no real way to know if the charity involved is focused on the needs of the charity, the tools, or the donor.

To complete the transformation to philanthropic planning, particularly for the top 10 percent of all donors, these models need to take the next step of integrating charitable gift planning with the needs of Older and Younger Boomers, Gen X, and Millennial donors in a more sophisticated way that not only helps them meet their charitable goals, but also integrates their philanthropy into their tax, estate, and financial planning using a comprehensive strategy. Not only does such an approach make it more likely that donors will maximize their philanthropy, it also ensures that they will craft a more meaningful legacy for their families and the charities they support.

It will require charities to develop significant relationships with their donors to understand what impact they want to have today, what outcomes they hope to achieve for tomorrow, and what legacy they desire to create during their lifetimes and beyond.

In order to reach this goal, charities can no longer work directly with donors without involving professional advisors. Professional advisors have access to the important details about their client's tax, estate, and financial planning. Their expertise is critical to the philanthropic planning matrix. Charities, donors, and professional advisors must work collaboratively to coordinate all of the different variables to fully integrate donor wishes into overall planning. When such an approach is implemented, the result is the creation of overall plans that:

- Meet donor personal planning goals.
- Reinforce and pass donor values to future generations.

- Create meaningful legacies for the donor, the donor's family, and the charities the donor supports.

These combined charitable, estate, and financial plans will be tax efficient and values based, ensuring that the donor/client is able to realize a vision of philanthropy. This philanthropic planning model can be illustrated graphically as follows:

$$\frac{\text{Gift Planner} + \text{Professional Advisors} + \text{Philanthropic Planning}}{\text{Donor with Charitable Intent}} = \text{Philanthropy}$$

The model depicts a planning situation where a donor/client with charitable intent is the common denominator and a gift planner (or fundraiser) working with the donor's professional advisors can complete a philanthropic planning process that leads the donor to become a philanthropist.

CASE STUDY   THE TWO-LAWYER FAMILY

Using the philanthropic planning model, I met a wonderful couple from Washington DC who wished to support the work of a particular charity. The husband and wife were transactional lawyers from the Older Boomer cohort, but freely admitted that they were not estate planning experts. Both were divorced with children from the past marriages, but had no children together. Neither one had a current will, but the wife had an old estate plan in place that still named her prior husband.

As the charitable gift planner, my first role was to discuss their interest in our charity. It became apparent very quickly that they truly believed in the mission of the charity and had several ideas about how they might perpetuate that mission going forward.

With two of the four variables in the Philanthropic Planning Model accounted for, we began a series of meetings where I used questionnaires to guide them through a process of self discovery, which will be discussed in detail in Chapter 6. During that time, the couple discovered that they had slightly different values and plans for their children. It was clear that until we could overcome this obstacle, we would be at an impasse.

Seeing an opportunity, at this stage I asked if we could bring their own advisors to the table to discuss how to implement their

(continued)

goals for themselves, their children, for passing their values, and for our charity.

Approximately nine months later, the family set up a complex estate plan that accounted for their blended family, the different values and inheritances they wanted to pass to their children, and their joint interest in supporting our charity.

Only with all four elements of the Philanthropic Planning Model could we complete a meaningful charitable gift. When one part was missing, the process stalled. — BMS

The Philanthropic Planning Model takes into account the many variables required to turn a regular donor into a philanthropist. It can be more time consuming than the typical gift or estate planning discussion, but the rewards will far outweigh the additional time required to complete the process. Once charities and advisors learn to work within this Model, it will increase gifts, donor satisfaction, and the efficacy of overall planning.

In Summary

The fundraising model has become more donor-centered over the last 250 years to meet the needs of different generational cohorts. With the emergence of the New Philanthropists, charities and advisors need to adopt a Philanthropic Planning Model for the top 10 percent of their donors. This planning process produces an integrated solution meeting the philanthropic and planning needs of donors and their families.

CHAPTER 2

The New Philanthropists

With the basic Philanthropic Planning Model in place, the next step is to address the unique generational characteristics of donors that make it necessary. By its nature, donor-centered philanthropic planning is driven by one thing—donors. When donors come to charities with different backgrounds and experiences, the fundraising community must evolve to meet their needs. At the start of 2011, a major shift occurred in the donor world. For the last 40 years, charities built their fundraising operations, solicitation methods, and stewardship programs to appeal to the needs of the Depression, World War II, and Post-War Cohorts (Traditionalists).

During that time, these cohorts were in their peak earning years. They had come of age at a point in history which gave them a profound sense of community and the need to be charitable. In 2010, the last of the Traditionalists reached the retirement age of 65. While they will continue to be an important charitable giving audience going forward, their influence and ability to give is now starting to wane.[1]

To fill this void, the charitable community has already started to rely upon the Older Boomers and the generations that follow to pick up the charitable mantle. These are the New Philanthropists. If charities and advisors are to work effectively with these next generations of donors in the Philanthropic Planning Model, they need to understand what about fundraising and planning techniques appealed to the Traditionalists and what existing and new strategies will be effective with the Older Boomers, Younger Boomers, Generation X, and Millennials going forward. To do so, charities and advisors need to learn how they think. The same tools and ideas that worked for Traditionalists will not meet the needs of the New Philanthropists.[2]

DEFINING GENERATIONS

Generations can be familial or cultural. Familial generations are parent-child-grandchild relationships. In philanthropic planning, they come into play when a philanthropist wants to pass or preserve assets and values for future generations, such as children and grandchildren. This topic will be covered in Chapter 6.

Cultural generations are groups of people who were born in the same "era" or time period and grow up sharing the same cultural experiences. These individuals developed latent values and feelings when they were coming of age, roughly between the ages of 17 and 23, based upon shared events or defining moments. This is a special time in human development, when individuals become aware of love, economics, and politics for the first time. As children become adults, they develop their core value systems which carry through for the rest of their lives. When a group of people come of age at the same time and experience many of the same things, their generational cohort develops an identity based upon the significant cultural and historical events going on during those years. These cohorts also tend to value that which was missing when they came of age. For example, those who came of age during the Great Depression value financial security.[3]

Generational cohorts will vary by country because experiences when coming of age in each country will differ. For example, Older Boomers growing up in the United States will have a strong association with the assassination of John F. Kennedy, while people of that same age growing up in China will likely not see this as a shaping, seminal event of their lives. As time goes by, and the world becomes more and more interconnected, cohorts are beginning to look more and more alike, particularly for the youngest generational cohorts.

Generational cohort theory is not new. It was first developed by German philosopher and sociologist Karl Mannheim in 1928 to explain the political attitudes and behavior of German youth after World War I[4]. In 1959, American demographer Norman Ryder adopted Mannheim's thesis in his seminal work *The Cohort as a Concept in the Study of Social Change*[5]. Ryder called for more empirical research to validate the coming-of-age hypothesis. In 1985, Drs. Howard Schuman and Jacqueline Scott of the Institute of Social Research at the University of Michigan at Ann

Arbor completed a study titled "Generations and Collective Memories,"[6] which confirmed that different generational cohorts are shaped by the confluence of personal and national events and memories from adolescence and early adulthood. Participants in the study listed 33 historical events over the prior 30 years which had impacted their thinking, and the ones they ranked as most important were those that happened when they were ages 17 to 23.[7]

With no formal authority for defining generational cohorts, the definitions and names vary. It is less important to get particular years exactly right, since experiences will differ the least between the last two years in a cohort. Since smaller cohorts tend to develop more closely aligned values, it is best to use the shorter year ranges when defining the cohorts for fundraising and planning purposes.

Even though generational cohorts provide an interesting and helpful lens to view prospects, it is important for fundraisers and advisors to remember that no one prospect is a generational cohort. Each person has a unique set of experiences and values which drive his or her behavior. While cohort generalizations help in understanding how a group may react to particular information or the best way to present giving and planning ideas when marketing, in the end what truly matters is how the individual acts on the information.

Traditionalists (Born Pre-1946)

The Traditionalists are actually made up of three distinct generational cohorts, the Depression Cohort (born 1912 to 1921), the World War II Cohort (born 1922 to 1927), and the Post-War Cohort (born 1928 to 1945).

Depression Cohort (1912 to 1921)   The Depression Cohort came of age (turned 17 to 23) during the Great Depression. They faced severe economic challenges, significant unemployment, and struggled to find work just to survive. The need for financial security trumps all other values for this cohort. They are compulsive savers, with many saving into their 80s for things like future medical costs or to leave an inheritance. They would rather live at a reduced lifestyle than spend from core savings and they avoid debt as much as possible. They want to be sure that their families never struggle through another Great Depression.[8]

| CONCEPT | DEPRESSION COHORT |

- *Defining Moment*
  - *Great Depression*
- *Shared Values*
  - *Practical: Everyone needs a sense of purpose*
  - *Savers: Be conservative where money is concerned; doing without has its rewards*
  - *Safety and Security: Safety and security must be guaranteed*
  - *Friends and Family: Social connectedness is vital*
  - *The Good Life: Comfort and convenience are nice luxuries, not requirements for living.[9]*

The Depression Cohort has made significant bequests in support of charities, holding onto their wealth until they were 100 percent sure they no longer needed it. Their charitable giving tends to be to unrestricted endowment, ensuring that charities will have what they need in their "rainy day fund" and not tying the hands of the charity to put the money to use where it is needed. They know that charities are the lifeblood of those without during difficult economic times and want to ensure that they can meet that need when the time arrives.

When approaching the Depression Cohort with fundraising or financial planning messages, the information should be simple and presented in a straightforward manner that is easy to process. Using visual pictures or cues will help enhance comprehension of written and spoken messages. Face to face communications in a location where the prospect is comfortable will maximize the opportunity for success. At this stage of their lives, print communications, advertisements, and promotional materials for the Depression Cohort should be uncluttered and simple in structure, with no reverse type. Printed materials are preferable to radio and television, so the donor can process information at a slower pace. If radio or television must be utilized, longer ads with repeated messages will lead to better comprehension.[10]

For many members of the Depression Cohort, adult children are now heavily involved in their decision-making process, particularly around charitable giving. These children come from different generational cohorts with different sets of values. They may impose those values on the parent,

DEPRESSION COHORT AND LOYALTY

I have met and worked with several donors who are in this cohort and they have shared terrible stories of the Great Depression. As the economy has struggled through the Great Recession, several have drawn parallels to their experiences in the 1920s and 1930s. Their interest in charitable gift annuities (CGA) has given me the opportunity to get to know them better and they have been motivated by the fixed rate of the CGA and their ability to "lock in" a rate that they can count on amidst economic uncertainty. In all cases thus far in my experience, these donors have made very modest, but consistent gifts to both the American Cancer Society and to Meridian Health. They have told me of their loyalty to the two organizations due to personal experiences where the organizations helped them or their family. —REW

even though the gift will come from the parent's resources. Adult children may also feel that any resources dedicated to charity will come out of their own pockets. When discussing philanthropy, a values-based approach using both familial and generational cohort values may be required to secure more significant charitable gifts.

World War II Cohort (1922 to 1927)   The World War II Cohort came of age during the Second World War. Their shared sacrifice for the common good gave them a sense of purpose, to defeat a common enemy. They are the most patriotic of the cohorts. The World War II Cohort is still saving, having learned during war time to ration and conserve. However, they do spend a bit more than the Depression Cohort did at the same age, so they might be labeled cautious savers and spenders. This Cohort is also extremely brand loyal. That loyalty tends to go beyond the brand to the people who sell them products. The most effective way for charities and advisors to retain relationships with the World War II Cohort is to hold onto the staff members who have built personal relationships with these donors.

CONCEPT   **WORLD WAR II COHORT**

- *Defining Moment*
  - *World War II*
- *Shared Values*
  - *Patriotic*
  - *Respect for Authority*
  - *Romantic*
  - *Self-Reliant*[11]

The World War II Cohort gives for the common good. As with the cohort before them, they tend to make their largest gifts at death through bequests, but they are very charitable during life as well, giving one-third more to charities than the national average. The World War II Cohort has always seen civic duty as a core responsibility, from supporting the war effort to the public service groups that gained prominence after the war, all of which were designed to contribute to the greater good of society.[12]

These donors see themselves as active and demanding consumers and expect one-on-one concierge-level treatment, which used to be the norm. They often seek out rebates, coupons, and discounts, so matching gift and challenge programs where a third party matches or enhances their contribution will be especially attractive to them. They still read newspapers, magazines, and advertisements fully, so the best way to reach them is with messages in print. Because of their thorough review of details, family members often look to them for advice and trust their judgment. This type of trust, coupled with the desire to volunteer can be a powerful tool for referrals—as they encourage others to be philanthropic to the charity's cause.

The World War II Cohort is a small group that came together to save the world. They delayed personal gratification for the good of others. They would like to be remembered for those sacrifices, so the idea of immortality is important to them. Gifts that will continue to remind the world of their sacrifices, which immortalize them or their generation, such as naming buildings or endowment funds, will continue to be popular both during their lifetimes and as bequest gifts.

Post-War Cohort (1928 to 1945)   The Post-War Cohort grew up in a time of unprecedented economic growth and social tranquility. There was a duality to the time period, marked by the ability to spend money for the first time since the Depression but marred by their fear of communism. This created a culture of "fitting in" so as not to be labeled different. Being a part of the crowd became a way of life. Cars, television, and music were all significant parts of the culture in the 1950s, with the emergence of many new cultural icons. The Post-War Cohort helped to create the middle class and sought out prosperity. They also faced the Korean War, McCarthyism, school dress codes, and the emergence of the civil rights movement.[13]

As they have reached retirement, the Post-War Cohort has moved away from acquiring materials objects, a key component of their formative years, and is now focused on sharing experiences with their spouses, families, and friends. Many see the current phase of their lives as a second childhood and are looking at activities to fill it. They are a bit conservative with money like their Depression Cohort parents, but splurge now and then like their Baby Boomer children. Because of the GI Bill, many in this generation have a college education. Due to the economic prosperity, they are likely

CONCEPT   **POST-WAR COHORT**

- *Defining Moments*
  - *End of World War II*
  - *Strong Economy*
  - *Move to the Suburbs*
  - *Cold War*
  - *Korean War*
  - *McCarthyism*
  - *Emergence of Rock and Roll*
  - *Civil Rights Movement*
- *Shared Values*
  - *The American Dream*
  - *Conformity*
  - *Stability*
  - *Family*
  - *Self-Fulfillment*[14]

to have significant savings, pensions, and home equity, which means they are ripe for charitable giving and financial planning.

The Post-War Cohort came of age in a time of much greater prosperity than their predecessors and is more likely to make lifetime charitable gifts, rather than waiting until death. They do not have a great deal of trust that their Baby Boomer children are going to use inherited wealth effectively, so they tend to limit what their children will get. Knowing that the rest of the funds are available, they are giving to charities while they are alive. Many have been drawn to the stability of charitable gift annuities, seeking out the security that was not available in their formative years due to the Cold War. Because this cohort wants to fit in, giving clubs are an excellent motivator for charitable gifts.

The Post-War Cohort is aware that their Boomer children have not saved enough to care for their families. They are actively seeking to help pay for grandchildren's education—a need which can be met through commuted payment gift annuities and term of years flip charitable remainder trusts.

Due to their intense focus on family, they put a premium on passing their values to future generations, including the value of philanthropy. For those of high net worth in the Post-War Cohort, this creates tremendous opportunities for collaborative planning among advisors, philanthropists, and charities. They are the first of the cohorts in which some members might be open to the Philanthropic Planning Model.

With a focus on family and group activities, the Post-War Cohort also desires volunteer opportunities. When they are helping others, they feel they are contributing members of society. Charities need to create real volunteer opportunities in which the Post-War Cohort is doing something active, such as nurturing youth and providing guidance, rather than just sitting around at meetings.

Transitioning

While each of the Traditionalist cohorts is unique and as a result behaves differently, charitable fundraising for this group has been largely the same. In fact, it was around the behavior of these three cohorts that fundraising programs have been built over the last 40 years. For all of their differences, each of the Traditionalist cohorts came of age at times when they could trust charities. If charities showed that they had a valuable mission, the Traditionalists would support it, often with modest current gifts and larger gifts at death. Most of the time, these gifts were unrestricted, with the donor trusting the charity to put the gift to good use where the need was greatest.

The New Philanthropists (Born 1946 to Present)

Unfortunately for charities, the experiences of the generations born after 1945, including Older Boomers (born 1946 to 1954), Younger Boomers (born 1955 to 1964), Generation X (born 1965 to 1976), and Millennials (born 1977 to 1984) have been less favorable when it comes to trust, and charities will no longer receive large, unrestricted gifts from this group. To be successful, charities and advisors will need to learn more about the shared values of these generations and how that translates into charitable giving.

Older Boomer/Leading Boomer Cohort (1946 to 1954)   The Older Boomers came of age in the 1960s, a time of tremendous upheaval in America. When John F. Kennedy was elected, it was an extension of the prosperity coupled with the transfer of authority from an older cohort to a much younger one. His assassination in 1963, followed by those of his brother Robert in 1968 and Martin Luther King, Jr. in 1969, signaled an end to the status quo. Suddenly Older Boomers were faced with leadership they did not trust, fighting a war in Vietnam that they felt was needlessly sacrificing lives, and major political upheaval at the Democratic National Convention in Chicago in 1968.

Despite these challenges, Older Boomers came of age in a time of economic prosperity. They had grown up in the 1950s and the expansion of the economy continued unabated through the 1960s. They used these economic good times to pursue a lifestyle reminiscent of the one they had grown up enjoying in the 1950s. When Neil Armstrong walked on the moon, it was tangible evidence of America's technological and economic superiority. This economic prosperity and low unemployment caused many Older Boomers to adopt carefree attitudes and experiment with free love and indulgence. As these ideas took hold, the importance of the individual over God, family, and social institutions began to grow.[15]

> **CONCEPT   OLDER BOOMER COHORT**
>
> - *Defining Moments*
>   - *Assassinations of John F. Kennedy, Robert F. Kennedy, and Martin Luther King, Jr.*
>   - *Vietnam War*
>   - *First Man on the Moon*
> - *Shared Values*
>   - *Personal/Social Expression*
>   - *Protected Individualism*
>   - *Youth*
>   - *Health and Wellness*

As the Older Boomers have aged, they have found conflict between their shared values and individualism and the responsibilities of society and family. They have difficulty accepting aging when the youth culture they created in the 1960s said not to trust anyone over 30. Most Older Boomers find that their middle-aged conservative outlook is in direct conflict with the anti-establishment views they held in their youth.[16] Balancing self-gratification, personal fulfillment, and new experiences against their circumstances today of being married with families and managers at work has played a major role in their view toward charities and involvement in the charitable community.

With the importance of individualism, it is much more difficult to coerce Older Boomers into charitable giving or activities using guilt or for the greater good of the group. You do not see many Older Boomers involved in civic groups or other volunteer activities, unless they involve their children. Older Boomers, the first generation with predominantly dual-income families and organized afterschool activities for children, do not have time for volunteer activities.

Social justice was an important part of the youth movement of the 1960s. As Older Boomers matured, they no longer had time for the causes they championed in their formative years. With increased affluence, Older Boomers have started giving in support of these causes and give more to charity than any other cohort. As they have aged, Boomers have become more socially liberal, giving to charities for the homeless, mentally ill, and disadvantaged children.[17] They also tend to give to causes that can change the world. Just as they have changed every phase of life as they reach it, Older Boomers want to cure disease, solve world problems, and save the planet.

Older Boomers have directed and restricted their gifts much more than any prior generation. They do not trust charities (which represent the establishment) to use the money effectively, and instead want to control how gifts are allocated. Older Boomers need to understand and be shown the impact their gift will have and the long-term outcome it will create. They need to verify that charities are using their gifts the way they intend, or they will not make additional gifts.[18] This is a fundamental shift in behavior and one to which charities need to adapt. As Older Boomers become the primary source of revenue for charities, the days of ever-increasing, unrestricted annual fund receipts will come to an end.

As Older Boomers retire, it will prove harder to encourage them to make outright cash gifts of any type. Older Boomers have never saved. They have always felt that they deserve the best of everything and have not been afraid to borrow to get it. When home values were growing and the stock market was booming in the 1990s, Older Boomers felt they would have enough for retirement. When children left home, instead of downsizing Older Boomers moved into more luxurious dream homes with large, flexible spaces for entertaining. With the Great Recession and the burst of the housing bubble, they are now moving into smaller, easier-to-care for homes, but still have limited savings to fall back on for charitable gifts once they stop earning. They have also gotten used to paying others to complete mundane tasks for them, to allow them time for jobs and caring for their parents and children. As they retire and have more time, it is likely that Older Boomers will retain these services to allow themselves time to pursue leisure and recreation activities, which will further limit the availability of cash for charitable gifts.

Older Boomers have also indicated that they intend to spend their savings, to the extent they have them. This is the first generation that is looking forward to the inheritance it will receive, rather than the one it will leave. They have an overwhelming feeling that they did enough for their children while the children were growing up—paying tuition and providing money for down payments on homes. Older Boomers believe that they should enjoy what is left rather than save it for kids, dying with a zero bank balance.[19] This, of course, would leave little for charities. Those that do plan to leave something behind feel it is more important to pass along values and keepsakes rather than money.[20]

The Employee Benefit Research Institute estimates that nearly half of Older Boomers may not be able to afford even basic living expenses in retirement. In all likelihood, this means that many Older Boomers will end up moving in with their Millennial children.[21] Interestingly, this may not turn out to be a huge challenge, as 60 percent of Millennials believe that families have a responsibility to have an elder parent come live with them if that parent wants to.[22]

One step advisors and charities can pursue is to help the more wealthy of the Older Boomers pursue alternative avenues for giving. Assets other than cash, such as appreciated stock, hedge fund interests, art, collectibles, and real estate are frequently the best assets for Older Boomers to give. In many cases, Older Boomers will no longer want or need certain collections or vacation homes as they move on to the next phase of their lives. These assets can be used to fund restricted gifts for causes they believe in.

To appeal to Older Boomers, charities need to show what is in it for them. Many Older Boomers are looking for ways to increase their income in retirement, pay for college education for their children, and pay for care for their parents. Using charitable gifts to promote social justice while also meeting personal planning needs is a win-win with the Older Boomer Cohort. If those gifts are then funded with less precious, non-cash assets, charities and advisors will have met the needs of this cohort.

When marketing to Older Boomers, charities and advisors should be conscious of physiological changes in vision which impact Older Boomers and the Traditionalists, adjusting print advertising accordingly. By employing 12 or 13 point type in high contrast (black on white or yellow), eliminating glossy stock, using sharp contrasting colors, and limiting the use of blue/grey/violet, marketing will be more accessible to Older Boomers. Marketing needs to reflect an emphasis on individualism, excitement, and fun. Broad, multi-cohort appeals will hold little interest for Older Boomers, they need appeals focused on them and retaining their youth.[23] For example, the Boy Scouts might show an Older Boomer and a current scout out in the wilderness kayaking together and then explain how the Older Boomer's gift made that trip or program possible. The posed shot of an Older Boomer watching or sitting as the Scout completes an activity has to be retired.

Younger Boomer/Trailing Boomer Cohort (1955 to 1964) The Younger Boomers came of age during times of high inflation and the first major economic downturn since the Great Depression. They lived through the oil embargo with its long gas lines, the end of the Vietnam War, the Watergate Scandal, and President Nixon's resignation. They watched the nuclear meltdown at Three Mile Island and witnessed the toxic waste at Love Canal. Younger Boomers would have seen the Nixon resignation and the fall of Saigon as images of American arrogance, deception, and failure. The oil embargo and subsequent recession marked the end of two decades of prosperity. The environmental and corporate scandals of the 1970s would add to their distrust of big business and government. After being promised the moon (literally) but confronted with a different reality, Younger Boomers are pessimistic about their economic future and feel disadvantaged. With Older Boomers holding the best jobs, vacation homes, and material possessions, the Younger Boomers feel left behind, trusting only in themselves.[24]

The Younger Boomers have become a spending generation. They buy for convenience and to feel better about their missed youth, but do so with an eye to economics, knowing that they need to conserve limited dollars. Frequently they seek out status objects. Since they had to compete for everything in their formative years they remain competitive, particularly with Older Boomers who often stand in their way.

Younger Boomers are often control freaks and micro-managers, seeking out situations where they decide what happens. They do not trust the

---

CONCEPT   **YOUNGER BOOMER COHORT**

- *Defining Moments*
  - *Fall of Vietnam*
  - *Watergate*
  - *Nixon Resignation*
  - *Energy Crisis*
- *Shared Values*
  - *Lonely Individualism*
  - *Cynicism/Distrust*
  - *Health and Wellness*
  - *Family Commitments*[25]

government or others, instead trusting themselves and money. Younger Boomers do share the Older Boomers' desire to be healthy and exercise.

Most Younger Boomers fought the good fight up the corporate ladder, following in the steps of the Older Boomers. But around 1999, many of them started to re-evaluate and began to look for ways to find work-life balance. They started spending more time with family and in the younger portion of the cohort, many women are electing to spend their time raising their children rather than pursuing careers outside the home. The women who do continue in the workforce are putting in longer hours which require men to do more at home. Blended families have become the norm due to the high divorce rate.[26] For advisors, blended families create tremendous opportunities to assist Younger Boomers with estate and college planning for children from different parents.

Younger Boomers tend to use their homes to retreat from their challenging work life. Their homes have become more extravagant over time and full of indulgences for themselves and their children. Younger Boomers are not loyal to one company and will change jobs to find the next opportunity. This adds stress, but has allowed them to increase income levels. It also causes them to have multiple benefit packages and retirement plans, which give advisors and charitable gift planners the opportunity to assist them in consolidation.[27]

Younger Boomers, alienated by the politics of their youth, have little interest in ideological issues. However, issues that directly impact their families will get their attention. Charities need to focus their missions and how they impact the lives of the Younger Boomers and their families. If a charity cannot make this connection, it will have difficulty gaining access to Younger Boomers. Local hospitals and arts organizations can do particularly well with the right messaging. Similarly, charities helping to cure diseases will do well with appeals to Younger Boomers who have had family members afflicted.

For Younger Boomers, their time is far more valuable than money, but money is still important because it can buy conveniences to save time. Coming of age during a recession with high inflation, they love to haggle and will use technology to find a bargain when possible. Charities embracing this tendency with matching gift and challenge programs will achieve good results. Gift structures which allow Younger Boomers to meet a

Jersey Shore University Medical Center is the Regional Trauma Center for Central New Jersey and as such has cared for many families and their loved ones over the years. Both annual and capital/major giving has seen many Younger Boomers respond to the messaging around the hospital caring for them. A recent gift planning marketing piece highlighted a story where a couple, Sandy and Bill, appreciated the care given to their son and how it motivates their giving annually and through their will. Others can appreciate their decision and several have also made commitments for similar reasons. —REW

personal planning objective, such as supplementing retirement income, should be successful.

With the sexual revolution behind them, they have more control over their fertility and are less likely to have kids than the generations that came before them. This makes them good targets for more significant gifts, even though they may have less capital than the Older Boomers. Bequest gifts could become popular with Younger Boomers with no kids, particularly for the residuary of their estate.

When marketing to Younger Boomers, charities and advisors should be conscious of their distrust of the government and institutions. Charities need to show Younger Boomers the impact their gifts will have, the outcomes they will create, verify usage of the funds, and provide accountability by showing the gift at work. Traditional stewardship reports will not be effective with this cohort. Younger Boomers are even less likely than Older Boomers to make unrestricted gifts. Characterizing Younger Boomers as realistic idealists with concerns for practicality and results will make marketing more effective.

Due to their lack of time and desire to be with family, charities should make giving convenient and easy. If charities make giving difficult, including the process of making or verifying the gift, then Younger Boomers will simply walk away. They do not have time to deal with charities that cannot deliver what they need, when they need it.

Stewardship should not revolve around thank-you events, giving clubs, or other tools appropriate to prior generations, but should instead focus on showing the impact and outcomes of gifts, thereby verifying and accounting for the use of donated funds. If a Younger Boomer feels like a modest gift is making a major difference, the charity is likely to get another gift.

Generation X/Baby Buster Cohort (1965 to 1976)   Generation X (Gen X or Xers) has often been referred to as a "slacker" generation. Because they followed the two Boomer cohorts, which meant that the Boomers could no longer own the youth movement, Gen X became suspect in the media (which was run by Boomers). Even the name of this cohort, trying to define them as generic and different from the main stream, shows a generational bias by those who came before.

Gen X grew up in the 1960s and 1970s during great social upheaval. Divorce rates were skyrocketing and mothers were entering the work-force, causing some to label Gen X latchkey kids. As Gen X came of age, the stock market crashed, the economy went into recession, the national debt hit new highs, AIDS ruined the sexual revolution, and the United States fought the first Persian Gulf War. The space shuttle Challenger exploded in 1986, taking with it the innocence of a generation and teaching them that there are no guarantees. Politically, the Berlin Wall fell in 1989, which would mark the beginning of the end of the Cold War. Xers graduating from college in the early 1990s entered the worst job market since World War II. As Gen Xers began adulthood, little promise and opportunity seemed to await them. They had a growing disenfranchisement from a system that had cheated and failed them.[28]

Despite the slacker hype, Gen X found its way, with many working in high-tech jobs. They tend to be hard workers, but put their own interests ahead of the team or company. Gen X also values work-life balance. Their values are so different from the Boomers who came before them that it often results in generational clashes. Boomers feel that Xers are whiners who do not want to pay their dues and show proper deference while Xers see Boomers as "self-righteous, materialistic control freaks who had their fun at other people's expense and spend way too much time politicking at

---

CONCEPT   **GENERATION X COHORT**

- Defining Moments
  - Large National Debt/Stock Market Crash of 1987
  - Challenger Explosion
  - Fall of the Berlin Wall
  - First Persian Gulf War
  - AIDS Crisis
- Shared Values
  - Free Agency/Independence
  - Dependence on Friends Over Family
  - Cynical About Future
  - Street Smart
  - Pursuit of Quality of Life
  - Acceptance of Violence, Sex[29]

---

the office."[30] Working on teams with Boomers has highlighted the differences in these cohorts, as Xers have little patience for the lack of independence such work requires.

Because they often feel they do not fit in, many Gen Xers gave up the corporate life and are entrepreneurs who have started a wide range of successful businesses, particularly in technology. They are far less risk-adverse than the generations that came before them, which allows them to be successful in these ventures.[31] Business ownership allows for more flexibility and a better quality of life than in the corporate world. Since entrepreneurs are usually quite charitable, this may open opportunities for fundraisers going forward, provided charities are open to taking an interest in such businesses.

Gen X seeks out many of the things that they did not have in their coming-of-age years. They have delayed marriage and children until they were ready to take on those commitments. As a result, they have lower divorce rates and demand work-life balance from employers. After witnessing the divorce of so many of their parents, more than half of all Xers now cohabitate prior to marriage. In many cases, they simple elect not to get married and have a "life partner."[32] This trend should not be ignored by charities or planners. There are significant planning and tax implications for Xers who live together for extended times. Unfortunately, the database platforms at most charities struggle to manage non-married couples. Regardless of their own beliefs on this issue, charities need to recognize that this will be the norm and create systems to address marketing and mailing to reach these donors appropriately.

Xers lean more heavily on friends than family, since family was often not present when they were growing up. They watched parents who had no work-life balance, and they pursue it in their employment, even if they make less money to do so.

Xers came of age during a time of government scandals, from Iran-Contra to Whitewater. They have little faith that government social welfare programs will be there for them and are taking financial matters into their own hands at a much younger age than the Boomers. They participate at a higher rate in a wide range of retirement savings, health care savings, and tax-free investment accounts.[33]

Gen X has had extensive exposure to other cultures through television, movies, travel, the Internet, and broader diversity in their peer group. Having come of age during the end of the Cold War, Xers see themselves more as world citizens than the generations which came before them. They are part of a larger culture and want to explore it. They also want their charitable gifts to make that world a better place.

Charities with an environmental bent will also do well with Xers. When they were coming of age, the Exxon Valdez oil spill and Chernobyl nuclear disaster raised awareness. Coupled with the discovery of the hole in the ozone layer, emphasis on global recycling, and interest in global warming, Gen X will give and volunteer to save the planet.[34]

Gen X loathes forced social functions. They want to choose who they socialize with rather than have others, like employers, choose for them.[35] Charities should not try to steward Xers with social events unless the event and attendees are truly something of interest to the participants. Within the next 20 years, the sit-down donor stewardship events, such as legacy society luncheons and fundraising galas, will lose their effectiveness.

For this same reason, organized religions will also have a more difficult time soliciting gifts from Xers. While most consider themselves spiritual and believe in God, they are less committed to a particular church or religion.

Gen X came of age during the recession of the early 1990s. With few job prospects, many continued in school and earned advanced degrees that are now helping them to earn promotions and financial rewards. College and universities can use this interest to promote giving. Xers have become life-long learners and will continue to want access to on-line education. They also want education available to their own children. Gifts to educational institutions will become a priority if positioned in this way.

Gen X tends to trust the judgment of a peer. Using peer-to-peer solicitation methods will prove effective, provided the mission is one in which both share a belief. They are looking for ease, convenience, value, and customer service. Charities soliciting Xers need to provide easy electronic ways for Gen X to give, such as texting, but also need to have real people available through the entire multi-channel spectrum to answer questions, and provide a high level of customer service.

Due to the difficult times in which they came of age, they are the most fiscally conservative cohort since World War II. They are price conscious and have little brand loyalty. If a charity does not deliver impact, outcomes, accountability, verifiability, and involve the donor in the gift, expect an Xer to make the next gift elsewhere. With no brand loyalty, there is no annual fund loyalty. The Xer needs to be tied to the mission to continue to support the charity.

When marketing to Gen X, charities and advisors need to drop the pretense. Xers do not feel the need to be attractive or rich, they just want the facts. Rather than spin, charities should use humor, music from their coming-of-age years, subtlety, irony, irreverence, and unexpected twists. Language such as "best, finest, world-class, you will benefit by . . . this is in your best interest" will get their attention.[36] Marketing showing families together will be particularly effective, since Xers yearn for the stability of family life that was largely missing from their childhoods. They prefer custom solutions, so gift plans that allow them to structure their gifts in a way to fit their own needs will be ideal. While they are probably too young for most of the traditional tools of gift planning such as charitable gift annuities, over time they will be interested and will want flexible planning tools. This will tap into Gen X's entrepreneurial spirit and maximize results for the charity and advisors.

Millennials/Generation Y/Generation Next/Echo Boomer Cohort (1977 to 1984?) Millennials are the youngest cohort and they are still coming of age. Any conclusions drawn about them this early will likely need to be adjusted as they develop their identities and values more fully.

My wife and I are members of Gen X. We found that many of the traits apply, but that there are other factors which cause us to be generous in our giving in a way that reflects our personal life experience. We recognize that five organizations have been helpful to our family and make annual gifts to three of them with additional annual gifts to about four other charities each year. We have included all five in our estate planning by naming them as beneficiaries of an insurance policy that we maintain just for that purpose. Of course, with my wife being an accountant and with my financial planning background and position as a gift planner, we have come to understand the value of giving and have chosen to plan for our giving through both annual gifts and with the aid of a planned giving tool. We have also made three modest major gifts based on our feeling that it was important to invest in the project that was presented to us at the time. I share that here because as we'll discuss later in Chapter 6, these cohorts offer a general understanding of people born in these timeframes. As you get to know the individual donors and perhaps as you get to go through the philanthropic planning process with them, you will certainly find that you still need to uncover their personal motivations to fully appreciate their point of view and their goals. —REW

Where this cohort will end for sure is still unclear, but it seems likely that the "Great Recession" starting in 2007 will trigger the end of the Millennials and the start of another generation, which for the purposes of this book, will be referred to as the "Great Recession" Generation.

Millennials generally grew up in diverse, two-income households where they needed to develop a high level of self sufficiency, although fully one quarter of Millennials grew up living with just one parent. They are the most technologically savvy generation to date, coming of age at a time when information is readily available on a wide range of devices and platforms. This technology has allowed them to avoid personal interaction in a way required of previous generations, the impact of which is yet to be known. While past generations looked at cars or clothes for social status, technology is the measure for Millennials.

> **CONCEPT**   **MILLENNIAL COHORT**
>
> - *Defining Moments*
>   - *The Internet*
>   - *Good Economic Times*
>   - *Columbine High School Shootings*
>   - *September 11 Terrorist Attacks*
>   - *Wars in Iraq and Afghanistan*
> - *Shared Values*
>   - *Hopeful About Financial Future*
>   - *Heightened Fears*
>   - *Change is Good*
>   - *Tolerance/Diversity*[37]

Millennials grew up and started coming of age during the good economic times of the mid to late 1990s and have a positive feeling about money. Despite a brief economic downturn after September 11, the economy again roared back to life to give Millennials a positive view of their economic future. For this reason, the Great Recession of 2007 is likely the launch point of another generation which will come of age with a far gloomier economic view.

Despite the economic good times, Millennials fear for their safety. The 1999 shootings at Columbine High School were the most horrific example of the rapid uptick in school violence that has led to increased security at schools.[38] The terrorist attacks of September 11, 2001, created feelings of vulnerability and insecurity that exceeded those of the attack on Pearl Harbor in 1941. Feelings of patriotism and altruism increased, but it is not clear if they have truly stayed with Millennials coming of age at that time. This insecurity was further fostered by the wars in Iraq and Afghanistan, in which Millennials are the foot soldiers. Two-thirds of Millennials say you cannot be too careful when dealing with people.[39]

The Clinton impeachment scandal confirmed for Millennials that they should not respect authority, a belief that was only reaffirmed when no weapons of mass destruction were found during the invasion of Iraq following September 11. This generation does not believe politicians or the establishment can tell the truth and look at them with a jaundiced eye. Even so, they tend to be less skeptical than prior generations and believe that government regulation and intervention can be a help.[40]

Despite these challenges, Millennials seem more hopeful, idealistic, and social-cause oriented than Gen X, with more structured life goals. It is likely that this is due to both the good economic conditions and that they were raised by Older Boomers who were more optimistic and outgoing than the Post-War parents of Gen X.[41]

Unlike the generations before them, which struggled with change, Millennials see change as a natural part of life. Since they grew up with constantly evolving technology, they see the world through a different lens than older cohorts. Most Millennials treat their smart phones and other multi-tasking devices like a body part.[42]

Millennials are attending college at record rates, but are borrowing to do so. They recognize that they will need good jobs upon graduation in order to pay back that debt. They seem more focused on the degree than the learning behind it, which makes them less engaged in the learning process. Because of these significant student loans, many Millennials are returning home after college, oftentimes not taking full financial responsibility for themselves until age 24 or later.[43] This is a far cry from their Boomer parents, who could not wait to get out of their parents' homes to start their own lives.

When entering the workforce, Millennials are not seeking to climb the corporate ladder. They see office cubicles as prisons and do not want their work to consume them the way it did their parents. They are looking for careers that have social impact, such as teaching, rather than pursuing business or finance. They would like to have jobs that pay well so they can afford the finer things in life, but not at the expense of overall happiness. Millennials are more comfortable working in teams than Gen X, probably because they were raised in that environment by Older Boomer parents.

Millennials' dating and marriage habits are also different than the generations that came before. Many more relationships are starting on the Web rather than face to face, since they are not as socially adept at interaction as Gen X. Millennials also report that they are waiting longer to become sexually active, with a fair number reporting that they are remaining virgins until marriage, reversing a trend started by their Older Boomers parents. They are also getting married younger, having children earlier, having more children, and frequently having one parent stay home with the kids. This is made possible by technology that allows the parent at home to work from the house part time, telecommute, or job share, options that did not exist in prior years. It is a return to more traditional values to increase the stability in their lives.[44]

Despite embracing more traditional values, charities cannot return to the fundraising methods used for Traditionalists, as Millennials' expectations are completely different. Millennials have learned from their parents that it is possible to change the world and they are eager to get started. They do not have patience for the way charities do business. If they see a problem that needs to be solved, and a charity cannot help them to do it, they will seek out another charity. If that does not work, they will form a new charity or a for-profit business to meet the identified need. Millennials are most likely to give when they are fully engaged with an organization with a compelling cause in which they trust the leadership.[45]

Millennials also want to be involved. Unlike their parents, who had little time to volunteer once they started climbing the corporate ladder, Millennials have the time and ability to work on causes they believe in. While they do not have significant resources to donate to these causes now, they do have the time to invest. If charities can provide them with meaningful volunteer opportunities, where they can see their good ideas put to work, they will develop relationships and become larger donors when their financial circumstances allow.[46] One way for charities to engage Millennials would be through reverse mentoring, allowing Millennials to help Boomers and Xers with technology or ideas on how to appeal to Millennial prospects.[47]

Unlike Gen X, Millennials are both brand conscious and brand loyal. For social causes that they believe in, it creates an opportunity to link with them and encourage them to continue to give to the charity's mission.

Because Millennials expect change, marketing for them must be kept fresh and multi-channel. A static Web presence will not garner return visits. While consistent advertisements worked well for older cohorts, Millennials want and expect something new. .

For the present time, charities should try to obtain small, annual donations dedicated to the area of importance of the donor. Charities will have little success garnering unrestricted gifts, as the individuality of this generational cohort will demand that their gifts go to the part of the cause about which they are passionate. Over time, gifts from engaged Millennials will grow, if they are properly cultivated and retain their trust in the charity's leadership.

Emergence of the "Great Recession" Generation?   The end date for the Millennial Cohort has not yet been determined. Although it is too soon to tell, the change in generational cohort may very well be marked by the Great Recession of 2007 to 2009, which has caused severe economic hardship, particularly for those in their formative years and trying to find jobs out of high school or after graduating from college. The recession has caused rampant unemployment and underemployment, frequently resulting in two and three familial generations under one roof to save on expenses. The crisis has been marked by 1960s-like protests against Wall Street and corporate greed. Current projections indicate that this next generation will have a lower quality of life than the generations that came before them, resulting in the continued decline of the middle class. It is expected that the next generation's career earnings and advancement will never fully recover from the Great Recession.

While charities and advisors may not yet be approaching this cohort, it is important to pay attention as their values develop to determine how to approach them in the future. If they share the pessimism of the Younger Boomers or the independence of Gen X, two generations that came of age during difficult economic times, they may prove a difficult audience for charities to capture. It is still too soon to tell.

CONCEPT   **GREAT RECESSION GENERATION (BORN 1985 TO ?)**

- *Defining Moments*
  - *Great Recession*
  - *2007 Mortgage Crisis*
  - *Rampant Unemployment*
  - *Election of Barack Obama*
- *Shared Values*
  - *Too soon to know*

In Summary

By understanding the values behind the Traditionalists and the New Philanthropists, charities and professional advisors can begin to craft strategies to approach them in creative ways which appeal to those values. While the strategies for Traditionalists are well established and have proven effective over time, they will not work with the majority of New Philanthropists, who came of age at a different time and have a fundamentally different world view. With the Traditionalists having reached retirement age, it is critical that charities and advisors adjust the way they work with the New Philanthropists to ensure their support for charitable causes.

CHAPTER 3

Identifying Prospects for Philanthropic Planning

With the emergence of the New Philanthropists necessitating that charities and advisors adopt the Philanthropic Planning Model, the next step in the process is for charities and advisors to identify the best prospects for philanthropic planning from this group.

PROSPECT MOTIVATION

Every individual has an estate. Unlike the iconic Jed Clampit who struck oil and moved his family to Beverly Hills to live above their former standing, most people have grown their wealth over time. And while some have more meager assets, each individual has a pool of assets that the Internal Revenue Service (IRS) considers as part of our gross estate. This is our personal property, real estate, checking and savings accounts, life insurance, stocks and bonds, employee benefits, gifts received, inheritances, art, and collectibles.

To begin planning, the basic question of "what do you have that makes up your estate?" starts the discussion. "How much tax do you pay now and how much will you owe on it?" then begins to approach an idea about tax planning. "What do you hope to accomplish with your assets?" works the conversation toward financial planning. "What cause has touched you or your loved ones, lives?" can bring in the concept of charitable gift planning. And "Who do you hope to get your assets when you're gone?" can bring about your thoughts on estate planning. Every individual should have a plan, since every individual has an estate, and every individual should be asked to consider a charitable legacy as part of that plan.

CONCEPT	BE PREPARED

As Eagle Scouts, Brian and I have grown up with the Boy Scout motto of "Be Prepared" and it can have multiple applications, but it is certainly appropriate for planning and considerations for one's future. It's never too early to start planning and the better prepared you are, the better off your loved ones and your estate and your charities will be when you are gone. —REW

Many have referred to three distinct phases in an adult's financial life—Phase 1 is the Asset Accumulation phase which encompasses most of successful people's working years, Phase 2 is the Asset Preservation phase when people enjoy their retirements as they settle into new communities, engage in hobbies and travelling, and spend time with their family and grandchildren, and then Phase 3 is the Asset Distribution phase when mature adults reflect on life and reach an age of enlightenment where they come to terms with their own eventual death and consider how they might leave their legacies. Interestingly, any adult can be in any phase at any time. While the phases are usually linear, in the twenty-first century both retired billionaire Millennials and members of the Depression Cohort continue to work and save in order to leave a legacy.

IDENTIFYING A LIST OF PROSPECTS

Since it is impossible to know which phase of life a prospect may be in, charities and advisors need to use other tools and techniques to identify individuals who should be approached for philanthropic planning. Everyone in a charity's prospect pool can be a prospect for philanthropic planning. For most charities and professional advisors, identifying those individuals who are the most open to this type of conversation is the key to building a successful program.

For many individuals, giving back to one's community and supporting charitable organizations is an important consideration in the construction of an estate plan. Often these individuals consider charitable gifts which fund something that is very important to them, and may wish to memorialize themselves or loved ones in the process.

While almost everyone is a candidate for philanthropic planning, and therefore it is important to promote philanthropic planning widely, certain individuals may be more open to the message than others. According to studies by the Planned Giving Company, 91 percent of future gifts come from donors who have given loyally to the annual fund of the institution named as a beneficiary of a will or retirement plan. Their data indicates that 41 percent of donors open to the gift planning message have contributed 10 or more consecutive years and 77 percent of such donors have made at least 15 gifts to the benefitting charity during their lifetimes.[1]

The best prospects for philanthropic planning are a subset of a charity's gift planning prospects—individuals who have consistently given over many years to an organization. However, once the gift planning prospect list is created, the donors with giving capacity in the top 1 percent become principal gift philanthropic planning prospects, the next 9 percent become major gift philanthropic planning prospects, and the remainder of the list is ranked by gift planning capacity for general gift planning outreach and marketing purposes. Figure 3.1 is a visual representation of the four tiers of prospects to be considered in the philanthropic planning and gift planning contexts.

If a charity had unlimited resources, it could use a philanthropic planning approach with all four tiers of the pyramid. Unfortunately, with

FIGURE 3.1   **PHILANTHROPIC PLANNING PYRAMID**

Source: © 2012 Gift Planning Development, LLC

limited staff, volunteers, and budget, charities need to focus their personalized attention on those prospects that have the greatest capacity to make charitable gifts and the greatest likelihood of doing so.

The first step in identifying philanthropic planning prospects is to create a list and rating criteria for gift planning prospects. Many charities already have such a list, but if they do not, it is a fairly easy exercise to build one. This system should be particular to the charity and its prospects, but likely will resemble Table 3.1.

Once the charity has created its rated list of gift planning prospects, the next step is to overlay a wealth screening on the identified list. Any donor with a rating of 1 through 12 who has a wealth score in the top 1 percent of the prospects for the charity should be removed from the gift planning pool and placed in the principal prospects pool for philanthropic planning category. Similarly, any donor with a rating of 1 through 12 who has a wealth score in the next 9 percent (90 to 99 percent) should be removed from the gift planning pool and placed in the major prospects pool for

TABLE 3.1   GIFT PLANNING RATINGS

Rating	Description
1	Known gift planning donors
2	Prospects who have inquired about gift planning in the past but not captured in rating 1
3	Donors who have given for 15 or more years not captured in ratings 1 and 2
4	Donors who have given for 10 of the last 15 years not captured in ratings 1–3
5	Donors who have given for 7 of the last 10 years not captured in ratings 1–4
6	Donors who have given for 5 of the last 7 years not captured in ratings 1–5
7	Donors who have given for 3 of the last 5 years not captured in ratings 1–6
8	Current or former board members not captured in ratings 1–7
9	Long-term volunteers and those tied to the organization long-term through personal or family associations but not captured in ratings 1–8
10	Current or former staff members with at least some giving history, but not captured in ratings 1–9
11	Donors and prospects previously rated 1–10 but who fall off the rating system when ratings are reviewed (typically every year)
12	Individuals who have turned down gift planning conversations, but really are saying "not now" (qualified prospects)
13	Prospects who have asked the charity not to pursue gift planning conversations.

philanthropic planning category. The methodology for approaching these prospects is outlined in Chapters 6 and 7 respectively. The balance of the gift planning-rated prospects remain in the gift planning pool. The methodology for approaching them will be addressed in Part III of the *Companion.*

Professional advisors likely know who the public philanthropists are in their community. However, because so many people keep their philanthropy private, it is important for advisors to ask about philanthropy in their work. Advisors might include the following questions on their client intake questionnaire, which will help identify those with philanthropic intent:

- Do you consider yourself to be philanthropic?
- If you could change the world in one meaningful way, what would it be?
- Are there causes that move you or touch you personally?
- What organizations have you supported in the past with charitable gifts?
- What organizations, if any, do you hope to support in the future?
- What organizations, if any, do you hope to support through your estate?
- What impact would you like your charitable giving to have?
- Are there long-term outcomes you hope to create using philanthropy?
- Do you want us to consider your philanthropic goals when putting together your (insurance, financial, investment, estate) plan?
- Do you want to use charitable giving to help pass your core values to your children or grandchildren?
- Do you want your family to be aware of and share in your philanthropy?
- Are you interested in learning about tax benefits of charitable giving for you and your family?

By asking these simple questions, advisors begin to explore with clients their interest in philanthropy and the likelihood that charitable giving should be part of their plans. If clients express an interest, then the materials in Chapter Six will help advisors work collaboratively with charities to apply a philanthropic planning model to their plans.

In Summary

Philanthropic planning prospects are the top 10 percent of loyal donors to a charity. By creating a list of gift planning prospects with a wealth overlay, charities can identify those individuals who would be interested in and have the capacity for philanthropic planning. Professional advisors should use a questionnaire approach with their high-net-worth clients to determine if they have an interest in philanthropy.

CHAPTER 4

Creating a Fundraising Environment for Philanthropic Planning

Having identified the need for a philanthropic planning approach and the best prospects for such conversations, charities need to set the stage to build a philanthropic planning program which fits with their unique set of donors and mission, while creating an environment where philanthropic planning can thrive. To do so, it needs to create a donor-centered organizational culture, draft an internal case for philanthropic planning, build or add to existing individual gifts infrastructure including annual gifts, major gifts, principal gifts, and gift planning, and finally engage staff and volunteer leadership in the creation of the program. Philanthropic planning relies upon an existing and functioning individual gifts operation. Without it, it will be impossible for charities to find success in philanthropic planning.

LAYING THE FOUNDATION FOR PHILANTHROPIC PLANNING

Each charity seeking to build a philanthropic planning program should have previously developed a solid mission, vision, and positioning statement, a strategic plan and a case statement that clearly articulate the purpose of the charity's existence, the plan to achieve its mission, and the case for why it is important. An organization cannot engage in philanthropic planning without leadership having a clear sense—a vision—of the organization's direction, familiarity with the organization's activities, and an understanding of how those activities relate to the mission and how those activities serve the greater community.

Adopting a positioning statement to work along with the charity's mission and vision statements will form the foundation of the charity's fundraising efforts. A positioning statement describes how a charity is unique. It describes how it positions itself in the marketplace. In other words, it identifies the charity's niche. Gary J. Stern states that "when you have successfully positioned your organization, people recognize who you are and what you do. It makes sense to them."[1]

The long-term vision for the organization in conjunction with the organization's mission should be reflected in a strategic plan. This plan guides the organization, its staff, and its volunteers as they work toward annual goals that steadily grow year over year as the organization grows. A strategic plan is an organization's blueprint for carrying out its mission statement. It is initiated, implemented, and periodically reviewed by an organization's staff and board. A strategic plan, which should cover three to five years, is a prerequisite for establishing a general, individual gifts fund development plan and, subsequently, its philanthropic planning program. It identifies institutional priorities, plots a course for achieving goals and objectives, lays out performance assessment, and provides for midcourse corrections. The planning process should involve both the advancement team and key volunteers, including board members and even major donors. These key constituents have a vested interest in the organization and should show a level of responsibility that causes their later support. This is exactly the reason to involve board members and donors. Their buy-in today should lead to their financial support tomorrow.

The organization's mission and strategic plan drive the organization's case statement. The case expresses potential reasons why the prospective donors might want to contribute to the advancement of the cause. It describes the organization's goals and objectives and explains the role of philanthropy in achieving those goals. It also covers the programs and services provided. There is one large case for the organization, from which smaller individual case statements are developed for various constituencies or programs.

With the mission, vision, and positioning statement, a strategic plan, and a case statement in place, a charity has built a culture supportive of philanthropic planning and can begin to build its philanthropic planning program.

The Internal Case for Philanthropic Planning

In order for an organization to sustain a philanthropic planning program, it needs to develop an internal case. The internal case for philanthropic planning explains and justifies why it is critically important for the charity to build and sustain a philanthropic planning program to secure the organization's long-term goals and objectives. Without a case, it will not be long before staff or board leadership changes and the commitment to philanthropic planning wanes, causing the charity to return to a transactional, short-term advancement effort.

In order for donors and advisors to remain confident that the charity is committed for the long-term and that the donor's wishes will be carried out in the future, they need confidence that the charity is committed to the process and its long-term vision. The case is a vital piece of that puzzle.

Each charity drafting a case should consider the following elements:

Purpose of the Case—The first step in drafting a case for philanthropic planning is the development of a statement of purpose. The purpose of the case is to:

- Invoke the highest purpose of the organization's existence—its mission—and demonstrate how the fulfillment of its long-term mission will be strengthened through a philanthropic planning approach that encourages partnerships with donors and advisors, ultimately leading to integrated philanthropic planning solutions;
- Focus on the needs of the donors—how through the philanthropic planning process, the organization's donors can be assured that their support will enhance the part of the mission that is most important to them, and that they can establish a meaningful and permanent legacy that meets the organization's needs while also meeting their own needs;
- Provide the rationale behind the philanthropic planning process;
- Identify a range of long-term resource needs and objectives; and
- Serve as the springboard for creating a variety of communication and marketing efforts in support of the organization's philanthropic planning and gift planning programs.

Intended Audience—The case is focused on the organization's internal audience, particularly the staff and volunteer board, to help change the organizational perspective on giving. It is impossible to win over external audiences if staff and volunteer leadership have not adopted and endorsed this approach. The case serves as a constant reminder and educational tool to ensure the organization stays on this path. Many charities lose their focus when board members change or a new executive director is hired. An internal case, with buy-in from the existing executive director and board, will ensure that the culture shift to philanthropic planning will last.

Content—The philanthropic planning case has 10 core elements including:

1. Description of the long-term mission and historic significance of the organization.
2. Definitions of philanthropic planning, legacy, and endowment gifts.
3. Stories of donors who have made significant legacy and endowment gifts in the past that are supporting the organization today, including the impact those gifts have had on those it serves and the long-term outcomes those gifts have created for the organization.
4. How philanthropic planning will help donors create their own legacies and ensure the organization's long-term future.
5. How philanthropic planning fits with donors' overall plans for present and future generations of their families, to ensure a meaningful legacy beyond the charity.
6. Information about the organization's values and philosophy about long-term resource management, including legacy and endowment policies.
7. Information about specific tools that will help donors achieve their long-term objectives for the charity, for themselves, and for their families.
8. Information about donor recognition and stewardship, to ensure that the charity maintains the legacy for all time.
9. The name and position of the person at the charity who will coordinate the effort to encourage philanthropic planning.
10. A clear commitment to donor-centered service and confidentiality.

Goal—The goal articulated by the philanthropic planning case is not a dollar goal. Instead, it is a goal of sustainability using this approach, even during difficult times. The true measure of success for the case is how effective the organization becomes in engaging donors in the long-term mission and their desire to support the charity not for just today, but in perpetuity.

Focus—The focus of the philanthropic planning case is to encourage a culture at the charity which supports and encourages donor-centered relationships that lead to future and endowment gifts. The relationships are not between individual donors and fundraisers, but relationships among individual donors, their families, their advisors, and the charity's mission. Donors who are tied to the mission become long-term supporters. By engaging their families in the process, the charity ensures that their legacies will be carried out, and may even find a new generation of potential donors. A true donor-centered philanthropic planning approach also invites all of the advisors working with the donors to participate in the process. A strong case will focus on why these kinds of gifts are important to the charity, to ensure the charity maintains this approach and the culture is supported by proper resources now and in the future.

Uses—The philanthropic planning case statement has six main uses:

1. Change the culture—The case statement reminds the volunteer board and staff how a donor-centered philanthropic planning approach enhances the charity's mission today and tomorrow.
2. Tell the story—Volunteers and staff need to be reminded of the impact and outcomes from gifts. The stories of matured legacy and endowment gifts are rich fodder to show impact and outcomes. Not just the immediate impact a gift has when it matures—for example, to build a building, but the impact it has later, when that building is used to care for sick animals which are then adopted by loving families, or whatever the mission might be. The reach of these gifts is long term. Long-term stories demonstrate the power of these gifts to fulfill a charity's mission.
3. Obtain feedback—Volunteers and staff often have reasons not to support philanthropic planning. Sharing the case allows the charity to hear those thoughts and build consensus on the importance of long-term support.
4. Form the basis for communication materials—The stories outlined in the case statement often can be reworked to show donors and

prospects the long-term outcomes created by philanthropic planning.

5. Test the market—The case statement allows the charity to determine if the organization is ready to pursue philanthropic planning. If the organization faces significant opposition to adopting a well-articulated case, it will need to spend more time educating volunteers and staff about the importance of this approach, as the organization is not yet ready for donor-centered philanthropic planning. However, feedback will help the charity to refine the message so that it hits the target. When the case is strong, it is easily reworked to become the basis of communication materials. When the case is not compelling, it will fail with insiders and potential donors alike.

6. Recruit volunteer leadership—The case statement shares the organization's fundraising philosophy with prospective volunteer leaders. If they do not agree with the case, it gives the charity an opportunity to educate them or to avoid putting them on the board.

Steps for Writing the Case Statement—Writing an internal case can be a wonderful exercise for a charity, bringing together staff and volunteer leadership to get behind this new philosophy and approach. To begin, a charity should assemble a planning group consisting of volunteer and staff leadership and ask participants the following questions:

- What is the nature of the work of the organization?
- What services and programs are provided?
- What kind of outreach does the organization provide in the community?
- Who uses the organization's services?
- What is the immediate impact and what are the long-term outcomes of the organization's efforts?
- How can these outcomes be illustrated or measured today, tomorrow, and in perpetuity?
- How will making a gift to the endowment allow the organization to offer more or better services?
- How will making a gift to the endowment make an impact on the organization, the community, and the cause?
- How will other people important to the donor view this gift?

- How can the organization engage the families and advisors to donors in this process?
- Why is it important to set up a legacy gift now?

With these questions answered, the planning group should collect information about the organization and its long-range plans. Conversations with all constituents (staff, administration, trustees, donors, prospects, donor and prospect families, and professional advisors) will provide understanding of the audience for which it is being written.

Once the case has been drafted, the planning group should provide the draft to stakeholders, gathering reactions to the draft from volunteer and staff leadership using a questionnaire that asks if the case statement:

- Elicits reasons to participate in a program of philanthropic planning and long-term support.
- Tells volunteers and staff how gifts will make a difference now and in perpetuity.
- Evokes a sense of history and the long-term importance of the organization's work.
- Offers proof that the plan will work.
- States the benefits to the donor, the donor's family, professional advisors, and other interested parties clearly.
- Is concise.
- Is donor-centered rather than organization-centered.
- Emphasizes opportunities for donors and their families rather than needs for the organization.
- Is presented in a logical order.
- Is readable, with short sentences, paragraphs, and enough blank space.
- Is readable, with typeface large enough and appropriate to the organization.
- Is complete, without being over done?

To ensure the case truly reflects a sustainable philanthropic planning philosophy for the charity, the planning group will need to relinquish pride of authorship, writing and rewriting the case until it expresses the philanthropic planning vision for the particular organization.

An internal case can take many forms, depending upon the organization. Appendix A includes an internal case for Le Moyne College. Because they were just beginning their program, their case is focused more on the need to launch a basic gift planning program. Notice how Le Moyne has integrated particular donor stories and outcomes into the case to make it more compelling. As their program evolves, Le Moyne will develop a more comprehensive philanthropic planning case, similar to the sample internal case in Appendix B.

THE ROLE OF AN INTEGRATED ADVANCEMENT PROGRAM

A philanthropic planning program is part of a charity's comprehensive, individual gifts advancement effort. Each individual gifts program starts with its donors, and perhaps most importantly, its first-time donors. The philanthropic planning program relies on loyal donors who have grown in their support of their favorite charity. These donors start as individuals who believe in the mission and make a modest gift to support it. Without them feeding the philanthropic planning pipeline, the program will ultimately fail.

Annual Giving in the Philanthropic Planning Context

An integrated advancement program includes annual giving, major/capital giving, principal giving, and gift planning. These four approaches, both individually and collectively, support the organization's needs over the course of its operation with the basic annual income to support the organization's core, capital funds needed for special programs, buildings, and other physical plant requirements, and future gifts to add new and enhance existing endowments.

Annual giving is the primary fundraising method used to broaden support, upgrade giving levels, and provide operating support for on-going programs. The annual giving program should continue to be developed as it fulfills the following purposes:

- Provides income for unrestricted and restricted programs
- Renews donor support annually
- Cultivates donors to increase giving levels
- Solicits new donors to broaden the base of support

- Identifies potential new board members and organizational leadership
- Identifies major gifts prospects
- Builds donor loyalty
- Identifies gift planning prospects
- Identifies philanthropic planning prospects

Unfortunately, too many organizations focus on the components of annual giving at the expense of other individual giving opportunities. In addition to a direct mail campaign, there are multiple special events that clog the calendars of just about every community. Ask business leaders how many invitations they get to support charity golf outings each year and the number will astound. Special events are overused in the United States. Cultivation events which focus on educating prospects about the charity's mission and building meaningful relationships will yield larger major and/ or legacy gifts than the modest contributions made to events. Events also hold less appeal to Generation X than other methods of engagement, meaning that this important cohort is being missed in the event culture prevalent today. If charities would spend resources to cultivate the 10 percent of donors who give 90 percent of the donations instead of spending their energies trying to get gifts from the 90 percent of donors who give 10 percent of the revenues, overall giving would be greater and costs for fundraising would be lower.

CONCEPT THE INTEGRATED APPROACH

Brian and I have both had the pleasure of developing gifts from many sources. Whether the referral came from an annual giving officer, a major gift officer, or was the result of strategic marketing, we have met people who came to know the organizations that we represented from just about every source you might consider. The one thing to take from this outcome is that while we need and should plan for a dynamic philanthropic planning program, the integrated approach where an organization develops relationships in all disciplines has proven to be effective for assisting with the identification and development of legacy gifts. —REW

There is no magic formula for determining the right mix of approaches, it varies from organization to organization depending on their needs, but it is clear that a balanced approach with annual giving, major giving, principal giving, and gift planning receiving equal marketing and development support from the staff will lead to the best results.

Gift Planning In the Philanthropic Planning Context

Before attempting to build a philanthropic planning program focused on serving principal and major gift donors, charities should first focus on ensuring they have a strong gift planning program to meet the needs of those constituencies. This walk before you run approach will provide charities with a strong base on which to build the programs discussed in Chapters 6 and 7.

In mature fundraising programs, traditional planned gifts, made up of life-income gifts (charitable gift annuities, pooled income funds, and charitable remainder trusts) and realized estate gifts (matured gifts from wills, living trusts, life insurance policies, and retirement plans) comprise 25 percent to 40 percent of total individual gifts receipts (excluding corporations, foundations, and government grants). If structured outright gifts and endowment gifts (which together with life-income gifts and estate gifts make up the universe of legacy gifts) are also included, the percentages are even higher. A legacy gift can be made with any asset and can be outright or deferred. What makes it unique is that the donor is actively thinking about how the gift helps the organization for the long-term as well as how the gift integrates with the donor's tax, estate, and financial planning.

Effective gift planning programs promote legacy gifts in a donor-centered approach. They are generally divided into three core areas including infrastructure, donor interaction, and communications and marketing. Within those three core areas are seven essentials that often determine the success or failure of a gift planning effort.

Infrastructure
Mission, endowment, and leadership: For a gift planning program to thrive, the organization must have a long-term mission and leadership committed to endowment building.

Making the case: An internal case for gift planning is a critical long-term vision statement which helps sustain a robust gift planning program over time. It answers the question of why an organization needs gift planning and why now. It provides a rationale and commitment to gift planning to share with future volunteer and staff leadership. The gift planning case contains many of the same elements that were described in the philanthropic planning case, it is simply a more basic version focused less on values and complex planning and more on long-term support of the charity.

Policies, procedures, and guidelines: There are a wide range of policies, procedures, and guidelines required for an effective gift planning program, largely because gift planning touches so many different areas of individual gifts. Part IV of the *Companion* outlines several areas which warrant attention from charities including tracking, reporting, gift acceptance policies, gift counting and valuation guidelines, gift recognition policies, gift procedures, gift agreements, and charitable registrations.

Donor Interaction

Identification of gift planning prospects: To build a donor-interaction program for gift planning, the charity must first identify prospects who are open to the gift planning message. Chapter 3 provides a methodology to identify the best gift planning prospects. Charities should use this tool to create a target audience for donor interaction.

Communication and Marketing

Stewardship: While strong gift planning programs include both outright gifts and gifts that mature in the future, most charities do little to steward these gifts. This often disenfranchises donors whose gifts will not come to fruition until a later time. Mature gift planning programs receive more than 50 percent of their life-income gift receipts from repeat donors. Similarly, most estate commitments are revocable, requiring an effective and robust stewardship program to ensure that donors continue to name their favorite organization as a beneficiary or increase the amount coming to it over time. Details on building an effective gift planning stewardship program are discussed in Chapter 12.

Marketing: A strategic marketing and communications program for gift planning should be built on a donor-centered, moves-managed based, philanthropic planning platform. Such a program is designed to find new prospects or to get existing prospects to self-identify as ready to consider a gift. Part III of the *Companion* provides detailed information on how to build such a marketing program to appeal to identified gift planning prospects.

Map to success: The final core element for an effective gift planning program is a long-term strategic plan. Each charity needs to build this plan for itself. Appendices G and L provide a sample gift planning marketing plan and a philanthropic planning timeline, respectively. Combined, they provide the start of a roadmap for how a charity can plan for a successful gift planning program.

The Role of Your Board and Volunteers in Gift Planning   With the seven core gift planning elements in place, involving your board and volunteers is the next step in the evolution of the program. Like most development programs, the board and volunteers can have a role in both gift planning and eventually philanthropic planning. Education about the charity's integrated advancement approach will position the charity's focus on the top tier of donors since they will now understand where each piece of the puzzle fits to create the big picture.

Educating Board Members About Gift Planning Fundraising is one of several key responsibilities of every non-profit board. Often special events, annual giving, and major gifts are at the top of the list when boards discuss vehicles to raise revenue. Obviously, they will not want to leave out what should be a key component of their overall development plan—gift planning.

Board members and volunteers want to make a difference. They want their efforts to be appreciated and their work to be meaningful. Training board members and volunteers is necessary if charities expect them to assist in gift planning. They need to be comfortable if they are to suggest legacy gifts to people they are cultivating for the organization. Training will allow them to do it successfully.

It is not necessary to acquaint board members with all that encompasses the gift planning area, but informing them on how it establishes long-term relationships with the donors of the organization, how it can provide future funds, and how it encourages donors to think about assets as potential gifts can be the building blocks for further discussions.

During the educational process, the charity has the opportunity to raise the board's awareness for their own potential for giving. When board members consider the benefits to a donor, it may trigger the thoughts for a personal gift. It should be a given that for the board to be helpful in developing legacy gifts, they should have given in that way themselves.

Setting Board Expectations

The Greatest Gift is a Portion of Thyself.

—Ralph Waldo Emerson

With the board educated, they are now in a position to understand gift planning and to support it. The charity should let them know what is expected of them as it relates to their own giving and their role as an ambassador of the organization's mission in the community. Roles should be defined as well as the extent of their legal responsibilities and board involvement with the gift planning program.

The board typically establishes investment policies and guidelines that include parameters for who makes investment decisions, where and how funds are to be invested, parameters for an acceptable rate of return, and how gifts of stock are handled, to name a few. The board establishes policies regarding management, marketing, and promotion of the gift planning program. If the people in charge of delivering the programs and services of an organization are not in agreement with the process of soliciting contributed income, they will not be effective advocates for the charity's fundraising efforts. They will determine what types of gift planning vehicles will be offered as well as a minimum amount to accept for each instrument. For example, some organizations use $5,000 as a minimum for charitable gift annuities while others use $10,000 as the threshold.

Board members should be ambassadors sharing the organization's mission, values, and programs throughout the community. After making their own gifts, board members should help to identify and cultivate prospects and open doors for the fundraiser to build relationships and solicit gifts. Noted major gift development expert Karen Osborn tells us that a culture of philanthropy exists when 100 percent of the board gives joyfully at a level commensurate with his or her ability; are informed and passionate ambassadors telling the story, introducing the institution to others; gladly and freely sharing expertise and wisdom; and seeing philanthropy as an aspect of every committee's role.[2]

By making use of their networks, board members make the organization stronger and able to survive change. Andrea Nierenberg, the author of

Million Dollar Networking, talks about being known, being liked, and being trusted as you build relationships and an alliance that fosters opportunities for business.[3] Perhaps one of the best resources charities have for marketing is the complex network created by boards and volunteers who serve organizations. Not only are they committed to the mission, but with training and support, they can serve as the best ambassadors in their spheres of influence. They are already known, are liked, and can be trusted by their peers as they assist charities with building stronger relationships in the community. They should become the biggest advocates for the gift planning program in the charity's market area. Considering that 85 percent of the adults in the United States die without having made a valid will, it becomes clear that there is much work to do. And factoring in—according to the *Campbell & Company Study (2007)*—that more than one out of four Americans (31 percent) are considering making a charitable bequest, the opportunity is there.[4]

The Role of Volunteers

> *No matter how big and powerful government gets, and the many services it provides, it can never take the place of volunteers.*
>
> —President Ronald Reagan

Gift planners and fundraisers working for charities are important players on the philanthropic planning team, but they can enhance their opportunities by partnering with others. Four groups of people can assist fundraisers in their pursuit of success—board members, professional advisors, a gift planning advisory board, and loyal volunteers.

Not all volunteers are willing fundraisers. No matter how much training, they may never feel comfortable with approaching others to follow their example and make a legacy gift. Every volunteer can and should participate in gift planning efforts. By saying that everyone has to play a role, but not everyone has to play the same role, charities provide for everyone's talents to have a place while not requiring that each make the ask. Volunteers can be matched with a skill and activity that is both fitting and rewarding. Each stage in the moves-management process can play to individual strengths, connections, capacity, time, and willingness to serve. This allows volunteers to have a different, but complementary, role in the gift planning process and share in the ultimate success of the giving effort.

CONCEPT QUITE A ``STARR``

One of the most knowledgeable donors that Brian and I have met over the years has to be Starr. She has served on the foundation board of one of the hospitals in Meridian Health for more than a decade and has also been very active in one of their auxiliaries. Starr can be seen wearing a star of some size either on her clothing or as an adornment since she is well known and enjoys people recognizing her and remembering her name. I have come to know her quite well over the last few years and had asked her to serve on our Meridian Philanthropic Planning Council. As a donor who is not a financial advisor, it is helpful to get her perspective after a meeting or seminar since she clearly has a different viewpoint. She regularly participates and stays as up-to-date on charitable gift planning information and tax law as it relates to her situation as any person I have met. She is the consummate planner and the outcomes of her planning have given her a comfortable living. About six months ago, I asked if she would mind sharing her story and her plan for her charitable giving with our other auxiliaries around Meridian Health. She agreed and has done a fabulous job going on the road with me talking about why she is so excited to both support her favorite hospital and why she has done eight charitable gift annuities for both her college and the hospital. You can't replace the enthusiasm of a volunteer or the sincerity of a message delivered from the heart. She is our shining Starr! —REW

Some suggestions for alternative roles include thanking donors through phone calls, letters, or hand-written notes, identifying donors from their many networks and circles of influence, leading committees to support fundraising efforts, and, if they are willing, assisting with gift solicitations.

Giving USA and Independent Sector estimate that 63.4 million adults volunteered in America in 2009 for more than 8.1 billion hours. Assuming that volunteer time is worth the average wage, or $20.85 per volunteer hour, the total value to nonprofit organizations was at least $169 billion in 2009.[5] Volunteers are certainly valuable.

Volunteers, like board members, need to be educated about gift planning and why it can be an effective part of an organization's advancement program. Again, if they can consider a personal gift, their commitments will be greater and their impacts will lead to greater success from their efforts. Most gift planning programs do very little to engage loyal volunteers outside of board members. To build an effective program, consider:

- What groups make up the charity's loyal donor base?
- How can the charity create volunteer opportunities that engage these groups but are not unwieldy to manage?
- What return does the charity want from its investment in volunteer groups?
- How will the charity measure success?

Once a charity determines who makes up their loyal volunteer group, it can survey those individuals to determine volunteer opportunities that interest them. After all, it is better to let volunteers determine for themselves how they want to engage with an organization on an ongoing basis. Traditionalists are happy to volunteer where charities need them, including serving on committees, staffing the gift shop, or filling in when asked. They see it as a civic responsibility. The Baby Boomers want to be able to pick the areas where they provide volunteer support to an organization. They are not willing to simply serve on the "golf committee", because that is where you need them. Because they started their families later in life than the generations before them, they generally have less time to volunteer, and only in recent years have they started to pick up the mantle from the Traditionalists. Generation X typically wants to volunteer to work on the program they are supporting with their financial gifts. They have far less interest in volunteering for other institutional priorities. Millennials tend not to volunteer for charity unless they have a say in how the program for which they are volunteering will be run. Millennials bring great energy and fresh, new ideas, but also have the lowest tolerance for the bureaucracies found at most established charities.

Consider the following sample of possible tasks for loyal volunteers that could advance a gift planning program:

- Making stewardship calls to other donors
- Profile in magazine, newsletter, or on web site along with impact stories
- Use of home, office, club for reception, vision meeting, service discussion; helping plan and implement

- Hosting committee meetings
- Use of their site for a foundation board meeting
- Potential donor screening sessions—participating, hosting
- Helping with fundraising strategies
- Making in-person cultivation, solicitation, and/or stewardship visits
- Helping with event mailings
- Writing letters to legislators and participating in other broad-based advocacy opportunities

Lastly, loyal volunteers who have worked with the charity for a decade or longer are not only ideal candidates themselves to make a legacy gift, but they also have a passion for the mission that has grown over many years and they are excited to share their story with others about why they do what they do. Certainly volunteers can play a vital role if charities engage them in ways that interest them.

The Role of the Board and Volunteers in Philanthropic Planning

When the board and volunteers are well-versed in gift planning, they are ready to take the next step to become acquainted with philanthropic planning.

An old fundraising chestnut is that people don't give to people, and people don't give to causes, they give to people with causes. One of the most beneficial ways for a board member to assist with philanthropic planning is to invite the prospective donor to sit down to discuss what has been a very important matter to them. As a peer, having a trustee involved in the development of the relationship is a wonderfully efficient way to build trust as the planning concept is presented.

According to The Advisory Board (2007), trustees can achieve great results in three main areas:

1. Initiating relationships with top prospects
   - Informing strategy development
   - Making the initial contact
   - Participating in the first meeting

2. Deepening and sustaining relationships with top prospects and donors
   - Participating in ongoing face-to-face interactions
   - Communicating between meetings
3. Soliciting large gifts
   - Attending solicitation meetings
   - If the case warrants, asking for the gift.[6]

In addition to referrals to donors, charities can also gain introductions to professional advisors through their board members. Whether they are trust, estate or tax attorneys, accountants, insurance professionals, investment advisors, financial planners, bankers, or real estate brokers, professional advisors can be strong partners in developing the philanthropic planning program.

As will be discussed in Chapter 5, professional advisors can be positive advocates for philanthropic planning. There should be two groups that can assist with spreading the word about philanthropic planning—those who are affiliated with the charity and those who are active volunteers as part of an advisory board. The best gift planning and philanthropic planning officers in the country have a sound conceptual knowledge of how each of the gift planning vehicles works and are also able to communicate them to prospects. It should be understood that only very few will ever become tax experts even if they study full time—so a general knowledge and the ability to work with others will provide the best opportunity for success. Additionally, while there are quite a few attorneys who serve nonprofit organizations as gift or philanthropic planners, most fundraisers do not need to be legal experts if they can work closely with trust and estate planning attorneys on matters that require their attention.

Board members and volunteers can assist with involving Tier One (principal gift) donors in projects and in ways that deepen their connection to an organization. In addition to board membership, there are always committees and other important roles that should be matched to the donors' interests. Northern Trust conducted a study of high-net-worth donors in 2007[7] and found that 42 percent wanted to support a cause that they personally believed in and 26 percent spent more than 100 hours as a volunteer. The Tarnside Curve of Involvement[8] in Figure 4.1 illustrates the continuum of progressive commitment. The curve is a simple concept that

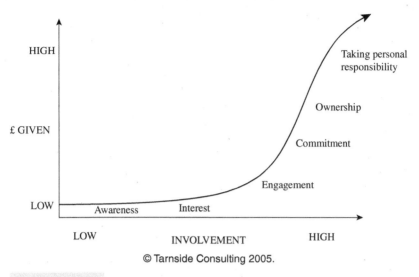

© Tarnside Consulting 2005.

FIGURE 4.1   THE TARNSIDE CURVE OF INVOLVEMENT

Source: Reproduced with permission from Tarnside Consulting, UK (www.tarnside.co.uk)

is easily understood by fundraisers and which encourages a specific way of discussing levels of interest.

The more involved people become in the cause, the more personal and financial resources they will commit and the greater the likelihood that they will participate in the philanthropic planning process. Board members can be very influential partners in the process to progressively move interested donors along the continuum toward a greater commitment.

CONCEPT   **INVOLVEMENT**

While working with the American Cancer Society, I can recall a meeting where we asked some of our best donors to sit down and discuss prospects for a capital campaign for the Hope Lodge in New York City. As we all know, you can get a great deal of feedback from donors and volunteers who might want to help you expand your reach after they themselves had made a gift to a project. We held the meeting in a very inspiring setting at the AT&T Global Communications center where we learned how communication grew over the centuries from drums that were beat to send messages
(continued)

long ago to the complex technology of today that gives us all a clear signal when we dial our phone. But the message that rang true for me came from one of our couples that were there to assist. In their remarks, they continued to refer to "their hospital" when speaking about a hospital that was near and dear to them. It was where they had made a transformational gift to provide some amazing support for a project that was serving thousands in their community. They were happy to support us and provide a place for people to stay free of charge while they had cancer treatments as an outpatient in Manhattan, but nothing spoke volumes about how they had taken personal responsibility like when they continued to use the words "our hospital." They had made a commitment to us, but they were an owner who had invested in their hospital and it was clear that they were as involved as a couple could be in their favorite cause. —REW

In Summary

This chapter has recounted the required elements that should exist for an integrated advancement program to be effective and lead an organization to the point of installing a philanthropic planning program. It outlines how an organization with all the pieces in place can enlist the support of its board and other volunteers in developing donors for each of the four levels of the philanthropic planning pyramid: principal gifts, major gifts, loyals, and everyone else. Not only can board members and volunteers be helpful in the process, but top-tier donors can be cultivated by involving them in the very process that has brought them along their journeys toward becoming philanthropists.

CHAPTER 5

The Role of Professional Advisors

he first four chapters of the *Companion* have focused on defining
philanthropic planning, why there is a need for philanthropic planning, identifying individuals who would benefit from philanthropic
planning, and preparing charities to pursue a program of philanthropic
planning.

$$\frac{\text{Gift Planner} + \text{Professional Advisors} + \text{Philanthropic Planning}}{\text{Donor with Charitable Intent}} = \text{Philanthropy}$$

These chapters have directly addressed all of the components of the
philanthropic planning model but one: the role of the professional advisor.

ROLES OF PROFESSIONAL ADVISORS IN THE PHILANTHROPIC PLANNING PROCESS

Professional advisors are the final element in the Philanthropic Planning
Model. To truly meet the needs of philanthropists, experts in the areas of
finances, taxes and tax law, insurance, real property, charitable giving, and
retirement benefits need to collaborate on a comprehensive plan. Everyone
needs to be at the table.

The Partnership for Philanthropic Planning (PPP) periodically completes surveys of donors. The number of donors who reported learning
about the most basic gift planning option—a charitable bequest—from
their legal or financial advisors increased from 4 percent in 1992 to 28 percent in 2000.[1] More recent studies have shown that a growing percentage
of Gen X and Millennials prefer to receive this information that way.[2]

And nearly 70 percent of charitable remainder trust donors reported learning about the option from their advisors.

An increasing number of charitable gifts are being structured by professional advisors, and very often, charity is not included in their conversations. This is an unfortunate development as charitable gift planners can assist advisors by providing information about services offered by the charity, donor motivations for giving, and charitable gift options. This frees the advisor to focus on his or her practice area. Together, advisors and gift planners can structure the right gift, with the right asset, at the right time, toward the right project, for the right cause. Working independently, many things may not go right.

Each of the following has an important role:

- *Attorney*—Probably the most important advisor an individual or couple will have in planning an estate is a capable trust and estate attorney. Not just any lawyer, but one skilled in helping to plan the distribution of assets rather than waiting to simply go through probate. A skilled lawyer can prepare the proper documents (wills, trusts, power of attorney, medical and charitable directives, etc.). This attorney should be someone with whom the individual or couple is comfortable expressing their views and wishes, and who will fairly represent all the options available. Seeking references from family, friends, and other professionals is best when looking for this advisor so conducting one's practice in a way that leads to good referrals is ideal.

- *Accountant or tax specialist*—A Certified Public Accountant or other tax specialist who is current on tax law including estate tax law and property valuation methods is an equally valuable member of the team. The advice of a strong accountant familiar with the financial transactions of the individual or couple will be helpful in planning for the various goals and the eventual distribution of the assets.

- *Insurance agent or specialist*—If life insurance makes up a larger part of an estate or if life insurance is being used as an estate planning tool, an agent is an important member of the philanthropic planning team. A Wealth Replacement Trust can be a helpful tool in maximizing the assets that are passed to heirs in the appropriate circumstance and an insurance specialist who can complement the planning process could be advantageous.

- *Bank trust officer*—Because of their long-standing relationships, the bank trust officer can often provide information about assets or help complete an inventory assessment. Similarly, they can serve the role of trustee should the situation warrant the use of one or more trusts.
- *Nonprofit fundraiser*—Knowledge of fundraising techniques acceptable to the charity and strong donor relationships associated with development make the fundraiser/gift planner a good resource for all stages of philanthropic planning. Additionally, the fundraiser can provide information about the charity's gift acceptance policies and gift agreement process.

DISPELLING THE MYTHS: COMPETING OR COMPLETING

There is a common misconception that charitable gift planners and professional advisors are in competition with each other. Gift planners have been known to refer to for-profit advisors as the "Dark-Side" in a Star Wars reference to the evil side of the "Force." By implication, gift planners are saying that they are on the side of good. This misconception has grown from anecdotal evidence from gift planners who have "lost" gifts because advisors have "killed" them. The perception in the gift planning world is that advisors discourage donors from making a gift to a favorite charity because the advisor either does not understand the workings of the gift plan or does not value the individual's charitable intent.

Similarly, many professional advisors are hesitant to include fundraisers in their conversations with clients because they could slow the process or suggest gift structures which do not work in the context of the plan. When working with insurance and investment advisors, many gift plans can unnecessarily and negatively impact the bottom line.

To maximize the benefits to the donor/client, fundraisers and advisors need to learn to work collaboratively. As Robert Sharpe, Jr. points out, fundraisers and advisors should look toward completing instead of competing. By working together, a gift planner and the donor's advisor can help the individual to make an informed decision. Through education and a relationship with their local fundraisers, advisors can begin to develop a new part of their practice and help out the many worthy causes that support their communities.

How Professional Advisors Can Promote Philanthropic Planning

Many advisors assume that their clients are not charitable. Some are not, but most are very supportive of their favorite causes and want to include them in their planning if the advisor asks about charitable giving. According to *Giving USA*, individuals account for between 84 and 88 percent of total annual giving. Knowing that up to 85 percent of clients are anxious to receive guidance about philanthropy from their advisors, and that almost 60 percent would give more if they were better informed about giving options and the effectiveness of their contributions, advisors should ask all of their clients the following question:

> "Hypothetically speaking, if you are set to inherit a million dollars from your great aunt with a condition that you have to give half of it away in order to receive the other half, what organization(s) would you like to support and why?"

The answer could lead to a wonderful discussion about charitable intent and the many philanthropic tools available to the client. And wouldn't everyone agree that proper planning can mean positive outcomes for their client? Wouldn't every advisor want to help their client to:

- Increase current income
- Decrease current income taxes
- Eliminate capital gains taxes
- Reduce or eliminate possible federal estate taxes
- Conserve assets for family and loved ones
- Diversify and professionally manage client assets

It can all happen while also helping a client to make a significant contribution to charity.

Much can come to the advisor who brings up the topic of charitable giving with their client. In addition to increased income, increased client loyalty, the ability to manage money for more than one generation, referrals from other professionals, and community influence, advisors can gain satisfaction in knowing that they were helpful in the process of supporting important charitable missions. The following steps can be helpful:

Steps for Advisors to Follow with their Clients

- Determine client planning objectives.
- Determine/evaluate donative intent of client.
- Match philanthropic tools to obtain client objectives.
- Attempt to capture philanthropic assets to maximize benefit to donor and succeeding interests.

Steps for Advisors to Follow with Nonprofits

- Determine personal interests and identify nonprofit organizations that match.
- Learn about philanthropic tools and types of gifts accepted by nonprofit organizations.
- Support the mission of the chosen organization.
- Include gift planners, in cases involving their organization, early in the process.

FORGING NEW RELATIONSHIPS

One of the closest relationships that I enjoy with a professional advisor evolved out of a phone call that I made in the fall of 2002 to advisors who were members of the Estate Planning Council of Northern New Jersey. I called one and asked for 20 minutes to meet at his office in Ridgewood, New Jersey. As we all know, giving busy people a chance to take an appointment in their office gives them little downtime, but for their time during your meeting.

When I arrived, the gentleman in Ridgewood said "in more than 25 years as a certified financial planner (CFP), it was the first time a planned giving officer (PGO) had called him." We had a great first meeting, ended up extending it an additional 20 minutes and have forged a wonderful collaboration that has led to many donor/client meetings, many referrals, and several business trips and speaking engagements together as well as more than $5 million in planned gifts. Paul W. Hansen, CFP, CLU, ChFC, CSPG, CAP is a terrific example of a professional advisor who understands philanthropic planning and has aligned his practice at Morgan Stanley Smith Barney with the nonprofit sector to grow his assets under management. —REW

Would Advisors Benefit from Specialized Training in Charitable Planning?

The marketplace for charitable giving is robust. According to *Giving USA*, individuals and estates account for more than $250 billion in charitable gifts each year. Those professional advisors with the ability to determine if a person is charitable and understanding the individual needs of that client can build a substantial charitable giving part of their practice.

Whether it is a fundraiser for a nonprofit organization or a financial advisor who uncovers a client's interest in giving, many philanthropic tools are available. They can include:

- Annual Gifts
- Major Gifts
- Bequests
- Charitable Remainder Trusts
- Charitable Lead Trusts
- Pooled Income Funds
- Charitable Gift Annuities
- Private Family Foundations
- Donor-advised Philanthropic Funds

By helping the donor/client to decide what type of gift to make, and sharing knowledge of the advantages and disadvantages of each, a gift planner and a professional advisor working collaboratively can assist the donor/client in making an informed decision. Hall (1997) cites a study conducted for *The Chronicle of Philanthropy* by Prince & Associates and Private Wealth Consultants where researchers polled 603 donors, each of whom had a net worth of at least $5 million and had contributed at least $75,000 using one of several types of planned gifts. When asked what donors wanted in their charitable advisors, 97.9 percent stated an expertise in the technical details of executing the planned gift.

For professional advisors who want to enhance their practice in this area, there are many different avenues to gain this knowledge. Several organizations offer educational opportunities to not only expand advisors breadth of understanding in charitable gift planning, but also provide a designation that is recognized in the charitable sector. The American College in Bryn Mawr, Pennsylvania, a standard bearer in the financial services field for designations such as Certified Life Underwriter (CLU), Chartered Financial Consultant (ChFC), and Certified Financial Planner (CFP®), offers the Chartered Advisor in Philanthropy (CAP) designation with almost equal interest among for-profit and nonprofit professionals. For a more specialized program, Cal State—Long Beach in Orange County, California, offers a Certified Specialist in Planned Giving designation (CSPG). There are also several certificate and master's degree programs in Fundraising Management and similar nonprofit management curriculums.

Two professional organizations specializing in philanthropic planning, the Partnership for Philanthropic Planning[3] (PPP) in Indianapolis, Indiana, and Advisors in Philanthropy[4] (AiP) in Rocky Hill, Connecticut, welcome professional advisors as members. Each offers an annual conference and a wide range of educational opportunities throughout the year to provide professional advisors with supplemental information about charitable giving. Many of the offerings include continuing education credits for a wide range of professional advisors.

METHODS FOR FUNDRAISERS TO ENGAGE AND PARTNER WITH PROFESSIONAL ADVISORS

Just as there are steps that professional advisors can take to work more effectively with fundraisers, fundraisers need to take steps to understand the role of advisors and work more collaboratively with them.

As noted earlier, there is a common misconception that charitable gift planners and financial advisors have different motivations and priorities when dealing with their donor/client. When either party believes this to be true, it often becomes a reality. Fundraisers need to understand that advisors have a different perspective on the donor/ client. While a gift planner wants to position the charity to receive current and deferred gifts in maximum amounts, financial advisors usually promote asset preservation and conservation of personal resources. These opposing notions can put the donor/client in the middle. A client must clearly articulate his or her wishes so advisors can calculate the value of their charitable intent.

Be aware of the challenge that can appear when a gift is being developed and planned. Depending on how the donor was discovered, the donor/

client's advisors can be leery of supporting the charitable gift since the idea did not originate with them. Gift planners need to encourage donors to affect collaboration amongst their advisors—including financial planners, accountants, attorneys, and insurance specialists—in their charitable planning.

Although communication among a donor/client's advisors has historically been poor, each can positively support their donative intent. When forces are combined, the result can bring about a wonderful combination of professionals. With the donor's financial well-being and personal motivations to give as the common denominator, professionals from the for-profit and nonprofit worlds can work together toward a common goal.

Education can go a long way toward building a bridge between gift planners and professional advisors. Limited knowledge of charitable giving options among many advisors can cause them to avoid discussing charitable giving concepts. Without formal training and education in philanthropic planning, many professionals are left unprepared to help their clients fulfill their wishes. The necessity of additional tax knowledge can also add to their anxiety. In the end, a lack of understanding about a concept can often lead to rejection. Similarly, advisors may fear that uneducated fundraisers could foul up a well-thought tax and estate plan by suggesting strategies to the donor/client without being aware of the balance of the plan. Taking the time to communicate can eliminate the challenge and build an important relationship as well.

Does an Advanced Degree or Certification Create Credibility with Advisors?

Fundraisers who display knowledge and skills for philanthropic planning will impress professional advisors, regardless of whether they hold a certification or an advanced degree. Fundraisers without strong skills will alienate professional advisors just as quickly.

For fundraisers who expect to do a significant amount of work with professional advisors, adding a credential which is recognizable to advisors does provide some initial credibility and ease of entry. The key is to be knowledgeable and build on that credibility by providing helpful and timely advice that positively reinforces the advisor's relationship with the charity's donor.

The best step a fundraiser can take is to become and remain educated. Attend seminars and conferences hosted by the Partnership for

Philanthropic Planning (PPP) and the Association of Fundraising Professionals (AFP). When faced with an unfamiliar gift situation, research it before going to legal counsel for answers. While the authors have backgrounds in financial planning and law, most of their gift planning knowledge came from working directly with prospects in need of help and professional advisors who provided advice along the way.

For those fundraisers who do want to pursue additional studies, consider the CAP or CFP® programs.

Engage Professional Advisors

For the philanthropic planning process to be successful, fundraisers should seek out ways to collaborate and partner with advisors.

Seven Proven Ways to Develop Support from Advisors

1. Look to the organization's own board and volunteers for advisors who already support it in some way. Meet with them and get to know what they do. Discover how the fundraiser and the advisor can develop more opportunities for success.
2. Provide helpful materials to advisors who regularly meet with individuals. The *Federal Pocket Tax Guide* is one useful reference tool. Create other guides that can assist them with the mission. Share brochures with them so they might provide them to the appropriate clients.

AN EXAMPLE OF COLLABORATION

At Meridian Health Affiliated Foundations, I worked with Fred Schoenbrodt, Esq. to develop two pieces as a tool for advisors—a booklet that describes in detail the New Jersey Estate and Inheritance Tax as well as a brochure that offers a simpler explanation for advisors and for possible use with people like executors. Fred's expertise as a knowledgeable trust and estate attorney who is very familiar with New Jersey tax law is invaluable to Meridian Health. In addition to his current volunteer role as Co-Chairman of the Meridian Philanthropic Planning Council, Fred and his partners at Neff Aguilar, LLC, have represented many estates where Meridian Health is a beneficiary. —REW

3. Create a Board of Advisors—that is, a group of advisors who can provide assistance in special cases involving complex gifts and can also meet periodically to discuss ways to prospect and market the organization's need for support from the community. Not only is their expertise invaluable in certain circumstances, but many advisors have become wonderful marketers as they have grown their own businesses. As shared in the example previously, the Meridian Philanthropic Planning Council serves as a resource for the efforts at Meridian Health.

4. Bring them in on cases that need an expert. Consulting with them early on can mean the difference between a "yes" and a "no". Don't forget how advisors make a living—opportunities for both the organization and the advisor will go a long way to strengthen the relationship and their future support.

5. Encourage their involvement in projects or special events that can be helpful to them and the organization. If advisors become a part of what the organization does, they will grow in their understanding of the mission.

6. Invite an advisor to bring a client who they feel is interested in the organization to an event. In turn, the fundraiser should invite a donor who might need some of the services provided by the advisor. Try this at events such as a golf outing. The donor will spend the round riding in the cart with the advisor while the fundraiser has the chance to get to know the advisor's client in a comfortable setting over a six-hour period.

BE SURE TO ASK FOR WHAT YOU TRULY NEED

I'm reminded of a letter that was sent to author Rudyard Kipling at a time when he was the most popular and the best paid writer in England. Upon reading that he earned 50 pence per word, some Cambridge University students sent that sum to him along with a request for one of his very best words. Kipling replied with a single-word telegram: "THANKS". —REW

7. Offer referrals. One of the best ways to increase support from advisors is to offer them referrals. Since they, like fundraisers, are looking to gain new opportunities to grow their businesses, referring a possible new client to them and even introducing them to a fellow advisor who might be a resource for them is both welcomed and appreciated.

By looking at donors/clients through the eyes of their professional advisors, fundraisers can better understand the relationship and how they can effectively fit into the relationship.

Support Professional Advisors in Their Work

When working with a prospect on a charitable gift, fundraisers have the choice to lead by example and engage professional advisors, or they can continue to work in a silo with the prospect and discover later that the gift does not fit with the prospect's overall plan. Clearly it is in the fundraiser's best interest to lead by example by reaching out to the prospect's professional advisors and open a conversation (with the prospect's permission, of course!).

Fundraisers should grab this opportunity to lead. Dale Carnegie said that a leader's job includes changing your people's attitudes and behavior. He offers the following principles to support leadership of others:

- Begin with praise and honest appreciation.
- Call attention to people's mistakes indirectly.
- Talk about your own mistakes before criticizing the other person.
- Ask questions instead of giving direct orders.
- Let the other person save face.
- Praise the slightest improvement and praise every improvement.
- Give the other person a fine reputation to live up to.
- Use encouragement. Make any fault seem easy to correct.
- Make the other person happy about doing the thing you suggest.

The authors have used each of these principals when working with advisors and colleagues alike and while they do not always work, the general spirit of each of Carnegie's principles are important in each relationship and in dealing with many situations that have arisen.

Steps for Fundraisers to Enhance Collaboration with Advisors

"The rare individual who unselfishly tries to serve others has an enormous advantage. He has little competition."

—Dale Carnegie

Fundraisers can expand their reach with engaged professional advisors who understand philanthropic planning and how it can help grow their practice. Consider the following steps to begin the process of cultivating and building sustainable relationships with interested professionals.

Steps for Fundraisers to Follow with Advisors

- Identify advisors with interest in the charitable giving market.
- Educate advisors about philanthropic tools and types of gifts.
- Support advisors in their business.

Once the fundraiser has identified the professional advisors to be approached, reach out to them (or better yet, get a referral to them) and set an appointment. For the first meeting, plan to arrive on time and consider the following:

- Offer your greeting.
- Offer "Resource Notebook."
- Share "Sample Charitable Gift Annuity (CGA) Proposal."
- Ask "What can I do to help you grow your business/practice?"
- Discuss seminar and business-cultivation opportunities.
- Offer referrals.
- Ask for referrals.

After the meeting, be sure to follow-up with a call or letter. Additionally, consider the following:

- Send a thank you.
- Offer a referral to another advisor.
- Send an additional resource.
- Continue a discussion about events.
- Invite the advisor to a golf outing, gala, research tour.

CONCEPT TWENTY MINUTE APPOINTMENTS

While a young professional in the financial services industry, I learned of an insurance agent that asked for 16 minutes to give his pitch. He used an alarm clock and would set it on the desk or table at the beginning of the meeting set for all to see that it would go off in 16 minutes. He would then proceed to do all the talking over the next quarter of an hour. At the end, the prospective customer would either say "yes" or typically "no". He ran his business by seeing as many people as he could over the course of the day, week, month, year, averaging between 10 and 12 appointments per day with a plan to close one for a little more than 200 new term insurance policies per year. Not a terrible strategy for selling a product, but one of sorting through many prospects with the hope to find a few.

As we work with advisors and donors, we need to value each and every meeting as the start of a new relationship so I don't advocate that you use the "quick hit" approach. I have often asked for 20 minutes, not 10 which is unrealistic, or 30 or more which can seem a bit much, but 20. I have found after introductions, we both get about eight minutes to describe what we do and if all is going well, to respect the initial request that I had made and to continue to build that initial foundation of trust (being on time for the appointment was one of the first important steps), I then would remind the person that we had reached the 20 minutes that I had asked for, but if he/she agreed, I was enjoying our conversation and had some more time if his/her schedule allowed. It has served me well for more than 20 years. —REW

- Send an annual letter with the new *Federal Tax Pocket Guide.*
- Make a quarterly phone call or e-mail.
- Send additional referrals.

Charities should create a packet of materials which would be helpful to professional advisors or serve to educate them about charitable options. The following tools have proven useful:

- Planned Giving Resource Notebook
- Gift Planning Newsletter
- Quarterly Charitable Estate Planning Updates

- *Federal Tax Pocket Guide* (updated annually)
- Gift Planning Options Pocket Guide
- Client Support—Q&A Resource and Proposal Service
- Leave Behinds: cookbooks, atlas, *Estate Planning for Women*

Charities should not limit their options to just these tools. By being creative and responsive to advisor suggestions for how they would like to interact with the charity, charities can create custom solutions to engage the advisors in their community.

Create a Professional Advisors Network

Gift Planning Advisory Boards or Councils were the mainstay of traditional planned giving programs of many nonprofit organizations. It used to be that experienced gift planners were the best resource for the financial services professionals to network for asset management opportunities and gift planners provided most of the education to the sector. Charitable organizations were the planned giving experts from the 1950s through the 1990s. Planned Giving Advisory Boards were wonderful outlets to share the technical know how and provided user friendly ways for professional advisors to enhance their client's tax-planning strategies. Both groups enjoyed a mutually beneficial relationship.

But with the growth of the financial services industry, it became common that financial planners now had the information that they formerly needed from gift planners. Many even listed "charitable gift planning" on their list of services. And charitable remainder trusts and private family foundations were offered more for their tax advantages than for the outcomes that could come from an investment in social capital. So for today's gift planner considering a gift planning advisory board, enlisting the interest of professional advisors can be more challenging.

To understand how charitable gift planning can fit into the practice of many professional advisors, charities need to consider what advisors view as their clients' top five priorities—preserving wealth, avoiding excessive taxes, accumulating additional wealth, passing wealth to children, and preserving the family business.[5] If charities then consider the seven most important goals of the affluent, they will find that there is a unique opportunity to engage advisors for philanthropic planning as it fits in their business model.[6]

1. To assure a comfortable retirement
2. To build a sizeable portfolio
3. To protect their estate from taxes
4. To protect their family against premature death
5. To leave an estate for their heirs
6. To finance their childrens' college educations
7. Charitable gift planning

There are several issues to consider in the planning process as it relates to both the donor/client and their assets.

Client	Assets
Current income requirements	Available assets
Future income requirements	Appreciate assets
Inflation protection	Current yield
Need for liquidity	Future performance
Need for diversity	Valuation concerns
Asset protection	Marketability
	Restrictions on transfer or sale
	Selling costs
	Debt
	Qualified plan assets

The donor/client then has several considerations to address when prioritizing goals for planning. With regards to their heirs, how much is enough or rather how much is too much? What values would they like to pass along when their wealth is transferred? Are there any special needs that should be considered and would a timed inheritance be appropriate to the situation? As it relates to their giving, what is the purpose of their community support? Are their advantages to the type of gift as it relates to their tax situation? Have they involved their children in the process so they fully understand their wishes? And with regards to their taxes, is there a strategy for current and future income taxes, capital gains tax, gift tax, estate tax, and income in respect of a decedent (IRD) taxes?

Additionally, there are now many segments in the ranks of professional advisors, and each segment has differing needs and interests relative to their work in philanthropic planning. Similarly, this diversity can be a tremendous asset to a gift planning advisory board. Before embarking on the development of such an undertaking, consider what services the advisory board can offer.

There are two special groups of advisors that can serve both their needs and the mission of the charity—a gift planning advisory board and a professional advisors network. Drop a pebble into a puddle and watch the ripples, the waves would be most intense near the impact of the pebble. Similarly, a gift planning advisory board should be the one or two dozen professional advisors who are most committed and most intense about the charity's mission. Beyond that closely held group, there are many advisors who may show some interest and might interact with your organization from time to time. Creating a professional advisor network would allow them to network with both the charity and their fellow professionals.

The American Cancer Society (ACS) offers a program called the National Professional Advisor Network (NPAN). NPAN is a resource for attorneys, accountants, financial planners, and insurance professionals who wish to stay informed. It was created by the American Cancer Society to make it easy for advisors to stay current about planned giving options, to give access to information about current developments at the Society, and to provide a tool to help clients touched by cancer. The ability for an advisor to share key resources for their clients going through a cancer experience can build loyalty by reinforcing their role as a trusted advisor.

Through NPAN resources, advisors can receive:

- Up-to-date information about charitable giving and estate plans.
- Updates on tax laws affecting charitable gift planning.
- Sample illustrations of charitable concepts to help clients understand all aspects of a gift.
- Sample legal documents to licensed attorneys.
- Education through sponsored seminars and workshops.
- Information on ACS gift opportunities.
- Resources for clients and their families who are dealing with cancer.

Whether a charity creates a gift planning advisory board or a professional advisor network, support from this new constituency will rise or fall with the attention given to it. If it is watered and fed, it can grow and flourish. If it is neglected, it will wither and cease to exist. Thoughtful consideration of a strategy and the vision for how professional advisors can assist the charity can save the charity time and energy and could lead to some exciting successes.

The Role of the Professional Advisors Network   A Professional Advisors Network is a special program that provides resources and opportunities for professionals such as attorneys, accountants, financial and estate planners. It is both a list that is maintained by the charity to share with donors who may need assistance from professionals and a resource to the charity when an advisor is needed in its work with donors.

The goal of the program is to help advisors to effectively explain and structure gift planning options for their clients with charitable intent. By becoming a resource for advisors, gift planners not only establish a pipeline for regular communication and education of those that can assist them, but it also positions them for future opportunities to structure gifts for clients that advisors uncover.

CASE STUDY   PROFESSIONAL ADVISOR NETWORK—MERIDIAN HEALTH AFFILIATED FOUNDATIONS

The following is a sample of the language used to encourage participation in the Meridian Professional Advisor Network . . .

Make a Difference with Philanthropic Planning

Meridian is synonymous with caring in our community and many of your clients have had a personal experience at our health system and may want to support us. Whether it's a new grandchild, a corrective procedure, or a battle with cancer, your clients have been touched by the Meridian hand and may want to make a difference for others through a planned gift.

Philanthropic planning is a way to combine your clients' charitable interests and their overall financial, tax, and estate planning
(continued)

goals. Your clients are able to support a cause they care about and often can improve their own financial situation.

Grow Client Relationships

As their financial advisor, your clients come to you for professional guidance. They trust you to look out for their best interests and to educate them about all of the financial planning options available.

A Comprehensive Healthcare Organization

Meridian's Brand Promise is to provide the best healthcare experience. As a major healthcare provider, Meridian provides programs and services throughout our community through six distinct hospitals. Meridian Health is committed to improving the health and well-being of the residents of New Jersey by providing quality patient-centered health care services delivered in the hospital, community, and in-home settings, and to advancing medicine through clinical education and research.

We foster a culture of excellence within a collaborative environment. We actively seek innovative solutions, technologies, and partnerships to support sustainable financial growth and to ensure communities we serve have access to a comprehensive continuum of integrated services that meet their present and future health care needs.

For all who participate in our professional advisor network, we offer support for charitable gift planning through our proposal service, and valuable tools (like tax guides and our will and trust planning kit) and resources that save time when working with clients. We send regular e-newsletters to offer timely information and resources designed for legal and estate planning professionals to keep them posted on tax law and other changes that affect charitable gift planning. We provide opportunities to network with other professionals who value Meridian's mission through continuing education seminars, donor/client cultivation lunches and dinners, and golf outings and other events. —REW

Knowledge about charitable gift planning can help professional advisors build client loyalty and relationships by reinforcing their role as a trusted advisor. Clients may also appreciate their advisors involvement in support of an organization that they themselves value so it can foster a positive community spirit.

By offering an organized outlet for involvement by professional advisors, charities create an opportunity for synergy with advisors and their clients. Bob Burg in his book entitled *Endless Referrals* talks about positioning one-self as the expert and only logical resource in a particular field. Charities which cater to professional advisors will be in the minority and will close more gifts.

Measure the Success of Your Partnerships with Professional Advisors

To evaluate whether partnerships with advisors are working, charities should develop benchmarks. Each year, the charity can compare its performance against the benchmarks and prior years to determine if it is doing a good job engaging advisors and ultimately in creating opportunities for philanthropic planning.

CASE STUDY   BENCHMARKING—MERIDIAN
                              HEALTH AFFILIATED
                              FOUNDATIONS

To measure the effectiveness of our work with advisors at Meridian Health, I track the following benchmarks:
- Meeting new professional advisors.
- Recruitment of new professional advisors to the Meridian Professional Advisors Network and possibly also the Meridian Philanthropic Planning Council.
- Introductions to clients—A helpful measure of the level of commitment from the advisors to our program's mission. An advisor who is just interested in meeting your organization's donors without offering to bring new people to you is not participating fully in building the relationship.

(continued)

MPAN—The Meridian Professional
Advisor Network

I spend one third of my time dedicated to building MPAN as follows:

- Utilize MPAN support materials and the Crescendo software to provide a service to professional advisors throughout the Meridian service area.
- Complete at least 100 face-to-face visits annually with advisors to cultivate relationships and develop planned and major gifts.
- Remind advisors that several events are available for the cultivation of their clients. Hospital tours, galas, our wine and martini tasting, golf outings, and so on, can all give advisors a chance to introduce their interested clients to us.
- Advisors have and will suggest major gifts to their clients if they know that we are looking for them and they can identify their clients' donative intent.
- As a result of our meetings with professional advisors, a total of 40 new members to the Meridian Professional Advisor Network is the goal each year. —REW

To reach its goals, a charity should create a plan and establish its agenda. Make its own performance dashboards and work with a sense of urgency. Prioritize and complete what matters most first. Know what the goal is and keep it in focus while working the plan. Prepare for activities and be responsible for the vision of success. In the end, the number of gifts closed as an outcome of the activity with professional advisors would be the best evidence of how the work is leading to results.

Follow the Model Standards of Practice

Several professional organizations have adopted guidelines for personal conduct in gift planning. It is imperative that fundraisers who strive to generate support for the mission of a nonprofit organization be diligent in their preparation and support of donors and that they work with the donors' advisors to support what is best for them.

"One hundred times a day I remind myself that my personal and professional . . . life depends on the fruit of other (people), living and dead . . . and that I should make every effort to give in the same measure in which I have received and am receiving."

—Albert Einstein

While Einstein certainly was speaking about his own work, his words are all too appropriate to inspire both the gift planner and the advisor. The Model Standards of Practice for the Charitable Gift Planner, as adopted by PPP (formerly the National Committee on Planned Giving), encourage all individuals who work in the charitable gift planning process to "work together to structure (gifts that achieve) a fair and proper balance between interests of the donor and the purpose of the charitable institution." The Model Standards continue, "It is the hallmark of professionalism for Gift Planners that they realize when they have reached the limits of their knowledge and expertise, and as a result, should include other professionals in the process. Such relationships should be characterized by courtesy, tact, and mutual respect."[7]

Similarly, the Association of Fundraising Professionals adopted a Code of Ethical Principles and Standards of Professional Practice that encourages members to "recognize their individual boundaries of competence" and involve the help of advisors in meeting the needs of donors. When soliciting gifts, "members shall take care to ensure that all . . . materials are accurate and correctly reflect the organization's mission and use of solicited funds." Members also "recognize their responsibility to ensure that needed resources are vigorously and ethically sought and the intent of the donor is honestly fulfilled."[8]

Additionally, David Cordell in the *Journal of Financial Planning* (2004) offered an alternative Platinum Rule since applying the Golden Rule fails to acknowledge cultural and personal difference, "Do unto others as they would have you do unto them." In so doing, we are applying the other person's standard to ourselves rather than forcing our standards on them.

In Summary

With the donor's financial well-being and personal motivations to give as a common denominator, professionals from the for-profit and nonprofit world can work together toward a common goal. The ability to know when to lead and when to follow in each situation along with a willingness to compromise is a must. Understanding, balancing, and in some cases, reconciling the interests of the various parties is the key to successful philanthropic planning efforts.

PART TWO

Working with Philanthropists

P art I laid out why changing demographics require charities and professional advisors to adopt a philanthropic planning model. It suggests how charities can configure their operations to follow the model and how charities and advisors can work together to identify the New Philanthropists. Chapter 3 introduced the four tiers of the Philanthropic Planning Pyramid, illustrating how charities and advisors should prioritize their work with both Traditionalists and New Philanthropists.

Ideally charities and advisors would have the time, volunteers and staff, to work with all philanthropists equally. But with limited resources, charities and advisors need to provide the highest level of attention to those philanthropists who are capable of making the most meaningful and institution-changing gifts, as charitable giving by high-net-worth households to nonprofit organizations accounts for about two-thirds of all individual giving and half of all charitable giving in the United States.[1] Part II details how charities and professional advisors should interact with Tier One and Tier Two prospects in a philanthropic planning model.

CHAPTER 6

Integrated Solutions for Principal Gift (Tier One) Philanthropists

Principal gift or Tier One prospects make up the top one percent of all donors and drive individual gifts philanthropy in the United States. This group expects concierge-level treatment, with charities and advisors working collaboratively to integrate individual goals, objectives, and values with philanthropic plans, particularly as the New Philanthropists seek to do their planning. A philanthropic planning program allows for the integration of high-net-worth donors' values, including the charities they care about, into their financial and estate plans, complimenting traditional tax and estate planning, encouraging partnerships with the donors' own advisors and promoting family strength, unity, and involvement. Charities and advisors offering philanthropic planning to their top donors and clients are truly offering them a tremendous service that will serve them and their families for multiple generations.

WHO ARE THE PRINCIPAL GIFT PHILANTHROPISTS?

"Let me tell you about the very rich. They are different than you and me."
"Yes. They have more money."

That famous literary exchange between F. Scott Fitzgerald and Ernest Hemingway took place more than 70 years ago, and yet the question persists.

In philanthropy, charities and advisors wonder whether the most generous philanthropists represent a fundamentally different charitable mindset, or whether they simply have more money to give.

Chapter 3 identified the group of prospects who will be the target audience for principal gift philanthropic planning. They are the loyal donors to charities with a net worth of more than $9,000,000 or an annual income of more than $500,000 that places them in the top 1 percent of the population (as of this printing).

What differentiates prospects for philanthropic planning from traditional principal gift prospects is the loyalty aspect. Traditional principal gift prospects may be far less loyal and still consider large, transactional gifts to fund particular projects which are important to them but may not be part of a larger plan for themselves or the charities supported. Traditional principal gift prospects are also more likely to come from the three Traditionalist generations. They trust charities and do not feel it necessary to engage in the type of long-term, values-based planning sought by the New Philanthropists.

Prospects for philanthropic planning are much more engaged by the mission of the charity and this engagement leads to an integrated planning process with advisors and family to produce a true philanthropic plan. They see the charity as part of their family, and planning for its future is as important as planning for their heirs. A higher percentage of philanthropic planning prospects will come from the New Philanthropists, and that percentage will grow as advisors and charities reach into the Younger Boomers and Generation X. They are the most eager to find integrated solutions for themselves and their families.

Unique Characteristics of High-Net-Worth Donors/Clients

Dove, Spears, and Herbert wrote about the Super Affluent—the top 1 percent of the population with mega-estates that are managed by the most sophisticated attorneys and advisors in the country. Their estates are so large that most do everything they can to avoid significant estate taxes. In the past, they have frequently looked to charitable giving to help them retain control of their wealth, through vehicles such as private foundations.[2] It allowed them to keep control while also offering prestige. Until recently, the question of how to pass values and not just valuables had not been addressed with many in this group.

Almost all affluent Americans give to charities and as their wealth increases, the percentage of those who contribute also rises. According to Spectrem Group, 80 percent of total U.S. households donate money each year to more than 1.35 million charities, social welfare organizations, and religious congregations. Ninety-seven percent of households with a net worth in excess of $1 million give to nonprofit organizations annually while 99 percent of households with a net worth in excess of $5 million give. Of this last group, an estimated 75 percent of those donors receive no tax benefit from their charitable gifts.[3]

The affluent market is continuing to grow and is expected to grow at 8 percent per year. According to the Spectrem Group, in 1995, there were 11.2 million individuals with more than $1 million of investable assets. That number grew to 19.4 million by 2000 and then 33.5 million by 2005.[4]

Table 6.1 shows the results of the 2010 Study of High-Net-Worth Philanthropy, which reported on the percentage of income used by high-net-worth families (those with more than $1 million in assets excluding the value of the primary residence) to make charitable gifts in 2009.

When it comes to estate distribution to charities, families in the $1 to $5 million range give between 8 to 9 percent of their assets while those in the $5 to $20 million range give about 15 to 16 percent and those with more than $20 million give about 41 percent of their assets.[5] This compares with lifetime distributions in 2009 of 0.8 percent of net worth for families in the $1 to $5 million rage, 0.4 percent of net worth for families in the $5 to $20 million range, and 2.2 percent of net worth for families with more than $20 million.[6]

TABLE 6.1   **PERCENTAGE OF HOUSEHOLD INCOME USED FOR CHARITABLE GIVING IN 2009**

Household Earnings	Percentage of Income Given to Charity
Less than $200,000	16.5
$200,000–$500,000	8.8
$500,000–$2,000,000	8.0
$2,000,000+	8.7

Data source: Bank of America Merrill Lynch 2010 Study of High-Net-Worth Philanthropy

Philanthropy is one of the top four financial issues for ultra-high-net-worth investors:

1. Tax minimization—91 percent
2. Asset management—89 percent
3. Estate Planning—73 percent
4. Philanthropy—51 percent[7]

The seven most important goals of the affluent according to a 2001 Spectrem Group Survey: "Trends and Opportunities in the Affluent Market" are to:

1. Assure a comfortable retirement
2. Build a sizable portfolio
3. Protect their estate from taxes
4. Protect their family against premature death
5. Leave an estate for their heirs
6. Finance their childrens' college educations
7. Charitable giving[8]

These findings are consistent with the experience of professional advisors everywhere who find that when working with high-net-worth individuals, they plan for themselves, their families, and the charities and social causes which have touched them, in that order.

Motivation for Giving   The Bank of America Merrill Lynch 2010 Study of High Net Worth Philanthropy by the Center on Philanthropy at Indiana University studied 800 random households in affluent neighborhoods with an income of greater than $200,000 and/or a net worth of at least $1,000,000 excluding the value of the primary residence. The average wealth of respondents was more than $10 million, while half of all respondents had a net worth between $3 million and $20 million. The study in its current form has been conducted biennially since 2006 and predecessor studies go back to the 1990s. The data provides insights into high-net-worth individuals and their philanthropic preferences. Table 6.2 shows the motivations to give by at least 50 percent of the households in 2009 and 2007.

All of the top five responses from 2007 remained on the list for 2009, but there were some significant differences, particularly a drop in the

TABLE 6.2   MOTIVATIONS FOR GIVING TO CHARITY 2009 AND 2007

Motivation	2009 Rank	Percent	2007 Rank	Percent
Moved at how gift can make a difference	1	72.4	3	66.9
Feel financially secure	2	71.2	4	65.3
Giving to an efficient organization*	3	71.0	N/A	N/A
Support same causes/organizations annually	4	65.9	2	70.7
Give back to community	5	64.7	1	81.2
Political/philosophical beliefs	6	52.1	5	58.5
Volunteer for the organization*	7	51.9	N/A	N/A

*Not asked in 2007
Data source: Bank of America Merrill Lynch 2010 Study of High-Net-Worth Philanthropy

percentage of households that are motivated to make gifts that give back to the community. The results show that most affluent people continue to give out of a sense of wanting to make a difference. About one-third of respondents cited communication about the impact of gifts as an important factor when making gift decisions.[9] The study did not ask about whether taxes motivated gifts.

In 1994, Russ Alan Prince and Karen Maru File published *The Seven Faces of Philanthropy: A New Approach to Cultivating Major Donors.* Their research built upon a concept first introduced by Teresa Odendahl in *Charity Begins at Home: Generosity and Self-Interest Among the Philanthropic Elite*, who used anthropological methods to study patterns in philanthropic motivation among 140 wealthy donors. Odendahl's study showed the importance of distinguishing giving from philanthropists who gave because of their multi-generational family tradition versus people who gave personally earned assets. She also indicated the importance of religious giving.[10]

Prince and File researched 218 affluent persons who had made a major contribution to nonprofit organizations and identified seven distinct segments—the seven faces of philanthropy.

1. *The Communitarian*—Doing Good Makes Sense (26.3 percent of donors surveyed)—they give because it makes sense to do so. Typically local business owners who find that service and donations to local nonprofits are good for business.

2.   *The Devout*—Doing Good is God's Will (20.9 percent)—they give because it is God's will for them to help others. Almost all (96.4 percent) of their giving is to religious institutions.

3.   *The Investor*—Doing Good is Good Business (15.3 percent)—they give with one eye on the cause and the other eye on personal tax and estate consequences. Investors calibrate their giving to take advantage of tax and estate benefits and want to work with nonprofits that understand these concerns. Investors are most likely to support community foundations and other umbrella nonprofits.

4.   *The Socialite*—Doing Good is Fun (10.8 percent)—they are part of the social networks that interact with a select group of nonprofits and find that social functions benefiting charities are a great way to give and help make a better world while having fun doing it.

5.   *The Altruist*—Doing Good Feels Right (9 percent)—they give because they feel it is morally imperative and give out of generosity. Altruists are known to make giving decisions without input from advisors and are not usually interested in having an active role in the charity. Often they give anonymously.

6.   *The Repayer*—Doing Good in Return (10.2 percent)—they tend to have been a constituent first. They have personally benefited from the charity and now give out of a feeling of loyalty or obligation.

7.   *The Dynast*—Doing Good is a Family Tradition (8.3 percent)—Typically inheriting their wealth, they give from their socialization out of a tradition that their family has stood for. However, younger dynasts will seek out different charities than their parents.[11]

The Prince and File study provides a slightly different vision of what motivates high-net-worth individuals to give. As with the discussion of generational cohorts, understanding these profiles can assist fundraisers to identify likely areas of interest and touch points when working with high-net-worth donors. They can serve as the starting point in the discussion about philanthropic planning.

Perceptions of Philanthropy   Philanthropic planning is a methodology designed to give meaning to life while supporting all that is important to the philanthropist. In 1943, Abraham Maslow's Hierarchy of Needs offered a theory around motivation as it relates to human development. After the basic physiological (survival) and safety needs are satisfied, he suggested that social needs, esteem needs, and ultimately self-actualization become the driving force in one's life. Dr. John Dewey, an American philosopher said that the deepest urge in human nature is "the desire to be important." Sigmund Freud talked about the desire to be great.[12]

Julie Salamon wrote about Rambam's Ladder. Rambam, better known by his name Maimonides was a twelfth-century physician, philosopher, and scholar who developed a ladder with eight rungs to illustrate the progression of charity as he pondered the issues of righteousness and obligation. As a person increases their level of generosity, they may move up from a lower to a higher rung. At the top of the ladder is the gift of self-reliance.

> *8—Responsibility:* To hand someone a gift or loan, or to enter into a partnership with him, or to find work for him so that he will never have to beg again.
>
> *7—Anonymity:* To give to someone you don't know and to do so anonymously.
>
> *6—Corruption:* To give to someone you know, but who doesn't know from who he is receiving help.
>
> *5—Boundaries:* To give to someone you don't know, but allow your name to be known.
>
> *4—Shame:* To hand money to the poor before being asked, but risk making the recipient feel shame.
>
> *3—Solicitation:* To hand money to the poor after being asked.
>
> *2—Proportion:* To give less to the poor than is proper, but to do so cheerfully.
>
> *1—Reluctance:* To give begrudgingly.[13]

The concept of voluntary versus involuntary philanthropy suggests that if a donor does not take advantage of tax savings from charitable giving, the donor gives anyway to the social programs provided by the government. The ability for high-net-worth families to consider social wealth and follow three steps can lead to a determination of a vision for giving:

1. Taking inventory—Where have you made a difference?
2. Taking aim—Where and how do you want to make a difference?
3. Taking shape—What must you do to make that difference?

Certified financial planners Monroe M. Diefendorf, Jr., and Robert Sterling Madden offered the concept of Three Dimensional Wealth as a new approach to financial planning that requires a person to turn their thinking inside out. Instead of using a wealth accumulation strategy of save, spend, and give what's left over, they offered a new strategy of give first, save, and then spend what's left over. Three-dimensional wealth integrates who you are, what you have, and how you can make a difference to lead the philanthropist to do something of significance.[14]

Tax Considerations   Over the years, commentators have debated the impact of tax incentives for charitable giving. The High Net Worth Study surveyed participants about the impact of changing tax laws on their expected giving behavior. When asked how their giving would change if income tax charitable deductions were eliminated, 32.6 percent said their giving would stay the same, 48.3 percent said it would decrease somewhat, and a significant 18.7 percent said it would decrease dramatically.[15]

Just the opposite was true when high-net-worth donors were asked about the elimination of the estate tax. Of those surveyed, 7.8 percent indicated that they would somewhat decrease their estate gifts if there was no longer an estate tax charitable deduction. In contrast, 47.5 percent indicated it would not impact their estate giving, 26 percent felt it would somewhat increase, and 17 percent said it would dramatically increase.[16]

Decisions and Distributions   Giving from high-net-worth couples is generally done together, with 54.6 percent of households reporting joint decision-making. Another 38.6 percent of households said that each member of the couple made his/her own charitable giving decisions and 6.8 percent involve at least one additional person. The majority of gifts go to causes that both partners consider important, but respondents reported that 35.6 percent of households gave to a cause important to just one spouse. Gifts were spread over a wide range of causes, with the highest percentage going to basic needs (84.8 percent) and education (80.1 percent) by total number of gifts. This is in contrast to overall individual giving patterns, as tracked in *Giving USA*, which consistently reports religious organizations as the top charitable subsector.

More than 15 percent of high-net-worth families gave to a private foundation, donor-advised fund, or charitable trust in 2009, a significant decline from the 21.7 percent that did so in 2007. Despite the apparent decline in the number of high-net-worth households making gifts to these types of gift entities, the largest share of charitable dollars (22.1 percent) went to them, followed by education at 19.3 percent and religion at 13.3 percent.[17]

Giving by Entrepreneurs   Entrepreneurs are consistently more charitable than other high-net-worth individuals. Entrepreneurs are individuals or households where 50 percent or more of their net worth comes from a family-owned business or startup company. They are far more generous than those individuals who acquired wealth by inheritance, investment asset growth, or investment in real estate.[18]

A 2010 study by the Fidelity Charitable Gift Fund surveyed 146 entrepreneurs about charitable giving. More than half of the entrepreneurs surveyed (53 percent) indicated that charitable giving is a key part of their estate plan. They cited three key factors that motivated their giving including: gratitude for help received; empathy for those less fortunate; and financial resources and freedom.[19]

The group also expressed their personal attitudes toward philanthropy. Ninety percent indicated that they donate their time as well as money to charities, 66 percent make charitable gifts on the basis of earning to returning, and 48 percent make gifts because it was part of their upbringing or family traditions.[20]

Fully 25 percent indicated that their financial advisor/attorney/CPA/tax advisor regularly advised them on the tax benefits of incorporating charitable giving into their overall financial plan.[21]

The Role of Professional Advisors   High-net-worth households tend to be more strategic about their charitable giving than others. Nearly 73 percent reported that they have a strategy and/or budget around charitable giving. Accountants are the top advisors turned to by high-net-worth families, relied upon by 67.5 percent of households when making a charitable giving decision. Attorneys came in at 40.8 percent while financial and wealth advisors jumped from 27.8 percent in 2007 to 38.8 percent in 2009. Nonprofit personnel were consulted just 24.1 percent of the time.[22]

When high-net-worth households consulted an advisor, 90 percent of the time it was the client who contacted the advisor. The only type of advisor above 10 percent was nonprofit personnel, who initiated the

TABLE 6.3 HIGH-NET-WORTH HOUSEHOLDS WHO CONSULTED OTHERS WHEN MAKING CHARITABLE GIVING DECISIONS BY TYPE OF ADVICE OR SERVICE (PERCENT)

	Attorney	Nonprofit Personnel	Accountant	Bank or Trust Co. Advisor	Independent Financial/ Wealth Advisor	Peers or Peer Networks	Community Foundation Staff	Other
Tax/Legal Assistance	55.9	3.9	73.1	26.9	33.7	11.1	1.3	9.5
Advice/Setup Foundation, Trust, or Donor-Advised Fund	32.8	11.7	11.9	23.9	18.1	21.0	29.1	19.0
Mission Definition/Creation	2.1	36.9	1.7	3.0	7.3	42.0	20.3	23.8
Management of Invested Charitable Assets	2.1	15.5	3.5	37.3	28.5	6.2	27.8	19.0
Other (Back Office Admin., Gift Structure/Timing)	7.2	32.0	9.8	9.0	12.4	19.8	21.5	28.6

Data source: Bank of America Merrill Lynch 2010 Study of High Net Worth Philanthropy

conversation 15.7 percent of the time. Interestingly, the only advisors which high-net-worth households were dissatisfied with were nonprofit personnel, but only 1.3 percent of the time.[23]

Utilization of Philanthropic Tools   More than 46 percent of high-net-worth households reported that they currently have a will in place with a specific charitable provision and 11.7 percent more indicated that they would consider doing so in the next three years. Nearly 21 percent have set up an endowment fund with a particular charity and 17.5 percent have a donor-advised fund. More than 15 percent of high-net-worth households have a charitable remainder trust, charitable lead trust, or charitable gift annuity and 8 percent would consider adding one in the next three years. Just 12 percent have a private foundation.[24]

Volunteering   More than three-quarters of high-net-worth donors reported volunteering in 2009, logging more than 307 hours on average. This compares to 26.8 percent of Americans generally who donated time the same year, according to the Bureau of Labor Statistics. The high-net-worth group increased both its percentage of volunteering and total hours compared to 2007.[25]

There was a direct correlation between the number of hours volunteered and giving levels, with those donating more time also making more significant gifts. Volunteers reserved their largest gifts for the organizations where they served on the board or had an oversight role, followed by organizations where they felt their gift would have the largest impact and where they volunteered the largest number of hours.

Children and Values   More than 85 percent of high-net-worth households use philanthropy to help share their values with children (the average age of children for respondents was 31 years old). More than 70 percent have family traditions involving children in charitable giving such as making gifts to organizations where they belong or receive direct benefits (33.7 percent), having family discussions about giving throughout the year (27 percent), volunteering as a family (18 percent), discussing religious traditions around giving (16 percent), and making family-level decisions about charitable giving during the holidays (10.1 percent). Those households with more family traditions tended to involve children in the decision-making process, while those with less did not.[26]

Fully 85 percent of high-net-worth families educate children about charitable giving through their own personal efforts and the family's network of peers. No other source of education broke 50 percent. Religious organizations were cited by 45 percent of households, other nonprofits were listed by 21.4 percent, and professional advisors were under 5 percent. Interestingly, children's own efforts were the way 19.4 percent of households educated children about philanthropy.[27]

| CASE STUDY | RAISING CHARITABLE CHILDREN |

It is never too young to teach children financial responsibility and the values of charitable giving. Several years ago, I read Carol Weisman's book, *Raising Charitable Children* (F.E. Robbins & Sons Press, St. Louis, MO, 2006). At the time, I had three young daughters at home and realized that even though I worked in the charitable sector and my wife and I told our children about our philanthropy, there is no greater way to learn about philanthropy than to experience it.

Our daughters have always had responsibilities around the house. There are those that they have to do as members of the household and a few for which they are paid for helping us out. It gives them spending money so that my wife and I are not always being asked to pay for a movie ticket or a trinket at Five Below and causes them to learn the value of a dollar. After reading Carol's book, we made an agreement with our daughters that each week their earnings would be divided into three parts. The first part went into their purse for them to use as they saw fit. The second part went into a brokerage account and was invested in a total stock market index fund. (My daughters were none too pleased with me regarding the second category when the Great Recession hit, but I guess they had to learn that the market goes up and comes down!) The final part went into an account for charity.

Around November of each year, we would sit down and determine which charities had been important to them that year and I send off a check on their behalf, with a note from each of them explaining how they got the money and why they had chosen to support that particular charity. Some years my daughters pool their money for the same charity and in other years they each

(continued)

pick their own. The YMCA, Girl Scouts, our church, and the Kelberman Center (the local autism center) have been common choices.

A couple of years back, it got to be the week before Christmas and the girls had not decided which charities they wanted to support. At the last Mass of the weekend, our priest reminded us about the "Giving Trees" in the sanctuary. Each year our parish collects presents for those in need in our community, to ensure that they have what they need and no child misses out on Christmas because of economic hardship. Each of us normally picks one or two stars off of one of the giving trees and we go out as a family and buy the presents, wrap them up, and return them to the church the next week. Well 2008 had been a particularly hard year in our community (as in many communities) and there were both more stars than usual and fewer parishioners who were able to take stars and help those in need.

After Mass, the girls turned to my wife and said "We need to go take more stars." We agreed and walked up to the sanctuary to pick out a few more people to help. As we did so, the church slowly emptied out, and we found ourselves standing there alone, with a tree full of unclaimed stars. A few minutes later Sister Martha, who runs the religious education program, came by and our girls asked her "What happens to the unclaimed stars?" Sister Martha told them, "The Church does what it can, but the rest do not get any presents."

My three daughters turned to me and said "Dad, we can't let that happen! What are we going to do?" One of my daughters then said, "Why don't we take all of the stars? We can pay for it from our charity money." The other two readily agreed, but as I counted the stars and did the math, it was pretty clear that there were far more stars than there were dollars in that account. I told my girls that I was not sure that they were going to be able to cover it. They asked if there was anything we could do. After giving it some thought, I suggested to them that if we cut back on their own presents for Christmas, we could probably afford to take all of the stars. They didn't hesitate for a second.

Since then, it has almost become a tradition to attend the last Mass before Christmas and take the remaining stars. I have no doubt that my children will grow up understanding the power of philanthropy—all because of a few stars and the wish that no one should have to miss out on Christmas. – BMS

Interpreting the Data

The data reveals some interesting facts about high-net-worth families. As with most families, when they consider their future they plan for themselves, their families, and the charities they support. This means that charities and advisors who can help plan for all three will be more effective than those who try to plan for just the donor.

The top 1 percent of all donors, the mega-wealthy, make both bigger lifetime and estate charitable gifts as a percentage of their total net worth, particularly estate gifts. They give from assets according to a strategic plan and have an estate plan that includes a charitable bequest. They are also more likely to utilize the full range of charitable tools available to them. Entrepreneurs are particularly generous among this group, providing a key target audience for charities and advisors. By engaging high-net-worth entrepreneurs in the cause and with volunteer opportunities, charities can maximize giving.

The most wealthy do not give as large a percentage of their income to charity each year as the next 9 percent, those who make $200,000 or less. It is likely that the next 9 percent do not have plans as sophisticated as the top 1 percent, which accounts for this difference.

The most wealthy tend to give back in their local community, with well over 60 percent of all gifts directed near to home.

While taxes do not motivate charitable giving for the top families, they do want their gifts to be tax efficient. They would give less than they do now if the income tax charitable deduction was rescinded and would give more than they do now if the estate tax were eliminated, as they would have more assets overall to distribute.

High-net-worth individuals rely heavily on advisors, particularly (CPAs), but the role of wealth advisors/financial planners is increasing. They want to pass their values to children and use philanthropy as the tool for doing so.

With these key findings in mind, charities and professional advisors can begin to design an approach to appeal to high-net-worth families.

BUILDING A PHILANTHROPIC PLANNING MODEL

Philanthropic planning is the art of integrating donors' philanthropic objectives with their overall tax, estate, and financial planning to create a meaningful legacy for both families and the charities they love. Instead of asking for a gift in a vacuum based upon organizational needs, this process encourages a deep relationship and institution-changing gifts that meld the institution's strategic vision with the hopes and dreams of donors for themselves, their families, and future generations. It is true values-based legacy building to help both the family and the institution now and for the future.

This approach requires significant investment of time in each prospect, as well as openness by the institution to accepting non-cash assets. Nearly 80 percent of resources held by high-net-worth individuals are in a form other than cash or appreciated stock. Alternative assets such as business interests, closely-held stock, hedge funds, real estate investment trusts (REITs), and more all must become part of the discussion in order for the institution to tap into this wealth from high-net-worth donors. With the economy continuing to struggle and the divide between the rich and poor growing wider, a larger and larger percentage of total gifts will come from a smaller and smaller population of high-net-worth donors.

To be effective, the model must address the identified needs and motivations of the target audience of Tier One prospects. This group is clearly motivated by a desire to take care of themselves, their families, and the charitable organizations that have touched their lives. They have a sense of responsibility to give back with time, treasure, and talent to the communities and institutions that helped them achieve their success. Tier One prospects want to work with their advisors to make their philanthropy tax efficient, utilizing the best philanthropic tools for the job to craft a meaningful and appropriate plan to meet their needs today, their families' needs tomorrow, and the needs of charities permanently. Most are eager to include their children in their planning to help pass their value system to the next generation, using charitable giving as the primary tool to do so.

Philanthropic Planning Models for Charities

Each charity needs to build its own program to work with these prospects. The program should be unique to the mission of the charity and the needs of its top philanthropic planning prospects. A growing number of charities have built models to meet the needs of this important group of prospects, each with its own unique elements to appeal to their donors. One of the earliest models to be developed was at Harvard University by Charles W. Collier. His book on the topic, *Wealth in Families,* was the first of its kind in the charitable community. It followed the research of James E. Hughes, Jr., and his seminal work on the topic, *Family Wealth: Keeping It in the Family*.[28]

■ EXAMPLE   THE HARVARD MODEL—WEALTH IN FAMILIES

The Harvard model is based largely on asking families the important questions around relationships. Collier suggests that there are three organizing principals that are essential to creating effective families including: 1) creating and telling family stories to give meaning to the experience of the family; 2) balancing the tension between being an individual in a family and being part of the whole to create a succession plan; and 3) assisting children and other family members to find a driving passion that they turn into meaningful work, to discover their true calling. Essentially, the Harvard model suggests that philanthropic planning prospects need to create and articulate a sense of family, encourage family members to embrace their passions in their work and life, and finally determine how that family will continue into the future.

To reach these lofty goals, Collier recommends that families start by exploring a series of questions about family wealth. The five core questions are:

1. What is really important to your family?
2. What are your family's true assets?
3. What should you do to guide and support the life journey of each family member over time?
4. How wealthy do you want your children to be?
5. Do you feel you have a responsibility to society?

The answers to the questions are less important than the process of answering them. Collier suggests that the successful family is the one that knows who it is, what it stands for, and where it is going and that if a family can define what's important before deciding what to do, children will thrive, family will flourish, and society will benefit.

To reach these goals, the Harvard model walks families through the following steps:

- Exploring the meaning of wealth.
- Defining a financial inheritance—how much is enough?
- Family parenting: Managing family.
- Psychological parenting: Managing oneself.

- Financial parenting: Managing money.
- Philanthropic parenting: Managing financial care.
- Family meetings: Managing the enterprise.

   To assist families in reaching these goals, Collier utilizes two questionnaires. The first questionnaire is designed to encourage the family to begin to explore their wealth, their philanthropy, and the future of the
family. It asks families to discuss their principles, their hopes and goals
for their children, and the values they hope to pass on through their philanthropy. The second questionnaire helps families to carefully define
their values and how they would use philanthropy to achieve those values. Over a period of months, and sometimes years, Collier would work
with families and eventually their advisors to explore these questions
and implement plans to fulfill their vision and carry family values
forward.[29]

Families that utilize the Harvard model have a much better sense of their
values and the role that philanthropy can play in carrying those values forward for future generations. They understand that this does not just happen, but requires regular family meetings to ensure that the goals of the
family remain in sight. The Harvard model does not technically raise
money for Harvard. But for those families who believe that higher education is one of their core values, and providing for higher education is a
noble purpose, then from such discussions there will be gifts to support
Harvard as well as other charities. In making those gifts and supporting the
life journey of each family member, the values of the family will carry
through from generation to generation while supporting the society that
has fostered the family's success.

EXAMPLE   THE PRINCETON MODEL—FAMILY PHILANTHROPY INITIATIVE

The Princeton model was developed by Jane Corwin and Ron Brown at
Princeton University. They had discovered that their high-net-worth
donors avoided real conversations regarding their deeply felt values
about family, wealth, and philanthropy because too often they had been

(continued)

surrounded by people and fundraisers who saw them as pools of money, rather than people. This impeded conversations about what really mattered most to them and how charities could help them achieve their most important goals.

The Family Philanthropy Initiative is built around a limited invitation (10 to 25 participants), interactive seminar entitled "Conversations about Family, Wealth, and Philanthropy." It is different from the Harvard model, which takes place over a long period of time, sometimes years, in that each seminar lasts roughly 24 hours. While each seminar is hosted by Princeton and the gift planning staff is present, they hire an outside moderator to oversee these sessions to allow participants to speak more freely.

The seminar starts with a dinner with no agenda, allowing the invitees to get to know each other and develop a group dynamic. The following day, the group participates in three 90-minute sessions led by an estate-planning attorney facilitating a session on families that successfully manage relationships as well as wealth; a family psychologist leading a discussion of family and relational issues of wealth; and an expert in family foundations initiating conversations about how to make good family philanthropy into great family philanthropy. The discussion leaders do not make presentations, but instead encourage individual participation. The goal is to get the participants talking about each of these topics to explore what is important to them and exchange their ideas. Corwin reports that when the sessions go well, participants leave feeling empowered, knowing they are not the only ones struggling with these issues but leaving with some new alternatives to try.

Princeton has a strict policy that the seminars are not fundraising events and no Princeton priorities are discussed. Instead, participants are encouraged to discuss all of their charitable interests and goals. Conversations have been far-ranging, including discussions of

- If monetary wealth is to be given to children, how much and when?
- How can I improve the joy of working with my family foundation?
- How can our family foundation decide between supporting capital and operating needs?
- How can I involve my children so they develop good values of their own, rather than imitating my values?

Princeton found that the participation has covered all of the generational cohorts, but has skewed significantly toward Generation X.[30]

While the Harvard and Princeton models use two completely different approaches to philanthropic planning, they cover much of the same ground. In both cases, they look to facilitate family discussions around the purpose of wealth, planning for wealth, and how philanthropy helps families to navigate these issues and pass values to future generations.

Neither institution uses these conversations to try and raise money, yet both report that donors who participate are more generous than they were before. Considering that high-net-worth donors report that they give more to charities where they are engaged, this result is no surprise, but it may be counterintuitive to those not familiar with this dynamic.

They are, at their core, values-based planning models. The Harvard model helps to facilitate the conversations over a period of months or years in a series of meetings with a set of important questions, while the Princeton model is less formal and occurs in just one day, allowing the families to take the lead themselves after the session has concluded.

Philanthropic Planning Models for Professional Advisors

Professional advisors can also build an area of their practice to help identify high-net-worth clients to integrate their philanthropic goals with their tax, estate, and financial planning. Just as charities should design their philanthropic planning model to meet the needs of their high-net-worth donors, advisors should put together a program to meet the needs of their practice's clients.

Tracy Gary has put together a strategy called "Inspired Philanthropy." While targeted at individuals, it provides a roadmap to advisors on how they might pursue philanthropic planning with their clients.

■ EXAMPLE   THE INSPIRED PHILANTHROPY MODEL

The Inspired Philanthropy model offers a two-part system for individuals to develop their identity as a philanthropist and create a giving plan, followed by strategic ways to leverage that giving. The model suggests that clients initially take nine steps:

1. Familiarize themselves with the nonprofit world and how it works.
2. Discover their values and motivations as philanthropists.

(continued)

3. Develop a system of giving based on a comprehensive giving strategy.
4. Create a mission statement.
5. Decide how much to give.
6. Choose where to give.
7. Create a personal giving plan.
8. Learn about different giving vehicles.
9. Understand organizational giving from entities such as family foundations and corporations.

Once a client has developed their philanthropic identity and created a giving plan, Gary encourages them to leverage their giving through:

- Engagement with groups they support.
- Creating greater plans for their families, heirs, and humanity.
- Growing and partnering with the next generation of givers.
- Pursuing transformative philanthropy.

Clients who follow the Inspired Philanthropy model will fully understand the philanthropic world, their own philanthropic goals and objectives—based on their values, how those goals can be realized through engagement with charities, and how they can affect meaningful change for the long term (transformational philanthropy) through partnerships within their families, with the next generation, and with other philanthropists.[31]

Advisors would be well served to adapt some version of Gary's model to apply to their philanthropic clients, even providing them with her materials. Clients would return much more ready to discuss their plans having completed the steps in Gary's workbook.

Even though Gary comes at philanthropic planning from a different place than the charities, many of the elements in her model mirror those in the Harvard and Princeton models. It is a values-based concept that suggests clients need to determine their own values and passions first, creating their own mission statements, then find charities to support which pursue that mission. In so doing, philanthropists can pass their values to future generations.

While Gary appeals directly to clients, Rod Zeeb and Perry Cochell of the Heritage Institute created a system to train professional advisors to work with high-net-worth individuals. Their system, known as the Heritage Process, was a multi-step program that advisors could use with clients to sustain family wealth and unity across generations. Its most recent iteration, Heritage Planning, includes a 12-element process advisors can use with clients to integrate philanthropy into their planning.

EXAMPLE   THE HERITAGE PLANNING MODEL

The Heritage Planning model is based on the idea that most parents want to pass not just their assets to the children, but also who they are, their stories, values, life lessons, traditions, and experiences. Unfortunately, heirs are usually not prepared to receive either their financial inheritance or their emotional inheritance (who they are). To help families navigate these challenges and thrive across generations, Heritage Planning uses a 12-element process and assessment exercise to be facilitated by the family's wealth advisor.

1. Foster strong and effective communication, and build trust between generations.
2. Develop, maintain, and regularly revisit the family's vision for the present and the future.
3. Meet regularly as a family.
4. Promote a balanced definition of the meaning of wealth.
5. Keep the family business (including investments) separate from the business of being a family.
6. Identify the roles necessary for the family to be successful (non-financially as well as financially).
7. Inspire individual family members to participate for their own individual reasons.
8. Train and mentor each generation.
9. Facilitate the genuine transfer of leadership from generation to generation.
10. Require true collaboration between your professional advisors.
11. Create mechanisms for ongoing family governance.
12. Do it now.

The Heritage Institute trains professional advisors and fundraisers in the Heritage Planning model and offers a certification program, the Certified Wealth Consultant, for those who complete the training. These individuals are well-prepared to walk clients through this vigorous process. It more closely resembles the one-on-one support of the Harvard model than the one-day seminar offered in the Princeton model or the self-guided Inspired Philanthropy model. The Heritage Planning model recognizes that to retain both family unity and prosperity across generations, the business of being a family must be planned for, tended, supported, and celebrated.[32]

A TOOL TO BEGIN THE PROCESS

We have described many models as a guide to follow when conducting a philanthropic planning process with donors, but how to begin? While I worked with the American Cancer Society (ACS), Paul Hansen and I developed one approach that gave interested donors an introduction into the concept of philanthropic planning. Working with local leadership, we held a "Healthy, Wealthy & Wise Dinner" at a popular upscale restaurant. We would ask the ACS Regional Vice President and members of the board to help us identify folks who would appreciate attending an event where we would present information that would be helpful to them. The components of the event included a speaker for each of the areas—healthy, wealthy, and wise. The first was either a prominent ACS leader or an oncologist to speak about the current situation in healthcare and cancer treatment, the second was a money manager who would speak about the current stock and bond market and the economy, and the third was Paul tying in the two with an introduction to how a donor's financial and tax goals could be married to both support fighting cancer and meeting their objectives through philanthropic planning. With this introduction, we then followed up with a personal consultation that would seek to uncover the donor's needs. If they saw a value in addressing those needs, we could then work through the process to understand and prepare a customized plan to provide a solution. —REW

The Heritage Planning model contains many of the same elements found in the other models, but in a more comprehensive and involved way. It helps families determine their identity, what they stand for, and how to create a future where children will thrive, family will flourish over multiple generations, and society will benefit.

Core Elements Common to All Philanthropic Planning Models

Because each charity and professional practice is unique, it is not possible to create one set of steps or an operating model to meet the needs of all charities and advisors. Each of the four models presented have unique elements and approaches that may be an effective fit for particular charities or advisors, and other charities and advisors may come up with additional ideas to most effectively reach their audience of Tier One donors/clients.

Chapter 1 introduced a concept model for philanthropic planning, suggesting that it requires a charitable representative and professional advisors working together with the donor with charitable intent as the common denominator, in order to facilitate true philanthropy. Each charity or professional advisor should use this as the basis when considering how to build a model for its own constituency.

$$\frac{\text{Gift Planner} + \text{Professional Advisors} + \text{Philanthropic Planning}}{\text{Donor with Charitable Intent}} = \text{Philanthropy}$$

Several common elements do appear in the four philanthropic planning operational models and likely would be helpful for most charities and advisors seeking to meet the needs of Tier One donors/clients.

Typically this type of planning involves families. When donors/clients do not have families to pass wealth or values, they will need a less vigorous process than philanthropic planning to explore their legacy and philanthropy. For those cases, the Gary model is readily adapted to meet their needs to understand their own philanthropy and how to pursue it.

For those prospects/clients with families, it is important that they be philanthropic. If a family is not philanthropic, it is much more difficult to engage them in the process of philanthropic planning. It may not be impossible, as sometimes in the process of defining values a family will discover philanthropy, but this is not the type of family that an advisor or charity wants to be the first ones through a new philanthropic planning program. Charitable intent truly does make a difference.

Defining Values All four models start by asking donors/clients to define what is really important to them and to their families. These are the values that they hold most dear. One way to open the values discussion is to ask "50 years from now, your great grandchild is asked to write a history of your family. What does that story say? What are the themes that carry through from now until then? How does that great grandchild know you, your guiding principles, and what you held most dear during your life?" Most families, when confronted with these questions, will have in-depth conversations to define their values, perhaps even writing a family mission or vision statement, as suggested by Gary and Heritage Planning. For those that struggle to define a value system, charities and advisors might suggest the list offered by Collier in *Wealth in Families* or recite the (Boy) Scout Law, "A scout is trustworthy, loyal, helpful, friendly, courteous, kind, obedient, cheerful, thrifty, brave, clean, and reverent." Whatever the value system, a family needs to understand what it believes before it can take the next step of evaluating the resources it has available.

Assets and Exploring the Meaning of Wealth   Family assets include far more than financial wealth. Each of the families in the philanthropic planning process will be wealthy, of course, not because they have to be (philanthropic planning works for everyone, regardless of financial wealth), but because charities do not have the resources necessary to invest substantial resources in conversations at this level with the full spectrum of prospects and clients cannot afford to pay advisors for this level of advice unless they are planning at a high level.

Despite their financial wealth, families have other important assets that are integral parts of the philanthropic planning process. Hughes and Collier define these assets as family capital and they include: human capital (passions, talents, expertise, and dreams), intellectual capital (knowledge, learning process, conflict management), and social capital (ties to society, philanthropic nature). Gary and Zeeb both discuss the importance of utilizing the talents of family members and embracing their passions. Truly wealthy families have not only financial assets but engagement with each other and the world to pursue human, intellectual, and social capital.

Limiting Financial Inheritance   In its own way, each of the four models suggest that families can leave too much of a financial inheritance to children, so much so that they are not inspired to pursue a meaningful life on their own. They suggest that families and advisors need to evaluate the question of "How much is enough?" and apply it to those who stand to inherit financial wealth. The family needs to discuss this issue until everyone is comfortable with the answer, or it will be impossible to get on with the business of the family. The generation currently holding financial resources needs to know what is left for social capital and the generation that stands to inherit needs to be comfortable with the idea that it will not all be handed to them.

The Business of Being a Family Most families do not ever consider how they are governed. They have fallen into roles with a division of labor that even if it is not perfect, keeps the household and family running. When family members leave the household, adjustments are made to allow the family dynamic to continue. Sometimes this works well, but frequently it does not.

The most successful families think about family governance. They treat the family like a business with a succession plan and structures for family decision-making that foster communication and encourage the growth and development of all family members (both living older generations and future generations). They plan for the transfer of leadership from generation to generation and seek to mentor each generation whenever possible.

Of equal importance, they keep the family business separate from the business of being a family. While many family members may work in the family business, its goals and objectives are different than those of the family. It contributes to the financial capital, but the family should be more concerned with the human, intellectual, and social capital. One could argue that the purpose of the family business is to provide financial capital so that family members can pursue their passions, education, and philanthropic interests.

CASE STUDY	"WHO'S GOING TO BE THE ADULT NOW?"

My parents both died at age 66. My father passed away first and my mother passed away 16 months later. They ran the family CPA practice together, one in which I and my four older siblings all participated in one form or another. I helped my mother to sell the practice after my father died. Even though my father was the professional CPA, my mother had been the matriarch of the family. She ran both the household and the business with a precision that we used to say would make General Patton proud (Patton was a World War II hero of our father).

In the hour after my mother passed, my siblings and I were sitting in the living room of the house in which we had all grown up, dealing with our loss. After a time, one of my sisters broke the silence and asked the question "Who's going to be the adult

(continued)

now?" By this stage of our lives, we had all left home, gone to college, started families, and pursued careers. By all measures, each of us was well into adulthood. What my sister was really asking was "Who's going to lead the family?"

My mother had always served that role. Once we moved out of the family home, we each would talk to Mom once a week and she would relay that latest news to the other siblings. Mom coordinated holidays and made sure we were invited to events with our extended family. When it was time to buy a present for a wedding for a distant cousin, Mom would buy the gift and send it from all of us, and we would send her a check. Without Mom, there was no one left in charge, no arbiter of last resort when a question about the date or location of the family Christmas was in dispute. There was no one to govern the family.

It took our family years to figure out how to handle governance after Mom passed away. Today, each of us has found a role and tries to provide leadership in that area. It is a team approach with which I, as a member of Generation X, feel most uncomfortable. It does seem to work better for my older, Boomer siblings. Imagine the challenges our family would have faced if in addition to scheduling holidays, we were also trying to figure out how to continue the family business or deal with the distribution of significant wealth. Without a system of family governance, the business would have been harmed and wealth squandered. It is an area that high-net-worth families, particularly those run by entrepreneurs with family businesses, need to consider both for the business, and for the family. —BMS

Communication—Family Meetings Communication is at the forefront of each of the models. Family meetings to discuss the business of the family and how it is handing the four elements of family wealth are vital to the health of a family over generations. Each member of the family brings special skills and abilities that enhance the family as a whole. The family meeting provides the forum and opportunity for those skills to come to light and be used effectively for the common good and to expand the different elements of the family's capital. Families that cannot communicate are destined to go "shirtsleeves to shirtsleeves" in three generations.

Philanthropy   Even though the process is called "philanthropic planning," the only model which puts a premium on philanthropy is the Inspired Philanthropy model, and even it does not suggest particular charities or organizations. This may take time for some charitable organizations to accept. After all, they have been working for years in a transactional mindset and are seeking to raise money for their own missions. Yet what each of the models suggests, and what is backed up by the authors' own experiences working with high-net-worth families, is that philanthropic planning needs to be about all of donor family's interests, not just philanthropy, and certainly not just one charity. What charities will find, if they are willing to take on philanthropic planning, is that by facilitating the process, collaborating with others, and being part of the team, their best and most loyal donors will not disappoint them when it comes times to draw up the philanthropic priorities as part of the overall plan.

Creating a Plan   "Failing to plan is planning to fail." This truism rings true with any endeavor, but especially with philanthropic planning. Each of the four models suggests that families develop short-, intermediate-, and long-term plans that identify family values, provide for the growth of family wealth, include the terms of family governance, plan for the present and future of the family and heirs, and encourage transformative philanthropy.

The Princeton model takes the least steps in this area, simply starting the thought process and encouraging families to meet with a representative of the University to help take the next steps. The other models are more defined, with a plan as one of the core steps. Every charity and professional advisor working with Tier One families in the philanthropic planning process should strive to help that family come up with a meaningful, written, sustainable plan.

Collaboration Among Professional Advisors, Charities, and the Family   While families may desire to focus on their human, intellectual, and social capital, they also must attend to their financial capital, particularly if there is a multi-generational family business. The authors have worked with many such families, most of which have a bevy of advisors, and rarely do the advisors speak to each other. Almost never do the advisors speak with charitable representatives from the organizations that are important to the family.

The philanthropic planning model requires that professional advisors and charities work together, with the donor/client as the common denominator. This collaboration will lead to effective, comprehensive planning. Even though the donor/client is the common denominator, that does not mean that the donor/client or family has the expertise to be the leader in bringing these players together. The Princeton model suggests that a moderator might be the solution. The Heritage Planning model trains a Certified Wealth Counselor to serve in this role. The Harvard model uses the charitable representative to coordinate the effort while the Inspired Philanthropy model tries to educate the donor family to lead the process.

In many ways, philanthropic planning is a cycle characterized by the results of group interaction being fed back to the group and becoming input for future interactions. Using empowerment, whether it is the fundraiser or advisor as the leader, group members can utilize their talents, abilities, and knowledge most effectively toward the strategy that is supportive to the donor/client family. Stephen Covey wrote that when you fully empower people, your paradigm of yourself changes. You become a servant. You no longer control others; they control themselves, you become a source of help to them.[33]

Kirkman and Rosen studied 112 teams in four organizations. They wanted to see if empowerment was an important factor to the team's success. They found strong support for the notion that empowerment does in fact lead to better team outcomes. They also found evidence that empowerment has four very closely related dimensions:

1. Potency—teams feel they have some degree of power to accomplish a goal.
2. Meaningfulness—teams experienced their tasks as important, valuable, and worthwhile.
3. Autonomy—the degree to which team members experienced freedom, independence, and discretion in conducting their business.
4. Impact—when a team produces work that they feel is significant.[34]

The Tubbs Model of Small Group Interaction organizes the important small group variables into three major categories:

1. Relevant Background Factors—attributes of the individual participants that existed prior to the group's formation and that will endure in at least some modified form after the group no longer exists.

Each member of the philanthropic planning team has a personality that will need to blend. This mix will certainly have an effect on the chemistry of the team.

2. Internal Influences—these factors affect the actual functioning of the group.

Group size is a key factor in philanthropic planning. Obviously the following are important people to have around the planning table:
- The donor/client, their spouse, and family members
- The fundraiser(s)
- The closest advisors including the donor's financial planner, attorney, accountant, and so on.

As Tubbs found, typically, the smaller the group, the higher the individual satisfaction of group members with the discussion.

Tubbs also wrote about status and power and how they can strongly influence group outcomes. For example, if a couple is engaged in the philanthropic planning process with a fundraiser for their favorite charity, and they ask that their estate attorney join in the discussion to advise them, this person will have a higher level of status in the group.

Leadership is an important internal influence. In philanthropic planning, the fundraiser can lead the process, but can do well to step aside if the donor sees another advisor as the natural leader to conduct the process.

Group norms establish what is comfortable or normal in the process. Professionalism should be the underlying theme amongst all in the planning process. Although communication among a donor/client's advisors is often poor, each can positively support their donative intent. When forces are combined, the result can bring about a wonderful combination of professionals.

3. Consequences—the benefits that result from the group process. The benefits are the reason the group was formed—solutions to problems/gaps, improvements in interpersonal relations, improvements in the flow of information between and among people, organization change for the better.[35]

Positive developments can emerge from the process to assist and move toward closure for the donor/client family. Again, for philanthropic planning to function with the precision of a fine watch, many gears and parts must work together in synchronization to keep accurate time and serve to maintain consistency of purpose. Philanthropic planning allows for all of the donor/client's needs and goals to be addressed with a comprehensive strategy and integrated solutions.

While there is no one "right" way to collaborate, all advisors and charities in the process should recognize the need for someone to quarterback the team and ensure that one of them is taking on that role. The best way for that to happen is for all of the advisors, fundraisers, and the family, or at least the primary donor/client, to meet together from time to time to keep everyone informed and the plan moving forward. The natural leader will emerge during those conversations.

The Art of Listening   While not explicitly stated as a formal goal for any of the models, they all rely upon fundraisers and advisors being skilled listeners. Most people are not born with good listening skills, it is something that must be practiced and developed. Good listeners remain focused, exhibit effective supporting behaviors, and maintain a proper attitude. Professional advisors and fundraisers alike will benefit from spending a little bit of time focused on improving listening skills before taking on the philanthropic planning process.

Effective listeners are aware of their body language. They make regular eye contact, nod appreciatively, and lean forward toward speakers to express interest. It is important to avoid gestures that close off the body, such as crossing the arms, and restless activities such as tapping or twirling a pencil. Speakers should feel like they have the undivided attention of the listener. Turn off mobile devices and mute the telephone (if the meeting is in an office). *There is nothing more disrespectful when conducting philanthropic planning than to take a phone call during a meeting or to be checking texts, tweets, and e-mail under the table.*

To assist in the listening process, fundraisers and advisors should practice asking open-ended questions. These are questions which require more than a yes or no answer. By using open-ended questions, donor/client families will talk more, allowing personal planning and philanthropic goals to come to the fore. It is often helpful to repeat back what has been said. It forces the listener to truly internalize what has been said and allows the speaker to reinforce key points or correct any misinterpretations.

While listening to what is being said, it is equally important to listen for what is not being said, to allow for follow up questions. For example, if the question concerns the amount of a reasonable inheritance and when it should occur and the family is avoiding the amount part of the question, it should be re-asked.

Finally, consider that the donor/client may not be a great communicator. Asking clarifying questions will ensure that the donor/client's intent is fully understood.

Concierge Stewardship   As with listening, none of the models listed "stewardship" as an important component, but all talked about engaging multiple generations of a family in philanthropy to ensure that values are

---

CASE STUDY   **TAKE NOTES**

I do not have a great memory. It is a challenge that I have struggled with over the years. Because of this, I took to asking donors for permission to take notes during meetings. Most were happy to allow me to do so, a few were not. For those who would not let me take notes, I would finish the visit, then drive around the corner and use my mini-cassette recorder (I know, I'm dating myself a bit here) to do a "brain dump." These recordings would become the basis of my visit reports later.

For those donors who allowed me to take notes, I always tried to use good listening skills and only record key points. Otherwise, they might only see the top of my head as I was scribbling away. On one such visit with an 83-year-old donor, she gave me permission to take notes. We started chatting and I recorded a few things here and there, but was so engaged in the conversation, I was probably writing down less than I should have been. At one point, she stopped speaking, pointed to my pad and said "Brian, I think you should write that down—it's important." She was right. That one comment led me to introduce her to a faculty member whose program she ended up funding. By taking notes, but not taking notes, she told me exactly what I needed to know to fulfill her philanthropic goals. —BMS

passed from one generation to the next. If charities and advisors engage in philanthropic planning with a family, they should expect that part of the plan developed in the process will be an ongoing relationship. No plan is static and each family engaged in a meaningful dialog about its future will want to continue to engage the charities and advisors which helped to put it together.

This ongoing relationship is "concierge stewardship." It is the one-on-one support, help, and affirmation that charities and advisors will continue to provide to these families across generations as they implement their plans. For charities, this likely involves keeping the family abreast of the successes of their philanthropy, showing impact and outcomes from gifts, inviting them to events, and to serve as volunteers in meaningful ways. It may even involve putting them on the board. Contact for no reason at all will usually be welcome, just to check in and say hello. For advisors, this is the highest level of customer service a practitioner can offer. Proactively contacting the family when laws change or might change that impact the plan that has been put together, checking in to determine if a family meeting might be in order, and providing information on new investment opportunities are all good ways to stay in touch.

The key to concierge stewardship, compared to other customer service that charities or professional advisors might offer, is its proactive nature. Rather than waiting for something to happen, the charities or advisors proactively reach out in anticipation of a need. For high-net-worth families, this level of service will ensure that charities and advisors stay in their good graces and continue to have meaningful relationships.

In Summary

Philanthropic planning best serves the needs of high-net-worth, loyal New Philanthropists. While there is no one philanthropic planning model which best serves the needs of this entire group, there are common elements which charities and advisors can utilize to provide these services including: defining values, exploring the meaning of wealth, limiting financial inheritances, the family as a business, family meetings, philanthropy, planning, collaboration, listening, and concierge stewardship. Charities and professional advisors must build their own philanthropic planning model based on these components, but designed to meet the needs of their own constituencies.

Charities and advisors need to learn to ask questions that prompt family discovery, instead of serving the interest of the charity or the advisor. Open-ended questions will help families to understand their identity, know what they stand for, and plan where it will go. As Collier states, if a family can define what is important before deciding what to do, children will thrive, family will flourish, and society will benefit. The philanthropic planning model will help families to remain unified and prosperous across generations while supporting the causes about which they are passionate.

Charities and advisors working with high-net-worth, New Philanthropist families in a philanthropic planning model will create loyal, multi-generational relationships that will transcend the transactional approaches utilized with the Traditionalists. While building an appropriate model and then the relationships it requires takes time, the rewards will be far more substantial for charities, advisors, and the families that go through the process.

CHAPTER 7

Working with Major (Tier Two) Donors

All charities would like to have the time, volunteer, and staff resources to treat all donors like principal gift donors—providing concierge-level treatment and working in full collaboration with professional advisors to integrate individual goals, objectives, and values with philanthropic plans. Unfortunately, resources are limited, requiring a different approach for the next group in the pyramid, Tier Two (major donors).

For major donors, using a more traditional moves management approach adjusted for philanthropic planning techniques will help to meet the donor's goals and garner support for charities without requiring the significant outlay of time required by the pure philanthropic planning techniques outlined in Chapter 6.

INTRODUCTION TO MOVES MANAGEMENT

Moves management is a process designed to help fundraisers build long-term relationships between donors and charities. Pioneered by David Dunlop of Cornell University and detailed by William Sturtevant in his book, *The Artful Journey: Cultivating and Soliciting the Major Gift* (Institutions Press, 2nd Edition, 2004) it provides a mechanism to move suspects into prospects, prospects into donors, and donors into repeat donors.[1]

Each organization creates its own steps in the moves management process, but most use some variation on this pattern:

- *Identification/Education*—Process of identifying potential prospects through various means, including, but not limited to, peer/list review, referrals, research, database screening, marketing responses, attendance at events, and so on, and then sharing information about the mission of the charity to engage them in its work.

- *Qualification*—Process of evaluating an identified suspect to determine if the suspect has both the capacity and propensity to become a prospect. If not, will the suspect have such capacity in the future, or can a relationship with the suspect be developed to increase propensity for the future.
- *Cultivation*—Process of building a relationship between prospects and the charity to engage the prospects in the life of the charity, to learn about the prospects' and their families' passions.
- *Solicitation*—Process of approaching prospects to ask them to consider increasing their level of involvement with the charity through a significant gift commitment to support an area they are passionate about while also meeting personal planning objectives for their families.
- *Negotiation*—Ongoing process of solicitation, after the ask has been made, to find the right fit between the prospect's passions and personal planning objectives and the charity's objectives. This process includes the creation of a carefully crafted gift agreement with the responsibilities of both parties clearly defined, with the help of professional advisors.
- *Stewardship*—A donor-centered process where the charity provides a contemporaneous thank you within seven days, indicates in the thank you what the gift was used for, reports back to the donor within six months on the long-term outcome the gift has created or will create, recognizes the gift publicly (when desired), and provides ongoing support and connection, as cultivation toward additional gifts.

IDENTIFICATION/EDUCATION

As before, the first step in this process for major gift prospects is to identify them. Using the tools outlined in Chapter 3, the charity should already have an identified pool of major gift prospects who are interested in using philanthropic planning tools to maximize their philanthropy while also supporting the charity. Tier Two prospects are the loyal donors who have wealth markers below what the charity defines as a principal gift prospect, but above the loyal donors who do not have the capacity to make significant gifts. Each charity needs to define these levels for its own mission and constituency, since a major donor to a large research university is very different from a major donor to a small town food bank. The number of zeros at the end of the number should never be the measure; it should be the value of the impact of the gift on the charity and on the donor.

QUALIFYING PROSPECTS

With the pool of loyal major donors identified, the next step is qualifying those prospects. Philanthropic planning for major prospects helps the prospect to identify his/her passions and make a structured gift that benefits a charity today and in the future while also meeting the prospect's personal planning objectives. The very best way to close these gifts is through personal relationships. For identified major gift prospects, this starts with the personal qualifying visit.

Qualifying Visits

Probably the most difficult prospect visit to schedule and handle, other than the solicitation visit, is the qualifying visit. Volunteers are uncertain how to handle them and fundraising staff often dread facing a litany of rejection before finally landing a qualifying visit. In some ways, calling to request a qualifying visit is a lot like playing baseball—only 3 out of 10 identified prospects reached will say yes. In baseball, a .300 batting average makes the player a Hall of Famer. In philanthropic planning, it makes the fundraiser a hero for the organization. Until an identified prospect has been qualified, the organization cannot pursue a meaningful relationship. While many fundraisers look to research to fill this role, the reality is that a fundraiser can learn more in a single qualification visit than a researcher can discover in a full day of searching.

CASE STUDY   THE ETHICS OF QUALIFYING VISITS

When I was working for Middlebury College in Vermont, I scheduled a qualifying visit with a woman who had inquired about a planned gift several times but never actually been visited. The visit was one of several that I had planned as part of a trip to New Jersey. As the day for the visit approached, I called each of my

(continued)

appointments to confirm, but did not hear back from this one prospect. Since she represented my first appointment of the trip, I elected to go anyway, figuring the prospect might just be out for the day or too busy to call back.

When I arrived, there were lights on but no one answered the door. I knocked several times, figuring that the prospect, who was elderly, might have difficulty hearing. Just as I started to walk away, a woman in her late 80's came to the door. It was the dead of winter, but she was dressed only in her light cotton nightgown with bare feet.

She asked who I was and what I wanted. I responded that I was from the College and had scheduled an appointment with her. She looked confused, so I showed her a copy of the letter I had sent to her describing the reason for the visit and confirming the date and time. When she saw the letter, it jogged her memory and she invited me in. We walked to the back of the house, which had only a few pieces of furniture but a large number of packed boxes. When we got to the kitchen, she pulled her copy of my letter out from under a magnet on her refrigerator and said, "Is this you?" I responded that indeed it was. She then said "I thought you would be older."

I did my best to conduct the qualification visit, first asking if I might get her a robe, to which she told me no. I asked her a series of questions about the College and her time there, but she was not particularly responsive. She did share that she would like to set up a charitable gift annuity, since it would pay her a high income. After about 20 minutes, she fell asleep peacefully in the chair in the kitchen. I quietly left her a note and my business card, thanking her for the visit.

When I got back to my office a few days later, I called her daughter, who was also an alumna. She told me that she had been expecting my call. She shared that her mother was suffering from dementia and the reason her home was packed up was that she was moving into a continuing care facility. She went on to let me know that her mother thought I was a very nice young man, but there would be no gift annuity.

When I wrote my donor report, I rated the prospect as "do not solicit", since she was no longer able to make decisions for herself. Not exactly the qualification visit result I was hoping for after actually landing the appointment. I did stay in touch with the daughter from time to time and learned that her mother passed away a year or so later. Imagine my surprise when in response to my condolence letter I received a card from the daughter. She wrote, among other things, "A lot of charities came calling on Mom just before she moved into the facility. They all got her to provide a small check even though she was really not competent to make decisions. You were the only one who called me to let me know something might be wrong and then checked up on Mom afterwards. Enclosed is a gift that Mom would have liked the College to have." With the card was a check for $10,000.

Philanthropic planning means that we follow the platinum rule all the time, treat others as they would like to be treated. While it does not always result in a gift, it is simply the right thing to do. If you treat your prospects well, from the first qualifying visit through the last stewardship visit, helping them meet their own goals while supporting your charity, they will take care of you. Treat them poorly, and you are bound to be left out. —BMS

Obtaining Qualifying Visits   Obtaining a qualifying visit is not as simple as picking up the telephone. While that might have worked back when only a few charities were visiting prospects, those days have long passed. Today, a fundraiser must be strategic when seeking to obtain qualifying visits.

The audience for these visits is those individuals on the second tier of the Philanthropic Planning Pyramid in Figure 3.1, or major prospects. The charity should believe that the prospects have both the capacity and inclination to make significant gifts, but perhaps not gifts that rise to the level of principal gifts for that charity. This group will want and need personalized attention, and frequently will want to make gifts helping them meet personal planning objectives, but they will not receive full philanthropic planning services from the charity.

The fundraiser needs to identify this audience and then begin contacting them regularly, on a schedule. If a fundraiser is making enough requests for visits each month, the fundraiser will garner sufficient interest to meet the fundraising goals of the charity. After all, the fundraiser cannot ask for gifts if the fundraiser is not seeing donors, and the first step is to reach out to those prospects.

1. Prepare the Prospect for the Call For most prospects, particularly those with only a passing familiarity with the charity, it is important to prepare the prospect for the call. A simple letter or e-mail takes the curse off of the call. Ideally this note will be on personal letterhead for the organization, clearly identifying the fundraiser and the reason for the visit. The more personalized the letter, the more effective it will be. Details about the prospect's relationship to the charity add credibility. Handwriting the letter adds a special touch, particularly for the Traditionalists, who have more difficulty turning down a visit when they feel you have invested time in asking for it. Make sure that the letter includes a full range of contact information, including name, telephone number, cell phone number, e-mail address, and web address.

2. Prepare to Make the Call Preparation for the call will help provide both the fundraiser and the prospect with more comfort during the call. A thorough review of the prospect's history with the charity is important. Review any written files and the prospect database, and ask other fundraisers or volunteers who may have had a prior relationship with the prospect what they know. The fundraiser should try to visualize the conversation from the prospect's perspective and prepare for any questions that may come up. Most prospects have some issue which troubles them about the charity. The fundraiser should anticipate what that issue is and be prepared to answer it. If there are no clues in the file, it does not mean that there is not an issue. Before making the call, the fundraiser should practice in front of a mirror, with a smile, stating in succinct language the reason for the visit. Over time, most fundraisers develop mental scripts which can be used to overcome objections, explain away difficult circumstances, or put prospects at ease. Until this comes naturally, only by practicing can a fundraiser be prepared to deal with these situations. Finally, the fundraiser should have the original note to the prospect, a clock, and a calendar at the ready before picking up the phone to dial.

3. Place the Call With all of the preparation in place, it is time to make the call. The fundraiser should smile while dialing to set the right tone, projecting happiness and energy. When the prospect picks up, the fundraiser should match the pace and tone of the prospect.

Once while making a presentation to a large group at a national conference about how to conduct visits, I reached the portion of the presentation about qualifying visits. This particular presentation had been delayed due to technical difficulties and I was pushing pretty hard to cover all of the material so I could catch my flight home. Just as I said, "when calling a prospect for a qualifying visit, be sure to match the pace and tone of the prospect", a voice rang out from the back of the room saying "Slow down, we're not all from New York, you know." Point taken. —BMS

The first thing to do is remind the prospect that the fundraiser is following up on a personal letter or note. This reminder will help to remove the fear that this is a sales call or another call the prospect does not want to take. Next, the fundraiser should recite the purpose for the call. Keep in mind that most prospects know why a fundraiser is calling. Over the next few minutes, the fundraiser should ask for the appointment, set the time and location, and hang up. The goal is for these calls to last not more than five minutes. The longer the fundraiser is on the phone, the greater the likelihood that the prospect will decide not to take the meeting, or that the meeting will not be necessary because everything has been handled on the phone.

When the authors present on this topic, one of the most common questions from the audience is "When is the best time to call?" The right answer, of course, is when someone is there to answer but not when it interrupts something important. Since it is nearly impossible to anticipate this, fundraisers must develop their own approaches which are effective for them. Try testing different times of the day and days of the week, tracking how often someone actually answers the phone. This will provide some initial data to use to establish calling patterns.

Start with these guidelines—for the Traditionalists, call just after the lunch hour. They tend to be up early and out doing activities, but return home after lunch for a break. For the Older and Younger Boomers, try calling first thing in the morning at work, before the work day gets started.

A second option would be to call after work hours at the office, maybe at 5:30 p.m., after the administrative assistant has left for the day. Most successful Boomers work long hours and you can reach them at the office at these times. For Gen X, call on the cell phone during the work day. Gen X likes to have work-life balance so they tend to work fewer hours than Boomers, but also are more reliant on cell phones. By calling the cell phone, you are more likely to get through. By calling during work, you are less likely to interrupt personal time with family, which many Gen X members protect more vigorously than time at work. Millennials tend to work non-traditional hours, so the cell phone is definitely the best way to reach them. Since they are less likely to have started families, early evening is often a good time to get them to answer.

When making these calls, most fundraisers run into gatekeepers. Gate-keepers take many forms including a spouse, administrative assistant at work, voicemail, and caller ID to name a few. It is important to treat human gatekeepers the same way that the fundraiser would treat the prospect. If the gatekeeper is on the fundraiser's side, it is much easier to gain access to the prospect and schedule the meeting. Technology can also be a gate-keeper. The fundraiser should be sure that the caller ID that comes up when calling a prospect is the name of the charity. When leaving a voice-mail, the fundraiser needs to be clear about the nature of the call and the charity involved. Overcoming gatekeepers is an art in and of itself, and a skill that fundraisers must learn to be successful.

4. Handle the Objections   The most challenging part of the phone call to obtain the qualifying visit is overcoming objections to the visit. There tend to be four types of objections to the visit including: indifference to the charity's mission, lack of effectiveness, personal circumstances, too busy/scheduling conflicts.

Indifference to the Charity's Mission   If a donor is going to move from being a modest supporter to major donor, the individual needs to have a passion for some aspect of the mission and the capacity to make a major gift. If the donor is not passionate about some aspect of the mission of the charity, and is motivated to make the occasional gift because a friend has asked him/her to do so, it will be difficult to get that individual to take a meeting. There is tremendous value in having this conversation regardless of whether the donor takes the meeting or not. If by having the conversation, the fundraiser learns that the donor is not a major prospect for the charity, the donor can be moved off of the major gift prospect list and continue to be solicited for annual gifts and events. Qualifying prospects includes the step of moving a suspected prospect to "no longer a major gift prospect." It frees the fundraiser to be able to add a new prospect to the list to be qualified.

In some cases, the donor has capacity but for some reason has not had enough exposure to the charity's mission. It could be that the charity has not been sending out materials about the fulfillment of its mission, or that the prospect has not had time to read the materials. If the fundraiser learns that this is the case, he/she can propose that the meeting be to discuss the mission and how gifts are making a profound difference for those served by the charity.

Lack of Effectiveness   There are a large number of donors who have a passion for an aspect of the mission of a charity but will not give it the full measure of their support because they believe the charity is not being effective in delivering on it. There are countless reasons that donors may believe this about a charity from bad reports in the press, something a peer said, information provided by a competing charity, and more. Until the donor shares this information, it will be impossible for the fundraiser to move the conversation forward. Use the phone call to identify the issue. The fundraiser will not be able to address it completely on the telephone, but by acknowledging that it is an issue to the donor, and promising to discuss it more fully on the visit, it will open the door to further conversations.

Personal Circumstances   Many donors do not see themselves as having the ability to make major charitable gifts. The very term *Major Gifts* is off-putting to a large portion of this audience. A donor receiving a call from a Major Gift Officer is likely to cite personal circumstances as making them unable to meet. After all, the donor does not want to meet with a fundraiser and then have to share that he or she does not have the capacity to make a gift at that level. It is better not to meet at all.

When placing these calls, fundraisers need to reinforce for donors that the visits are to thank them for their loyalty, share more about the charity's mission, and learn about why the donor is passionate about that mission. The gift conversation will come later, if the donor has the capacity and inclination. If the donor expresses concerns about personal circumstances which would stand in the way of making a gift, the fundraiser needs to share that if the conversation reaches that point, the charity has tools available to help the donor meet personal planning objectives while also supporting the charity. The balance of the conversation can happen on the visit—just put the donor at ease so that the visit can happen.

Too Busy/Scheduling Conflicts   Both advisors and fundraisers will deal with donors/clients who simply do not have the time to attend to their planning. It is up the advisor/fundraiser to find a time that the donor does not realize is available and use it to schedule the meeting and move the conversation forward. This usually occurs one of two ways—first, the donor has a life event, crisis, or unfortunate circumstance and decides to make planning a priority. These are the times when it is very important for fundraisers to have relationships with advisors. If the donor appears on the advisor's doorstep and asks to do planning because of the birth of a child, the death of a loved one, a change in employment, retirement, the graduation of the last child from college, the pending sale of a closely held family business, or another life event, the donor is likely not thinking about the charity. But if the fundraiser has a good relationship with the donor's advisors, the advisor is much more likely to remind the donor to include charitable intentions in planning and bring the fundraiser into the conversation, as described in Chapter 5.

The second way that these meetings happen is on the fly. Donors do make time to attend charity events, serve on Boards, eat meals, coach Little League®, and a myriad of other activities. If the fundraiser can find a way to piggy back on these commitments, it may be possible to get the conversation started. Once the discussion has momentum, a donor who is passionate about an aspect of the charity's mission will take the subsequent phone calls and meetings required to complete the gift. The key is to make it as simple and easy as possible for the donor to begin the process.

Appendix C includes a list of 20 common objections, quantifying the type of objection and how a fundraiser might overcome it. Notice how each response is open ended, allowing the conversation to continue or the visit to be completed. Unless a prospect is truly hostile to the mission, a fundraiser should be able to overcome most objections and obtain the initial qualifying meeting.

FINDING TIME ON THE GOLF COURSE

You never know when or where you'll meet someone and have an opportunity to begin a gift discussion. I recall that I took a day off to play golf with my friend Chris who had accepted a position to be vice president of marketing for an insurance company in San Francisco. He normally would invite me to play one of the many municipal courses near Princeton and I suggested that since this was the last time we would play in a while that we would play a private course that I had access to. He agreed and we enjoyed a fabulous day. As we sat in the clubhouse and enjoyed a late lunch after our round, I saw a regular supporter of one of our American Cancer Society golf outings. We invited him to join us and had a fun time talking about golf, San Francisco, and his second home in Bermuda. Turns out he was looking to sell it and was considering options that would help him to realize some income. He asked me if we could talk further about the possibility of a Charitable Remainder Trust. We met a few weeks later and the gift discussion was in motion. —REW

5. Schedule the Meeting At the end of the call, the fundraiser should set a time, date, and place for the initial meeting. While this seems like an easy step in the process, it has tripped up more than one fundraiser over the years.

Consider the age and status of the donor when proposing a time, date, and place. For example, many Traditionalists prefer not to be driving at night. A lunch meeting or mid-afternoon tea might be better than a dinner meeting. Since the donor has likely never met the fundraiser before, it might be uncomfortable either having the meeting at the donor's home or having the fundraiser pick the donor up for the meeting.

The Boomer cohorts may be far too busy at work to take time out for a fundraising meeting and likely will want to meet after hours for dinner or drinks. Gen X donors will prefer to have meetings during working hours, to protect their family time, while Millennials tend to be most flexible about time and location.

Since a fundraiser cannot know the personal circumstances of the donor, it is best to allow the donor to pick the time and location. This ensures that the donor will be in a comfortable environment at a time that works for him/her. It also avoids a potentially awkward situation if the fundraiser takes the donor to a restaurant or other meeting place which is too high scale or low brow for the donor. This is a more donor-centered and effective way to get the first meeting.

Once the meeting is scheduled, it is important to confirm the meeting. It is best to confirm using whatever medium works for the donor. By asking the donor how, such as via mail, e-mail, an electronic calendaring program, text, tweet, and so on, and with whom the fundraiser should confirm, the fundraiser will be sure that the meeting gets on the calendar. When confirming, the fundraiser should include all contact information so that the donor will know how to reach the fundraiser if something goes wrong.

The fundraiser should reconfirm the meeting time and location the day prior to the actual meeting. On the day of the meeting, the fundraiser should arrive a few minutes early and bring along a calendar, in case the donor needs to reschedule at the last minute or wants to schedule another meeting to follow up the current session.

SCHEDULING VISITS

When I was a gift planner for the University of Pennsylvania and Middlebury College, my territory was the entire world. Needless to say, I did not get to some locations very often, and it was frustrating when I would call and a donor would be open to a meeting, but there was a scheduling conflict. Over the years, I began to learn that sometimes it was not a scheduling conflict at all, but that the donor really did not want to see me.

In order to know whether a donor really had a conflict or was politely saying "no thank you" and trying to spare my feelings, I began to plan my travel a year at a time. I would look at my prospect pool and determine how many visits I needed to make in a given location that year. For example, if I needed to make 15 visits in Seattle, Washington, this year, I knew that I would likely make two trips to Seattle, each lasting two to three days. While I knew I could complete five visits per day,

I was also realistic that there would be cancellations and travel time to and from the west coast.

After scheduling my two trips, I would start calling the 15 donors with whom I needed to schedule visits. I would offer up each day of my first trip individually. If none of those dates worked, I would then offer that I was returning to Seattle two months later, would any of the dates for that trip work. By the time I went through five or six days, some several months in the future, if the donor was still not available, it was pretty likely that it had nothing to do with my timing but rather the prospect just did not want to take the meeting. At that point, I took the donor off my prospect list as a person who would not take a visit. This allowed me to move on to other donors and stop bothering someone who was just not passionate about our mission. — BMS

Planning for Qualifying Visits   The qualifying visit should be a very purposeful meeting. It is the opportunity for the fundraiser to learn more about the capacity, passions, and personal planning objectives of the donor. Most fundraisers make the mistake of going into qualifying visit meetings with no written agenda. Without an agenda, the fundraiser does not have clear, articulated goals of what the fundraiser hopes to learn in the session. Appendix D includes a Sample Qualification Visit Preparation Worksheet. Fundraisers can use this worksheet to develop their own template to plan for qualifying visits.

Conducting Qualifying Visits   Donor-centered philanthropic planning requires the fundraiser to ask open-ended questions and listen carefully for what is being said, as well as what is not being said. The less a fundraiser talks and the more he/she listens, the better the result will be for the charity and for the donor, since the donor's wishes will be paramount. Chapter 6 details some of the listening skills which should be applied to all visits, including qualification visits with major prospects.

To assist fundraisers, Appendix E contains a list of sample qualifying visit questions which are designed to get donors talking. Professional advisors can use these same questions to get a client to open up about passions and philanthropic priorities. These questions are broken into three categories including general questions, capacity questions, and propensity questions. Appendix F includes an additional list of questions about the personal planning objectives of donors. While the questions in Appendix F might not be used until the fundraiser starts cultivation visits, they are a powerful tool to help understand what might stand in the way of a donor considering a meaningful gift and allows for the fundraiser to start providing creative gift planning solutions to meet these needs.

At the end of the qualifying visit, the fundraiser should thank the prospect, summarize the meeting, and articulate next steps. A qualifying visit should not end until there is a clearly defined next step with the prospect, or the prospect has been disqualified and can be removed from the prospect list.

Following Up Qualifying Visits   There is nothing more important after the qualifying visit than the contemporaneous thank you note. Many fundraisers wait too long to complete a thank you. When working with either of the Boomer cohorts or the Traditionalists, a written thank you is the appropriate medium. If the fundraiser is on a multi-day trip, the thank you note should be written and sent from the road. There will be an opportunity to send a more formal follow up letter when the fundraiser returns to the office, but this initial note, showing appreciation, will be a huge help in building the relationship. For Gen X and Millennials, it may be more appropriate to use an e-mail thank you, depending upon the donor. Keep in mind, however, that even if a written thank you seems trite to a Gen X or Millennial donor, it will make the visit more memorable.

One of the great losses to the fundraising industry with the widespread use of database systems has been the call report. While today's systems are far more functional and effective than the manual entry of past years, the call report gave fundraisers a clear and consistent set of rules for what should be recorded after a qualifying visit. In today's systems, the entire report ends up in free text, often with key elements missing, or it has be recorded in several different modules across a range of fields, and some are forgotten. As a general rule, fundraisers should record the following data after a qualifying visit:

- Background on the donor, including family members, family history, and personal and professional bios.

- Sense of engagement and history with the charity.
- Areas of interest at the charity about which the donor is passionate.
- Where the area of interest falls on the donor's philanthropic priorities.
- Other charities the donor supports.
- Capacity of the donor or observations of wealth from the visit (type of car, house, art, and other assets observed).
- Personal planning objectives the donor has which may impact philanthropic planning.
- Answers to questions written up prior to the visit.
- What the donor agreed to do.
- What the fundraiser agreed to do.
- Next steps and timeline for completion.

Once this information has been compiled, the fundraiser should complete the follow-up steps promised and remind the donor of any action items. Following up the visit will rarely be the donor's first priority, so appropriate reminders from the fundraiser of particular tasks will go a long way toward moving the process forward to cultivation.

Cultivating Prospects

Once a prospect has been qualified and the charity has some confidence that the individual has both the capacity and the inclination to make a major gift, the next step in the process is to cultivate the relationship between the donor and the charity. This allows the donor to better understand the mission and goals of the charity and the charity to better understand the passions the donor has for one or more areas of the charity's mission and the personal planning objectives of the donor.

Sharing the Charity's Mission

When cultivating a relationship, the charity needs to begin to build connections with the donor. The first step is to identify existing connections. This should have happened during the qualifying visit. Most donors come to the attention of a charity because they have used its services, benefitted from its services, had family or friends who have benefitted from its services, or had a friend who asked them to become involved.

Introducing Others into the Conversation   Once the initial qualifying visit has been made, and the charity has learned a little bit about how the donor wants to be engaged by the charity, the next step is to build on that level of engagement. Depending upon the organization, this may be through assistance with programs, participation in activities, ongoing use of the services, and more.

In every case, it is vital to help the donor build multiple points of contact and connections within the charity. It is commonly said that fundraising is a relationship-building effort. This is absolutely true. Unfortunately, with the increase in professional fundraisers has come the misconception that the relationship is between the fundraiser and the donor. In fact, the relationship is between the donor and the charity. The professional fundraiser's job, and the job of any volunteers working with the donor, is to enhance the relationship with the charity and its mission over time. The charity's representatives must help connect the donor to the area at the charity about which the donor is passionate. That way, if the staff member or volunteer moves on, the relationship is not lost. By introducing others into the conversation, it also increases the likelihood that one of those people will share an area of the mission which is so compelling that the donor will want to invest in it.

Cultivation Visits   The cultivation visit should be a logical progression from the qualifying visit. The fundraiser should use the cultivation visit to further quantify the donor's particular areas of interest at the charity and passion for the mission; discover other charities the donor supports and why; ask about personal planning objectives the donor has which might stand in the way of philanthropy; and inquire how the donor uses professional advisors. The questions in Appendix F should provide guidance on how to ask about these topics. By the end of the visit, the fundraiser should have clear action steps for moving the donor's relationship forward with the charity. It may be the introduction of additional staff people or volunteers, attendance at an event, or participation in an activity. The key is to use the cultivation visit to identify how the donor wants to be engaged by the charity and to provide that level of engagement, deepening the relationship over time.

It may take several cultivation visits to move a donor from the cultivation phase to the solicitation phase. However, the fundraiser should develop a strategy for moving each donor through this process. Frequently fundraisers will spend years cultivating a relationship, when in fact all the fundraiser and donor are really doing is having lunch or playing golf on the charity's expense account. While this analysis may seem a bit harsh, if the fundraiser is not actively planning how each meeting and conversation moves the relationship forward, it can stall in the cultivation phase and end up costing both the fundraiser and the charity significant time and resources. Fundraisers should use the planning worksheet in Appendix D to ensure that each visit has an articulated goal and progress is measured against that goal.

There are some in the charitable community who would argue that using moves management and planning visits in this way is contrary to the philanthropic planning, donor-centered approach. That in a philanthropic planning, donor-centered world, you allow the relationship between the organization and the donor to evolve organically, providing information related to the donor's passions and opportunities for interaction.

While the organic model may seem attractive, it is actually not in the best interests of either the donor or the charity. The donor who is passionate about one or more aspects of the mission and wants to be supportive is interested in learning more about the charity during these interactions. He/she becomes invested because of the valuable work that the charity does that touches these passions. The donor is busy and likely wants to see these meetings as productive. Long term, since the donor wants to pursue these passions, he/she wants this relationship to lead to a logical conclusion that meets both the needs of the charity and the needs of the donor.

If the charity is spending significant resources on the donor in the form of both dollars and personnel time and it is not leading anywhere, that time is being taken away from other potential donors or from mission-based work. The only reason to invest this type of time in a donor is to build a relationship in a purposeful way that leads to gifts of time, treasure, or talent to the organization. A charity that does not see this as the end goal of a cultivation strategy, or which has no end game, is not utilizing charitable resources efficiently. Both the donor and the charity ultimately want to see the mission furthered, which cannot happen if these cultivation visits are not purposeful. Donor-centered does not mean that long-term outcomes for the charity are ignored along the way.

Understanding the Donor

Cultivation strategies will vary depending upon the donor, his/her philanthropic motivations/passions, personal planning objectives, and reliance upon advisors. It is important to follow the platinum rule of treating the donor as the donor wants to be treated during the cultivation process. While this will be different for each person, there are some common elements which can be identified by generational cohorts.

Traditionalists (Born Pre-1946)   For the purposes of this book, anyone born prior to 1946 falls into the Traditionalists, made up of the Depression, World War II, and Post-War Cohorts. This is a group that grew up with an "us versus them" mentality born of World War II and the Cold War. A few members of this generation may also have memories of growing up in the Great Depression. Because of this, they will want to make gifts that put ideas to work—practical solutions to problems and needs of the charity.

For the last couple of decades, charities have received billions of dollars from this group in the form of unrestricted bequests. They trust that the charities will put the money where it will do the most good and know that there are great needs to be met. In so many ways, they are the golden generation for estate gifts.

When cultivating this group, fundraisers should focus less on the use of the gift and more on the good works of the charity. The mission itself will have more power than long-term outcomes created by legacy gifts. Passions are less important in this cohort than the ones that follow, but if a donor is passionate about an area of the mission, it should be fully explored and the gift directed to it.

When advisors are working with this group, it is very important to help them determine how much is enough to leave to their kids. This generation often feels that their children waste too much money and do not need a lot of help. If advisors can help Traditionalists to recognize that they have enough to care for themselves and to leave a modest inheritance for children, the rest can come to charity outright or though a bequest, with the bequest being the preferred vehicle for most of these donors.

Older Boomers (Born 1946 to 1954)   The Older Boomers are the first of the generational cohorts that do not have an inherent trust of charities. They came of age in the 1960s amid tremendous political upheaval and unrest. They associate charities with the establishment and the establishment was bad. Since they see the world with jaundiced eyes, this generation wants to make it a better place and tends to focus their philanthropy accordingly, provided they can verify that their gifts are making a difference.

To meet the needs of Older Boomers, fundraisers first have to identify the passions of the donor. This generation is not likely to give to help a charity meet its needs, but instead will focus their philanthropy on their passions. But to be successful, the fundraiser will need to show how the gift will have an immediate impact on the world and how it helps to solve the long-term problem (creates an outcome) that the donor is passionate about. Fundraisers also need to create an infrastructure to verify that gifts are being used as the donor directed.

Most Older Boomers have not saved enough for retirement. Many of them are looking for their charitable gifts to also meet personal planning needs. The most common needs expressed by Older Boomers are to to provide for my future retirement income; to provide income for my elderly parent or loved one; and to pay for my grandchildren's education.

With these core personal planning goals intertwined with their charitable giving, professional advisors have an important role to plan with this generational cohort. Advisors might suggest a flip charitable remainder trust, a deferred gift annuity, or a flexible gift annuity to help provide future retirement income. A charitable gift annuity or a charitable remainder annuity trust might be the vehicle of choice to provide for an elderly parent or loved one.

In all cases, the fundraiser needs to cultivate the donor by talking about the area within the mission about which the donor is passionate, followed by the donor's personal planning needs. When the donor believes that the mission is right and the personal planning need is correctly identified, the advisor can then suggest the right tools to accomplish both the financial goal and the charitable goal. Working alone, neither the fundraiser nor the advisor can make this gift happen. But working together, with the fundraiser focused on donor passions and the advisor focused on structure, amazing gifts will result.

Younger Boomers (Born 1955 to 1964) The Younger Boomers share the distrust for charities with the Older Boomers. They also have a healthy cynicism for the world, since the Older Boomers stand in their way to get the best jobs, vacation homes, and lifestyle. Like the Older Boomers, they want to see the impact and outcomes created by their gifts. But because of their cynicism, they want more than to just verify that their gifts are being used as intended, they want true accountability in the process.

Younger Boomers will require a much more robust cultivation process from fundraisers to overcome this cynicism. Appealing to their passions will be vital, to help them feel confident their gift is going to achieve something important. They also will want formal gift agreements, so that they can include verification measures about their gifts. Because they have less wealth than the cohorts that came before them and may not be to the distribution phase of life (they are still accumulating wealth), the cultivation process may be extended. Younger Boomers are more likely to want their philanthropy to meet their personal planning needs than even the Older Boomers, because they have less wealth and feel like they will not have the opportunities to earn as much as the generation before them. Providing for future retirement income, for elderly parents, and perhaps for children's education will be their personal planning objectives. Until these issues are dealt with, they will not be prepared to make meaningful charitable gifts.

Professional advisors play a key role in helping Younger Boomers plan for the future. This is the time in life when most people finally can see what the future holds and put their long-term financial and estate plans in place. This may not be when the first will is drawn, but it will be the one upon which future wills will be based. Advisors need to ask Younger Boomers about their passions, if they have charities they want to support, and what kind of legacy they want to create.

Generation X (Born 1965 to 1976)   Gen X approaches philanthropy differently than the generations that precede them. They came of age during charity and business scandals, making them less likely to want to give. They also are still in the accumulation phase of life and generally not ready to make really significant outright gifts.

Charities frequently talk about the need for donors to give of their time, treasure, and talent. The way to cultivate Gen X donors is to ask first for their time and talent. Gen X wants to volunteer and put their passions into action. Unlike the prior generations, Gen X is far less interested in serving on a board or committee. These donors are much more interested in actually getting into the field and making a difference, bringing their passions to life. Unfortunately, most fundraisers and charities do not have these kinds of volunteer opportunities available. If the mission touches a Gen Xer and there is a volunteer opportunity to go with it, these donors will then make gifts.

While a few Gen X members might be thinking about supplementing retirement income, this generation is currently focused on family. They are trying to figure out how to pay the ever-increasing cost of college and how to protect their children in case something should happen to them. They are a perfect group for fundraisers to approach about writing their first wills and putting in place effective insurance. When they do, they can create a meaningful legacy by naming the charity as a contingent beneficiary of the will, retirement plan, or life insurance policy in an area important to the donor.

Professional advisors are especially important to Gen X. As detailed later, in Table 8.2, Gen X trusts their professional advisors and prefer to obtain estate planning and charitable bequest information from them rather than fundraisers. Since this is the age when most individuals complete their first wills, the advisor can form a special, lifetime bond with the donor by discussing the entire financial and estate plan, how the Gen Xer wants to support his/her family, his/her passions, and the charities to include in the plan.

Millennials (Born 1977 to 1984?)   Millennials are in the accumulation phase of life and are still figuring out what will be their life-long passions. Many of them do not yet have families and are just starting to make their way in the world.

Millennials have an unusual ability to filter information, which leads to quick decision-making. As a cohort, they want to be involved personally with a charity, making things happen. They will get involved with a broader range of charities if the mission touches them right now, even though it may not be something they support for the rest of their lives. Millennials do not have any patience for the traditional ways that charities tend to do business. If a charity cannot find a way to let a Millennial help, the Millennial will find another charity, start a competing charity, or create a for-profit business to make money while supporting the cause.

Cultivation for Millennials should be a very short process. Since they are not making life-long decisions to support the charity, the charity needs to focus on what is the passion of the moment. If the charity can have a series of moments with Millennials, the gifts will eventually turn into a lifetime of support.

Planning is not particularly important to most Millennials, so fundraisers need to partner with advisors in the community to bring advisors to Millennials. Most Millennials have not been educated about wills, retirement planning, financial planning, budgets, or life insurance. Their knowledge of these areas is frequently limited to what they have read online. If fundraisers connect Millennials with advisors who can educate them and then allow Millennials to do additional research on their own, it is possible for advisors then to suggest charitable gifts to this cohort. Millennials have retirement plans and life insurance through their employers and can easily name charities as the beneficiaries. This is a good first step in building long-term relationships.

SOLICITING PROSPECTS

Once a fundraiser has built a relationship with the donor, understands the passions which tie the donor to the charity, and has cultivated a meaningful dialog, it is time to start the gift conversation. With proper cultivation, the solicitation is one of the easiest steps in the philanthropic planning process.

How the Philanthropic Planning Approach is Different from Other "Asks"

Philanthropic planning focuses less on the needs of the charity and more on the passions of the donor. Carrying this approach to its logical conclusion, the fundraiser should not be thinking about making an ask. For decades, fundraisers have used the transactional approach. In that approach, the fundraiser meets with the donor, determines the capacity, finds an area of interest at the charity, and then asks the donor to make a gift at the level of his/her capacity to the area of interest.

In the philanthropic planning context, it will be clear when it is time to approach a donor about a gift. The fundraiser will have provided the donor with opportunities to fulfill his/her passions through participation with the charity, and the donor will be ready to do more.

THE RIGHT ASK AMOUNT

When I train fundraisers on using a philanthropic planning approach, I am often asked "How do you figure out the right amount for the ask?" This is actually far easier to do in a philanthropic planning approach than it is for a traditional major gift ask.

By the time I am having a gift discussion with the donor, there are no surprises. We have talked in depth about his/her passions and the areas of the charity which he/she wants to invest in. I have previously shared information and gotten feedback from the donor about what he/she liked and did not like about the different ways that the charity was pursuing the area of passion.

At this stage, the donor normally *approaches me* and says "I want to make this happen, how can I do it?" I typically respond by saying "The total cost of the project is $5 million. In order to complete it, we need several lead donors and many additional supporters. Where do you see yourself in that continuum?" Most of the time, the donor will give me a number. I then articulate what that number will help us accomplish. If the number is less than I was expecting, I raise some of the personal planning issues that the donor has shared with me previously, perhaps that he/she does not have enough saved for retirement, and ask if that is the impediment to really accomplishing this gift.

Since the donor is already committed to the project, helping remove the impediment to completing the gift is usually rather easy. We figure out together how the donor might accomplish both, in this case, a gift of appreciated stock with a portion used to fund a flexible gift annuity, and complete the gift with the help of the donor's advisors. The back and forth is always to help the donor meet his/her dual goals of funding an area of the charity's mission that he/she is passionate about while also assuring that his/her personal planning needs are met.

In my entire career, I have probably not put a number on the table for a major ask more than a dozen times. The rest of the time I have used this method of philanthropic planning to great success. —BMS

Preparing for the Solicitation Visit

Before the fundraiser schedules a gift discussion visit, the ideas to be shared should be vetted with the donor.

The Pre-Solicitation Visit   The process of making a solicitation is just that, a process. The fundraiser has built a relationship and learned about the donor's passions. At this stage, the fundraiser should schedule a visit with the donor to test the fundraiser's understanding of the donor's passions, the particular area the donor seems inclined to support, and the estimated gift amount. By asking questions about these topics on a pre-solicitation visit, it allows the donor to get used to the idea of what is coming and also allows the fundraiser to change the approach, if needed, before a gift discussion occurs. In some cases, if the donor is really ready, the fundraiser will actually have to put the donor off until the fundraiser is sure that everything is in order.

Who Should Participate in the Solicitation Visit?   In the traditional, transactional fundraising model, the head of the organization or a board member makes most of the high-end asks. In the philanthropic planning model, the people who have the relationships with the donor should be the ones participating in the conversation. This usually includes the fund-raiser and those who have become engaged with the donor along the way as the relationship has expanded. For example, in an education setting, the fundraiser may have brought the dean and a faculty member doing research which is of interest to the donor to cultivation meetings. Those are the individuals who should be on the team when it is time to discuss a gift with the donor. In this case, the head of the organization or a board member would not be a natural fit, since they have not been talking to the do-nor over the course of the cultivation. If it is a solicitation which requires the head of the organization or a board member and he/she has not yet been involved with the donor, the cultivation process is not yet complete. The first time a donor meets the head of the organization or a board member should not be to discuss completing a gift.

The number of people on the solicitation visit should be careful considered. It should be the right group that the donor would naturally expect, but generally no more than three, and better if it were two. According to

Walton in the February 1999 issue of *Fundraising Management* on the psychology of major gifts, soliciting in teams is more effective than asking for gifts alone:

- Team members can use individual strengths to present the case for support and can gain energy and competence from each other during the process.
- One member of the team can speak, while the other team member can listen and observe the prospect's body language.
- There is less chance the charity will miss something the prospect has said, or has shown through body language, than if the conversation happened alone.
- Also, it lets the prospect know that he or she is important enough to merit two people from the organization. It elevates the prospect to the top tier of supporters for the group.[2]

Scripting and Rehearsing the Solicitation Because asking for a gift can be challenging for those involved in the process, many charities have taken to "scripting" a solicitation. The fundraiser writes up a script for the various parties attending the meeting and they practice to make sure everyone knows their roles and purpose. The script includes who will make the ask, the amount of the ask, and the purpose of the gift. The script also includes alternatives, so if the donor turns down the gift, the charity can determine if it was the purpose or the amount which was the problem and salvage some portion of the gift. In the transactional model, it ensures that the gift conversation happens early in the meeting and is articulated in an appropriate and effective way. It also takes some of the burden off of volunteers and the head of the organization, who may not be comfortable with this type of solicitation.

In the philanthropic planning model, the approach needs to be fundamentally different. Through the cultivation and pre-solicitation processes, the charity should already know what area/ideas the donor is passionate about and have vetted with the donor how the charity is pursuing that area. Because this is a partnership, with the charity providing an opportunity for the donor to pursue his/her passions, there should be no surprise ask or amount. It is an organic conversation that has come from months and sometimes years of cultivation, which has been revisited several times before the solicitation meeting. This usually means that there is no formal "proposal" to be presented to the donor at the meeting. This is replaced by discussion of the terms of the gift agreement in the negotiation process.

Asking for the Gift

In the philanthropic planning model, the solicitation will frequently begin with some variation of the language,

> We have been talking about _____ for several months, which is clearly very important to you. Together, we believe we can help you to realize your goal of _____ for those served by our charity. The last time we met, we discussed your support for this area and how we could partner together to make your vision a reality. The total cost to complete this project is going to be $_____. Where would you see yourself in making this happen?

If the donor raises objections to the project, then the solicitation conversation was premature or the charity failed to understand his/her passions and needs to take a step back. If the donor raises concerns about the amount, the fundraiser should ask questions about the personal planning issues that may stand in the way of the gift, and see if there are gift planning solutions to them. The fundraiser should also explore alternative assets, since the donor may not be thinking of those assets. In many cases, if professional advisors have not been consulted by this point in the process, it is time to ask to involve them to help the donor realize his/her passions while supporting the charity.

At the conclusion of the solicitation meeting, the fundraiser and other representatives of the charity should summarize the conversation so that everyone understands the results of the meeting. Assuming that the donor wants to go forward, but needs time to consider what has been proposed, the next step is to negotiate the details of the gift.

NEGOTIATING THE GIFT

Once the charity and donor have agreed to the framework of the gift, in particular the area/passion to be funded and the costs associated with it, the fundraiser needs to provide the donor and advisors with a gift agreement. The gift agreement outlines what the charity has agreed to, what the donor has agreed to, the assets to be used to make the gift or the gift structure, and how the gift will be recognized and stewarded. It is important that the gift agreement include all of the terms of the agreement with the donor, as it will govern the future use of the gift. Chapter 14 contains a summary of what an effective gift agreement should contain and Appendix R is a sample gift agreement.

Typically the fundraiser will provide the donor and the advisors with a copy of a draft gift agreement within a few days after the solicitation visit. It may require additional conversations with the donor to clarify key points, particularly if the gift is going to include a segment to help the donor meet a personal planning objective. Advisors have a key role and should be sure that the agreement meets all of the donor's goals and protects the donor against changes in staffing at the charity. Even if the donor has a great relationship with the charity, the gift must be properly documented.

Once the draft is delivered, there are usually one or more negotiation visits where the donor, advisors, and representatives of the charity clarify the details of how the donor's gift will meet the philanthropic goals of everyone involved. When all of the details have been ironed out, the final gift agreement is executed by the donor and the charity and the real work begins—making the vision a reality.

STEWARDING THE DONOR

With the gift completed and the gift agreement signed, the final step in any gift conversation is thanking, recognizing, and stewarding the donor. Donors expect some very basic elements: a contemporaneous thank you (within 48 hours) stating the gift has been put to the use where directed, appropriate recognition with similar donors, follow up reports showing the impact of the gift today and eventually the long-term outcomes of tomorrow, and an on-going relationship with the charity so that the donor can see those passions at work. If the gift also was designed to meet a personal planning objective, regular updates should show that this additional portion of the gift is progressing (or explain why it is not). For those donors who elect to complete legacy gifts as part of this process, additional details about stewarding legacy gifts can be found in Chapter 12.

Introduction to the Seven Touches Philosophy

Regular interaction and communication is an integral part of the successful stewardship program. Care must be given to not only offer information that consistently keeps donors abreast of the outcomes of their investment, but to also position the case for making the next gift to an organization. The topic of frequency has been debated—too much and a donor could tune out the noise which comes across as static, too little and a donor might not ever hear the harmony of the sound that could lead to their full commitment. Over the course of a year, seven touches has been proven to be both efficient and effective in delivering a clear message that matches the tone that is sweet music to the donor's ear.

Seven distinct moves offer seven opportunities for the donor to understand that they are important to the charity. Seven messages that are singular, but when positioned together work toward a complete concept of reminding the donor both why they are giving and what their support is accomplishing.

Seven Touches

1. *Prompt Thank You Letters*—Consistent thank you letters within 48 hours of their giving. A tiered recognition plan that involves multiple thank yous as giving levels increase will offer the greatest impact to position repeated giving.

2. *Impact Reports*—Donors are inspired by the results of their giving. Positive outcomes that are a direct result from their investment in a program will motivate a donor to give again.

3. *Annual Report*—Just like a program report that shares how donor support led to success for an aspect of the organizational mission, an informative annual report that depicts the overall picture of a charity will build trust in their ability to efficiently reach and surpass goals. Similarly, transparency and accountability lead to donor loyalty as they continue to become engaged in mission delivery.

4. *Volunteer Recognition Card*—Sent in April during Volunteer Recognition month, it highlights the charity's appreciation of its donors' active involvement in the mission of the organization. Whether they are board members, committee members, or other volunteers, committed donors appreciate recognition.

5. *Birthday Card*—Sent out the first week of each month (or three days prior to the donor's birthday if possible), a greeting on the birthday says that the organization is paying attention to the donor in a very personal way.

6. *Thanksgiving Card*—At a time of year for expressing thanks, thanks to donors should be a priority.

7. *Personal Phone Call*—Make a personal phone call in early December to wish donors a Happy Holiday.

To truly offer a donor-centered approach the examples above should be amended to match the constituents of the particular organization. The meter of the approach is proven, but the touches should be tailored to the donors and the charity's mission.

CASE STUDY   **SEVEN TOUCHES IN ACTION**

Sam often told me of all the mail he would get from his alma mater, his church, his professional association, and other organizations. He would send me the pieces with a note to let me know that he was paying attention and that he wanted to help. I took care in using the seven touches approach with Sam and he told me how he appreciated it since he could count on my call before the holidays and as a retired executive, he appreciated the financials and other information in the annual report. He would often call me after getting something in the mail to say thank you. I said, "Sam, why do you call me to say thank you?" He would reply, "Because you and the American Cancer Society are showing me how much I matter to you." Sam taught me how to say thank you in a new way—the donor-centered way—where we think about how our donors feel and what they want and then put those ideas into action. In addition to his annual giving and volunteering, Sam became a "Champion" in "The Society" by including the American Cancer Society in his will. —REW

Perspectives of Different Generational Cohorts

When dealing with major donors, the stewardship of each gift should be customized to meet the expectations of the donor and documented in the gift agreement. Unlike in the past, when a one-size-fits-all approach was applied to stewardship (because charities were only stewarding the Traditionalists), differences in generational cohorts now require a more robust stewardship effort to meet different generational expectations. Use the seven touches to help craft a plan that meets the needs of each of the cohorts.

Traditionalists   The Traditionalists have an inherent trust that a charity will use a gift effectively. Because they want to see ideas put to work, their stewardship should include reports and personal contact telling them about how their gifts have had an impact. At a minimum the stewardship should show how the charity is pursuing its mission in the area the donor is passionate about. Donor stories are particularly effective in getting the message out that the gift has been put to work and is achieving results.

Older Boomers   The emergence of the Older Boomers as the primary donors to most charities was the impetus for many of the changes in fundraising outlined in the *Companion*. Their behavior is fundamentally different than the generations which came before. In the case of stewardship, most Older Boomers are giving to make the world a better place, not just to impact the local community. The vision is larger so the stewardship must account for it. Older Boomers make gifts to areas of the charity's mission about which they are passionate. They expect to get progress reports on the impact that their gifts are having on the targeted areas/populations. They also want to see multi-year progressions, showing how that impact is creating long-term outcomes—solving the problem they wanted to solve. Older Boomers will seek out the opportunities to serve on the board and advisory committees as a way to verify that gifts are being used as they intended and progress is being made.

Younger Boomers   The Younger Boomers, much like the Older Boomers, do not trust charities. They are looking for many of the same things as Older Boomers—the impact of gifts and verified long-term outcomes.

However, because they are a bit less trusting of charities than the Older Boomers, they also want accountability. If they feel that the staff is not getting the job done, they will stand up and try to redirect the charity. Their stewardship needs to be all about actual results.

Generation X Gen X looks at philanthropy differently from the preceding generations. Because they are less focused on their careers and seek more work-life balance, they want to use some of that time to do work for charities, particularly in the areas where they have made gifts. Gen X is much less interested in serving on boards and advisory panels to rubber stamp decisions made by the staff or the Boomers in leadership positions on the board. They tend to be loners who are not interested in socializing with other supporters of the charity. Instead, they want to make gifts that allow them to be personally involved in the work of the charity in the area they are passionate about. They still need to see the impact and long-term outcomes of gifts, and will want to see reports to verify that gifts are being used as intended and providing results, but they will feel most engaged when they are actually doing something meaningful. This is perhaps one of the most difficult areas for charities, as most are not prepared to provide real, quality volunteer opportunities for Gen X.

Millennials Because Millennials are still in the accumulation phase financially and have sacrificed earnings to achieve the work-life balance, most of them are not yet making big gifts as they lack the resources to do so. Instead, they seek to actively participate (personally help) to solve a particular, identified problem that they are passionate about. If they find such opportunities, they will support them within their means. But Millennials are different from the other cohorts because they will not let a lack of resources stop them from making a difference. They are truly activist philanthropists and their stewardship must reflect this. If charities cannot provide Millennials with opportunities to personally help, they will lose them as volunteers and donors.

Other Segments Substantial research has been done on how to maintain relationships with other segments that might be focused on the mission of a particular charity. If a charity appeals to distinct groups, or segments its population based on other factors, such as gender or sexual orientation, then the stewardship program must account for these differences as well. There is no one, right answer. Rather, each charity must build its stewardship program to meet the needs of its constituent base.

The Role of Professional Advisors

Professional advisors play an important role in the stewardship of donors. While the charity is focused on illustrating to the donor how the gift is impacting the mission, it is up to the professional advisors to ensure that the mechanics of the gift continue to move forward as required by the gift agreement. It is far more likely that the professional advisor will be aware of life-changing events which might impact the philanthropic plan, since donors think to meet with their advisors long before they go back to a charity to discuss a gift plan. Similarly, advisors will be monitoring changes in tax laws which could impact the donor and have a better handle on how to deal with those changes for a particular situation.

Complex Asset Gifts   There are many different types of assets that individual donors will use to make major gifts. Most charities are not experts and cannot provide guidance when such gifts are proposed or after they are completed. Some of these gifts, such as gifts of closely held stock, involve holding periods when the charity and donor are, in effect, both investors in the asset. Professional advisors cannot provide advice about a gift structure and then walk away. Their help is needed from the time the gift is proposed until the charity has liquidated the asset. By actively participating in this process, advisors can avoid charities making mistakes that negatively impact their clients.

Similarly, charities often are not prepared to effectively handle gifts-in-kind such as art, collectibles, books, and automobiles. These are complex areas requiring a true partnership with the advisor before, during, and after the gift to ensure that the client is protected.

Bequests and Living Trusts   By far the most common philanthropic planning tool is to include a charity in the donor's will or living trust. Professional advisors need to stay abreast of changing estate tax laws to ensure that a charitable bequest does not negatively impact other tax planning in the estate documents and the client's wishes are carried out.

For example, when the estate tax exemption amount jumped to $5,000,000 per year in 2011 and the code allowed for the portability of the unused estate tax marital deduction, the estate planning attorney should have prompted the client to review any formula clauses in the will to determine if any adjustments to the plan were required to meet the dictates of the new law. If the advisor can bring the charity into the conversation at the appropriate time, it helps the donor, the charity, and the advisor's relationships with both.

Retirement Plan Designations   Over the last several years, more and more charities and donors have come to realize the significant tax benefits of naming a charity rather than children as the beneficiaries of a retirement plan. Unfortunately, many donors and charities are not well informed about the rules and regulations regarding these types of gifts and do not keep abreast of tax law changes. Donors need advisors to provide them with assistance when naming the charity as a beneficiary and then to monitor the situation as tax laws change.

WATCH THOSE BENEFICIARY DESIGNATIONS

A few years back I was contacted by the company that holds my 401(k) and Individual Retirement Accounts. It was not a nice letter, but one of those "information notices" in very small legal print that no one tends to read. This particular notice shared that the brokerage had found over the years that many of its clients had not been keeping the beneficiary designations on their retirement plans up to date. The person would die, and an old IRA would name an ex-spouse rather than a current spouse, or recently born children or grandchildren would be excluded, and so on. The brokerage had decided to do something about it. On a date one or two months hence, it would automatically update the beneficiary designations on all of my retirement accounts in their custody to reflect the same beneficiaries as I had named on the most recently filed "change of beneficiary" form. The company was unilaterally changing the beneficiaries on all my retirement accounts based on the form filed for only one of my accounts.

(continued)

I immediately called the brokerage to direct them not to do this, since I had intentionally filled out my retirement plan beneficiary forms for different beneficiaries. Two months later, much to my dismay, I received notice that all of my beneficiaries had been changed—despite my directive not to do so. In two cases, the letter stated that I had not ever filed a beneficiary form, even though I had a hard copy in my file.

It became very clear that I need to keep hard copies of change of beneficiary forms for all accounts, and check with the broker every year or two to be sure it is still on file. For advisors, this is an excellent way to steward your clients—remind them to check their beneficiary designations from time to time, or the family members/charities they want to support may not actually receive their gifts. —BMS

Life Insurance Many donors elect to name charities as beneficiaries of life insurance policies. While the authors are not huge fans of this type of philanthropic plan except in unusual cases, the practice remains fairly widespread. Unfortunately, when structured poorly, these policies can end up costing significant dollars or can lapse after a substantial investment. Advisors should monitor life insurance policies set up for charitable purposes to ensure that they continue to meet the goals of the donor.

Charitable Remainder Trusts If the donor has set up a charitable remainder trust as part of the gift plan, the professional advisor should monitor the investments, check to see that payments are made on time, and prompt the issuance of the Form K-1 and filing of Form 5227 for tax purposes by the trustee. The advisor can prompt the client to check in with the charity from time to time to ensure that the ultimate use of the proceeds from the trust remains viable.

Charitable Gift Annuities Charitable gift annuities are simple contracts between the charity and the donor. However, donors often have questions before executing the contract, and later about tax reporting. There are some complex nuances when gift annuities involve more than one life, the donor is not a beneficiary, appreciated stock is used to fund the gift annuity, and when there are two annuitants who are

CASE STUDY	THE BAD LIFE INSURANCE PLAN

I have served two organizations where life insurance was used in a bad way. In both cases, I heard a story of how a life insurance agent had been brought in to help donors to turn their gifts into something more with just one gift. With the hope that the interest rates at the time would continue to fund universal life insurance contracts with a single premium, contracts were signed with donors or their young children named as the insured and the charity named as both the owner and beneficiary. Needless to say, most did not last with poor performance due to the economy and non-payment of additional premiums.

Life insurance can be a wonderful tool when used properly. If an older donor, who no longer has a need for a paid-up policy, were to wish to make a gift by donating their policy, the charity would have the option to either hold it till the donor passed to realize the full value, or to take the cash surrender value by cashing it in. Even simpler than naming a beneficiary in one's will, a donor could name a charity as the beneficiary in their life insurance policy. And perhaps the best use is inside of a wealth replacement trust where the life insurance can replace the value of a gift to charity so that the donor's heirs receive an amount that they might have gotten without the encumbrance of estate taxes. —REW

not married. The gift and estate tax consequences can be significant. It is important for the professional advisor to be involved throughout, to ensure that the gift is set up correctly, and then monitor the payments and Form 1099s afterward to confirm that it is being executed and reported as required.

IN SUMMARY

Chapters 6 and 7 focused on how to apply the philanthropic planning model to principal and major prospects in a one-on-one approach, integrating the work of fundraisers and professional advisors in a more meaningful way than has been done in the past. If charities wish to increase their fundraising performance, donors want to ensure that their passions are carried out, and professional advisors seek to effectively advise and retain their clients over multiple generations, the philanthropic planning model achieves all of these goals.

PART THREE

Marketing to Prospects and Those Interested in the Mission

Parts I and II discussed how donors, advisors, and fundraisers could work together in a philanthropic planning context to meet the needs of donors and charities alike for both today and in the long term. This requires a fundamental change in approach, where the needs of the prospect take a much higher priority, particularly for the Older and Younger Boomers, Gen X, and Millennials. The focus was on the one-on-one discussions typically found in principal gifts and major gifts fundraising and provides a framework for how such gifts can be discussed, negotiated, and completed to maximize the benefits for prospects and their families while also producing meaningful charitable gifts.

Part III is directed primarily at charities that wish to reach a broader audience of prospects, beyond those who are met with during one-on-one meetings. Charities simply do not have enough resources to meet with everyone individually and need to focus their personal visits on the prospects with the greatest capacity. Part III outlines effective ways for charities to share information about their missions and gift planning opportunities with these additional prospects, without requiring personal visits until the prospects have self-identified as either interested or having greater capacity than suspected. Importantly, it does so using the philanthropic planning, moves management-based approach outlined in Parts I and II instead of the traditional, gift vehicle-based approach used since the 1970s.

CHAPTER 8

Marketing on a Moves Management Platform

The gift planning marketing effort is designed to reach all of those individuals who feel a strong affinity toward a charity. A review of the Philanthropic Planning Pyramid introduced in Chapter 3 (see Figure 8.1) shows four levels of prospects to target. The top level—made up of principal prospects—and the second level—made up of major prospects who have been regular, consistent donors—have already been addressed through one-on-one visits with a complete or partial philanthropic planning approach, as described in Part II. Even so, charities should still market more basic gift planning to these prospects since they have an inclination to gift planning and the additional marketing only reinforces the messages shared in the personal visits.

The third level of the pyramid shows loyals, the regular, consistent annual donors which a charity does not believe have the capacity to make principal or major gifts. This group is in the marketing sweet spot for more basic gift planning opportunities. They are extremely loyal, but are likely not to warrant a personal visit and full philanthropic planning process unless they express an interest and have sufficient resources. Gift planning marketing should always be targeted to meet the needs of this group, since this is where a charity will acquire significant bequest intentions, gifts from retirement plans, gifts from life insurance, and gifts that meet personal planning objectives without having to go through an entire, one-on-one philanthropic planning effort.

The 2007 study, *Bequest Donors: Demographics and Motivations of Potential and Actual Donors,* conducted by the Center on Philanthropy at Indiana

FIGURE 8.1   PHILANTHROPIC PLANNING PYRAMID

Source: © 2012 Gift Planning Development, LLC

University found that less than 10 percent of individuals over age 60 would even consider adding a new charity to benefit through an estate gift. In fact, the younger the individual, the greater the likelihood that he or she would consider a new charity. Research supports that if charities and professional advisors want to find the best prospects for gift planning, the first place to look is to existing donors, those who are committed to the cause and give regularly. For charities, it is fairly simple to create an initial list of prospects most open to a gift planning message. The charity should review its database to find donors who have given:

- 15 or more years
- 10 of the last 15 years
- 7 of the last 10 years
- 5 of the last 7 years and
- 3 of the last 5 years

Add to that list, to the extent that they are not already included, those who have made some gifts and are:

- Current or former gift planning society members.
- Individuals who have expressed an interest in gift planning with the organization in the past by returning a reply card or other device.

- Current and/or former board members.
- Current and/or former staff members.
- Long-term volunteers.
- Tied to the organization long-term through personal or family associations.
- Strong in philosophical or religious belief in helping others or in giving back.
- Others who are strongly tied to the mission in a meaningful way.

Together, this group represents those who believe closely in the charity and will support it financially. They are the most open to both a philanthropic planning message and providing long-term support. The process for creating and ranking this list was detailed in Chapter 3.

The final group on the pyramid is made up of everyone else interested in the mission. While it may seem counterintuitive to market to everyone else after carefully selecting a gift planning audience, the reality is that everyone who dies with any assets at all can elect to leave something to charity. As the saying goes, "You can't take it with you." If the prospect believes in the mission, the marketing plan should contemplate ways to reach the prospect as part of the effort in case the prospect wants to include the charity in his or her long-term plans. The trick is to reach that audience without incurring significant expense, since the likelihood of getting a gift is far smaller than with the identified groups in the top three tiers of the pyramid.

MARKETING IS NOT GIFT PLANNING

Chapter 1 includes the definition of *charitable gift planning* as the process of cultivating, designing, facilitating, and stewarding gifts to charitable organizations. It uses a variety of financial tools and techniques for giving; requires the assistance of one or more qualified specialists; utilizes tax incentives that encourage charitable giving, when appropriate; and covers the full spectrum of generosity by individuals and institutions; and is based on powerful traditions of giving in the United States.[1]

Gift planning marketing is none of those things. Mark Elliott, long-time gift planner and senior development advisor to Bucknell University, talks frequently about how gift planning marketing sells the "sizzle" and not the "steak". The goal of gift planning marketing is to get a prospect to raise his or her hand and say "Yes, I'm interested in this—please send me more information." The goal is not to provide prospects with every last detail of how a charitable gift plan works, or to do so with so much insider language that it makes the marketing inaccessible to the very prospects a charity is seeking to reach.

Unfortunately, most gift planning marketing efforts today do just the opposite, providing more information than any prospect will read and in language that only a lawyer could understand.

A classic example was the gift planning community's response to the IRA Charitable Rollover. When the IRA Charitable Rollover was first signed into law, charities saw an opportunity to share this good news with their prospects. Most of these advertisements were in the form of oversized postcards. The typical headline read something like "IRA Charitable Rollover Finally Passes—Act Now!" Most of these postcards then went on, in excruciating detail, to explain all of the rules and procedures to complete such a gift. There was no mention of the charity's mission or how the prospect could help meet his or her personal goals. The postcards assumed that a prospect would know what an IRA Charitable Rollover was, that the prospect wanted all of the technical information, and that the prospect wanted to support the charity in question. There was no information about outcomes to be created by the gifts and therefore no sizzle.

Fast forward to 2010 and 2011 when the IRA Charitable Rollover was extended for the third time. Many charities rolled out postcards with the headline "The Third Time's the Charm!" followed by another, subheading "IRA Charitable Rollover Renewed!" For prospects who had not been following the IRA Charitable Rollover since 2006, the headline meant nothing. Both the headline and subheading used insider language that is inaccessible to prospects. By not tying the message to the charity's mission, the postcard could be for any charity, anywhere and had no sizzle.

USING MOVES MANAGEMENT

To be successful, gift planning marketing needs to be different from one-on-one, relationship-driven philanthropic planning for principal and major prospects. Each marketing piece has to have a clearly defined purpose, content, audience, schedule, budget, and measures of success. Over time, a well-defined gift planning marketing plan will help to propel prospects through a moves management process of identification/education, qualification, cultivation, solicitation, and stewardship. Most gift planning marketing efforts to date have been "random acts of marketing." The charity has a gift planning program and when activity is slow or it just "feels right", the person responsible for gift planning sends out a postcard, designs a newsletter, plans an event, or takes some other action to increase activity. There is no gift planning marketing plan, little thought to how the piece or activity moves the gift planning effort forward, and frequently no tracking of the success of the effort.

Brian Sagrestano first developed the moves management-based gift planning marketing concept in 2004 while working at the University of Pennsylvania (Penn). Collaborating with his team, particularly with Colleen Elisii, associate director of gift planning marketing, they were able to develop a program that focused on meeting prospect needs while showing the impact and outcomes created by the gifts. After Sagrestano left Penn and started his consulting practice, Elisii continued to enhance the program, resulting in higher gift planning response rates, increased gifts, and a more fully engaged constituency. Sagrestano began sharing Penn's results at conferences, starting with the National Conference on Planned Giving (now the National Conference on Philanthropic Planning) in 2007. In 2008 he authored the gift planning marketing components of the Planned Giving Course, compiled by the Partnership for Philanthropic Planning of Greater Philadelphia. In 2011, Michael J. Rosen, CFRE, published *Donor-Centered Planned Gift Marketing* (John Wiley & Sons, Inc., 2011), part of the Non Profit Essentials Series from the Association of Fundraising Professionals (AFP) using many of the concepts and ideas developed by Sagrestano and his Penn colleagues.

MULTICHANNEL MARKETING

In order to put together a gift planning marketing plan built on this model, charities must determine how they want to communicate with their prospects. Too often, charities use a one-size-fits-all approach for delivering gift planning content. For much of the 1990s, the approach seemed to be gift planning newsletters. For the better part of the last decade, the tool of choice has been the oversized postcard. As charities select and then segment their gift planning marketing target audience, they need to use multichannel marketing techniques across the moves management steps to ensure that they reach the different identified groups and move them toward gift conversations.

There have been several recent studies examining how different generational cohorts receive information from charities. *The Next Generation of American Giving: A Study on the Multichannel Preferences and Charitable Habits of Generation Y, Generation X, Baby Boomers and Matures,* Vinay Bhagat, Pam Loeb, and Mark Rovner, (Convio, Edge Research and Sea Change Strategies, March 2010)[2] ("Convio Study"), surveyed 1,526 donors to non profit organizations in the prior 12 months to learn about their giving habits and how they receive information. On page five of the Convio Study it states: "Mail is the dominant charity information channel for Matures [Traditionalists], but information sources are far more varied for younger generations, with web sites and email communications being ranked as most important. Facebook and other social media register as somewhat significant charity information channels for Gen X and Y [Millennials]." The Convio Study data asked donors to select all of the different ways that they received information from the number one charity in their philanthropic priorities. The data is shown in Table 8.1.

TABLE 8.1   SOURCES OF CHARITABLE INFORMATION BY GENERATION

	Total	Millennials	Gen X	Boomers	Traditionalists
Mail	37%	26%	38%	36%	49%
E-mail/E-Newsletter	29%	29%	34%	28%	24%
Web Site	27%	36%	34%	22%	14%
Subscribe to Issue Updates from the Charity	12%	12%	14%	13%	9%
Facebook and Other Social Media	10%	17%	16%	5%	2%
Text/SMS	3%	7%	4%	1%	2%
Twitter	3%	7%	5%	1%	0

Data source: Convio, Edge Research and Sea Change Strategies, March 2010

The data shows that direct mail and e-mail marketing are currently the way that the majority of donors receive information from their number one charity.

The question the Convio Study did not ask was how donors *prefer* to receive information from charities. In February and March of 2008, Selzer & Company and the Stelter Company conducted a telephone survey with 901 adults aged 40 and over throughout the United States. The results of the study *Discovering the Secret Giver: Groundbreaking Research on the Behavior of Bequest Givers in America,* Larry Stelter and J. Ann Selzer, Ph.D. (The Stelter Company and Selzer & Company, Inc. 2008)[3] ("Secret Giver Study") indicate that despite all of the press about different delivery methods, 42 percent of survey participants want their first contact about a bequest gift to be via U.S. mail. Among other responses, only 8 percent wanted a personal call, 8 percent advice from a financial advisor, 6 percent contact by e-mail, and 3 percent an in-person meeting. Also significant, 39 percent were not sure how they would want to be contacted. Among prospects without a will in place, the number preferring to be contacted first by mail rises to a significant 67 percent.

The Secret Giver Study did not include an analysis based on generational cohorts. When contacted, Bev Hutney of Stelter graciously agreed to provide additional data from the study and divided it into generational cohorts as defined in Chapter 2. Unfortunately, because the study did not use individuals under age 40, the Gen X sample only represents 67 survey participants and there are no Millennial results.

When the Secret Giver Study data is recharacterized by generational cohorts in Table 8.2, it illustrates profound differences in how the cohorts wish to be first contacted regarding bequest gifts. As respondents get younger, they express a growing preference for both contact using e-mail *and* a desire for charities to work through their financial advisors. The increased reliance upon e-mail by Younger Boomers and Gen X show their overall comfort with the medium, as it came into active use during their working lives. Clearly charities can use e-mail as an effective delivery tool for these younger cohorts.

More interesting is the result that the younger cohorts show a greater preference for information to be provided through their financial advisors. This follows the findings in the *Future of Charitable Gift Planning: A Report*

TABLE 8.2   **PREFERRED SOURCE OF FIRST BEQUEST INFORMATION BY GENERATION**

	Gen X	Younger Boomers	Older Boomers	Post-War	WWII
Call you personally on the phone	10%	9%	8%	7%	6%
Send information in the mail	46%	53%	45%	29%	35%
Meet in person	6%	5%	2%	1%	2%
Work through financial advisor	21%	11%	7%	10%	2%
Contact by e-mail	16%	10%	8%	2%	2%
Other	3%	1%	2%	1%	0
Not sure	15%	24%	34%	55%	56%

Data source: The Stelter Company and Selzer & Company, Inc. 2008

of the NCPG Strategic Directions Taskforce, which found: "An increasing number of planned gifts are being structured by professional advisors, and . . . many donors are seeking technical advice from professional advisors."[4] As the younger cohorts reach their peak earning and giving years, it becomes incumbent upon charities and advisors to work collaboratively together to deliver the gift planning message and structure gifts according to donor wishes, as discussed in Chapter 5.

What remains consistent, regardless of generational cohort, is the desire of participants to get their first contact about bequests via mail. With that figure actually getting higher for younger generational cohorts than the Traditionalists, charities need to consider at least starting with more traditional messaging for younger donors, rather than jumping straight to social media options, although social media needs to be in the mix once the initial information about bequests has been shared.

While the Secret Giver Study did not have information on Millennials, *Millennial Donors: A Study of Millennial Giving and Engagement Habits,* Derrick Feldmann, Ted Grossnickle, Angela White, and Nick Parkevich (Achieve and Johnson Grossnickle Associates, 2010)[5] ("Millennial Donors Study"), asked 2,216 survey participants, (primarily Millennials with a few younger Gen Xers) how they would prefer to receive information from charities (not bequest information in particular) with the following responses shown in Table 8.3.

TABLE 8.3	HOW MILLENNIALS PREFER TO RECEIVE INFORMATION FROM CHARITIES

How would you like to receive information?

E-mail	93.1%
Text	3.1%
Blog	7.1%
Facebook/Social Media	24.0%
Twitter	3.8%
Print	26.9%
YouTube	3.2%

Data source: Achieve and Johnson Grossnickle Associates, 2010

It is clear that Millennials would prefer to get information via e-mail (continuing a trend illustrated in the Secret Giver Study data), followed at a distant second by print and Facebook. Interestingly, print still approached 27 percent while social media had a significant presence. Since the Secret Giver Study was completed in 2008, it is possible that this more current study shows the growing comfort that younger cohorts have with social media as a tool. Additional study is needed to determine if social media would be an acceptable way to make first contact with Millennials about bequests.

One of the interesting results of the study is that once Millennials are approached, they may give by a variety of methods, often not using the same method to make their gift as that used by the charity in its approach. This means that charities need to update their response measures and track multiple channels to determine which marketing is actually producing results. It is no longer safe to assume that because a gift came in via the web that it was solicited that way.

One of the recommendations coming from the Millennial Donors Study was to "develop a multi channel approach to communication and solicitation methods, recognizing that technology is a tool, not a solution."[6] This conclusion can be extrapolated to all generational cohorts—charities need to use multi channel approaches to open the door with prospects, reaching out to them in one or more ways that they prefer to be contacted. Whether charities use generational cohorts or another method to ascertain how prospects wish to be reached, the important lesson is to evaluate the charity's particular audience and reach them using communication methods that will be well received by the prospects. This may require a fair amount of testing to determine what really works for a particular constituency. As relationships are built, each prospect will show preferences which can then be followed in communicating with that prospect.

For those charities where the cost of testing makes it prohibitive, a multi channel approach offers the best opportunity for success, generally using more technology for the younger cohorts and more mail and print for the older cohorts.

CREATING A BRAND

For a charity to be effective marketing gift planning, it must have a look and feel which fits within the overall brand of the charity, but is unique to the gift planning marketing effort. Many charities elect to use their legacy society as the brand for their gift planning program. By creating a consistent brand which is known to donors, it allows the gift planning program to be seen as a unique entity. For donor-centered gift planning programs, donors will learn to trust the brand and be more likely to open and read all of the marketing across the multi channel effort.

TRACKING MARKETING EFFORTS/ MEASURES OF SUCCESS

When marketing on a moves management platform, it is important to track your results. In order to do so, each piece needs to serve a designated step in the moves management process. When a marketing piece tries to do too many things or take too many steps at once, it loses focus and effectiveness.

As noted earlier, each piece in the gift planning marketing effort should have a designated moves management purpose, clear content, an identified audience, a logical schedule, a reasonable budget, and identified measures of success. While tracking success sounds straightforward, in this era of multi channel marketing it is very difficult. Most fundraising software is designed to track each marketing piece individually and the only outcome it can record is a gift. Charities need to work with their software vendors or build systems which allow them to track in their databases the different

When Colleen Elisii and I were rebuilding the University of Pennsylvania's gift planning marketing program, one of the elements we reviewed was the University's gift planning newsletter. At the time, it was being sent to 35,000 people whom Penn had identified as gift planning prospects (people over age 50 with a giving capacity of $100,000 or more). The response rate to the newsletter was an anemic 0.02 percent. The newsletter opened with a donor profile on the front cover which carried over to the back cover, including a photo of the donor. Typically the donor profile highlighted the history of the donor with Penn and the structure of the gift (a gift annuity, charitable remainder trust, or bequest intention). It did not talk about the mission, the motivation of the donor in giving, or the outcome the donor hoped to create with the gift. The second and third pages usually included a detailed article about the gift vehicle used by the profiled donor. Frequently this article was accompanied by a chart showing payout rates. The final page closed with contact information. Inserted inside was a reply card and envelope that provided a wide range of check boxes for all types of gifts.

This newsletter had several major problems which led to the low response rate. The target audience was poorly defined, the donor profile did not emphasize impact and outcomes from gifts, Penn's mission was not included, and the response mechanism provided too many options. Most importantly, though, it tried to do too much in a single piece. The newsletter was trying to identify, educate, cultivate, solicit, and steward all in one four-page mailing.

Colleen and I redesigned with a clear focus on stewardship. The audience was changed to include members of the legacy society and anyone who had inquired about a gift planning opportunity in the last five years. The newsletter continued to have a donor profile, but it focused on why the donor wanted to support Penn and the outcome to be created by the donor's gift. This donor-centered, mission-based approach made the articles much more accessible and likely to serve a stewardship purpose, since many legacy gift donors want to be immortalized, particularly Traditionalists. The feature articles provided useful estate and financial planning advice with a gift planning spin, to keep legacy society members abreast of

(continued)

planning opportunities. A pull-out box included the latest tax updates which impacted charitable gift planning and estate planning, so that donors could keep their plans up to date. Finally, there was information about the gift planning staff and where they were traveling, so that donors could ask to see them if the gift officer had not called the donor to schedule an appointment.

On average, the new gift planning stewardship newsletter received the same number of responses as its predecessor newsletter. But it was mailed to 3,500 people instead of 35,000 at a substantially lower cost. Penn then used other communications tools and channels to identify, educate, cultivate, and solicit. —BMS

multi channel touches for each prospect to evaluate results. It is no longer possible to measure the success of a gift planning marketing program by the number of responses to a single piece. Instead, the charity needs to look at the entire marketing plan, all of the touches from the various communications tools and vehicles, and evaluate over the long term whether the overall effect is moving the suspect to a prospect, prospect to donor, and donor to repeat donor.

In the moves management context, the first step is to identify what the charity hopes to accomplish with an individual piece. Is it to educate the broadest group, "everyone else" as previously defined? Is it to get prospects to self-identify an interest in gift planning? Is it to cultivate identified prospects so that they are considering the options before them? Is it to actually solicit a prospect? Is it to provide stewardship to past donors?

Next, the charity needs to look at what type of direct response it hopes to achieve through the piece. Does the charity want a mail response, e-mail, phone calls, traffic on the web site, gift activity? If the response is something which can be tracked, does the piece have a tracking mechanism built in so that the charity can readily evaluate its performance?

Third, the charity needs to evaluate the overall effectiveness of the piece in the context of the moves management process. Did it move the relationship forward as anticipated? Were the responses of the type expected for the desired purpose?

Finally, the charity should look at the overall impact of the piece on the relationship with the prospect. Over time, does this piece serve the larger purpose, in collaboration with the other pieces in the moves management-based marketing plan, to move suspects to repeat donors?

If the donor-centered gift planning marketing effort is properly designed, the charity will be able to clearly measure increased performance from the gift planning marketing program including an increased number of:

- Gift planning inquiries.
- Legacy gift asks and commitments.
- Complex asset gifts and commitments.
- Strategy and planning discussions.

Without an effective plan, the charity will continue to produce random acts of marketing which can be tracked individually but do not help move the entire effort forward over time. Each piece has its own response rate, but the overall success requires evaluation over the entire moves-management spectrum.

Managing Costs

When confronted with this new model for gift planning marketing, most charities immediately and legitimately raise the issue of cost. Just as charities can only afford to directly visit with a subset of the total prospect base, the same holds true for gift planning marketing. With limited resources, a charity must be creative, investing in segmented, multi channel marketing in an affordable way. Frequently gift planning messages can be integrated into existing marketing and outreach efforts with no additional cost to the charity. For smaller charities, it may be the only way to offer multi channel marketing at all.

For those charities that can afford to invest in a more robust gift planning marketing program, including the use of testing, the results speak for themselves. In 2010 PG Calc surveyed their clients to find out their gift planning marketing budget and compared it to their total gift planning results. Charities using PG Calc have an active gift planning program.

As illustrated in Figure 8.2, charities with limited gift planning marketing budgets tend to get limited results. Once the gift planning budget reaches $15,001 to $50,000 per year, the gift planning results

What is the marketing budget for your planned giving program?								
	Total*	Average annual total dollars raised from closed planned gifts and realized bequests						
		Under $50,000	$50,001 to $100,000	$100,001 to $500,000	$500,001 to $5 million	$5 million to $50 million	Over $50 million	Other
Total	665	10%	12%	24%	31%	18%	3%	2%
No marketing budget	11%	34%	20%	13%	5%	1%	0%	13%
Under $5,000	17%	31%	41%	24%	9%	2%	0%	20%
$5,001 to $15,000	20%	20%	20%	33%	21%	8%	0%	7%
$15,001 to $50,000	25%	6%	13%	20%	37%	31%	0%	20%
$50,001 to $75,000	6%	0%	1%	3%	7%	15%	0%	7%
$75,001 to $150,000	8%	2%	4%	2%	8%	16%	24%	20%
Over $150,000	7%	0%	0%	3%	4%	17%	57%	0%
Don't know budget	8%	8%	1%	4%	10%	12%	19%	13%

FIGURE 8.2   GIFT PLANNING MARKETING BUDGET VERSUS RESULT

Source: © 2010 PG Calc

increase dramatically. This also represents the largest segment of the PG Calc client population surveyed, indicating that these are probably the more established programs which have been pursuing gift planning for some period of time. Newer programs tend to have smaller budgets and generate fewer gifts. The bottom line, if a charity invests in gift planning marketing, it produces results.

In Summary

Prospects in the bottom two layers of the Philanthropic Planning Pyramid should be approached in a fundamentally different way from the principal and major prospects at the top of the pyramid. While the top prospects receive one-on-one visits in a philanthropic planning approach, the bottom two groups receive less personalized attention. For a charity to be successful with these groups of prospects, it needs to build a donor-centered gift planning marketing effort on a moves management platform with multi channel, segmented marketing, using effective measures of performance at reasonable costs. Subsequent chapters will address how a charity can populate such a marketing plan for these two important prospect groups.

CHAPTER 9

Qualifying and Educating
Everyone Else

With a strategy and philosophy in place, the next step in building the donor-centered, moves management-based gift planning marketing program is to identify the segments and tools to be applied in each of the moves management steps. Appendix G includes a comprehensive University-style plan for the fictional GPD University, which can be adapted for use by all charities. Keep in mind the seven touches philosophy—that a prospect must hear the message seven times before it is absorbed.

Chapter 8 discussed the different moves management steps involved in the gift planning process. *Identification* was covered in Chapter 2. Within the identified group, *education* applies to everyone else as shown on the Philanthropic Planning Pyramid. A critical part of the process is educating potential prospects so that they raise their hands and charities can begin to qualify and cultivate them. This chapter focuses on how to provide information in a format that will educate the broadest group of prospects about a charity's mission so that they build meaningful relationships with those prospects who might be interested.

MAKE DONOR-CENTERED
GIFT PLANNING INFORMATION
BROADLY AVAILABLE THROUGH
EXISTING OUTREACH

Figure 8.1 illustrated the four levels of gift planning prospects. Identified prospects at the principal and major gifts level receive gift planning information one-on-one during their philanthropic planning visits and contacts.

Regular consistent loyal donors receive targeted information through a multi channel approach. However before discussing how to provide that targeted information, it is important to address how to reach the group defined as *everyone else*. Using existing outreach channels, it is possible to contact the broadest possible audience. While these messages are not segmented, they do provide an opportunity to touch those interested in a charity's mission at a low cost or with no cost at all.

In order to reach this broad audience, the first step is to create a communications inventory. When the authors work with a charity on its gift planning program, one of the first things they request is a list of all of the outreach to the constituency. The usual response "We don't have one of those" or of greater concern, "What is a communications inventory?" A communications inventory is a chronological list of all of the publications and outreach a charity sends and gives to those who might be potential prospects. For large charities, this can be a substantial list and likely is housed in the Office of Communications. For smaller charities, the list might only include a few items.

Once a charity compiles a communications inventory, it becomes a simple matter to evaluate each piece and determine how a gift planning message can be integrated into it. When gift planning messages are integrated into most or all of a charity's existing marketing, it is far closer to reaching its goal of seven touches for all of its potential prospects.

While it would be impossible to discuss all of the different multi-channel communications avenues open to charities when communicating with the broadest group of prospects, it does help to have some ideas for the most common types of communication offered and those which are emerging.

Existing Publications and E-Publications

Open the general magazine or regular newsletter for any charity with an active gift planning program and you should find an advertisement for gift planning. These charities have learned to start the seven touches process with everyone else through broad dissemination of information in the marketing piece that they send to their largest audience. Because this piece is already being designed and published, there is little actual cost to the charity to add gift planning messaging.

Creating Meaningful Ads In order to create meaningful ads for the general publication, first consider the audience members and their motivations. Most general publications are targeted at the entire mailing list of the charity. They encompass all of the generational cohorts, including people of a wide range of giving capacities, and frequently include people with only a passing interest in the charity. To deliver an effective message, a charity should consider what generally motivates an individual to consider a bequest or other gift and incorporate it into the advertisement.

A September 2008 study completed by Adrian Sargeant and Jen Shang ("Sargeant and Shang Study") of Indiana University on behalf of the Association of Fundraising Professionals focused on what motivates individuals to offer bequests to charities. They identified generic motives, organizational factors, and bequest-specific motives.[1]

Generic Motives The two generic motives identified by Sargeant and Shang for offering a bequest to charity were prestige and the need to give back/reciprocity. Those who cited reciprocity expressed an interest in either giving something back for the benefits they had personally received or to pay it forward for gifts from a previous generation of donors.[2]

Organizational Factors Factors about an organization that motivate bequest gifts include performance, professionalism, communication quality, and program quality. The Sargeant and Shang Study showed that bequest givers generally want to see evidence that a charity is both efficient and effective in its use of resources before they will consider long-term support. Donors translate their treatment by staff and volunteers for the charity as how the charity will utilize their gifts in the future. If the staff and volunteers are unprofessional, donors are less confident that their bequests will be used appropriately when they mature.

Donors also want to be kept informed about the organization. It is not enough to just send a newsletter from time to time. Donors like personalized communications and white glove or concierge-level treatment—it gives them confidence that a bequest or gift is important. Finally, the program itself has to be of good quality. People like to give to winners. If the program is failing, at risk, or is good enough without aspiring to greatness, donors are less likely to consider the charity for a bequest gift.[3]

Bequest-Specific Motives   The motives that donors cited that were specific to bequests included family need, taxes, the need to live on, spite, and making a difference. It should be no great surprise to discover that many donors will not consider a bequest gift until they are confident that their own needs and those of their close family, however it is defined, have been met. Most individuals are more altruistic to family than to charity. It may be more surprising to some that tax considerations are not particularly motivating for bequest gifts to charity. The study found that avoidance of taxes was a motive to start the estate planning process, not to consider a bequest. Many charities with gift planning programs have been finding this out in recent years, as mailings about tax benefits of gift planning tools have produced limited results.

For those who have visited charities in recent years and seen the names of donors on buildings, endowed funds, bricks and donor walls, the idea that donors want to live on, or be immortal, is literally documented. The fourth bequest-specific motive as defined by the study is spite. Put simply, some donors are motivated to include charities in their estate plans because they do not want their families to waste it. The altruistic motive is secondary to the goal of not allowing children to not work at all or spend the money on an expensive car. The last and perhaps most important factor motivating bequest giving is making a difference. "Participants recognized that one of the unique facets of a bequest gift was the ability to be able to make a big impact on the cause and a bigger impact than would typically be the case with lifetime giving."[4]

Combined, these motives provide powerful insight into how to put together meaningful ads. While each ad may not have all of the motivational elements, by including two or more in each ad, the ad is more likely to be successful.

TYPICAL GIFT PLANNING AD

The typical gift planning ad is centered on a donor profile. The ad tells the story of the donor's life, links the donor to the charity, explains in detail the type of legacy gift the donor has set up, including the tax benefits and income to be received, provides a chart of potential payout rates, and gives contact information.

> While these ads are prolific, they produce alarmingly low response rates. When we do an assessment of a gift planning program, they are usually the first thing that the charity wants to drop. These ads do not work because they are more focused on stewarding the profiled donor and giving every last detail about how the profiled gift type works than selling the charity's mission. Remember, ads are to sell the sizzle, not the steak. The ads need to focus their message on one or two of the motivating factors and stop trying to provide too much information.

While there are many different ways to approach ads that use these motivating factors, the LEAVE A LEGACY® ads produced by the Partnership for Philanthropic Planning encompass many of the best practices highlighted in the Sargeant and Shang Study. Figure 9.1 is one of the ads designed for this campaign.[5]

The ad includes several of the elements that will make it compelling to potential bequest donors. There is clearly a prestige and immortality element to the presentation, as the donor has died but lives on today to support the organization. The ad quickly ties the donor to the organization as the charity previously provided him with services. There is an obvious desire to give or pay back what was provided to him. It highlights the professionalism of the staff and how a staff member made a difference in his life which he is now paying forward for other children. Note that the ad does not include the details of how a bequest intention works or sample language to include a charity in the will. Instead it shows the immediate impact the bequest gift has had on the charity and those it serves, the long-term outcome it is creating, and the power of the giving tool. It is selling the sizzle, the motivating factors which will make others want to make a bequest, and then has a clear call to action at the end.

Use of Language   With effective messaging in place, focus next on the use of language in the ads. Careful attention to language will enhance the effectiveness of the ads. Most prospects tend to think in the abstract about the future. Ads that focus on continuing organizational values, enhancing future opportunities, or relief of suffering will appeal to gift planning prospects.[6]

Appeals for the future should also focus more on the "why" than the "how." By showing impact and outcomes from gifts and what successful achievement

Carpenter Dominic Mason died in 1989.

Tomorrow, he'll renovate the playroom at the local homeless shelter.

As a carpenter, Dominic renovated homes for his clients. As a child, he and his mother found a home in a shelter when times were hard. A counselor there showed Dominic a future filled with opportunity, and he never forgot that life-changing vision.

Thanks to a bequest in his will, a few more children will have a chance to build their dreams. Include your favorite cause in your will or estate plan. Contact a charitable organization, attorney, financial advisor or local LEAVE A LEGACY® program to learn how.

LEAVE A LEGACY®
Make a Difference in the Lives that Follow
www.leavealegacy.org

FIGURE 9.1   **LEAVE A LEGACY AD**

Source: LEAVE A LEGACY® is a registered trademark of the Partnership for Philanthropic Planning. LEAVE A LEGACY® promotes bequest giving in general; the trademarked name should not be used to promote a specific charity or company.

I worked closely with Northeastern University to develop a new gift planning marketing strategy based on the moves management model. While designing their ads, associate director of gift planning Matthew McDonald and director of gift planning Elizabeth Hill suggested a new way to implement the seven touches strategy. They carried the donor profile used each quarter in the alumni magazine into all of the other multi channel efforts in the moves management approach for the duration of the quarter. For example, if the quarterly ad profiled a donor who was meeting a personal planning objective of increasing retirement income (meeting a family need of having enough in retirement) while making a difference for Northeastern, then they would carry that story to their solicitation postcards, feature it on their web site, include it on their receipt stuffers, link to it with their e-newsletters, and more. By the end of the quarter, everyone receiving information from Northeastern would have had at least seven touches with the same look, feel, donor, and message. Best of all, after two or three years, the same marketing effort could be used all over again. — BMS

of the mission will deliver, ads will appeal to more prospects.[7] Similarly, prospects are more likely to give through bequests when the language in the ad shows a broader social significance of the work rather than focusing on just the charity or the situation at hand. Since these may change, speaking in broader terms makes prospects feel more comfortable with a future gift.[8]

When making gifts for the long-term, donors think of themselves in their ideal identity. They want their gifts to reflect the ideal version of themselves, rather than the way they currently see themselves. Their gift is helping to reinforce the legacy they want to create for themselves. By drafting ads that appeal to their ideal identity, which frequently involves making the world a better place, the ads will be more impactful.[9]

Ad Topics   The content of gift planning ads can cover a broad range of areas. However, since the vast majority of legacy gifts come from realized

Several years ago, I was working with a donor to a law school. Before my arrival, the donor had set up an endowed fund to provide scholarships to law students with demonstrated financial need. He had also promised an additional gift from his estate to bring the endowment fund up to $1,000,000. Over the intervening years, the donor had met each of the law students who had won the scholarship, learned their history, and seemed relatively pleased with his gift.

I went to visit the donor on a standard stewardship visit and had planned to update him on the goings on at the law school, share the latest report from the dean, and fill him in about the latest scholarship winner. The donor stopped me before I could even start the update by telling me that he had decided to remove the bequest from his will and instead was directing the gift to a local food bank. When I inquired as to why, he shared that in his community he is one of the biggest donors. He had been touched by the message of the food bank and how they were struggling to feed the hungry. He felt that his bequest gift would have more impact on the hungry in his community than it would on the law students at a top law school.

It was at that moment that I realized our stewardship of this donor had been a failure. We had introduced him to the students who had won the scholarship, and even told him their life stories, but we had not shown him what they had accomplished after leaving law school. The food bank was showing the donor an outcome, feeding the hungry long-term in the community—a why. We were showing impact on current students, a how.

We went back and researched each student who had won the scholarship. We found out what the students had been doing since graduation and put together portfolios for each one. Their accomplishments were amazing. One student had become a U.S. Supreme Court clerk and written important opinions; another had started a charity that was helping feed and clothe destitute children in South America; a third was running a free legal aid clinic in the donor's home city. When we shared these stories with the donor, he realized that his gift to the law school was not to help current law students, but to help all of those people whose lives those students had touched and would continue to touch after they graduated. He could finally see the why behind his gift how it would make a difference forever, around the world and right in his own community. It put the gift in a larger context for the benefit of all society and the donor's ideal self. —BMS

bequests and beneficiary designations on qualified retirement plans and life insurance policies, ads should focus primarily on these areas. If the charity offers more advanced gift planning options, the ads can also be used to show how a legacy gift meets a personal planning objective (as outlined in Chapter 7) while also supporting the charity. Just remember to keep the ads focused on prospect motivations using language that is most likely to appeal to the prospect audience.

Response Mechanisms When putting together ads, charities should consider the best response mechanism available. The mechanism(s) used will depend upon the delivery method of the ad. For example, an electronic ad may have either a hot link to the charity's gift planning response page on its gift planning web site, or an e-mail address (or both). A print ad may have a toll-free telephone number, e-mail address, and postal mailing address. Alternatively, if the print ad is in a magazine, it may have a tear-out postcard or reply envelope included.

Gift planning prospects usually want to be private. Whatever means they use to respond should be designed in such a way that their personal information is not revealed. The response tool should also be targeted. The authors have reviewed hundreds of gift planning reply cards and envelopes. Many of them contain more than 20 options, offering the entire universe of gift planning options that a prospect might consider. If the ad is targeted, the response vehicle should be as well. If the ad is about including the charity as a beneficiary of the prospect's will, then the check boxes on the reply card should only include naming the charity as a beneficiary of the will. It should not cover paying for grandchildren's education or ways to increase retirement income. By keeping the reply mechanism on point with the ad, it will get a higher response rate.

Web Site

If this book had been written just 10 to 15 years ago, this section would have discussed whether there was a need for charities to have a gift planning presence on the Web. Today, there are few tools more important to an effective gift planning marketing effort than a well thought out web site. The web site serves as an electronic brochure, open 24 hours a days, seven days a week, 365 days a year. Most prospects will research gift planning on the charity's web site before they ever call or email to ask about giving opportunities. As noted in Table 8.1, it is clear that regardless of age, prospects are on the Web and looking for information. Charities without a gift planning Web presence are at a tremendous disadvantage.

A gift planning Web presence consists of two parts. The first part is gift planning content and links on non-gift planning pages. It is vitally important in a donor-centered approach that all of the charity's Web pages include references and links to how prospects can support initiatives illustrated on the web site. Without these connections, even the most loyal prospects may not realize that the charity seeks their gifts. The second part of the Web presence is the gift planning web site itself. There are several components required to produce a high quality gift planning web site.

Properties of an Effective Gift Planning Web Site   Unlike ads, which are designed to sell the sizzle, the gift planning web site is more about the steak. It is the first place prospects go to find more detailed information about a charity's gift planning offerings. At the same time, a charity should not put so much information on a gift planning web site that it is overwhelming and causes a prospect to navigate away. It should be steak, not a whole side of beef.

Even though the web site will have more detailed content than a typical marketing ad, it should still use the same motivations, language, and donor-centered topics used for the ads, as outlined previously. Michael Rosen, in his book *Donor-Centered Planned Gift Marketing* (Wiley 2011), suggests that charities should visit their own gift planning web sites and ask the following questions:

- Is the planned giving section easy to find?
- Is it reader friendly and easy to navigate?
- Is text presented in easy-to-digest portions or does unbroken text scroll . . . down the page?

- Is it visually appealing?
- Does it look as intended regardless of the Internet browser used and the type of monitor used?
- Are the gift descriptions clear, engaging, and to the point?
- Is the focus on the benefits that a gift plan can provide the reader or, does it contain dry recitations of gift planning features . . . ?[10]

One of the most common challenges faced by prospects is actually finding the gift planning web site. Most use difficult names that are not indexed when a prospect does a basic search of the charity's web site. Gift planning content should be not more than two or three clicks from the charity's homepage and the gift planning home page should be readily found using the web site's search function and general search engines.

Setting Up a Gift Planning Web Site   The first question to ask when setting up a gift planning web site is whether a charity should create its own or purchase gift planning content from a vendor. The authors have drafted several gift planning web sites. It is both time consuming and detail-oriented work. Once the web site drafting is complete, it must be designed, maintained, and refreshed regularly.

There are currently at least a half dozen gift planning Web content vendors that provide a broad range of Web products. These vendors have talented, dedicated staff to ensure content stays up to date with the latest tax-law changes. They also refresh the pages regularly, supplying new information about the latest and greatest gift planning alternatives. In reality, there are very few charities with the resources to maintain a gift planning web site more effectively and efficiently than a vendor that supplies web sites to hundreds or even thousands of charities as one of its primary business lines.

Even so, the very best gift planning web sites are hybrids. Since the primary role of a gift planning web site is to provide educational material for prospects while motivating them to consider legacy gifts, it should be organized to do so. The charity should provide mission-based, charity-specific information to augment the content provided by the vendor about the specific tools and tax benefits. The donor stories should show real impacts and outcomes from new and realized legacy gifts. Only by combining technical information and the charity's story will a gift planning site be compelling.

Design the Web Site for the Four Tiers of the Gift Planning Audience   The gift planning web site should be designed to appeal to all four components of the gift planning audience shown in Figure 8.1: principal prospects, major prospects, loyal annual prospects, and everyone else. While the web site needs to address the needs of all of these groups, it should be focused more on the bottom two tiers than the top two tiers.

The top two tiers, made up of a charity's best prospects, should be getting gift planning information one-on-one from a gift officer or volunteer in the philanthropic planning process. However, these prospects will also come to a charity's web site to review options while contemplating their gifts. They may also send their advisors to the web site to review the options they are considering. With this in mind, the gift planning web site should have some high-level content for this audience. Information about gifts of complex assets, details of tax consequences of charitable gifts, the charity's tax identification number, and legal address should all be on the web site. The web site does not have to include detailed information about a charity's philanthropic planning effort—how it works closely with top prospects on integrated solutions. This information appeals to a small subset of Web users and promises services that cannot be delivered to a broad audience.

For the third tier, made up of loyal annual fund donors, the web site should focus on how to meet their personal planning objectives while supporting the charity's mission. One of the key hurdles for a legacy gift is the knowledge that personal planning for the prospect and the prospect's family are complete. For the majority of loyal annual donors, this is the top issue standing in the way of a more significant gift. They do not have the wealth of the top level prospects and regularly ask the question, "Do I have enough to make a gift of greater significance?" What fundraisers typically hear from these prospects is: "I would love to make a significant gift but. . . . " The gift planning web site should provide answers to these questions as outlined in Chapter 7.

The fourth tier, made up of everyone else interested in a charity's mission, seeks a web site that shares information about mission and giving opportunities in a non-threatening, easy-to-navigate manner. If the site is front-loaded with text and technical information, the charity will lose these potential prospects before the first click. To be effective, the gift planning home page needs to be clean, effectively use graphics, and limit the amount of information to a few key links.

Because the web site is targeted at a charity's entire audience, it needs to account for all of the generational cohorts discussed in Chapter 2. These individuals are spread across the four tiers of a charity's audience. Keep in mind generational differences as the web site is designed. For example, the Traditionalists will have trouble viewing white text on a colored background and will need the ability to increase the size of text on certain pages. They also prefer serif body copy such as Garamond and Times New Roman because they are easier to read.[11] Gen X and Millennials will be looking for shorter bits of information and a mobile version. The Boomers will want impact and outcome stories. By keeping the overall needs of each cohort in mind when crafting a web site, it can meet the needs of the charity's entire audience.

Key Components to a Gift Planning Web Site   Each charity should design its gift planning web site to reflect its mission, style, and personality. Even so, there are some core components that no web site should be without including:

- Clean, easy to navigate home page which is visually appealing.
- Information about how gift planning can support the charity's mission.
- Links targeted for each of the core audiences.
  - Information (limited and not on the gift planning home page) on complex asset gifts (principal and major prospects).
    - Unlocking the value of existing assets.
    - Maximizing children's or grandchildren's inheritance.
  - Information on meeting personal planning objectives (loyal annual donors).
    - Increasing retirement income.
    - Paying for college.
    - Providing for an elderly parent or loved one.
  - Information on impact and outcomes created by planned gifts (everyone else).
    - Crafting a meaningful legacy.
- Giving chart based on personal planning goals of the prospect showing gift options, tax benefits, and benefits to charity.

- Life stage planning tool based on generational cohorts.
- Planning tool targeted at other key constituencies (women and non-traditional couples).
- Donor profiles using the language and motivations described for ads.
- Sample bequest and beneficiary language.
- Gift calculator.
- Legacy society information.
- Information for professional advisors (including more detailed information on how the different types of legacy gifts work).
- Federal tax identification number and legal name of the charity.
- Contact names and information at the charity (this should be easy to find and use—prospects should not have to search for ways to contact the charity).
- Mobile version (for use on a tablet or smart phone).

Network for Good provides general fundraising web sites for more than 100,000 charities. Katya Andresen, chief strategy officer, suggests 10 elements for a strong home page which also should be applied to a charity's gift planning home page:

1. Something that tugs the heartstrings—an arresting image, a bold statement, the start of an incredible story.
2. A two-second statement that sums up who you are and what you do so that anyone glancing at the page gets it right away.
3. Clear, intuitive navigation that is organized according to the brain of the people who come to your web site and *not* your organizational chart.
4. A quick case or link to a case for why you're *the* organization to support.
5. A way to capture people whose interest has been captured (a great e-mail signup that entices people to provide their e-mail addresses).
6. A big donate button for people ready to give.
7. A third-party endorsement (ratings from Charity Navigator or a testimonial from someone).
8. Something that shows where the money goes or links to information on where donations go (this can be part of number four).

9.   Engagement opportunities—lots of them!

10.   Social media links—so people can take your message around the Internet.[12]

By applying the best tools for Web design with information that motivates gift planning donors, it is possible to design a page that gets attention once prospects have arrived. A web site with these components will appeal to all four audiences and the different generational cohorts, while motivating them to click through for more detail on the particular gift plan that interests them. Remember to use the language and motivations that will interest these prospects, particularly when writing donor profiles.

Driving Traffic to the Gift Planning Web Site   Even if a charity puts together an ideal gift planning web site, it will be of no use if there are no prospects viewing it. Including links to the gift planning page throughout a charity's multichannel marketing effort will maximize the opportunities for prospects to view the gift planning site and ask for more information. Viken Mikaelian, founder and CEO of PlannedGiving.Com and Virtual-Giving.Com, which provide planned giving web sites to more than 500 charities, suggests a seven-step process to increase gift planning traffic including:

1.   Make a complete inventory of all the publications/correspondence sent out by the organization.

2.   Place an interesting column or article, including the web site URL in all print pieces when possible/appropriate.

3.   Place a display ad with your web site URL in print pieces which showcase a donor and highlighting positive giving outcomes.

4.   Include a bold and striking link to your gift planning web site in your institutional mass emails.

5.   Send a personalized letter with a live stamp to your most loyal prospects, directing them to the educational content on your web site.

6.   Develop five or more compelling e-mail signature lines and make sure everyone at the charity uses them in their e-mail correspondence, with each linking to a particular page on your gift planning web site.

7.   Consider postcards as a punchy, inexpensive way to get the word out about a charity's program and web site.

Mikaelian concludes by suggesting that charities use their web sites as an online brochure, e-mailing prospects with links for particular information in addition to sending the information via mail.[13]

Charities should recognize that most prospects will not be coming back to a gift planning web site over and over again. The site is primarily there to provide information. The most important measures of success of the site are the number of unique visitors and the amount of time spent on each page. If a charity is getting a consistently growing number of unique visitors and they are spending a good amount of time on the web site, then the web site is producing the type of results the charity wants.

Social Media and Networking Sites

Tables 8.1 and 8.3 illustrate that while social media sites may not be the primary way that charities should reach a gift planning audience, they are an important tool in the multi channel approach that should not be ignored.

Crescendo Interactive provides gift planning web sites to more than 1,000 charities. In the Fall 2011 *Crescendo Notes*, senior vice president Kristen Schultz Jaarda, JD, LLM, commented on the NTEN, Common Knowledge, and Blackbaud 2011 nonprofit social networking survey. Of the more than 11,000 nonprofits surveyed, 89 percent now have some presence on Facebook and 57 percent are using Twitter. The average Facebook community size rose 161 percent in 2011 over 2010. The percentage of charities generating gifts through Facebook (in the $1 to $10,000 range), rose from 38 percent in 2009 to 46 percent in 2011.[14] Jaarda goes on to state:

> . . . [U]se of social media for non-profits can no longer be dismissed as a "fad." Its use is growing and charities can no longer afford to be without a presence . . . [I]f you are not there, some other charity will be out there making "friends" with your supporters who are "following" on a daily basis . . . While I advocate that a Facebook or Twitter page should never be set up solely for the purpose of raising money, gifts will be the result of a strong relationship. For planned gifts, it makes sense to regularly update your supports through social media since a solid ongoing long-term relationship is often the basis for a future gift.[15]

Just as 10 to 15 years ago charities were debating whether a gift planning webpage made sense—and now every charity with a gift planning program has one—in a few more years there will be no debate that charities need to be active in social networking. Now is the time to create or enhance a social networking presence. It will help increase the charity's reach to all generational cohorts, particularly Millennials and Gen X, the next generation of givers and leaders in the charitable sector.

Multimedia

With the advent of Facebook and YouTube, it is more important than ever for gift planning programs to include multimedia in their marketing and advertising. There is nothing more powerful than an outcomes-based video clip showing how a past gift has changed the world.

Webinars, Simulcasts, and Podcasts   Perhaps one of the most helpful tools developed in recent years is the ability to bring multiple parties together for a celebration, meeting, conversation, or collaboration using technology. Gift planning by its nature is complex. Prospects have many questions about how to apply the tools of gift planning to their own personal situations. Many financial advisors are still learning about gift planning tools. Due to the complexity of this material, sending it in the mail or via e-mail, or even discussing it on the phone is not always effective. A face-to-face conversation using technology such as Skype can go a long way toward a prospect or advisor feeling more comfortable with the material and moving forward with a gift discussion.

Similarly, when trying to educate an audience about gift planning, webinars, simulcasts, and podcasts are less expensive, convenient ways to get this information out, particularly as gift planning marketing reaches out to Older Boomers, Younger Boomers, Gen X, and Millennials who have adopted this technology.

CASE STUDY	PRINCETON UNIVERSITY MULTIMEDIA

Princeton University has adopted multimedia on its gift planning web site, http://giving.princeton.edu/giftplanning/. In 2011, when the IRA Charitable Rollover was nearing expiration, Princeton posted an audio simulcast of its conference call with its 55th Reunion Class. The purpose was to share with interested

(continued)

members of the class the opportunity provided by the IRA Charitable Rollover in a non-threatening, verbal way. The host of the call
was a member of the Class of 1955 and it included another Princeton graduate and tax expert to help explain how members of the
class could use the IRA Charitable Rollover to their advantage
while also supporting the class' reunion effort. The clip was also
available as a podcast/mp3 download.

   Princeton also created a planned giving video, which covers
why gift planning is important at Princeton. Coupled with the
many other, outcomes-based videos on Princeton's web site,
http://giving.princeton.edu/news/media/, it is difficult not to be
inspired to support the cause.

Videos and Public Service Announcements   Videos and public service
announcements (PSAs) can be tremendous tools to enhance the gift planning effort. The audio and video PSAs included in the LEAVE A LEGACY®
campaign are an excellent example of outcomes-based marketing. The video
PSA tells the story of three generous individuals, all who have passed away,
and the good that their bequests continue to do today. To view the video,
visit: www.leavealegacy.org/ultimategift_video.asp.

   With the technology available today, it is possible for every charity to
produce inexpensive videos to show the impact and outcomes of gifts.
These stories will motivate prospects to become donors and add great value
to the gift planning effort. For those charities already producing these types
of videos, adding a gift planning component will allow for broader usage
and increased results.

IN SUMMARY

Everyone can be a gift planning prospect. Because charities have limited
resources, they need to allocate those resources to the most likely gift planning prospects. Even so, by tapping into existing resources and marketing
efforts, charities can deliver gift planning content to everyone else. By
using language and messaging that motivates those interested in gift planning, a multichannel approach can produce real results, educating a broad
audience, and providing new and interesting leads for the charity's gift
planning effort at a low cost.

CHAPTER 10

Cultivating Loyals and Everyone Else

Chapter 9 discussed how to educate and qualify everyone else, those individuals who do not fit into the matrix of gift planning prospects defined in Chapter 2. Having established tools and techniques to educate those who are not identified gift planning prospects, the next step in the donor-centered, gift planning moves management marketing process is to determine the best ways to proactively cultivate those members of everyone else who raised their hands and expressed interest, plus the third tier of the Philanthropic Planning Pyramid, the Loyals. Together, the third and fourth tiers make a significant number of legacy gifts. Although neither group has the wealth markers coupled with loyalty that make them warrant major gifts attention, their gifts add up and provide significant and important support to the charities they love.

As always, it starts with mission. The prospects who are most engaged in the mission of the charity are the ones who are going to be open to a gift planning conversation. If the charity tries to lead with tax benefits or a gift planning tool, then the charity has two sales to make. First the prospect has to be interested in the tool, vehicle, or tax benefits, and then the prospect has to also be convinced about the mission. If the charity leads with the mission conversation, then applying the right tools and techniques to meet the prospect's personal planning objectives is not a sale at all, it is a natural flow from wanting to find a way to support a mission in which the prospect believes. If the prospect does not have an inclination/propensity toward a charity, then no gift planning appeal will be effective.

Each charity should develop its own, unique set of cultivation materials that are designed to engage the third and fourth tiers. The charity needs to evaluate its audience when creating these materials, selecting the right words, designs, and mediums to appeal to its core audience, or creating multiple versions that can be targeted at select audiences. Chapter 7 detailed some of the needs of the different generational cohorts and how they apply in the cultivation process. As the charity builds its marketing plan (see Appendix G for a sample plan), it should account for these different audiences and test different options to maximize the effectiveness of the effort.

As was noted in the last chapter, it is impossible to discuss every type of piece for each moves management stage. However, there are some key cultivation tools that no proactive, donor-centered gift planning program should be without.

BROCHURE PROGRAM

Gift planning brochures have been around for decades. The traditional "planned giving" brochure describes a gift vehicle and how it works in every last detail. Back when charities were the primary source of information about charitable gift planning, these were valuable resources to charities, donors, and advisors.

In the mid-1980s, Congress embarked on a substantial revision of the tax code. The Tax Reform Act of 1986 eliminated a wide array of tax shelters that had been utilized by banks, investment firms, accountants, financial planners, and other advisors to assist their clients in lowering their overall tax exposure. In an effort to provide alternatives, professional advisors began more vigorous use and education of clients about charitable giving tools and the tax benefits. As this movement grew, charities no longer were the keepers of information about planned giving, forever altering the landscape of charitable giving, they became one of many sources.

To differentiate themselves, and to appeal to those individuals most likely to make gifts from tiers three and four, charities today need to customize their brochures and publications to focus on how gifts help the charity achieve their mission while meeting donor personal planning objectives. These brochures should provide less-detailed information—leaving that space to professional advisors—instead focusing on what makes the charity unique. If the charity does not have the ability to test its materials or identify its core audience, the most likely audience is the Older Boomer cohort, and materials should be developed with them in mind.

General Brochure

Charities pursuing proactive gift planning programs should produce a general brochure. It serves as a fulfillment piece for those individuals requesting additional information about gift planning generally and can be used by staff and volunteers as a leave-behind piece for interested prospects. The brochure should include information about the charity's mission, how legacy gifts have helped achieve that mission, and real-life outcomes created by these gifts.

Charities should be careful not to have the general brochure focus too heavily on the details of gift planning tools and techniques. This is another sizzle piece, which is meant to capture the reader's attention, not provide every last bit of information about a legacy gift. The goal is to get the prospect to respond.

EXAMPLE   SAMPLE BROCHURE

Appendix H provides an effective brochure put together by Togo Travalia and Kimberly Andrien of SteegeThomson Communications and Ann Satterthwaite and Joseph Leive of University of the Sciences in Philadelphia (USciences), a client of mine. Their publication illustrates the core elements which should be found in a general brochure. The design is four color, on a quality stock which feels and appears elegant without seeming pretentious. The opening panel discusses the mission and how gift planning supports that mission, naming specific programs which have benefitted from legacy gifts or would benefit from legacy gifts. It also touches on how gift planning can help the donor meet personal planning objectives while supporting USciences.

The subsequent pages use real donors, in this case all living, to describe how their gifts will help USciences while also helping the donors. USciences could have also used some deceased donors, to create outcomes-based stories similar to those in the LEAVE A LEGACY® ads

(continued)

profiled earlier, but because they have a young gift planning program, living donor stories were the best and most effective stories available.

The brochure includes a summary of the USciences legacy society and the benefits of membership, without the typical oversell which normally accompanies these brochures.

The brochure closes with a brief summary of different personal planning objectives that the target audience will face and some charitable solutions that USciences offers, ending with a call to action. Included with the brochure is a reply card and envelope to allow the prospect to respond privately. —BMS

Personal Planning Brochures

If the general brochures are the sizzle of the cultivation marketing effort, then the personal planning brochures are the steak. The Planned Giving Company developed a process to evaluate charity databases and determine the best planned giving prospects. The loyalty prospect rankings in Chapter 2 are partially based on their research. At a 2011 presentation to the Partnership for Philanthropic Planning of Greater Philadelphia, they shared that only 6 percent of planned giving donors would also be ranked as major gift prospects using traditional wealth screening techniques.[1] This means that gift planning prospects are frequently not wealthy and do not view themselves as major donors.

The personal planning brochures should be designed to tap into this perception. By creating a series of brochures which focuses on meeting the needs of the donors and their families while also being charitable, it side steps the language and idea that such gifts are only for the well off. It allows donors to see themselves in the gift situation, which is why donor profiles of ordinary folks are such an important element of gift planning brochures. These materials can be less formal than the general brochure. Many charities simply design a masthead (branded letterhead) and print these materials from a color laser printer. Placed in a branded folder and mailed to the donor, or sent electronically as a PDF, it provides donor-centered information in an accessible and straightforward way.

CASE STUDY	PERSONAL PLANNING BROCHURES AT THE UNIVERSITY OF PENNSYLVANIA

As described earlier, the gift planning marketing program at Penn allowed us to monitor responses and survey donors to determine which personal planning needs or challenges most often stood in the way of the donors completing a charitable gift to the University. That research led to the creation of a group of personal planning brochures describing how donors could meet those needs while still supporting Penn. The most popular brochures focused on how an individual could create a legacy and take care of family. The rest balanced a need now with a gift to Penn later.

- *Crafting Your Legacy*—The most popular title offered in the series was *Crafting Your Legacy*. We were initially surprised to find just how philanthropic our donors were. Every time we gave them a chance to benefit themselves more than the University, they always chose the option that would do better by Penn. This brochure outlined how bequests and beneficiary designation gifts had changed the face of the University and invited donors to have a similar impact by making the same type of gift. Included was sample language for restricted and unrestricted bequests and information on naming Penn as the beneficiary of a retirement plan or life insurance policy.

- *Maximizing Your Children or Grandchildren's Inheritance*— For most donors, a charitable gift is third on the list of personal priorities, after making sure that their own needs are met and their family's future is secure. By creating a brochure that acknowledged that reality, and provided options for securing inheritance while also being charitable, it opened the door to a whole new group of conversations. This brochure presented case studies of a charitable lead annuity trust and a wealth-replacement charitable remainder trust.

- *Creating a Family Vision and Multi-Generational Plan*—We never got around to writing this brochure for Penn, but we should have since donors wanted it. I later wrote it for some other clients and they used it with good success. Values-based planning has become a big deal for Baby Boomers and this brochure introduces the concept. It would be a great addition for

(*continued*)

those fundraising programs which plan to pursue the principal gift strategies outlined in Chapter Six.

- **Unlocking Value in Your Existing Assets/Using Your Real Estate Creatively**—This brochure started as one brochure but because there was so much interest in gifts of real estate, and so much information to cover, we broke real estate out into its own brochure. The *Existing Assets* brochure used short, pithy descriptions to describe different assets that donors could use to make charitable gifts. Included were gifts of cash, stock, real estate, closely held business interests, life insurance, personal property, art, collectibles, retirement plans, and donor-advised funds. It also covered restricted and unrestricted gifts, and the purpose of endowment. The target market was those individuals who were committed to the mission, but perhaps were not thinking of the assets they could use other than cash or stock to make gifts. In a four-year period, Penn went from getting very few non-cash gifts, to receiving more non-cash gifts than we did life-income gifts. We found that while donors were not motivated to make gifts due to the tax benefits of alternative assets, once they discovered the tax benefits, they wanted to make those gifts of alternative assets as tax efficient as possible. It also opened another source of gifts for more wealthy donors who did not want to part with ready cash.

  The stand-alone real estate brochure used a question-and-answer (Q&A) format and some actual case studies to illustrate how real estate could be used to meet charitable giving and personal planning goals. The case studies talked about donors who had completed retained life estate gifts, turned a vacation home into an income stream, and outright gifts of highly appreciated property. The brochure also outlined the tax consequences if real estate was sold rather than donated. Lynn Malzone Ierardi, director of gift planning at Penn, was a significant contributor to the real estate brochure.

- **Increasing Your Retirement Income**—This brochure also started as a single brochure at Penn and later became a two-part brochure when I wrote brochures for other charities. For Traditionalists in the target group, particularly the Post-War Cohort that has saved a bit less than the other Traditionalist cohorts, the fear that they will run out of money in retirement is a great impediment to charitable giving. This brochure and the marketing materials that went with it helped them to overcome this fear. Set up as a Q&A with case studies, it addressed how to increase the income flow from low yielding investments by using them to fund a variety of life income gifts.

The initial surprise for us at Penn was the genuine interest in this topic from our Older Boomers, Younger Boomers, and Gen X. Our successful younger donors, most of whom were still in the accumulation phase of life, were worried about making gifts that could negatively impact their future retirement income. By providing them with a Q&A that showed how to make the gift now and still have secure retirement income directly from Penn later, it provided peace of mind and resulted in significant gifts.

- *Paying for College for Your Children or Grandchildren*—We took a bit of a risk publishing a brochure on paying for college, knowing that a certain group of our audience would feel like we had created the problem of high tuition and now were offering to solve it. The reaction to the piece was just the opposite— donors were pleased to have the information about ways to make a gift and pay for education, particularly for grandchildren. The brochure used case studies illustrating a commuted payment gift annuity and a term-of-years flip charitable remainder trust, but did not name these complex vehicles, to avoid including too much lingo. Because we were worried, we included significant information on how to save for college using non-charitable options, including Section 529 Plans, pre-paid tuition plans, and Coverdell Education Savings Accounts, all of which was well received.
- *Providing Income to Your Elderly Parents*—There are a growing number of families that have to provide for both their children and their elderly parents, because the parents' retirement savings were hurt by economic conditions or they simply have outlived them. Frequently there are issues where the parent does not want to take money from the child, even though the parent needs the help. This brochure used real-life examples to illustrate charitable giving techniques to help families through these difficult issues while also making a gift.

Several staff members at Penn helped to develop this original program, including Colleen Elisii, Meaghan Hogan, Deb Layton, and Lynn Ierardi. —BMS

Newsletter

As noted in Chapter 8, the authors are not fans of gift planning newsletters that try to do more than two steps in the moves management process in a single piece. These newsletters tend to lose focus and not serve any of the purposes well. Instead, the newsletter should be primarily for stewardship purposes with existing legacy donors. For more information on the newsletter as a stewardship piece, see Chapter 12.

For charities that are producing a gift planning stewardship newsletter, the secondary purpose of the newsletter can be to cultivate those individuals who have requested gift planning information in the last five years, but failed to act on it. It is a simple way to keep them engaged and informed about the charity's work without sending a fundraiser or volunteer to visit when resources are limited. The charity sends the same stewardship newsletter it is sending to existing legacy gift donors, and the stewardship information helps to cultivate these identified prospects, just as it helps to cultivate additional gifts from existing legacy gift donors.

Cultivation Tools to Encourage Prospects to "Raise their Hands"

The cultivation tools discussed so far would go to prospects that have expressed an interest in the gift planning program of the charity. It might be in response to the direct gift planning marketing from the charity or from the general, broadly disseminated gift planning materials the charity has made available. There are some cultivation tools, such as the prospect survey and the volunteer letter, that a charity can develop which are proactive and encourage identified gift planning prospects to raise their hands, which will allow the charity to engage them more effectively.

Survey and Wills Kit

Generating qualified gift planning leads is the elusive search for the holy grail that most charities chase in all of their direct mail marketing. Using a donor-centered approach, gift planners can increase results to their gift planning marketing using content that appeals to their interests and motivations for giving.

Hank Zachry of Caswell Zachry Grizzard has developed a gift planning survey tool that has proven to elicit an amazing response, frequently more than 12 percent. It is a survey that asks many of the questions a gift planner would ask in a qualifying visit in a form that is also soliciting the advice of the prospect. Prospects welcome the chance to share their opinions and at the same time share information that helps to identify them as qualified gift planning prospects. Zachary suggests that by offering a premium or gift such as a helpful tax brochure or a will planning kit, it motivates more individuals to respond.

CASE STUDY   MERIDIAN GUIDE TO PLANNING
                                                YOUR WILL

A will planning kit or a *Guide to Planning your Will or Trust* as we call it at Meridian Health, has proven to be a helpful giveaway for our survey participants. It is also a useful tool in other ways. Similar to a fact finder used in the financial services industry, it can offer a place for a new prospect to list all their information for your next discussion. It can be offered at your introductory meeting so that the prospect can take it with them to gather information about their assets and other associated facts. The information can then be incorporated into a plan that works for their situation as a charitable giving strategy is developed. If you are working with a tier one or tier two donor, it can help with the first phase of the philanthropic planning process.

As it is offered for a response to your gift planning marketing, it can serve the prospect as he or she prepares to meet with their attorney or advisor to give them a place to gather the information that they will need to assist them in preparing a will, and hopefully including your organization as a beneficiary.

Lastly, as we have offered it to our Heritage Club members who have already included Meridian Health in their will or estate plans. It is a useful tool for existing donors to list all their information for use by their executors. Kept in a safe place, it gives them one place to list assets, account numbers, contact information, and so on, so it can be easily accessed at a later date. —REW

In some cases, Zachary uses only a paper survey, but in others he will include an e-mail follow up linking to an electronic form of the survey. If a charity is surveying largely Traditionalists, then a completely paper survey should be effective. However, as the survey audience reaches into the Older Boomers, Younger Boomers, Gen X, and Millennials, increased use of technology will enhance results.

Direct mail to a broad mailing list of wealthy individuals not otherwise connected to the mission of a charity will no longer produce the results it once did. The Traditionalists will still respond if they recognize the name and believe that the charity does good works. Charities have found that sending this group a small gift will increase their yield, as the members of these generations feel badly that the charity spent valuable resources on them and want to pay it back. But with the Traditionalists past their peak earning and giving years, the true target of such appeals are the two Boomer cohorts and Gen X. When the Boomers get these mailings, they tend not to use the free items unless they send a gift, but often just recycle them. Gen X, on the other hand, will use the free item and not feel compelled to send a gift. Gen X feels it would be a shame to waste the free item, but since it was not requested, no reason to make a gift. Charities need to consider whether they should continue to send these types of items to Gen X and Millennials.

NOT ANOTHER CALENDAR

Anyone with an elderly parent or grandparent knows that it is no longer particularly effective to send a free calendar to entice a new gift from a repeat donor. On a recent trip to Florida to visit my wife's grandmother, Esther pulled out a stack of more than a dozen calendars. She offered them to my wife and kids, since she could not possibly use them all. When I looked through them, most came from animal organizations that Esther had supported in the past. I asked Esther if she had requested the calendars or even wanted them and she said "Not really. I like to look at the pictures, but then I give them away when I can." When I asked her if receiving a calendar caused her to make another gift, she confided, "Not anymore—it just got to be too many." —BMS

Using Volunteers

Chapter 4 describes the many different ways that charities can use volunteers in the gift planning program. When cultivating prospects in a donor-centered, gift planning marketing model, the volunteer letter described there can be quite powerful.

For a smaller charity, it might simply appoint a chair to the legacy society who then becomes the face and advocate of the program. For larger charities, like research universities, there might be a volunteer gift planning chair for each college, each department, each graduating class, and more. As long as prospects see the volunteer as a peer, the relationship is one the charity can foster.

In the marketing context, the volunteer will draft and sign correspondence that shares information about gift planning with peers. The letters might describe the volunteer's motivation to give and the programs impacted. It may speak about those who have benefitted. The message should be appropriate to the audience, and the volunteer should know that audience even better than the staff. Ideally the letters will cater to the generational cohort within the audience. These letters can be mailed twice a year to share information about the program. They bring a personal dimension to the marketing, which can sometimes be seen as too commercial.

In Summary

There are an endless number of marketing tools that a charity can develop to help cultivate relationships with gift planning prospects that do not require one-on-one visits or a significant investment of staff time. Each charity should look at its own program to determine what can be done easily and effectively that would appeal to the audience of loyals and those who have expressed an interest in legacy giving, but do not rise to the level of major and principal gift prospects. Each charity should develop, at a minimum, a small group of materials that can be utilized not only to cultivate relationships, but also as fulfillment materials when prospects do request information. Donor-centered brochures, newsletters, surveys, and peer-to-peer letters, coupled with the web site and other multi-media tools outlined in Chapters 8 and 9 will help the charity build relationships, even with prospects with which the charity does not complete one-on-one visits.

CHAPTER 11

Soliciting Loyals

Soliciting gifts in the donor-centered, philanthropic planning model is quite different than in the traditional gift planning model. Chapter 6 discussed the unique way to approach principal gift prospects. Chapter 7 suggested the best methods to develop relationships and approach major prospects using this model. Chapters 8 through 10 discussed how to culti-vate relationships with the bottom two levels of the philanthropic planning pyramid, the loyals and everyone else, without personal visits and time-intensive efforts of cultivation used for principal and major prospects. Assuming a charity has been successful and now has a group of cultivated loyals plus those from the everyone else category who have requested gift planning information, a charity can begin to solicit gifts from this group. Before beginning this solicitation effort, the gift planning program should establish consistent contact information, including a regular phone number and e-mail address which can then be routed to the current person respon-sible for gift planning. These basic tools provide consistency so that when staff leave and new people are hired, leads are not lost.

As with cultivation, there is no *right* solicitation model to ask these prospects for gifts. The audience should be segmented and the approach tailored for the identified group. If appropriate, generational cohorts should be considered and included in the segmentation. Ideally the charity would test each of the segments and solicitation channels prior to investing in large mailings or other multi channel outreach, to find those that are most effective. The balance of this chapter will describe some of the more effective solicitation methods, using the philanthropic planning methodology.

POSTCARDS

Postcards with a reply device have become the solicitation method of choice for gift planning programs, in many cases replacing the more traditional planned giving newsletter. Postcards have a unique advantage over a fundraising letter or text heavy newsletter: they are short. In a world where people are bombarded with thousands of marketing messages a day, the postcard can be succinct without requiring the donor to sift through pages of text.

The philanthropic planning postcard should be focused on the mission of the charity and the outcomes created by gifts. The message needs to be short and to the point. The postcard should contain powerful photography illustrating an outcome created by a gift, with a caption to explain how the gift helped produce the outcome. When discussing the gift itself, the postcard should focus on one of the donor's personal planning objectives outlined in Chapter 10. The card should close with a call to action and include reply opportunities via mail, e-mail, phone, text, tweet, Facebook, and Web.

KEEP IT SIMPLE AND APPEAL TO THE MASSES

Several years ago, while working for Middlebury College, I attended an educational seminar offered by Tom Smith, senior philanthropic advisor to the Vermont Community Foundation and a top notch gift planner. Tom shared with his audience a sampling of gift planning postcards. The vast majority focused on selling particular gift vehicles, with a significant number talking about charitable lead trusts and charitable remainder trusts.

Tom asked the audience how many of them had sent out a mailing about lead trusts in the past two years, and almost every hand went up. He then asked how many had received back more than five responses to this mailing—no hands. Finally, he asked how many of the gift planners had actually ever worked on a charitable lead trust to benefit their charity. Only one hand went up. Tom suggested to the group that perhaps their marketing dollars were best spent elsewhere, rather than selling high-end gift vehicles to a broad audience, when they would only appeal to a very limited group of prospects. —BMS

When putting together the postcard solicitation plan, only mail to the audience targeted by the postcard's message. For example, if the postcard is about increasing retirement income today, use a postcard design and target list for the Traditionalists in the charity's prospect pool. The photography can be more general in nature and less outcomes based. A peer-to-peer testimonial on the postcard might prove effective.

If the postcard is about increasing future retirement income, then the message should be much more outcomes-based and targeted at Older and Younger Boomers in the loyals group. The response mechanism should be more focused on electronic than print, but would still offer both.

For most charities, mailing five segmented postcards a year will be an effective strategy. For those following the seven touches philosophy, the

CASE STUDY   CHILDREN'S HOSPITAL OF
                                        PHILADELPHIA

The Children's Hospital of Philadelphia (CHOP) has been using gift planning postcards for several years. When they first started, you would see pictures of patients in the hospital setting with their parents or doctors, and the caption would suggest that you help those children. Those postcards were effective at pulling the heart strings, particularly for the Traditionalists, and resulted in some gifts to support the hospital. More recently, as CHOP has changed its focus to appeal to the immediate families of patients, it has started presenting postcards with photos of active children in more traditional settings, on the playground, at the beach, participating in soccer games, and the like. These photos include captions talking about the wonderful future in front of these children because of the state-of-the-art care they received at CHOP. These are outcomes-based stories, if the donor makes a gift, these great things can happen. The new stories appeal to the Older and Younger Boomers, Gen X, and Millennials who will be the next generations of donors to CHOP. —BMS

donors should be well cultivated by the time these pieces arrive. Consider the following schedule and topics:

Month to Mail	Topic
January	Beneficiary Designations-Retirement Plans (split card)
March	Increasing Retirement Income (split card)
May	Beneficiary Designations-Bequests (split card)
September	Increasing Retirement Income (split card)
November	Year-End Appreciated Stock and Other Assets

The months for mailing are targeted based upon donor interest in the particular topics at those times of year. Most individuals set up or update their estate plans at one of these four times: a) at the occurrence of a life event such as a birth, death in the family, new job or retirement; b) at the start of the year (usually late January or early February) based on a New Year's resolution to get their affairs in order or because of benefits/retirement plan changes at work; c) before leaving on a summer vacation, to assure that if something went wrong, their plans were up to date; or d) after a major tax law change.

A charity cannot predict when a prospect will have a life event, which is why the seven touches approach was created. By being continuously present, it is far more likely that prospects will think of the charity when going to see planners and make a change to their plans. Similarly, one of the reasons that charities want to be involved with professional advisors is to ensure that when prospects do have life events and go to see advisors, the advisors will remember that the prospects/clients want to include a charity and remind the prospects/clients accordingly.

While a charity cannot predict a life event, it can anticipate that prospects are more likely to see their planners in January/February and May and time mailings accordingly. These postcards are as much reminders as they are solicitations. Charities can also add an additional mailing whenever there is a major change to the law that might make prospects likely to amend estate plans.

The increasing retirement income cards mail in March, just when prospects are thinking about taxes and how unhappy they are paying the government, and September, when they should start to think about year-end planning. The final card, on gifts of appreciated assets, is always a supplement that goes out just ahead of annual giving appeals which will mail in December, to remind prospects to use these assets for year-end gifts.

> ### REPLY CARD TO THE ESTATE PLANNING ATTORNEY
>
> I recall several years ago seeing a reply card for a bequest mailing that did not come back to the charity. Instead, the charity asked the donor to fill in the name and address of the estate planning attorney on the reply device and mail it directly to the professional advisor to be put in the file. That way, when the donor came in to revise his/her plans, there would be a reminder in the attorney's file to ask the donor about including the charity in the estate plan. —BMS

Even though there are several different topics that could be covered in these postcards, charities should follow Tom Smith's recommendation and limit the messages to those with the broadest appeal. Typically 80 percent of gift planning revenue comes from bequests and beneficiary designations. This is the core market and should be attended to with at least two mailings a year. Among all of the non-beneficiary topics, increasing retirement income is the one that generates the greatest interest. By focusing two split mailings a year on this topic, it increases the likelihood of responses and gifts.

Split cards account for segmentation. For example, beneficiary designation cards can be split so that donors over age 70 $\frac{1}{2}$ get information on the IRA Charitable Rollover (in years when it is available) instead of standard language on creating a meaningful legacy. As noted earlier, charities should always segment the messages for these cards based on their identified audience.

E-mail Follow Up

While postcards are a great tool, it is important to follow them up with an e-mail sent between two and three weeks following the mailing of the postcard. This time frame is long enough so that those who would reply to the actual postcard will have done so, but not so long that readers will have forgotten receiving the postcard.

The e-mail should reaffirm the message of the postcard and provide a hot link to the section of the charity's gift planning web site which is dedicated to the type of gift covered by the postcard. According to Larry Stelter, president and CEO of the Stelter Company, if the charity has the ability to create and use personalized URLs, or PURLs, the charity may further increase results. In a donor-centered world, the more personalized the messaging, the greater the likelihood the message will be read.

Fulfillment Packages

Once a charity starts sending out donor-centered gift planning marketing materials, particularly solicitation materials, it should be ready with a standard set of print and electronic follow up for each piece. The fulfillment materials should include a letter, a description of the personal planning objective the donor is seeking to resolve, the solution or solutions being suggested by the charity, corresponding disclosure statements for each gift type outlined in the solutions, any necessary calculations, and the appropriate brochure packaged in a branded gift planning folder or e-mail device. These consistent response mechanisms will help to limit the amount of time an on-staff gift planner, volunteer, or consultant needs to spend responding to inquiries. If put together correctly, someone with gift planning expertise may not be required until it is time to follow up the fulfillment package with a phone call or e-mail.

In some cases, the charity may prefer to call the interested prospect prior to sending out materials. It allows the package to be more carefully tailored and personalized. Keep in mind that it is *always* preferable to have personal, one-on-one contact with donors who have inquired about gift planning. However, the idea behind the tiered system is to keep gift planners' time focused on prospects on the top two tiers of the Philanthropic Planning Pyramid. If the charity has enough staff and budget, then a phone call followed by a personal visit to everyone who inquires in response to the marketing program would be welcome and encouraged. Unfortunately, those resources simply do not exist for most nonprofits at the present time.

BEQUEST BUCK SLIPS

When loyal donors are asked why they have not included a charity in their plans, they consistently respond that either "No one asked" or "It never occurred to me."[1] To deal with this problem for principal and major do-nors, Chapter 7 suggests that each major gift officer's performance be measured by the percentage of his/her prospect pool asked to consider a legacy gift in a given year. Assuming a 20 percent per year ask rate, within five years the majority of the assigned prospects at a charity will have been asked to consider a legacy gift, producing tremendous results.

For those donors in the bottom two levels of the pyramid, charities need to find alternative ways to put the legacy giving message in front of them. One such tool is the buck slip.

Buck slips can be added to many different mailings sent out by charities to their donors. An excellent place to include a buck slip is with the receipt for a current gift. Donors are used to getting additional materials with other financial materials, and a buck slip is a simple way to encourage loyal donors to include the charity in long-term plans. Charities should be care-ful not to include buck slips with thank you notes, or if the receipt and thank you go in the same envelope. A thank you should never be diluted by an additional request for funds, even for a deferred gift. It should show true appreciation and thanks rather than serve as a vehicle to ask for another commitment.

A buck slip can also be sent with a check or the advice of a deposit with distributions from life-income gifts such as charitable remainder trusts and gift annuities. These donors have already made a gift to plan for the future of the charity and may be willing to add to their support through a bequest intention.

CONCEPT   USE OF THE BUCK SLIP

I have seen the buck slip used effectively at the American Cancer Society with their mass-mailing approach and have recently employed it with Me-ridian Health to highlight the IRA Charitable Rollover option. As described here, it is an easy way to encourage your existing donors to consider in-cluding your organization in their will or estate plans. The cost becomes very affordable when you print off several thousand and with your use in several places, it can add to your consistent messaging that can be helpful in building awareness. —REW

The buck slip should utilize outcomes-based marketing, talking about the wonderful outcomes created by past legacy gifts. Many legacy donors want to be immortalized, and a buck slip which does this will not only please their families, it will also illustrate to potential donors that after they have passed, their story could live on as well.

USE OF OTHER MESSAGES

There are a few other places where a charity can add a gift planning message to remind regular supporters that the charity would appreciate their consideration of including the organization in their will.

A fundraiser's e-mail signature offers a regular communication both externally to donors, prospects, and volunteers and also internally to fellow employees. By adding the phrase "Please consider including (insert the charity's name here) in your will or estate plan" to the external e-mail signature it will encourage donors and volunteers to consider this option. By adding the phrase "Please consider including (insert the charity's name here) as a beneficiary in your insurance or retirement plan," it will remind fellow employees that they can include the charity in their plans.

A similar phrase should be added at the bottom of letterhead or on the lower left hand corner of envelopes to keep the message front of mind.

If a fundraiser has the ability to include a recorded message on the phone system for those on hold, it may offer a place to provide information or to encourage a conversation with your organization about tax advantages of charitable gift planning. Dawn Jones, executive vice president at Chilton Hospital Foundation, has done this for years with good success.

GIFT ANNUITY ADDITION PROGRAM

Many donors who set up gift annuities with a charity will never rise to the level of major donors. For those who are not getting regular attention, it is possible to use the charity's stewardship program (outlined in Chapter 12) and just modest amounts of additional attention to keep them connected and possibly making additional gifts.

The Traditionalists, particularly the World War II and Post-War cohorts, have been tremendous gift annuity donors. Gift annuities have allowed them to make larger gifts than they thought possible while also providing secure income in retirement. Many of these individuals have become serial annuitants, setting up a new gift annuity each year to further enhance retirement income.

Benjamin Madonia, long-time director of planned giving at Hamilton College, has often commented on the fact that those donors who are effectively stewarded tend to make repeat planned gifts. Over the years, Hamilton and other liberal arts colleges like it have seen 50 percent or more of their new life income gifts each year come from repeat donors.

To encourage this behavior, charities should set up an automated system of letters to existing annuitants on their half-birthdays. These letters would express the thanks of the institution for making their original gift, tell an outcomes-based story of how gifts are making a significant difference for the mission, and then inform the donor of the new gift annuity rate available if the donor would like to set up a new gift.

Phone Calling Program

Over the last few years, phone calling programs have emerged as a gift planning solicitation method. In a multi channel marketing strategy, they provide an additional way to reach the third tier of the Philanthropic Planning Pyramid beyond print and electronic appeals.

MARKET COVERAGE

When I was at the University of Pennsylvania, we had a pool of more than 70,000 loyal donors spread over tiers one, two, and three. We built a model where we trained senior leadership and gift officers to discuss gift planning opportunities with their prospects and put incentives in place for those gift officers to ask their prospects to consider legacy gifts each year. We provided the gift officers with lists of loyals they could use as filler visits when they were on the road. We hired a team of gift planning specialists to support those gift officers and also conduct stewardship visits with our 2,600 Harrison Society members. Even with all of these personnel, we still were not personally touching the vast majority of our loyal donors.

The moves management-based marketing program we built to reach these loyals was state of the art. We touched our loyals in many different ways using print, electronic media, seminars, and more. They

(continued)

should have been reached by our message well over the seven times needed to raise awareness of our program. Even with all of these tools, we really missed the boat by not including a phone calling program.

We were approached with the idea by several vendors who had built excellent models. However, when we initially reviewed the costs, we felt like we would be paying a premium for the vendor to discover donors who had already included the University in their plans, but just had not told us about it, and that seemed like a waste of money. We also felt like we could simply make the calls ourselves and build stronger relationships for Penn. Since then, I have learned a few things. First, even if the vendor only discovered existing donors, wouldn't we have wanted to know about those people so we could steward them properly and further engage them in the life of the University? Second, there would never be enough time for the gift planners on the team to make the calls the vendor was going make—nor should they be making these calls. The gift planners should be focused on the top two tiers of the Philanthropic Planning Pyramid, not the third tier. If the phone calling had been targeted as a piece of the marketing program for the third tier, it would have in no way negatively impacted the first and second tiers and would have resulted in more touches and more gifts for Penn. If I could do it over again, a phone calling program would be a core element of my third tier marketing strategy. Only then would I feel like we had fully covered the gift planning market for the University. —BMS

Because phone calling is a specialized skill and can be costly, a charity needs to determine if it can complete the calling on its own or needs to hire an outside firm. Considering that phone calling is targeted at tier three loyal donors, charities going down this road will likely want to use an outside firm, keeping staff available to work one-on-one with tier one and two donors and any tier three donors who respond to the marketing plan or the phone calls. Michael J. Rosen, CFRE, suggests that a charity use the following steps when setting up a calling program:

- Determine the objectives of an outreach program.
- Define the largest prospect pool possible given budgetary constraints, institutional priorities, and the limited ability to visit with all prospects.

- Consider the organization's capacity to handle the post call follow-up work when determining the size of the prospect pool.
- Choose the calling model that can best achieve the objectives and that is most compatible with the prospect pool.
- Make sure that the callers are intelligent, mature, experienced, and articulate.
- Provide the callers with extensive training.
- Use a call outline rather than a hard script. Callers should stick to a structure and a call flow, but they should never actually read from a script.
- The letters and the calls used should be friendly and helpful in tone.
- Have a follow-up system in place to handle all responses, even from those who choose not to commit.
- Plan on visiting with those contacted, particularly those who commit.[2]

The Planned Giving Company recommended a six-stage approach to deliver a calling program:

1. Loyalty screening.
2. List review and approval.
3. Pre-call introduction letter.
4. Phase 1: Prospect qualification calls.
5. Phase 2: Gift planning conversations.
6. Confirmation/fulfillment/recognition/reporting.[3]

There are several reasons why a phone calling program is an effective component of the solicitation process including:

- It pinpoints the group from which 90 percent of your deferred gifts will come.
- Loyals always take your call.
- Average response rate is <u>37</u> times that of direct mail (15 percent versus 0.4 percent)!
- You can qualify your *whole* pipeline in a short time.
- You can verify and quantify gift commitments easily.
- You can resolve gift planning questions or issues that may block self-initiated action.
- You can uncover and count anonymous commitments (2 to 4 percent of the responses will be self-identifications).[4]

CASE STUDY   UNIVERSITY OF MISSOURI

Timothy D. Logan, ACFRE, vice president of planned giving services at RuffaloCODY partnered with Dr. James O. Preston, senior
director of development in the Office of Gift Planning and Endowments at the University of Missouri (MU) to conduct a multi-part
phone-calling program for MU. Due to the size and scope of MU,
the original calling program was a pilot, or test, allowing Logan
and Preston to determine the best way to conduct future calling
programs for the different units that make up MU. By testing first,
they were able to develop an effective, repeatable process.

Each project had several steps including: designing the data
pull; drafting the script (which in MU's case was always a survey);
mailing a postcard one to two weeks ahead of the call to inform
the prospect to expect a telephone survey on estate planning for
their alma mater; training for callers (which was attended by MU
staff to provide background and ultimately monitor some live
calls); graded responses with clearly articulated results ranging
from grade 1—the prospect has included the charity in his/her
plans—to grade 7—they just completed the survey but have no
interest in additional information; data upload to MU of the
results; Prospect follow up/fulfillment directly from the MU Office
of Gift Planning; second calls and follow up from RuffaloCODY
(approximately two to three weeks later) to those prospects
which had indicated an interest and requested additional information (grades three to five); additional follow up by the MU Office of
Gift Planning or the particular unit for which the calls were made.

Over the course of this effort, 5,381 prospects were entered
into the program, resulting in 3,743 completed calls, and 2,506
completed surveys. The surveys resulted in 232 or 6.19 percent
good leads. Of the good leads, 92 said that they had included the
University in their plans and the balance are in the cultivation process now.

By integrating phone calling into the MU gift planning program, which had already been using a donor-centered multi channel marketing strategy, MU increased its reach. The phone calling
uncovered 20 percent of the total expectancies recorded at MU
during the time period of the projects and 50 percent of the total
leads, adding nearly $4 million in expectancies to their program.[5]

In Summary

Soliciting loyals in the philanthropic planning context will be as unique as the charity completing the solicitation. Each charity should design a multi-channel strategy that illustrates how the donor and the charity's mission can benefit from these types of gifts. Using methods other than one-on-one visits will allow the charity to expand its reach, particularly to tiers 3 and 4 of the Philanthropic Planning Pyramid. While eventually a personal touch will be required, it is far less time intensive to use postcards and phone calls to determine who is sincerely interested and then work personally with that group.

CHAPTER 12

Thanking, Recognizing, and Stewarding Legacy Donors

"Thank you" are two of the most powerful words that a charity can say to a donor. And proper recognition and stewardship can be one of the most powerful ways over time to cultivate an annual donor into a legacy donor.

Thanking, recognizing, and stewarding are three distinct actions that charities need to take in response to all gifts, current and legacy. Thanking is the first obligation after a gift, followed by formal recognition of the particular gift and finally on-going stewardship of both the gift and the donor to show how the gift and donor are supporting the mission.

ANNUAL DONORS

In order to obtain legacy donors, a charity must first have a cadre of loyal annual donors to approach for legacy gifts. Without these donors, the gift planning program will fail even before it starts. The only way to create loyal annual donors is to build an effective program to thank, recognize, and steward this group from the time of their first gift.

In her seminal work, *Donor Centered Fundraising*, Penelope Burk states the three things a donor needs to know in order to feel the gift was successful and offer additional support: "1) that the gift was received . . . and you were pleased to get it; 2) that the gift was 'set to work' as intended; 3) that the project or program to which the gift was directed had/is having the desired effect."[1]

Thanking Annual Donors

The first step is to thank annual donors, and most significantly first-time donors, with a prompt acknowledgement within 48 hours that includes confirmation of the intended use of the funds. This approach illustrates to donors that the organization believes the gift is important and confirms that the purpose was not lost when the gift was processed.

"We Don't Value Your Gift"   Each thank you note should aspire to greatness. Charities often settle for thank you notes that are good enough.

FAILURE OF STEWARDSHIP

I make an annual gift each year to an organization that is consistently among the top three of my philanthropic priorities. On the pledge card, I designate my gift to the same endowment fund to which all of my gifts have gone for the last 15 years and to which my legacy gift is designated. At least two-thirds of the time when I receive my gift receipt, it says that the gift has been directed to that area, but it does not say whether or not it was put into the actual endowment fund for which it is designated. I then call the organization and in most cases, the gift has been allocated to the general fund rather than to the endowment. When I inquire as to why, I am informed that it must be a clerical error. After 15 years without satisfaction I have to question whether my much larger bequest will also be subject to a clerical error.

Further the thank-you letter I get from this charity does not discuss the area to which my gift has been designated, but instead speaks about the charity's general mission. The stewardship report the charity sends to me each year does not list my name because my annual gift is below the threshold level they have established to include donor names. It also does not include the particular area at the charity to which my gift has been designated because it is less important than some other initiatives in the same department (although it is definitely something they want to continue to raise money to support). Is your organization paying attention to these issues?

Charities need to look through the eyes of the donor when making these decisions, or risk alienating the loyal annual donors who will become legacy donors. —BMS

The thank you letter is not personalized, does not state the purpose of the donor's gift, and does not indicate the gift will be put to the intended purpose. Frequently it is not a thank you at all, but a computer generated gift receipt, postcard, or e-mail. Worse still, many charities have policies that donors below a certain gift level get a gift receipt but no thank you at all. Charities justify these types of acknowledgements on a lack of staff, a lack of budget, or the need to focus resources on fulfilling the mission. The message for donors is quite clear—"we don't value your gift." While charities will argue that this is not the case, that every gift is important, the thank you (or lack thereof) tells the donor how the charity values the gift.

CONCEPT

ATTRIBUTES OF A GREAT THANK YOU LETTER

1. The letter is a real letter and not a pre-printed card.
2. It is personally addressed.
3. It has a personal salutation (no "dear donor" or "dear friend).
4. It is personally signed.
5. It is personally signed by someone from the highest ranks of the organization.
6. It makes specific reference to the intended use of the funds.
7. It indicates approximately when the donor will receive an update on the program being funded.
8. It includes the name and phone number of a staff person whom the donor can contact at any time or an invitation to contact the writer directly.
9. It does not ask for another gift.
10. It does not ask the donor to do anything (like complete an enclosed survey, for example).
11. It acknowledges the donor's past giving, where applicable.
12. It contains no spelling or grammatical errors.
13. It has an overall can-do positive tone as opposed to a hand-wringing one.
14. It communicates the excitement, gratitude, and inner warmth of the writer.
15. It grabs the reader's attention in the opening sentence.

(continued)

16. *It speaks directly to the donor.*
17. *It does not continue to sell.*
18. *It is concise—no more than two short paragraphs.*
19. *It is received by the donor promptly.*
20. *Plus, in some circumstances, the letter is handwritten.*[2]

A great thank you will help the charity retain its donors, both new and loyal.

Retention and Lapsed Donors   Fifty percent of first-time donors never make a second gift to the same nonprofit organization. Why is donor retention so poor? When surveyed, donors say it is a failure to thank, recognize, and steward. And when you consider that legacy gifts are developed from loyal donors, it can provide for a bleak outlook for future philanthropic planning opportunities. Nonprofit organizations lose on average 30 percent of their overall donor pool each year. William T. Sturtevant stated that "it requires 4.5 times the effort, staff, and dollars to acquire a new donor as it does to keep one."[3] A charity's best effort is therefore spent maintaining and even building current relationships with donors.

CONCEPT   REASONS FOR LAPSED DONORS

- *Inadequate recognition.*
- *Inadequate involvement and information.*
- *Inadequate stewardship.*
- *Poor handling of complaint.*
- *Organizational changes.*
- *New leaders, programs, or policies.*
- *A similar organization is more attractive.*
- *Move to a different community.*
- *Life circumstances—aging, financial situation, death.*

Charities spend an enormous sum each year trying to lure back lapsed donors and identify new donors. Yet they consistently send a message to their modest annual fund donors that their gifts are not important. If charities were to spend a small portion of their donor acquisition budgets on meaningful thank you notes, they would retain a much larger percentage of their annual donors, turn them into loyal donors, and eventually convert them to legacy donors. As Burk shares: "On a gift-by-gift basis, budgeting communication and recognition relative to gift size seems to make sense, but it is actually the *opposite* of what we need to do if we want to retain more donors and increase the average value of contributions. We make the mistake of designing and budgeting communication as a post-gift activity instead of what it really is—the investment cost of securing the next gift."[4]

Investing In an Acknowledgement System   Most nonprofits have a system in place for acknowledgement and recognition. Charities need to ensure that their donor software allows them to send contemporaneous, personalized thank yous, track and link spousal and couple gifts, designate gifts to restricted purposes, provide for cumulative giving, and track all types of future gifts at both current and net present value. A charity should never be wondering if a donor made a gift, the amount of the gift, the purpose of the gift, was it acknowledged, and did it serve its purpose.

In addition to recording data, nonprofits should have a robust reporting capacity so they can track their performance issuing thank yous, using gifts as intended, and meeting donor restrictions. Only by measuring performance in these areas can nonprofits be sure that they are doing what they need to properly thank their donors.

Recognizing Annual Donors

Charities need to recognize all of their donors (providing they do not wish to remain anonymous). Giving may be its own reward, but a thoughtfully conceived, donor-focused recognition program is indispensable to the success of any philanthropic planning program.

Donor recognition has a two-fold purpose, to thank the donors for their gifts and then to encourage the donors (and others) to upgrade their gifts. Recognition begins at the moment that the donor makes the commitment. The initial sincere response lets donors know how thrilled the organization is to have them join in support of the cause.

Jerold Panas in *Mega Gifts* recommends finding a way to thank your donor seven times each year.[5] Seven distinct moves offer seven opportunities for the donor to understand that they are important to the charity. Seven messages that are singular, but when positioned together work toward a complete concept of reminding the donor both why they are giving and what their support is accomplishing.

CONCEPT   SEVEN TOUCHES

1. *Prompt Thank You Letters—Consistent thank you letters within 48 hours of their giving.*

2. *Impact Reports—Donors are inspired by the results of their giving. Positive outcomes that are a direct result from their investment in a program will motivate a donor to give again.*

3. *Annual Report—Just like a program report that shares how donor support led to success for an aspect of the organizational mission, an informative annual report that depicts the overall picture of a charity will build trust in their ability to efficiently reach and surpass goals. Similarly, transparency and accountability lead to donor loyalty as they continue to become engaged in mission delivery.*

4. *Volunteer Recognition Card—Sent in April during Volunteer Recognition month or November for National Philanthropy Day (or both), it highlights your appreciation of your donors active involvement in the mission of your organization.*

5. *Birthday Card—Sent out the first week of each month (or three days prior to the donor's birthday if you can), a greeting on the birthday says that you and your organization are paying attention to the donor in a very personal way. These cards, which must be signed by the person at the organization who has a personal relationship with the donor, create warmth. A non-descript card with an automated signature is not worth the cost of printing and postage to send.*

6. *Thanksgiving Card—While most of us get holiday/Christmas cards from multiple sources, how many Thanksgiving cards do you get? At a time of year when we are thankful for many things,*

expressing thanks to your donors should be a priority. But as with the birthday card, if it lacks the personal touch, better not to send it at all.

7. *Personal Phone Call—Make a personal phone call in early December to wish your donors a Happy Holiday. While you shouldn't bring it up in the call, it also offers donors a chance to offer a year-end gift.*

To truly offer a donor-centered approach, the examples here should be amended to match the constituents of the particular organization. The meter of the approach is proven, but the touches should be tailored to the donors and the mission.

CONCEPT RECOGNITION PROFILES

The following recognition profiles can help you to understand the individual motivations of your donors toward their stewardship. As with most generalities, there can surely be people who can be a combination of two or more of these profiles.

The Expectants: Bring it on. They look forward to being recognized often upon making their gift to your organization. They may be motivated to give for many different reasons, but if they fit this profile, they revel in the spotlight of you thanking them in a public setting.

The Moderates: Some attention, but not too much. They appreciate being recognized, but don't want you to overdo it. They would enjoy being part of the list of those recognized at an event or on the donor wall.

The Frugal: Don't spend any money on my recognition. They are fine with a thank you letter and appreciate a personal handwritten note, but they don't want money spent on a plaque or a donor wall. They would rather see their donation go to the mission of your organization than to anything that recognizes their giving.

The Secretive: Thank me personally, but not in public. They don't want the public recognition that often comes with a large gift. While their

(continued)

leadership in a campaign might be helpful to encourage others by their giving, they don't seek nor do they want to be recognized. In some cases, folks in this profile group will delay making their gift commitment until they are sure that their name will be cared for and not announced.

The Anonymous: Give because they want to support the cause, but want to remain anonymous. We often will see, anonymous on the donor wall in several places as there are a few people who don't want to be known. In many cases, we know the donor and need to respect their wishes as they ask to remain anonymous. In some rare other cases, the donor may have made the gift without even our knowledge of their gift.

Recognition methods:

- *Personal handwritten or typed letter.*
- *Phone call.*
- *E-mail.*
- *Certificate.*
- *Giving society.*
- *Publications (programs, reports, web site, etc.).*
- *Acknowledgment at events.*
- *Fund agreement.*
- *Plaque.*
- *Naming opportunities (donor wall, room, wing, building, etc.).*
- *Interaction with volunteer leaders, staff, and beneficiaries.*

While donors making regular annual gifts may not be major or principal gift donors, they are donors and deserve appropriate recognition opportunities. The size of the gift should matter less than the commitment to the cause. Charities should try to identify how donors wish to be recognized and deliver what donors want.

Stewarding Annual Donors

Stewardship programs are the most neglected aspect among thanking, recognizing, and stewarding. Recognition is essential, but a stellar stewardship program will transform donors into philanthropists.

Stewardship is the careful and responsible management of another's property or financial affairs; one who administers anything as the agent of another or others (source: Webster's Dictionary).[6] Stewardship implies an acknowledgement that a nonprofit is supposed to make a difference.

An effective stewardship program is a continuing and planned process of saying thank you, expressing appreciation, and reporting back on the use of and outcomes created by the donor's gifts throughout the span of a donor's relationship with a nonprofit. Stewardship activities must be transparent and accountable.

Hank Rosso described stewardship as a sacred trust that voluntary organizations accept when they place themselves in positions of responsibility for the public good. Serious regard for this trust represents the soul of stewardship.[7]

According to Susan O'Leary, director of research and product development for CharityAmerica.com, the challenge for stewards of donor relations programs is to move the recipient to actually read, appreciate, and act upon the message of the charitable organization. Donors are bombarded with too much mail, too many telephone calls, and so many asks for commitments. The best marketing efforts consists of saying "thank you" in a thoughtful, respectful, and unique way. Saying "thank you" displays courtesy and enthusiasm for the cause and provides an opportunity to honor donors and prospects, spread the word about the organization's mission, and invite donors to participate in future projects.[8]

In his article, *Remember to Say "Thank You,"* author Robert J. Lloyd expresses that feeling gratitude and not expressing it is like wrapping a present and not giving it. To give thanks one needs to show gratitude in actions by passing on the kindness to others in need of such a blessing. Roman writer, statesman, and orator Marcus Cicero (106 to 43 BC) said, "*Gratitude is not only the greatest of virtues but the parent of all others.*"[9] The messages are loud and clear—people like to be appreciated.

Annual Fund Buckets Charities make stewardship very complicated, when it can be quite simple. Once an effective thank you and recognition program is in place, stewardship needs only to provide donors with the final piece in the process, letting them know that their gift is having the desired effect or at least providing measurable results on their gifts at work.

The Traditionalists are able and willing to make unrestricted gifts. Their stewardship should be simple and straightforward, reporting back some of the key ways that the charity is using unrestricted funds to support the mission, preferably with some outcomes-based stories.

The New Philanthropists expect more stewardship of their gifts. One way to do this in the annual fund context is to establish four or five core areas or buckets and allow these cohorts to designate their annual gifts. While this may seem counterintuitive, as charities have spent the last 30 years or more encouraging unrestricted gifts, the reality is that most of the New Philanthropists want to restrict their gifts, including their annual gifts, to a particular purpose at the charity. By allowing gifts to be restricted to core areas, the charity can still have broad discretion over the funds while giving donors the ability to direct gifts to preferred areas. This has multiple benefits to the charity. First, the donor is designating the annual gift to an area which the charity had already intended to fund, so they are still budget-relieving dollars. Second, the donor has told the charity an area of interest, which could become the topic of conversation for a major or legacy gift. Third, the charity can create general stewardship reports for each of the four or five bucket areas, and effectively report back to donors in those bucket areas about the results of their gifts at work.

Annual fund donors who have been properly thanked, recognized, and stewarded will become repeat donors and feed the charity's major gifts and legacy giving pipeline. Without them, it will be increasingly difficult for charities to maintain their current level of fundraising.

LEGACY DONORS

Legacy donors, like annual fund donors, want to be thanked, recognized, and stewarded. Even though many of these gifts will come from tier three donors on the Philanthropic Planning Pyramid, legacy gifts are the largest gifts that people can make, and are many times larger than their annual fund gifts. They deserve the same individualized attention for thanking, recognizing, and stewarding that would be provided to all donors. The biggest difference for legacy donors is that they often are not around to see the benefit of their philanthropy, since the gifts normally mature after the donor has passed away. This makes it incumbent upon charities to create thanking, recognition, and stewardship mechanisms that can overcome this challenge.

Thanking Legacy Donors

As with annual fund donors, legacy donors seek a contemporaneous thank you at the time the donor informs the charity about the gift, indicating that the charity intends to use the money where it will be directed, and then providing reports of the progress of the program for the duration of the donor's life. By connecting a legacy donor to the people at the charity who are providing the service to be funded or who benefit from it, legacy donors will feel secure that their gifts will come to good use. The thank you process and the relationship that follows create a trust that the charity will use the gift as intended, even after the donor is not there to ensure that the charity does so.

Because legacy gifts will not mature until the future, legacy donors must feel confident that the charity's board members are engaged and committed to the future. Board members should be asked to join the legacy society, to increase their visibility and investment in the organization. Board members should also be utilized in the thanking process. It is very powerful for a new legacy donor to get a thank you note or telephone call from a board member. It makes it clear that the gift is valued and far more likely that the gift will be used for its intended purpose.

Recognizing Legacy Donors

Most charities struggle to effectively recognize legacy donors. Because these gifts usually do not mature until the future, there is often an element of fairness that comes into the conversation. Charities feel it is unfair to treat a legacy donor the same as a major donor, since the gift from the legacy donor has not yet been irrevocably transferred to the charity.

As Burk pointed out, however, recognition and stewardship for major and annual donors are not a post-gift activity but an investment in the next gift. The same holds true for legacy donors. The recognition and stewardship today are for the final gift, the one that comes when the donor passes.

The Role of the Recognition Society   The legacy/recognition society is the most common method of recognizing legacy donors to a charity. It allows the charity to publicly recognize gifts that will not mature until the future, as well as to immortalize those who have died leaving legacy gifts. It honors those individuals who support the charity's mission and love the organization enough to create a gift of great significance for it.

BE CAREFUL WITH THE TIMING OF YOUR RECOGNITION

Author Mark Twain was traveling in Europe and was startled to read his own obituary. His response was this oft-quoted cable to the Associated Press on June 2, 1897:

THE REPORT OF MY DEATH WAS AN EXAGGERATION.

Twain was not the only notable whose demise was reported prematurely. In 1899, when portrait painter John Singer Sargent was just 43 years old and living abroad, his death was reported in American newspapers. He set the following telegram to his patron and friend, Isabella Stewart Gardner:

ALIVE AND KICKING. SARGENT[10]

Name and Branding   Every charity that receives legacy gifts should have a legacy society to recognize those donors who have planned for the charity's long-term future. The name of the society should be unique and clearly identifiable with the organization. If a charity does not yet have a society, it should select a name that shares an important story about a legacy gift in the charity's past, or a donor who made a legacy gift. If the charity does not have any such gifts, it can use something generic like the Legacy Society or Evergreen Society, but change it to something meaningful as gifts are realized.

CASE STUDY   **GAMALIEL PAINTER'S CANE SOCIETY**

Middlebury College has perhaps one of the best legacy society names conceived. Gamaliel Painter was one of Middlebury College's founding fathers, a tireless advocate of the College in its earliest years and a vital benefactor. He was known to walk the cobblestone streets of Middlebury with the sound of his cane warning all of his approach.

Upon his death in 1819, Painter's generosity carried on in the form of a bequest that literally saved the fledgling school from financial ruin. Painter bequeathed more than his money to the College. In a codicil to his will, Gamaliel Painter also left his cane, a sturdy walking stick with a deep blue ribbon and a steel tip.

Throughout Middlebury's history, the cane has stood as a reminder of Painter's legacy of leadership and support. The original cane serves as the mace of the college, is passed around at convocation for each incoming student to touch and for each graduating student to remember. Each student receives a replica of Painter's Cane upon graduation from Middlebury and brings it back for Reunion. Upon special occasions, such as the 50th Reunion, a gold ribbon is added to the blue ribbon on the cane. Those in the Cane Society are given a white ribbon for their canes. At each Reunion, and at all convocations, the students, faculty, staff, and alumni sing the song:

"Gamaliel Painter's Cane" -1917
Verse 1: When Gamaliel Painter died, he was Middlebury's pride,
A sturdy pioneer without a stain;
And he left his all by will, to the college on the hill,
And included his codicil cane.
Chorus: Oh, its rap rap rap, and it's tap tap tap,
If you listen you can hear it sounding plain;
For a helper true and tried, as the generations glide,
There is nothing like Gamaliel Painter's cane.

Upon graduation from Middlebury, every student knows the story of Gamaliel Painter's Cane, understands the importance of bequest gifts, and knows about will codicils. When I worked for the College and asked alumni to join Gamaliel Painter's Cane Society, I didn't have to explain it—they knew what it was and the prestige that went with it. It meant something to be a member of the Society. Each year, when the president would address the Society, he reminded them that without Painter's gifts, and without their gifts, there would be no Middlebury College. —BMS

The society should have a brand that compliments and works in collaboration with the charity's existing brand using a symbol or mark, along with coordinating colors, look, feel, and design.

Membership Criteria   Membership in the society should be extended to all individuals and their spouses who have set up an endowment to benefit the organization, included the organization in their estate plans, named the organization as a beneficiary of a trust, life insurance policy, charitable lead trust, or retirement plan, or created a life-income gift (charitable remainder trust, pooled income fund, charitable gift annuity).

Membership Roster   One of the key elements of effective recognition is the creation of a membership roster for the legacy society. It says to the donor that the gift is important and that the charity is telling the world that it is important. Charities create membership rosters in many different ways. Some have patio pavers with the names of all current and deceased members. Others use a donor wall in a prominent location at the charity. As with so many things, to determine what works best for the donors to a particular charity is by asking them. A short survey of members about recognition will tell a charity a great deal about what members want in recognition and how to use recognition to appeal to potential legacy donors. Keep in mind the recognition profiles. Some donors will want no recognition and others will want to remain anonymous. Unless the charity has a large percentage of these types of donors, ignore those responses and create the roster based on the response of those individuals who want to be recognized.

Membership Benefits   Membership benefits should be customized to combine thanking legacy donors for their long-term commitment to the organization while showing them the long-term impact and outcomes created by their legacy gifts and those of others. Each organization should craft an Acknowledgement and Recognition Plan to articulate how the charity plans to steward these important donors. Some possible benefits of donor recognition society membership might include:

- New Members:
  - Thank you letter or personal thank you call from the board president.
  - Thank you letter from the CEO/president.
  - Certificate of membership.

- Memento (pin, paperweight, mug, clock, picture frame).
- Special mention in the annual report.
- Existing Members
  - Listing in the annual report (both before and after death—emeritus status).
  - Invitation to recognition society event (written, followed up by personal invite from a board member via telephone).
  - Birthday card.
  - Thanksgiving Day card.
  - Annual phone call from board member.
  - Social networking.
- Deceased Members
  - Acknowledgement to family.
  - Collection of gift.
  - Funds put to purpose donor intended.
  - Recognition after death.
  - Ongoing connection with family to show long-term impact of gift.

All members of the legacy society should feel well connected and recognized for their generosity, even though their gifts may not mature until the future.

Stewarding Legacy Donors

Stewardship of legacy donors will ensure that they feel a lifetime of commitment to and from the charity. The charity should have clear objectives for the stewardship program.

Stewardship is the art of managing the relationship between donors and the organization. A successful stewardship program will increase the charity's connection with most loyal legacy gift supporters, causing them to become more engaged with the charity's mission and desiring to help fund impactful programs that further its success. In fact, successful, mature gift planning programs receive up to 50 percent of their new life-income gifts from existing life-income gift donors who feel well connected and stewarded by the organization. Stewardship requires proper acknowledgement of donations of time, talent, and treasure, the three legs of donor participation.

Stewardship Events   Stewardship events have been a mainstay of gift planning recognition since the invention of the legacy society. These events will largely draw Traditionalists who appreciate the opportunity to hear from leadership about the organization and socialize with each other.

CONCEPT

STEWARDSHIP OBJECTIVES FOR GIFT PLANNING DONORS AND PHILANTHROPISTS

- *Organizational commitment to relationship building and donor-centered fundraising through all employees and volunteers—stewardship is everyone's job.*
- *Appreciation and fulfillment of the long-term outcomes donors seek to create through their philanthropy.*
- *Retention, renewal, and enhancement of donor support over a lifetime of giving and in perpetuity.*

<table>
<tr><td>CONCEPT</td><td>PURPOSE OF LEGACY GIFT STEWARDSHIP</td></tr>
</table>

- *Maintain and strengthen the relationship of legacy gift donors to the organization.*
- *Provide a vehicle for ongoing communication with legacy gift donors.*
- *Engage legacy gift donors with the organization and its mission on an on-going basis.*
- *Focus attention on the value of legacy gifts to the organization.*
- *Encourage others to consider and make legacy gifts.*

Some Older and Younger Boomers may attend these events for the prestige, but they will not attract Gen X, which does not care to socialize in this way. Millennials may attend once or twice, but this style of event is not meaningful for them. Put simply, stewardship events for legacy donors have a place right now, but within the next 20 years will need to be updated to meet the needs of the next generation or eliminated in favor of other types of legacy donor stewardship.

ANNUAL STEWARDSHIP EVENTS

At Meridian Health Affiliated Foundations, we have held an annual Heritage Club event for our planned giving donors for many years. Over that time, we have experimented with small, individual events for each of our hospitals and we have held one big event for the convenience of organization and attendance by our team. The format has included breakfasts, lunches, dinners, and even afternoon tea at a nearby Victorian Bed & Breakfast. The same Traditionalist cohort donors usually attend and those that joined us for tea last year really enjoyed it, but we needed something that would remind them of why they were giving.

Our loyal Heritage Club members needed an update on the hospital that they have generously supported with annual gifts and time as a

(continued)

volunteer. They wanted to hear about something new and innovative that showed that our medical centers are on the cutting edge of health-care. This year, we had Heritage Club Dinners in the President's Board Room at each of the hospitals. Most don't ever see the board room, and with the hospital presidents as the hosts, they not only felt special, but the presidents each gave their own personal briefing on the latest news and successes at their hospitals.

We had one of our top physicians present at each as well. Dr. Elkwood spoke about the Center for Paralysis and Nerve Regeneration at one of the dinners. From what he told our donors, Jersey Shore University Medical Center is one of only two hospitals in the country that is doing the type of surgery that he and his partner Dr. Kaufman are doing with phrenic nerve surgery—some amazing stories of improving the quality of life for patients with nerve damage.

And not only did our Heritage Club see, hear, and experience the food and the talks, but they also had company in the rooms. This year we invited the board of trustees as well as the executive committees of the auxiliaries to be with us. Not only did we have record attendance for each event, but those two groups of donors who both regularly give and volunteer their time were with us to hear about the value of the Heritage Club as another reminder that they too, could join and leave a legacy to their favorite hospital.

Key Elements to Make Your Event a Success

- Held at a location where you can provide real-life examples of the benefits that matured gifts have produced, creating immortality for those Traditionalists who have passed away and promising it to those in attendance.
- Lunch (even though your society will have individuals of many different ages, the Traditionalists tend to attend these events and do not want to fight rush hour traffic or drive in the dark).
- Valet parking.
- Speaker with a compelling message of impact and outcomes of legacy gifts on the organization.
- Induction of new members into the society.
- Remembrance of those members who have passed away since the prior luncheon.
- Token of appreciation for their support.
- Invitation to other special organizational events. —REW

There is no one, right way to offer stewardship events. Each charity needs to evaluate its donor group and determine what would appeal to them. If a charity is not sure, it should poll or survey the members to find out. The key is to continue to build the connection between the charity and the legacy donors to ensure that their gifts in fact come to the charity upon their passing.

Additional Materials—Multi Channel Approach   As with other communication, stewarding legacy donors should be approached in a multi channel way. With the emergence of the New Philanthropists, charities need to start using multimedia to illustrate the impact and outcomes of gifts. Web videos of interviews with donors and the individuals a charity supports, Skype connections between U.S.-based donors and work being done overseas, Web cams in remote villages around the globe where charities are building schools—all of these tools are available right now and connect donors to the work of the charity in a much more personal way than was possible even ten years ago.

To appeal to New Philanthropists, charities need their stewardship to make these connections. Using technology to reaffirm for them the results of their philanthropy, or their future philanthropy, will go a long way toward ensuring that legacy gifts stay in place and current gifts are increased for the same purpose.

Appendix I includes a list of more than 50 additional ways, small and large, that a charity can continue to provide stewardship to legacy donors that may prove helpful as an organization builds its stewardship plan.

Brochure   While it is important to use a broader range of technology for the New Philanthropists, there are still some key tools which charities need to keep in place for the Traditionalists. The legacy society brochure, which tells the story of the society and criteria for membership, should be a staple of every gift planning stewardship program until the Traditionalists have passed on.

Each charity should create a brochure unique to its culture and legacy society. If the brochure is appealing, with an effective reply mechanism, it will enhance membership.

Newsletter   The gift planning newsletter has served many purposes over the years. For decades it was the primary (and frequently the only)

▒ **EXAMPLE   UNIVERSITY OF THE SCIENCES**
REMINGTON BROCHURE

Appendix J includes a sample legacy society brochure from the University of the Sciences. The same team worked on this brochure and the general brochure discussed in Chapter 10. Notice how the brochure invites the reader to join the Society. It then uses four panels to tell the story of Joseph Remington and why his legacy is so important; why legacy gifts, and the prospect's legacy gift, would be so important to the University; what constitutes a legacy gift that qualifies for membership; and a call to action. Note that the call to action provides multiple ways to contact a real person about a legacy gift, including a confidential reply card which is found in Appendix K. The reply card for this brochure is far less detailed than the general brochure, since the focus of this brochure is to invite individuals to join the legacy society. It only asks for what the charity needs in order to take the next step with the prospect.

The text of the brochure is pithy and to the point. The design is consistent with the brand and colors established in the general brochure. The quotes bring a peer-to-peer ask component to the brochure. When you look at the pieces together, they belong with one another. The visual identity is undeniable, which makes them work together in a far more effective way than if each had been designed on its own. ▒

marketing tool used to share information about legacy gifts. As noted in Chapter 7, the traditional gift planning newsletter tries to accomplish too many steps in the moves management process. In the philanthropic planning model, it really serves two roles, to steward existing legacy society donors and to cultivate new gift opportunities from existing society members and those individuals who have requested gift planning information in the last five years. It should be produced three times per year on a regular schedule, which will make it an expected and desired piece in the mailbox or e-mail box of legacy society members.

A gift planning stewardship newsletter should typically include the following elements:

- *Donor profiles:* If the newsletter is to steward donors, it needs to include profiles that give a short history of the donor's relationship with the charity and what motivated the donor to make a legacy gift. To effectively cultivate others, these profiles should also show the impact and outcomes of gifts, so that other donors and potential donors can see how a gift produced the desired result, or will produce the desired result. In many cases, it will make sense to profile deceased donors, whose gifts have matured, so that the long-term outcome can be very clearly illustrated. These profiles *should not* spend a great deal of time or effort on particular gift planning tools and how they work. That information can be provided on the web site. To return to our earlier analogy, the information about tools represents the steak, and the stewardship newsletter, at least in the donor profile, should be selling the sizzle.

- *Financial planning articles:* Legacy donors are planners. They have planned for the future of one or more charitable organizations. By providing financial planning information, it positions the organization as a partner with the donor's financial advisors, rather than as a competitor. By showing a willingness to work with professional advisors (for example, having an advisor write a guest article in the newsletter), it will open the door to additional collaboration in a philanthropic planning process.

- *Tax law updates:* As noted earlier, each time the tax law changes, tax, estate, financial, and charitable planning will need to be updated. By providing information about tax law changes, the charity again shows itself to be a partner in the planning process with members and advisors, which makes it more likely the charity will have a seat at the table when it comes time to update those plans.

- *Contact information:* The newsletter should make it simple for society members to reach the person at the charity responsible for gift planning. If it is a large staff, list their names, contact information, and coverage areas. If it is a small staff, no coverage areas will be required.

When sending the newsletter, charities should ask their legacy society members how they would prefer to receive the content. While some members will prefer an electronic version, most still prefer to receive this content in print. By offering both, the charity can lower costs and connect with the members in a way that is more likely to result in them reading the publication.

Volunteer Opportunities   Stewardship of legacy donors frequently involves volunteer opportunities. Those donors who are most engaged with the mission of the charity are the best prospects for gift planning. Once they set up legacy gifts, they become even more engaged and want to do even more financially and personally.

The Traditionalists welcome the volunteer opportunities that have become the norm in charitable giving circles. Serving on boards or advisory committees, attending awareness raising events, hand-writing invites, and making phone calls are all good ways to engage Traditionalists.

Older Boomers will still serve in many of these traditional roles, but they find them less interesting than the Traditionalists. They are looking for more leisure time, particularly after working so hard for so many years. If the activities involve their children, they may have a greater interest in participating, particularly if they can show adult or teenage children that they are helping to pursue the social justice agenda of the Older Boomers' youth.

Younger Boomers are much less interested in traditional volunteer roles. They tend to see them as a time sink and of little value. If a particular charity impacts their family, they are more likely to donate time to the cause. Local hospitals and arts organizations will find ready volunteers in the Younger Boomer cohort, but not to serve on auxiliaries or committees. Charities need to find ways to engage Younger Boomers in the areas that their gifts will actually support. For example, if a Younger Boomer makes a gift in support of bringing the arts to inner-city schools, the volunteer opportunity should be to help create and promote the concert by those benefitting from the program.

Gen X wants nothing to do with traditional stewardship events or volunteer opportunities. This generation will only give and volunteer to causes that touch them personally. They are more environmentally conscious than the cohorts that came before, so charities seeking to save the planet will do well with them, provided the volunteer opportunities are real. Keep in mind that Xers do not like to work in teams and have an entrepreneurial bent. Volunteer opportunities need to allow them to be creative to help solve the problem which is of interest to them.

Millennials are much more flexible than the generations which came before, meaning that they can adapt to whatever volunteer opportunities charities have for them. But just because they are willing to adapt does not mean that charities should take advantage of that and try to push them into the same roles as Traditionalists. Millennials are full of positive energy, fresh ideas, and are plugged in. Charities that can harness that energy and give Millennials responsibility for a meaningful volunteer activity will find that the Millennials will come up with creative, new ways to achieve the goal of the activity which engage other Millennials. While most gift planning programs will not have a lot of Millennial donors until they get a bit older, those who can be engaged at this stage of life will be a welcome addition and will draw in others.

Volunteer opportunities, as with all aspects of stewardship, must evolve to meet the needs of the next generations of philanthropists. Charities have to adapt to their changing donor group for all stages of the moves management process, including stewardship.

Stewarding Philanthropists

While this chapter focuses on stewardship and recognition of Tiers Three and Four, it is important to mention the approach for Tiers One and Two. Just like stewardship of legacy donors, philanthropists need to feel a lifetime of commitment to and from the charity. The difference is in the delivery of stewardship activities. Throughout the philanthropic planning process, this group of donors was worthy of one-on-one attention and their stewardship should be no different. In addition to the methods described, organizations should offer stewardship that is personal and customized to their needs and objectives, or "concierge stewardship."

Unlike the approach for annual giving and legacy giving, concierge stewardship gives the donor exactly what they have stated that they want to see from the organization in their stewardship. A very creative and again, customized program is mapped out to provide the philanthropist with the seven touches that will remind them that they are valuable to the organization.

Like the concierge service at a fine hotel, the organization might offer a menu of items that it can provide for donors. Organizations will have distinctly different offerings that are chosen by the fundraiser, as the primary relationship manager for the organization, and are picked based on the fundraiser's knowledge of the donors and their wishes. This approach gives donors a very tailored stewardship regimen. For example, with a chance to show the outcomes of their giving, an organization might engage the donor in an experience that would give them a first-hand look. In healthcare, an opportunity to shadow a physician for an afternoon for rounds, or in higher education attending a lecture on a topic that is interesting to the donors in an area that was funded by them would be tremendous glimpses into the program that is a result of the donors' generosity.

Stewardship of the top two tiers of donors should be commensurate with their philanthropy. Concierge stewardship ensures that philanthropists are receiving the attention, information, and experiences that they expect as investors in the organization's mission.

IN SUMMARY

An effective thank you, recognition, and stewardship program will produce donors who feel appreciated and respected. They will be more engaged by the mission of the charity, making them more likely to direct gifts to meet organization needs and priorities. Over time, this increased level of engagement should lead to larger outright gifts.

Well-stewarded donors will eventually look for a wider range of charitable giving tools to integrate their philanthropic goals for all organizations with their tax, estate, and financial planning. They will become shareholders in the charities they support and engage others to support those charitable missions, becoming the best ambassadors for those charitable missions.

*   *   *

Part three has focused on delivering gift planning using a philanthropic planning approach to Tier Three and Four prospects on the Philanthropic Planning Pyramid. Using the outlined moves management platform to build this program will provide the maximum opportunities for success. Charities following this model should see increased interest in legacy gifts, more engaged prospects, and more satisfied donors. Each step in the process is critical in order to feed the next step. If charities jump to solicitation without educating and cultivating, the solicitations will fall flat. Charities that ignore stewardship put the success of the prior steps at risk. Organizations that take the traditional path and focus on old, wealthy people—

which do not identify the best prospects or tailor their message to generational cohorts—will see their results dwindle over time. The methodology outlined should be simple and straightforward to follow and will maximize gifts, both current gifts today and legacy gifts tomorrow, from Tiers Three and Four, which might otherwise be ignored by charities all together.

PART FOUR

Program Infrastructure

Successful philanthropic planning programs require a strong infrastructure to support them. Much like a house built on the sand, a
philanthropic planning program will not stand for long without building
several key elements to support it. Part IV of the *Companion* discusses how
a charity should build its program over a multi-year period. Chapter 13
details the elements and requirements in a plan for philanthropic planning
as well as how a charity tracks its overall philanthropic planning success
over five or more years. Chapter 14 outlines gift acceptance policies,
procedures, and agreements, along with gift counting and recognition
policies that need to be in place for a program to function. Finally,
Chapter 15 reviews the different types of charitable registration required to
comply with state regulation of charitable giving.

CHAPTER 13

Creating and Tracking Your Success

T here is an old phrase that "You should inspect what you expect." When building a philanthropic planning program, charities need to follow a plan and implement a process to keep track of their efforts.

Philanthropic planning does not fit nicely into one of the traditional development silos. It has components that stretch through each of the areas of individual giving (principal gifts, major gifts, gift planning, and annual giving). The plan and the tracking mechanisms must bridge these silos to ensure the long-term success of the effort.

CREATE A PLAN

A strategy is always the keystone to success in development. Creating a strategy and plan for philanthropic planning provides a foundation for leading fundraisers and volunteers, for balancing priorities, and for working with donors. It should include both goals and objectives and can then lead to action plans that outline the specific steps and activities that will drive the results.

As it is impossible to build a philanthropic planning program in one year with all of its various components, the plan should incorporate multiple years to implement each of the elements. The plan should include components for principal gifts philanthropic planning (tier one prospects); major gifts philanthropic planning (tier two prospects); loyal prospects and everyone else (tiers three and four) in the three core areas of donor interaction, marketing and stewardship, and program development, much as the

Companion is laid out. The marketing plan should focus primarily on reaching tier three and four prospects, with tier one and two prospects getting their primary gift planning information from one-on-one visits with board, volunteers, and staff. The plan will guide the organization's actions throughout the year and provide a benchmark against which to measure success.

As Henry Rosso pointed out many years ago, "The fund raising plan is the principal resource for setting and communicating priorities with staff and volunteers. Although successful managers adhere to the basic direction laid out in the plan, they are also flexible, responding to the changing fund raising environment and the emerging needs of the marketplace. They realize that the development plan is a dynamic tool that should be reviewed, evaluated, and revised on a regular basis."[1]

The outline of a plan has been provided throughout the *Companion*. Chapters 2 and 3 provide a methodology for how to select the right audience and segment it for philanthropic planning. Chapters 4 and 5 discuss the roles of Board members, volunteers, and professional advisors in partnering with charities to pursue philanthropic planning. Chapter 6 provides a model for building and approaching tier one prospects for philanthropic planning. It also includes examples from several sources, so that each charity can build a program tailored to its own needs. Chapter 7 provides a detailed method for approaching tier two prospects. Chapters 8 through 12 explain how to reach tiers three and four and includes in Appendix G, a detailed, sample marketing plan.

To help charities pull these materials together, Appendix L is a three-year sample plan timeline developed by Gift Planning Development, LLC for a college. Since not every charity will begin its philanthropic planning program at the start of a fiscal or calendar year, the sample timeline picks the random month of October to begin introducing philanthropic planning ideas. Each month, the timeline includes what the charity should do in each of the moves management steps, as well as for donor interaction and program development. While each charity will need to develop its own plan based upon its staffing, organizational structure, mission, and prospect population, Appendix L provides a framework that each charity can follow to conceive and implement such a plan.

Once a plan is implemented, charities should evaluate their performance against the plan each month and at the end of each fiscal year. If the charity has fallen away from the plan, it should determine why. If the charity is ahead of schedule, are there opportunities to take advantage of this success? Each area of the plan should have measures of success to determine progress against goals.

INDIVIDUAL PERFORMANCE GOALS AND MEASURING SUCCESS

In addition to the measures of success for the philanthropic planning plan, charities should also develop performance goals for individuals involved in philanthropic planning. Developing and assigning individual goals centered on core philanthropic planning activities helps to define fundraisers' roles, prioritize their efforts, and instill individual accountability. Individual activity metrics can also help fundraisers to manage their own performance, thereby helping the manager to lead the team.

Measuring Performance

The best measure of philanthropic planning performance is not dollars raised but increased activity with each of the four tiers of prospects. Tier one prospect visits/meetings, tier two, three, and four qualifying visits, cultivation visits, solicitation visits, asks/solicitations, stewardship visits, quality contacts, and internal prospect strategy discussions each month are all basic, but very necessary activities that when measured are indicators of success. Appendix M includes two simple, monthly activity reports that can be used by charities to track these important activities. These same activities are noted as monthly goals on the sample plan timeline found in Appendix L.

Dollar goals in philanthropic planning programs can be easily misunderstood since most people involved in nonprofit organizations are accustomed to recording success based on money raised and receipted. Some of the mechanisms of philanthropic planning yield an immediate, recordable gift, but many will be testamentary with residual gifts that will not be realized by the organization until long after the current fundraising team has moved on or retired. Others may be gifts of complex assets that cannot be valued right away, but will benefit the organization in a period of years. Still others may take a long time to develop as donors and advisors work together to implement a complex planning mechanism resulting from the philanthropic planning process. The effectiveness of a philanthropic planning program simply cannot be measured in just cash today, but needs to be measured using the activity measures noted earlier and the gifts yet to come.

Individual Activity Goals

It is human nature that individuals perform to the goals against which they are measured. For years, major gift fundraisers have been measured not against their activity or long-term relationships built, but against dollars raised in the current year. It should come as no surprise that organizations using such goals find that their fundraisers are using a transactional approach rather than an integrated, philanthropic planning approach.

Well thought out and articulated goals drive the right activity and keep fundraisers and the charities they work for on track. Setting goals and then measuring performance against those goals is paramount to the charity and the fundraiser reaching their goals.

Each charity must determine on its own appropriate activity targets for fundraisers. William Sturtevant, one of the fathers of moves management, offers a methodology for fundraisers who are developing major and planned gifts.

The first step in determining activity levels is to assign a fundraiser to a particular tier of prospects and recognize the other activities which may pull a fundraiser away from working with prospects. For example, a director of gift planning who has to manage the entire back office of the operation and also create and implement a gift planning marketing strategy is probably only spending 25 to 40 percent of his or her time working with prospects. When determining the performance measures, the director should only have 25 to 40 percent of the prospect goals of a full-time gift planner.

Philanthropic Planning Officers   Philanthropic planning officers who work with tier one prospects can only handle a modest number of relationships at a time. A reasonable estimate to start would be 75 families, but the number may be far less if the families are ready to have meaningful philanthropic planning conversations. Proper preparation for and follow

▪ EXAMPLE STURTEVANT PERFORMANCE GOALS RECOMMENDATIONS[2]

Contact Goal for Individual Fundraiser = Total Number of Prospects Under Management Divided by 4

For example: 100 prospects divided by 4 = 25 contacts or moves per week.

Contacts (Moves) Objectives and Mix Per Week

In this example, I use 100 as the base for contacts under management.

Standard	Qualifying Contacts	Cultivation Contacts	Solicitations or Asks	Stewardship Contacts
New Fundraiser	70% (18)	20% (5)	5% (1)	5%(1)
Experienced Fundraiser (3 to 5 years)	25% (5)	50%(13)	15%(4)	10% (3)
Very Experienced Fundraiser (5 years or longer)	5%(1)	65% (16)	20% (5)	10% (3)

A Contact (move) has an objective. It may be accomplished by letter, telephone, or personal visit. With good prospects, one contact (move) per month (12 per year) is desired, with four to five per year in the form of personal visits. A reasonable target for gifts secured is six per month by whatever method. This could result in $1 to $2 million per year, at first, with growth based on working more prospects and development of the program. Major and planned gifts typically have a longer time horizon than other types of gifts and don't neatly fit into 12-month cycles, but activity can be measured from the start. Once established, three-year rolling averages should give charities a better indication of trends. ▪

up to complex philanthropic planning meetings will make it impossible for the philanthropic planning officer to complete more than 100 visits per year, assuming no other responsibilities at the charity.

Fundraisers   A full-time fundraiser or gift planner working with tier two prospects in a philanthropic planning model should be completing 110 to 150 prospect visits per year. The goal in each visit category will vary depending upon the makeup of the prospects in the fundraiser's/gift planner's portfolio. For example, if he/she has a relatively new prospect pool with more prospects to qualify, qualification visits will be the top priority. Eventually, after a few years of working with the prospect pool, solicitation and stewardship visits will be the primary activity. Visit activity should result in 40 to 60 fully vetted solicitations/proposals per year. Quality contacts are activities that move a relationship forward, but may not rise to the level of an actual move from one contact purpose level to the next. Most organizations measure these as letters, e-mails, phone calls, and events. In a typical year, a full-time fundraiser/gift planner should expect to have approximately 350 to 500 quality contacts with prospects.

Gift Planning Specialists   For organizations that employ one or more gift planning specialists to serve as an internal resource to other fundraisers, the organization should also be tracking the number of prospect strategy discussions the gift planner has with major gift officers. For a full-time gift planner, this would amount to 125 to 150 strategy sessions each year. Note that the sessions may not be unique, in that the same prospect may be discussed multiple times in a year, or three or four prospects may be discussed in a single session. The key is to document the collaboration so that both the fundraiser and the gift planner can measure it.

The *Monthly Fundraiser Activity Report* in Appendix M tracks the collaborations by fundraiser, so that the gift planner and the fundraiser can see their progress both for the month and year to date. When these strategy sessions are tracked in the database, it is a simple matter to create a report similar to the sample, which can then be shared with all fundraisers each month. The report also tracks the number of new legacy society members and society-qualifying asks. The new members tally is merely to keep track of the overall growth of the society.

The true measure of collaboration and gift planning performance is the number of qualifying asks. The success rate or close rate is less important than the fact that prospects are being asked. An organization should set a goal for each of its fundraisers to ask 10 to 20 percent of his/her assigned prospects to consider a legacy gift each year. If the goal is 20 percent, within five years each fundraiser will have asked 100 percent of his/her prospect pool to consider a legacy gift. While there will be some exceptions, this method of requiring fundraisers to make legacy asks has proven to increase collaboration between gift planning officers and fundraisers to increase the number of legacy commitments and to increase the dollars received in legacy gifts, even though it is tracking activity and not success. As an organization involves volunteers in the solicitation process, a similar tracking effort should be made with them to ensure that gift planning is part of every prospect strategy, not just those pursued by the staff without volunteer assistance.

Gift and Commitment Reports

While the best measure of philanthropic planning success is activity, charities also need a methodology to track gifts for reporting purposes. Chapter 14 and its appendices discuss the different counting methods that charities should consider and how to record gifts based on the counting method selected.

When counting, charities should track results over multiple years, just as was suggested for activity. Multi-year tracking can help identify trends that provide charities with a basis to predict future giving and to determine an average for gifts. For example, if an organizational average for realized bequests over a five-year period is $55,000, then new estate intentions that are reported to an organization could be estimated at $55,000. This allows the fundraiser who cultivated the gift to be rewarded even though the gift will not mature in some cases for many years to come.

In Summary

To build an effective philanthropic planning program based on the model in the *Companion*, charities need to create a plan with performance goals, as well as provide individual fundraisers with appropriate performance goals that incentivize philanthropic planning behavior. The tracking mechanisms inherent to the traditional, transactional fundraising model are antithetical to the philanthropic planning process and will have the fundraisers working at cross purposes. Only when everyone is pulling in the same direction, having adopted the same philosophy, will the philanthropic planning model be successful—which starts with a clearly articulated plan.

14

Policies, Procedures, and Agreements

W hen building a philanthropic planning program, a charity cannot ignore the behind-the-scenes structure and materials that are needed to help the program run efficiently and effectively. Too often, these areas are ignored, which leads to difficulty when donors propose unusual gifts or want special treatment. It is far easier to turn down a multi-million dollar gift of contaminated real estate when the charity has a procedure for evaluating it, rather than waiting until the gift is proposed and there is pressure to accept it due to its overall value. Without policies and procedures, professional advisors will suggest non-traditional assets for gifts and charities may unnecessarily reject them or accept a gift they later regret.

GIFT ACCEPTANCE

Charities should create comprehensive gift acceptance policies and procedures and update them at least every other year. A gift acceptance policy (GAP) should be short, concise, and written in non-legal language so that it is readily reviewed and understood by employees and volunteers of the charity as well as donors. Charities should resist the desire to add gift acceptance procedures to a GAP, it makes the policy unnecessarily long and will require that the governing board review those procedures when updating and approving the policy. Gift acceptance procedures belong in a separate document which is written and maintained by the staff of the charity. It may take a charity 12 to 18 months to rewrite gift acceptance policies and procedures from the ground up and obtain board approval of the policies.

Policies

An effective GAP provides a charity with discipline around both gift acceptance and gift administration. A well-thought-out GAP should:

- Define the assets that are acceptable.
- Establish gift forms that are acceptable.
- Provide for the development of gift acceptance and administration procedures.
- Require the charity's leadership to think through different aspects of accepting gifts without a pending gift to cloud judgment.
- Engage the board and leadership in a discussion of alternative gift forms and assets.
- Educate staff, board, and volunteer leadership about critical issues around certain assets.
- Protect the charity from accepting assets that would unnecessarily subject it to liability or risk.

Drafting a Gift Acceptance Policy　Drafting a GAP is a group effort, including:

- Chief Executive Officer
- Chief Development Officer
- Gift Planning Staff
- Finance Staff
- Legal Advisor
- Board Oversight Committee Chair

In some cases, particularly for smaller charities, all of these positions may not exist. The exact position is less important than including those individuals who will have input into gift acceptance decisions and have the expertise to ensure that the GAP makes sense for the particular charity for which it is being written.

Core Elements   An effective GAP using a donor-centered, philanthropic planning approach will include the following elements:

- *Mission statement*—A statement of the mission of the charity, since all gifts accepted should be in service of the mission.
- *Purpose of the policies*—A statement articulating why the charity has a gift acceptance policy.
- *Responsibility to donors*—A statement of the fundraising approach, ethics, and donor rights adopted by the charity including:
  - Commitment to a donor-centered approach
  - Confidentiality
  - Anonymity
  - Ethical standards
- *Legal considerations*—A detailed grouping describing what the charity will and will not do legally, what services it provides, and when it uses counsel to assist in gift acceptance. Elements include:
  - Compliance
  - Non-endorsement of providers
  - Legal, tax, and financial advice
  - Preparation of legal documents
  - Payment of fees
  - Service as executor
  - Trusteeship
  - Use of counsel
- *Gift acceptance*—The governing board is the only entity that can accept gifts on behalf of a charity. In order for most charities to function, it delegates the ability to accept certain gifts to the staff and allows exceptions to be approved by a gift acceptance committee on which the board is represented. These provisions can be addressed as:
  - *Implementation*—typically delegated to the chief advancement officer.
  - *Approval of exceptions*—typically delegated to the gift acceptance committee.
  - *Gift acceptance committee*—this group should be small, to allow for quick gift decisions on exceptions to the gift acceptance policy. Normally it consists of the chief advancement officer, chief finance officer, and a member of the governing board.

- *Gift acceptance procedures*—the gift acceptance committee typically approves any procedures which require such approval.
- *Gift acceptance alternatives*—a statement that in the donor-centered, philanthropic planning environment, if the charity needs to reject an asset as a gift, it should try to help the donor find another charity which can accept it and share the proceeds.
- *Gift agreements*—a statement that the charity uses gift agreements, whether they are binding or non-binding, and when each type of gift agreement should be utilized.
- *Gift restrictions*—Defines which gifts may be restricted and for what purposes.
- *Types of property*—Defines the assets which are acceptable to the charity with and without gift acceptance committee approval. Elements might include:
  - Cash
  - Securities
  - Life insurance
  - Real property
  - Tangible personal property
  - Other property
- *Structured current gifts*—Defines non-outright gifts of assets that are acceptable to the charity with and without gift acceptance committee approval. Elements might include:
  - Bargain sales
  - Charitable lead trusts
  - IRA charitable rollovers
  - Matching gifts
  - Other structured current gifts
- *Future gifts*—Defines gifts that will mature to the benefit of the charity in the future and when they are acceptable to the charity with and without gift acceptance committee approval. Elements might include:
  - Subject to a payment interest—
    - Charitable gift annuities
    - Charitable remainder trusts/charity as trustee
    - Charitable remainder trusts/charity not trustee
    - Pooled income funds

- Not subject to a payment interest—
  - Gifts by will or living trust
  - Beneficiary designations
  - Retirement plans
  - Life insurance policies
  - Payable on death accounts
- *Donor recognition*—Establishes the parameters for naming, steward-ship, and other donor recognition offered by the charity to donors.
- *Reporting and valuation standards*—Recites the reporting, counting, and valuation standards adopted by the charity.
- *Periodic review*—Establishes the timeframe for periodic and special re-view of the policy.

Appendix N provides a sample gift acceptance policy containing all of these elements.

Approval and Review   Gift acceptance policies need to be approved by the governing board, since only it has the power to accept gifts on behalf of the charity. Charities can get into trouble if there is not a clear set of rules regard-ing who can accept gifts on its behalf, which is why this power is reserved to the governing board and then designated in a GAP to certain staff or volun-teers. Many of the charitable scandals of the last few decades have resulted because someone without authority accepted a gift on behalf of a charity and then put it to personal use. There must be controls in place within the policy (and procedures), to ensure the safety and proper handling of donations.

A GAP needs to be updated about every other year. A provision in the GAP which requires such a review in either even- or odd-numbered years ensures that such an update occurs on a regular basis.

Exceptions   A gift acceptance policy should cover the vast majority of gift situations a charity expects to encounter. This provides fundraisers, volun-teers, and donors with an understanding of those assets that can be accepted immediately and those that will require additional approval. With a clear set of approved gifts, exceptions to the policy will be rare and easily handled by a small gift acceptance committee made up of the chief advancement officer, chief financial officer, and a board representative.

Most donors want to complete gifts quickly, once they decide to move forward. A gift acceptance policy that only pre-approves gifts of cash and appreciated stock will result in a charity only receiving gifts of cash and stock. While this may sound appealing because such gifts are easy to manage and liquidate, it is not in the long-term interest of the charity. The vast majority of assets, with some estimates being over 80 percent, are held by individuals in other forms, such as retirement plans, real estate, life insurance policies, hedge funds, real estate investment trusts (REITs), art, collectibles, and more. Charities that have clear policies regarding acceptance of these alternative or non-traditional assets will find that their donors will make larger gifts using these assets, because it allows them to draw from a different pocket than the one normally used for charitable giving. In the philanthropic planning approach, charities need to offer these alternatives.

Engagement of Outside Professionals   When finalizing a GAP, a charity should have it reviewed by legal counsel. If the charity does not have in-house counsel, then it should hire outside counsel with experience working on charitable gifts. Charitable gifts can be complex legal transactions, and competent advice is always needed.

In addition to qualified counsel, charities should also develop relationships with outside experts with subject-matter expertise for the most common non-cash gifts. Since donors want to complete gifts quickly, if a charity already has relationships with experts in real estate, closely-held businesses, hedge funds, coins, art and other non-cash assets, it will be able to react quickly when approached about a non-traditional asset. This will allow the charity to accept a gift that others may not be able to accommodate and enhance the relationship with the donor.

RETAIN EXPERTS AS A RESOURCE

Since 2009, the History Channel has offered a show called *Pawn Stars* where a parade of individuals comes through the doors at a pawn shop with a wide range of assets, everything from antique guns to video games. The owners of the shop spend their days determining the story behind the item, if it is authentic, and the value. They then make an offer to the seller.

While the gentlemen who own the pawn shop buy and sell every day, for unusual or hard-to-value assets they have a series of experts they rely upon for advice. The experts are knowledgeable on collectibles from toys to antique arms. By having these experts on-call, the *Pawn Stars* can quickly determine the authenticity and value of the assets brought into the shop.

Charities should have similar experts ready when donors approach them about complex assets. It ensures that the needs of the donor are met and protects the charity from risk in the future. And it's a lot of fun.

Procedures

Most charities put in place a basic set of gift acceptance policies, but rarely give thought to formally implementing these policies with written procedures. Because each charity has a unique organizational structure, it is impossible to generate a sample set of gift acceptance procedures. However, there are some general guidelines to follow which will make creating these procedures simple.

Identify Areas That Need Procedures To do so, a charity should start with its GAP. For example, in section II.A of the sample GAP in Appendix N, it discusses that the charity is committed to a donor-centered philanthropic planning approach. Using this responsibility to donors, procedures can be written around how to work with professional advisors. The charity might include a procedure which indicates "Did we include the donor's advisor when sharing information about a gift of real estate?"

Each area of the GAP will have procedures to go with it. For complex outright gifts, those procedures will involve how to use the gift acceptance committee, how the gift should be reviewed, what materials should be reviewed, and more. The most common complex outright gift is real estate and many charities have gift acceptance procedures for accepting this asset that are available on their web sites.

If the charity cannot put together a comprehensive set of procedures, it can put together a procedure each time it is presented with a new type of gift, until the procedures have been fully drafted and formalized.

Use Checklists   Gift acceptance procedures are usually formatted as checklists to create a process for accepting a gift. For example, if a charity is accepting a bequest, it would have a checklist for each step in the estate administration process from the time it is first notified about the donor's death until the final distribution. In addition, there should be checklists to review the accounting statement and the release and refunding bond. Finally, the charity should create sample letters to the executor and family and an administration timeline for taxable and non-taxable estates.

These checklists, whether electronic or paper, will help ensure that each step in the gift administration process is completed.

Define Responsibilities   All gift acceptance procedures should provide clear guidance about who at the charity is responsible for each step in the process. When two different departments are responsible for a single task, no one is. The procedures manual will likely have roles for each of the departments in advancement plus responsibilities for counsel and finance.

GIFT COUNTING AND REPORTING

There has been considerable debate in charitable circles about how charities should count, report, account, value, and recognize/credit charitable gifts. Each has its own purpose, yet reporting five different numbers serves only to confuse both board members and donors and makes fundraising even less transparent.

In the donor-centered, philanthropic planning universe, effective cultivation and stewardship requires clear, fair counting and reporting for all types of charitable gifts. Each charity needs to adopt a set of counting and reporting standards that donors can understand and rely upon.

PPP and CASE Standards

In 2006, the Partnership for Philanthropic Planning (PPP) released revised guidelines for counting and reporting charitable gifts. The guidelines were designed to create consistency in counting and reporting, clarity, transparency, and accountability. They differed from what was then the industry standard Council for Advancement and Support of Education (CASE)

Reporting Standards and Management Guidelines. Since that time, while CASE has not embraced the PPP standards, they have said that the PPP standards are not inconsistent with the CASE standards.

PPP defined counting and reporting as follows: "Counting is the numeric summary of activity, results, and progress toward goals. Reporting is the process of convening to a lay audience clearly and transparently what has happened during a specific timeframe."[1] This contrasted with crediting, which PPP defined as follows: "Crediting is institution specific and represents the way each organization grants recognition to its donors. Such recognition need not stem from any of the factors of counting, accounting, or valuation, although a given organization may use any of these calculations as the basis of its donor recognition policies."[2]

The PPP standards call for a different way of counting and reporting. Rather than lumping all types of gifts together into one fundraising total, PPP divides gifts into three components: Category A: Outright Gifts— usable gifts today or during the reporting period; Category B: Irrevocable Future Gifts—gifts committed today or during the reporting period but not usable by the organization until after the end of the period; and Category C: Revocable Future Gifts—gifts committed today or during the reporting period and not usable by the organization until after the period, but in which the donor retains the right to change the commitment or the charitable beneficiary.

Using the PPP model, donors are given face-value credit for all gifts in all forms, whether the donor retains an interest in the gift or the gift is revocable. However, by using the three categories, it is clear to the donor, outside observers, and the charity exactly what assets are available today, what assets will be available tomorrow, and what assets may or may not be available in the future. This model is fair to all parties involved and delivers the transparency missing from the field. Appendix O includes a sample gift counting and reporting policy summary based on the combined CASE and PPP standards.

Generating Reports

In order to track gifts in the PPP categories, charities need to create new reports that account for the different categories of gifts. Appendix P provides two different sample reports. The first sample reflects gifts in each category by tender type. On the left column, the report shows the gift by category and tender type, with a listing for each donor under the tender type. As the reader moves across the report, there is additional detail for each gift, including the members of the prospect management team, the purpose of the gift, how the gift is structured, the date of gift and the amount. Notice that the gift structure and tender type are *two different fields*. Many charities combine these two categories together on their database, making it impossible to pull complete and transparent reports. For example, if a charity uses a single field and a donor funds a charitable remainder trust with appreciated stock, the charity will not have the ability to record both variables and later pull reports on tender type.

The second report in Appendix P shows gifts by tender type over a five year reporting period. This report lacks the donor-detail of the prior report, but allows a charity to track its total giving in each category for each of the five years, as well as the total giving in each tender type over five years. Over time, this report will help the charity to build an effective pipeline and evaluate whether it is doing enough to share different gift opportunities.

Appendix Q includes two additional reports. They are largely the same as the first group of reports, but instead of reporting based on tender type, they report based on gift structure. It allows a charity to evaluate the type of gift vehicles preferred by its donors in a given year or over a period of time.

Together, this group of reports, coupled with the sample gift counting policy document, provide a charity with an easy and effective way to adopt the PPP and CASE combined standards for gift counting and reporting.

Gift Crediting/Recognition

As noted earlier, gift crediting/recognition is a charity-specific method to recognize donors for their giving. Gift crediting need not be tied to how a charity counts or values gifts, and frequently is not. In the philanthropic planning approach, charities should adopt standards for recognizing gifts which are clear and simple to understand. In most cases, the best approach is to adopt the gift counting standards as the gift crediting standards. This provides donors with one set of numbers and standards to remember and keeps things rather straightforward.

That said, charities should be gracious in granting gift recognition. It costs little to recognize a gift broadly, but can provide wonderful stewardship for the donors so recognized. However the charity should avoid being so generous with recognition that donors begin to manipulate the system to minimize giving and maximize recognition. There are two common exceptions to giving recognition the same way that gifts are counted.

Gifts from Couples

When a couple makes a joint gift, the charity should split the gift, with half being counted for each. For gift recognition, both should be seen as having made the full amount of the combined gift. This is normally done using a soft credit, so that the fundraising totals for counting purposes show the actual amount, and the recognition shows the combined total of their gifts on both records.

Matching Gifts

Many corporations make matching gifts. For each gift their employee makes to a charity, the employer will make an additional gift to the same charity on the employee's behalf. In such cases, the corporation is given gift counting and recognition credit for the gift. But since the gift would not have come to the charity without the employee requesting it and making a gift of his/her own, the employee is normally given soft credit for the corporate gift for gift recognition purposes.

Gift Valuation

In addition to promulgating gift counting standards, PPP has also provided charities with Valuation Standards for Planned Gifts.[3] Last updated in 2009, these standards are designed to help charities reflect the actual value today of a gift, whether it is an outright gift, an irrevocable future gift, or a revocable future gift.

While the PPP Counting and Reporting standards suggested all gifts be recorded at face value in one of the three categories, the valuation standards allow all gifts to be compared to one another apples to apples. This means that all gifts, whether current or future, are valued in today's dollars.

With many charities focused on current gifts only, it is important to have a system of valuation of all types of gifts so that a charity can:

- Estimate the real value of funds raised through its fundraising efforts, including irrevocable and revocable future gifts.
- Compare the relative value of alternative gift forms for the charitable organization.
- Accurately reflect the present value of the ultimate purchasing power of all gifts.
- Permit easy tracking of effectiveness of fundraising programs.
- Allow for research into effectiveness of fundraising across the charitable community.[4]

The PPP Valuation Standards assume that all current gifts are counted in today's dollars, even pledges that can take up to five years to complete. This follows the CASE counting standards, which allow for up to five years to pay any pledge with no discounting.

The PPP Valuation Standards suggest a two-step process to value irrevocable future gifts. The first step is to determine the total future value of the gift at the end of the donor's life expectancy. To make this calculation, the charity or advisor will need to know the payout rate on the future gift (if any), the life expectancy for the payment beneficiary on the gift (or term of the gift if it is a term-of-years gift), and the assumed investment return. Most charities elect to use the Annuity 2000 table adopted by the National Association of Insurance Commissioners to determine life expectancy. The rate of return must be determined by the charity based upon its experience investing charitable gifts. A 6 percent total return with 1 percent expenses, for a net return of 5 percent is conservative but appropriate for this type of calculation at this time. If the investment climate changes, charities should adjust these variables accordingly.

Once the future value of a gift has been determined, the second step is to discount that future value back to present value. The variable used to determine present value is called the discount rate. The discount rate used by the charity should be the amount it expects costs to rise per year during the life of the gift. Many charities use the long-term inflation rate, while educational institutions frequently use the Higher Education Price Index (HEPI)[5] which tracks the major cost centers for those institutions and tends to be slightly higher than inflation.

▨ EXAMPLE   GIFT VALUATION CALCULATION[6]

A 75-year-old male donor with a life expectancy of 13.2 years makes a $10,000 gift to fund a charitable gift annuity paying 6.5 percent per year. The charity expects a net investment return of 5 percent over the life of the gift and uses the long-term inflation rate of 3.4 percent as the discount rate.

Step 1: Determine the total future value

$FV = Gift (1 + Net Return)^{LE} - Payout[((1 + Net Return)^{LE}-1)/Net Return]$

$FV = \$10,000 (1 + .05)^{13.2} - \$650[((1 + .05)^{13.2}-1)/0.05]$

$FV = \$10,000 (1.9041394) - \$650 (0.9041394/0.05)$

$FV = \$19,041.39 - \$11,753.81$

$FV = \$7,287.58$

At the end of 13.2 years, the annuity balance, or total remaining future value is $7,287.58

Step 2: Discount total future value back to present value

$PV = FV/(1 + Discount Rate)^{LE}$

$PV = \$7,287.58/(1 + 0.034)^{13.2}$

$PV = \$7,287.58/1.5547877$

$PV = \$4,687.19$

Current purchasing power of the gift to the charity in today's dollars is $4,687.19.[7] ▨

For revocable future gifts, the calculation is slightly more complicated. In addition to determining the future value and then discounting back to present value, the charity needs to apply a probability factor to estimate the likelihood of receipt of the gift because the donor can revoke or change it at any time. The probability factor will vary depending upon the relationship of the donor to the charity and the charity's overall experience. For example, if a charity has no relationship with the donor, the probability of the gift being realized is much smaller than if the donor is the retiring chair of the board. The PPP Valuation Standards include a chart of assumptions that can be used to calculate the probability of fulfillment.

Charities should always report the values of revocable gifts separately from irrevocable gifts due to the uncertain nature of the commitment, even though it has been discounted to account for revocability.

While the PPP Valuation standards are not the only option for valuing present and future gifts, they are the most comprehensive. When applied over time, they help charities to see the total value of their fundraising programs from all types of revenue in a way that other standards do not.

GIFT AGREEMENTS

Chapter 7 discussed why gift agreements are important in the donor-centered, philanthropic planning context. Gift agreements help to protect the relationship between the donor and the charity by ensuring that the donor's intentions are carried out. They also set the expectations of both parties. Some charities will use a fund agreement to detail the terms of the use of the gift and a separate pledge or intention card to document the actual transfer of assets for the gift. In either case, it is important that when such documentation is required, it is completed carefully and completely.

When Is a Gift Agreement Necessary?

Gift agreements are not required for every gift. If a donor makes a one-time, unrestricted gift, such as an annual fund gift, the formality of a gift agreement would be unnecessary. Ideally the charity would have some documentation from the donor indicating the unrestricted nature of the gift, such as a note in the memo line of the check indicating "Annual Fund." If the donor makes a multi-year, unrestricted commitment, a simple pledge/intention card can replace a more formal gift agreement.

As a general rule, charities should be utilizing gift agreements for all current restricted gifts as well as for all future restricted gifts, for which the donor wants certainty that the funds will be used exactly as intended. For this latter category, this is most common when the donor has named the charity as a beneficiary of a retirement plan or life insurance policy and cannot designate the purpose directly on the beneficiary form. While the Traditionalists may not request or expect a gift agreement, the New Philanthropists will be expecting the charity to have one ready to document the gift.

Binding or Non-Binding?

Each charity must determine for itself, with the help of competent counsel, whether to use binding or non-binding gift agreements for particular gifts. The general preference among charities is to avoid using binding gift agreements, as they tend to put off donors and lack flexibility. Non-binding gift agreements are more commonly referred to as Statements of Intent. Unfortunately, non-binding agreements do have risks associated with them, not the least of which is the lack of enforceability. While the charity may not plan to sue a donor who does not pay, the charity has no claim as a debtor against the donor's estate if the donor passes away while still owing on an outstanding commitment, making it very difficult to collect, even if the donor would have wanted the executor to pay.

There are several situations where a charity might prefer to use a binding gift agreement.

- *Enforceability*—If the donor is making a gift to the charity that the charity would need to enforce, it is wise to use a binding gift agreement. For example, if the charity is building and naming a facility and the donor is providing a significant portion of the funding, the charity needs to have recourse against the donor. The charity would ideally set a figure above which all gift agreements would be binding. It is the amount that if the donor reneged, the charity would be significantly harmed. This amount will be different for each charity.
- *Bonding (collateral for borrowing)*—Large charities with significant outstanding pledges can use the gifts owed to them as collateral for borrowing. If the gift agreements are non-binding, the lender may not be willing to let the charity use the intentions as collateral.
- *Demonstrating the seriousness of the charity's commitment to carry out the Donor's wishes*—In a donor-centered, philanthropic planning approach, a binding gift agreement shows that the charity is as committed to the gift as the donor. Many donors today want to be sure that the charity is bound to use the gift as the donor intends.

If a charity elects to use binding gift agreements, it should still use non-binding statements of intent when:

- *Donor intends to pay off commitment from a donor-advised fund (DAF)*—Donor advised funds are separate legal entities from the donor. The donor cannot bind a DAF to make a gift on his/her behalf. If the donor intends to pay from a DAF, the charity should use a non-binding statement of intent which clearly states that a portion of the gift may be requested by the donor to be paid from a DAF but that the DAF is under no obligation to make such a payment. When faced with a DAF gift, it is in everyone's best interest for the charity to speak directly with the DAF about its policies on gift agreements before executing a gift agreement or statement of intent.

- *Donor may pay commitment from a DAF and personal assets, still unsure*— When the donor is unsure of how he/she will make the payments, a non-binding agreement offers the maximum amount of flexibility. It is better to use a non-binding agreement than to have to fix a binding agreement later.

- *Donor may have commitment paid by others (family members, friends, matching gift company)*—If anyone pays a binding commitment on behalf of a donor, that is relieving the donor of a debt/commitment, which the IRS terms a private inurment. In such cases, the donor would have to declare such a payment as income. To avoid this eventuality, charities should use a non-binding gift agreement if the donor may be paying a portion and raising the rest from family and friends. If the donor is expecting a matching gift, a binding gift agreement can be used, but the donor's commitment needs to be limited to what he/she will pay, with a reference that the donor will submit the gift for matching but the matching company is under no legal obligation to make such a gift.

It is possible in some jurisdictions to create a binding estate agreement. It is simply a binding gift agreement that indicates either a) if the gift has not been paid by the time of the donor's death, it is an obligation of the estate or b) that the gift is to come from the estate and is a legal obligation thereof. In the latter case, the donor still needs to execute a valid estate document leaving assets to the charity.

Some charities prefer to have binding estate commitments on record so that they can count gifts. In a donor-centered philanthropic planning approach, this is exactly the opposite of what a charity should do. Most donors who select an estate gift *want* the flexibility associated with it, which is why they elect this gift form. By asking them to sign a binding estate commitment, charities are no longer meeting the personal planning goals of the donors. If charities adopt the PPP Counting and Reporting Standards, binding gift agreements are not required and donors will feel respected and appreciated.

CASE STUDY	USE OF A BINDING GIFT AGREEMENT IN A CAPITAL CAMPAIGN

While working with Virtua Foundation, Brian and I utilized a binding gift agreement for a couple who wanted to name a part of a new hospital by making a testamentary gift. Their gift was to be paid by life insurance, but would be a debt of their estate if they no longer had their policies in force. They were married with no children and thought this would be a great way for them to make a gift now with future dollars. For valuation purposes, we computed the future value of their gift based on their age and the present value needed for the naming opportunity. —REW

Types of Gift Agreements

Most charities should have several different prototype gift agreements which have been drafted and preapproved by counsel. This allows the charity to move forward quickly when a donor is ready to complete a gift. A pledge card can be used for gifts to the unrestricted endowment, additions to existing funds, and unrestricted gifts generally. The charity should develop gift agreements for gifts to create restricted endowments and gifts for capital projects. There should be binding, non-binding, and estate versions of all gift agreement forms.

Anatomy of the Gift Agreement   Each charity should work with its own legal counsel to draft the different types of prototype gift agreements. As a general rule, gift agreements should contain the following information:

- Heading/Name of agreement or fund
- Names of parties
- Introduction—
  - Information about donors
  - Motivation for gift
  - Intent for gift
  - Impact and outcomes donors hope to achieve through the gift

- Payment schedule
- Valuation of assets used to make the gift
- Legally binding or non-binding
- State law to apply
- Charity's commitment
- Management of the assets used to make the gift
- Saving language-purpose (Cy Pres)
- Morals clause
- Donor recognition
- Execution

Appendix R contains a sample gift agreement incorporating these elements.

Partnering with Finance and Legal Counsel

Gift agreements are a complex area of fundraising. The advancement office should not try to tackle them alone, but should instead work in close contact with both finance and legal counsel. Finance is responsible for allocating funds according to the terms of the gift agreement. If finance does not approve a gift agreement, it should not be executed. Legal counsel reviews all legal documents, and gift agreements should be no exception. The charity can be at substantial risk if it fails to follow donor restrictions on gifts.

Enforcing Gift Agreement Terms   Gift agreements are between the donor and the charity. However, because a gift must be irrevocable to be considered complete, the donor does not retain the right to sue to enforce the terms of the gift. In most jurisdictions, it is up to the attorney general to act to keep charities in compliance with the terms of the agreement. In recent years, courts in some jurisdictions have relaxed this rule, allowing the donor or the family of the donor to sue to get a charity to abide by the donor's wishes.

While the charity will rarely include a provision in the gift agreement that reserves the right of the donor to sue to enforce its terms, legal counsel for the donor should always make this request provided it does not make the gift incomplete for tax purposes. It is a provision that will give the donor much more leverage after the gift is completed should the charity renege on its part of the agreement.

Misuse of Restricted Funds   Misuse of funds can result in civil and criminal penalties against the charity and the individuals who work there. If an employee of the charity approves an inappropriate expenditure from a restricted fund, the employee and the supervisors of the employee can be subject to civil liability. There have been cases in some jurisdictions where employees have been held criminally liable for knowingly misappropriating funds. When in doubt, finance, legal counsel, and advancement should work together to determine if funds can be used for a particular purpose.

Repurposing a Restricted Fund   From time to time, it is no longer possible to use a restricted fund for its intended purpose. In such cases, finance, legal counsel, and advancement should work together to determine next steps.

The most common way to deal with such an issue is to contact the donor (if alive) or the donor's family to amend the agreement by consent. If that is not possible, there are two legal remedies available. The charity can petition for equitable deviation, wherein the court approves changes to the administration of the funds. Alternatively, the charity can submit a cy pres petition through which the court allows changes to the donor's restrictions. Charities should keep in mind that there is always the risk that the court could order the transfer of the funds to another charity which could use the gift according to the donor's restrictions.

To avoid this eventuality, the charity should discuss this possibility with the donor ahead of time and include an alternative use in the gift agreement. If the donor is uncomfortable with an alternative, the charity should include saving or cy pres language in the gift agreement, which allows the charity to repurpose the fund if it is no longer practicable to continue to follow the restrictions.

In Summary

The back office policies, procedures, counting, and gift agreements are the fine gears on the inside of the philanthropic planning watch. They need to be carefully created and monitored to ensure that the donor's goals and objectives are carried out. If a charity fails to attend to these details, it will negatively impact its relationships with current and future donors.

15

Registration

O ver the last several years, states have become much more active regulating the charitable giving industry, which makes up by some estimates, more than 10 percent of the total economy. Many states have passed rules requiring charities to register to solicit, register the names of any fundraising firms/counsel they utilize, register to do business, and register to issue gift annuities. A few states even require charities to register if they plan to serve as trustee of charitable remainder trusts. As charities put their infrastructure in order for philanthropic planning, a key component is compliance with state regulations.

Until recently, many charities have elected to ignore out-of-state regulations and simply comply in their home states. With the release of the new Form 990 from the IRS, charities that raise more than $25,000 will have a much more difficult time avoiding out-of-state regulations. Schedule G, Part I, Question 3 requires charities to list all states where the charity is registered or licensed to solicit funds or has been notified that it is exempt from doing so. This section effectively puts the IRS and states on notice if charities are not in compliance with their rules. Charities need to confer with legal counsel and comply with state regulations in jurisdictions where they solicit gifts or have a presence.

REGISTRATION TO SOLICIT

Registration to solicit is a complex area because each state has unique rules, regulations, exemptions, and fees. If a charity plans to solicit in a state, it should either register there or obtain an exemption. Soliciting in a state includes both targeted mail and electronic solicitations.

Garry Curtis Cannon, JD, and Marc Lee, CFRE, of Affinity Registration Services recommend the following suggestions in their webinar on registering to solicit:

- Register or determine you are exempt before you start fundraising.
- Register in your home state (state of domicile).
- Register in every state where you actively solicit funds, unless you are exempt.
- If you receive very little from a state (less than $250), stop soliciting there so you avoid the registration process.
- If you accept any gifts from Florida or New York, register there (unless you are exempt), since accepting any gift from those states requires registration.
- Follow the rules of each state for registration, reporting, and documentation.
- Renew your registration according to the rules of each state.[1]

Registration Requirements

Rules and fees regarding registration will vary from state to state. As of this printing, 38 states accept the Unified Registration Form, but each has its own unique requirements and supplemental materials. The majority of states require the following documents in order to register:

- Annual Registration Statement
- Audited Financial Statements
- Form 990

For an initial registration, most states will also require:

- Articles of Incorporation
- Bylaws
- IRS Determination Letter

Registration requirements are always changing. In most states, religious organizations are exempt from registration requirements, but each state defines religious organization differently. In some states, education and political organizations are exempt.[2] For the most up-to-date information on registration and exemption requirements, visit www.nasconet.org, www.multistatefiling.org, or www.fundraisingregistration.com.

Due to the complexity of this process, several vendors have emerged to assist charities with the registration process.[3]

- Affinity Fundraising Registration—www.fundraisingregistration.com
- Charitable Registry—www.charitableregistry.com
- Copilevitz & Canter—www.cckc-law.com
- Martignetti Planned Giving Advisors—www.mpgadv.com
- Montgomery, McCracken, Walker & Rhoads, LLP—www.mmwr .com/home/services/business/nonprofit-organizations/charity-reg-istration-service/default.aspx
- Perlman & Perlman—www.perlmanandperlman.com
- Webster, Chamberlain & Bean—www.wc-b.com

Whether a charity decides to register on its own or use outside help, it is important to assign one person at the charity to be responsible for keeping registrations current. The process for registering should be included in the gift procedures document discussed in Chapter 14.

CHARITABLE GIFT ANNUITY REGISTRATION

Charitable gift annuities are a significant component of the gift planning effort of many charities. They are a valuable tool that can be used to help meet a wide range of personal planning objectives for donors while also supporting the charities of their choice. Gift annuities are a highly regulated gift planning tool. As with registration to solicit, each state has its own rules and regulations regarding what a charity must do in order to qualify to solicit and issue gift annuities. These rules should be reviewed by legal counsel and finance in addition to advancement.

There are four different approaches used by the states regarding gift annuity registration including:

- *Initial notification/registration and annual filing*—The charity must notify the state that it plans to solicit and issue gift annuities to residents of the state, comply with any state-specific regulations on gift annuities (including investment restrictions, required reserve amounts, maximum gift annuity rates, and special language in gift annuity agreements) and file annual statements about its gift annuity program.

- *Initial notification/registration*—The charity must notify the state that it plans to solicit and issue gift annuities to residents of the state and comply with any state-specific regulations on gift annuities.
- *Certain criteria, but no registration or annual filing*—The charity must comply with any state-specific regulations on gift annuities, but does not have to notify the state that it will be issuing gift annuities in that state.
- *State statutes are silent on gift annuities*—Some states have not passed regulations on gift annuities. The charity needs to follow the rules of its home state (state of domicile) when issuing gift annuities to residents of silent states.

As gift annuity registration rules are constantly changing, it is important for the charity to name one person or office that will be responsible for maintaining current gift annuity registrations and to document its procedures.

For the most current state-specific information, visit www.acga-web.org, the web site for the American Council on Gift Annuities (ACGA). The ACGA not only keeps an up-to-date database of state regulations, it is also the organization that provides the recommended maximum rates which comply with the laws of all the states. If an organization plans to issue gift annuities, it should become a sponsor of the ACGA. For a modest fee, membership ensures that the charity will have the latest information on gift annuity rates and that the ACGA can continue to provide these suggested rates going forward.

For charities issuing gift annuities nationally, the registration requirements can be quite onerous, particularly for investing gift annuity reserve funds. Several vendors have emerged to assist with the registration process including:[4]

- PG Calc—www.pgcalc.com
- Crescendo—www.crescendointeractive.com
- Planned Giving Resources—www.pgresources.com

Due to the cost and difficulty of staying current with gift annuity registration, as well as the longevity and investment risk associated with issuing just a handful of gift annuities, small- and mid-size organizations may want to avoid registration by using a third-party charity to issue gift annuities for their benefit. The gift annuity contract is actually between the third-party charity and the donor, with the original charity simply receiving the funds when the gift annuity matures. The most common third-party charity is the local or regional community foundation, and for Jewish charities it is the local Federation. Typically the community foundation will provide the gift annuity and upon the donor's death, will set up a permanent fund at the community foundation for the benefit of the original charity. If the original charity does not want to create a permanent fund, it might consider gift annuities through Comerica Foundation—www.comerica.com or Dechomai Foundation—www.dechomai.org.[5] These third-party charities will return the remaining funds or residuum to the original charity when the gift annuity matures. Any decision to issue gift annuities through a third-party charity should be well vetted internally and approved by the governing board.

REGISTRATION TO DO BUSINESS

As charities register to solicit or to issue charitable gift annuities, they may discover that before they can complete these registrations, some states also require them to register to do business.

Requirements for registration to do business will vary by state. Unlike charitable registration to solicit, however, the process in each state is more straightforward because most businesses must register to do business. Many states will require the charity to have a bona-fide office or an agent for service of process in order to register. This is an address where those who want to sue the charity can serve legal papers. If the charity does not have a bona-fide office, there are several firms which for a monthly fee will serve as the charity's agent for service of process purposes.

The advancement office of the charity may want to check with legal counsel and the finance office prior to registering to do business. Not only is the process potentially costly, it may open the charity to having to defend lawsuits in far away jurisdictions outside of the fundraising context.

DUE DILIGENCE BY ADVISORS

With the increase in regulation, professional advisors should ensure that charitable gifts by their philanthropist clients go to charities that have stayed in compliance and retained their non-profit status or they take the risk that tax deductions may be disallowed for gifts to non-qualifying charities. While most charities soliciting funds are in good standing and have their tax-exempt status intact, more than 275,000 charities lost that status in 2011.

Under the Pension Protection Act of 2006, any non-profit that was required to file an annual information return such as a Form 990, 990-N, 990-EZ, or 990-PF, but failed to do so for three or more consecutive years would have its tax-exempt status revoked. In 2011, the IRS published a list of more than 275,000 charities that had failed to meet this requirement and for which it had revoked their tax-exempt status.

David Wheeler Newman, an attorney at Mitchell, Silverberg & Knupp, suggests that when making substantial charitable gifts, philanthropists or their advisors should check IRS Publication 78 to determine if the charity is, in fact, a public charity under IRS guidelines and then visit the IRS web site to confirm that the tax-exempt status of the recipient organization has not been revoked under the Pension Protection Act. Newman encourages the philanthropist or his/her advisors to memorialize this due diligence in the event the gift is later challenged by the IRS.[6]

In Summary

Charitable giving is a significant industry in the United States and regulated individually by the states. Charities pursuing a philanthropic planning approach need to adhere to the regulations in their home state and in other states where they do business, solicit, or issue gift annuities. There must be someone at the charity who is responsible for ensuring that these registrations are completed and kept up to date, or the charity puts itself and its philanthropists at risk.

Epilogue

We started our conversation about philanthropic planning by exploring time and the progress of fundraising over time. Philanthropic planning represents the next step in the natural evolution of fundraising. It is a more effective and efficient way to raise funds from the emerging New Philanthropists, designed to meet their personal planning needs, pass their values to future generations, and help them create meaningful legacies for their families, their communities, and the charities they support. It requires a true partnership among donors, advisors, and fundraisers. It is focused on the impact and outcomes created when extraordinary people are matched with exceptional missions to truly make a meaningful difference. We are excited to be working with philanthropists, advisors, and fundraisers at this seminal time.

We divided the *Companion* into four parts to provide a roadmap for advisors and fundraisers to work collaboratively with donors to make them philanthropists. In *The Emergence of Philanthropic Planning*, we laid the groundwork for the rest of the *Companion*, discussing why there was a need for fundraising to evolve to a philanthropic model. To do so, we shared information about generational cohorts, defined the New Philanthropists and introduced the Philanthropic Planning Pyramid of donors, illustrating the four tiers of prospects and how each should be approached. We then explained the new roles for fundraisers, professional advisors, board members, and volunteers when working with these New Philanthropists.

The second part of the book, *Working with Philanthropists*, outlined how charities, professional advisors, and philanthropists can work collaboratively in an integrated, donor-centered, values-based, philanthropic planning approach to meet the charitable and personal planning objectives of the top 10 percent of all philanthropists—what have commonly been referred to as principal and major gift prospects. It is truly the heart of the book, providing guidance for both charities and advisors on building a philanthropic planning method, based on some of the best practices in this emerging model. For most fundraisers and professional advisors, the Philanthropic Planning methodology represents a fundamental shift in approach from the transactional model used with Traditionalists for the last 40 years.

In *Marketing to Prospects and Those Interested in the Mission*, the third part of the book, we provided detailed information, strategies, and plans for how charities should approach the remaining two tiers of the Philanthropic Planning Pyramid. This donor-centered, moves management system of gift planning outreach to the loyal donors and those with an interest in the mission acknowledges that we would like to give all donors the same level of attention and support that we provide to our top philanthropists, but that we need to make choices in order to achieve the mission of the charity. But for those individuals who raise their hands and express interest, they immediately move up to level two of the pyramid, even if their wealth indicators may dictate otherwise.

Within the final section, *Program Infrastructure*, we provided the architecture to charities for building a donor-centered gift planning component as an integrated part of their fundraising effort. Without these key elements, the gift planning effort, and ultimately the philanthropic planning effort, will fail. Successful fundraising programs need to have a strong infrastructure to support this fundraising approach.

WHAT DO I DO NEXT?

Having read the *Companion*, the logical question to ask yourself is "What do I do next?" This is an incredibly hard question to answer, because each charity and each professional advisor take unique approaches to how they work with philanthropists. But when in doubt, start at the beginning.

We set up the *Companion* in a logical order to allow you to work from the front to the back to build your own model, based on the needs of your practice, your donors, and/or your charity. The first step is to develop an organizational recognition and commitment to the concept of philanthropic planning. Consider sharing a copy of the *Companion* with decision-makers, board members, and others working with you, even potential philanthropists themselves. It provides common ground for a discussion about how your firm or organization will pursue philanthropic planning going forward. Use Chapters 1 and 2 to guide your understanding of the new world we live in and how you need to adapt your work to continue to be effective in that new world.

With the important players acknowledging the need to adopt a philanthropic planning approach, use the tools in Chapter 3 to clearly define and identify the best prospects for this model. These are individuals who are in the top 10 percent financially who are also loyal and charitably minded. They are the exact audience that traditional planning and fundraising models are failing at present. They believe in the mission, but tend not to give to their full potential. Place these prospects in the top two tiers of the Philanthropic Planning Pyramid. Then identify the balance of the loyals and place them in the third and fourth tiers of the pyramid. For advisors, these are the individuals who will never be huge accounts, but they may be some of your well-liked clients, as they have a passion for charitable giving. For charities, these will still be significant and meaningful donors, but likely will not get the same level of attention that you provide to tiers one and two.

Now that you have identified the need and the right prospects, you need to document why you will pursue this approach to ensure institutional commitment for the long-term. Philanthropic planning takes time, and changes in board or staff leadership can significantly impact whether the program is continued. To ensure your advisory firm or your charity stays on course, draft an internal case (for charities) or a business model/vision statement (for professional advisors), which outlines why you are adopting this approach and how it will create more meaningful and significant philanthropic opportunities. Appendix B provides a sample case to utilize in this process.

The next step in the process is to find ways for everyone to work together. Philanthropic planning is truly a collaborative process with advisors, philanthropists, the families of philanthropists, and charities all involved and at the table, according to the philanthropic planning model:

$$\frac{\text{Gift Planner} + \text{Professional Advisors} + \text{Philanthropic Planning}}{\text{Donor with Charitable Intent}} = \text{Philanthropy}$$

For the process to work, everyone has to check their preconceived notions at the door and commit to achieving goals that meet the needs of the donor, the donor's family, and the charities, while working within the confines of the law to make the plan as tax efficient as possible. Sometimes tax benefits will be sacrificed to achieve the philanthropists' goals. Other times the amount for charity will be a touch more or less to meet a family goal. Unlike a traditional negotiation, when the best deal makes everyone around the table a little uncomfortable because they did not get everything they wanted, philanthropic planning should strive to create a balance that makes everyone feel that the goals of the philanthropist have been achieved for today and for the long term.

With these important preliminaries out of the way, advisors and charities can look to build their own philanthropic planning programs. Start with the top 1 percent of loyal philanthropists, those of means who have inclination to support one or more charities in a significant way. They are tier one prospects and will provide the greatest results for your effort. Not every prospect approached about philanthropic planning will be interested, but for those who are, it is an opportunity to make a lasting difference. If you have so many prospects that you never move on to the other steps, fantastic! But most advisors and charities have prospects at all four levels of the Philanthropic Planning Pyramid.

Build a program for tier one prospects based on the best practices outlined in Chapter 6. While each program will be unique, it should include a process which defines values, explores the meaning of wealth, considers an appropriate financial inheritance, encourages the business of being a family, fosters communication, planning, and collaboration, and is based on charitable intent. With these core elements, families can discuss their values and personal planning objectives and integrate them with their philanthropy into truly unique solutions. Just remember that once a plan is in place and implemented, the work is just beginning. Proactive, concierge-level stewardship is required to ensure that philanthropists stay with the plan and their support is secure.

Once the top 1 percent have been addressed, charities and advisors can move to the next 9 percent or tier two prospects. These are individuals who may not be able or willing to make principal gifts today, but we want to give them individualized attention to help them meet personal planning objectives while being charitable. For prospects at this level, charities and advisors need to build a moves management (charities) or sales process (advisors) that helps to move them through levels of engagement over time and build meaningful relationships. These relationships allow advisors and charities to identify the personal planning needs and illustrate how individuals can provide for themselves, their families, and their futures while also supporting the charities they love.

After meeting the needs of tiers one and two, the roles of charities and advisors diverge somewhat. Advisors usually do not personally handle individuals in tiers three and four unless the individual reaches out to the advisor. Charities, on the other hand, rely quite heavily on annual support from tiers three and four to help balance their budgets, staff their events, and for a wide range of other forms of volunteer support. These groups warrant charitable attention and serve an important place in the programs of charities. Unfortunately, with limited resources, it is difficult for charities to provide the same level of service as they provide to tiers one and two, which provide such a significant portion of the gift revenue for charities.

To meet this need in a less staff-intensive way, Chapters 8 through 12 provide an outreach and stewardship model for tiers three and four. We suggest that you build this model on the same moves management platform developed for tier two prospects (defined in Chapter 7) but without the same level of personal interaction. Keep in mind that even though it may look more like a traditional fundraising program than a philanthropic planning effort, it needs to retain philanthropic planning elements throughout. This will help to maximize effectiveness for the New Philanthropists going forward.

Finally, after building outreach and relationship programs for all four tiers of prospects, charities need to build an effective infrastructure to support the gifts that will result from these efforts. A failure to build infrastructure will ensure that the program will not be sustainable for the long term—and since sustainability is one of the key elements required by the New Philanthropists—charities ignore it at their peril. Appendices N through R provide many of the tools required to build the necessary infrastructure.

START TODAY!

Philanthropy has been defined as the voluntary action for the public good, and philanthropic planning is a means to that end—a way to make the action more efficient and the good more lasting. The tools and techniques of planned giving are part of the effort, but philanthropic planning is much more than a gift annuity contract or a testamentary charitable remainder trust. It is all about putting in the time and effort to explore all those aspects of the wishes of the philanthropist and how their goals can be realized. Working together, donors and their advisors use all the tools at their disposal to carry vision and values into the future. Those tools come from the worlds of estate and financial planning, charitable giving, psychology and family counseling, and many other specialized fields. When they intersect to enlarge a donor's legacy, the result is philanthropic planning. It is a wonderful, exciting process that you should start to pursue today.

Rewards of Philanthropic Planning

Perhaps one of the best rewards that any of us experience is the pleasure to meet some of the most amazing people through philanthropy. We both were fortunate to have met one of the stars of the twentieth century— Dorothy Young. She lived the fullest of lives. She had answered an ad in the show business paper *Variety* that said "Girl dancer wanted for Broadway show and tour of the United States." She loved to dance so she auditioned among 150 hopefuls and was chosen to perform in her first show on December 14, 1925, at the Shubert Theater in New York City with Houdini! As the "Radio girl," Dorothy performed with Harry Houdini and later continued her career on Broadway. She traveled around the world as part of a dance team and then studied art and oil painting.[1] Years later, she settled in Ocean Grove, New Jersey, where she continued to be active in support of Jersey Shore University Medical Center and Drew University. As a donor she was able to name the chapel at the hospital and to endow the Arts Building at Drew. She had enjoyed life and wanted to share her riches with others. As the last surviving member of Houdini's act, Dorothy passed away just shy of her 104th birthday, yet her legacy lives through her philanthropy.

There are literally thousands of stories that we can share about philanthropists who have made a difference locally and globally, just in our practice of philanthropic planning. We hope that you will embrace the opportunity to work with philanthropists in this way and truly make a difference in their lives, the lives of their families, and the charities which they support.

It Is Up to You

Bring who you are into what you do and who you represent. While writing the *Companion*, we often discussed our shared value system, which could be traced back to both sharing a generational cohort (we are both from Generation X) and we are both Eagle Scouts. We were brought up learning values and goal setting that continue to guide us to this day. Like a compass, trustworthy, loyal, helpful, courteous, and kind point the way in the backs of our minds as we interact with colleagues and those that we assist. We all have a unique set of values and beliefs that along with our knowledge and experiences contribute to who we are. When you couple that with a passion for representing an organization with a mission that is admired and appreciated by donors who have an inclination to give, all is present to contribute and support the process of philanthropic planning.

The late David J. Schwartz in his famous book, *The Magic of Thinking Big*, said that "Big thinkers are specialists in creating positive, forward-looking optimistic pictures in their own minds and in the minds of others."[2] To think big, you must use words and phrases that produce big, positive mental images. The population of high-net-worth individuals and ultra-high-net-worth individuals is growing. They want to be philanthropic if charities and advisors can share the vision of what can be achieved, they will invest and transform charitable organizations. What picture can you paint to show to the philanthropists that you meet? How can you engage other fundraisers and advisors to become allies in helping these philanthropists—many of the same people that you also know—to spend the time to plan? Setting goals and thinking big will drive you to success! Philanthropic planning can be the vehicle to get you there.

Will this new process take time to implement and catch on? Of course. But as time passes and the New Philanthropists become dominant, a new, donor-centered, philanthropic planning paradigm will emerge for fund-raising. By building your practice with the craftsmanship of a fine watch, you will have a philanthropic planning program that can meet the needs of philanthropists and change the world, one donor at a time. We wish you much success as you build your program. It is up to you.

Appendices

Sample Internal Case for Gift Planning—Le Moyne College

STATEMENT OF PURPOSE, MISSION, AND HISTORY

Le Moyne College is a diverse learning community that strives for academic excellence in the Catholic and Jesuit tradition through its comprehensive programs rooted in the liberal arts and sciences. Its emphasis is on education of the whole person and on the search for meaning and value as integral parts of the intellectual life. Le Moyne College seeks to prepare its students for leadership and service in their personal and professional lives to promote a more just society.

Founded in 1946 by the Society of Jesus, Le Moyne is one of only 28 Jesuit colleges and universities nationwide. Today it has grown to include more than 30 undergraduate programs of study and four graduate programs, and the 470-year-old Jesuit tradition upon which it was founded continues to thrive. The College's commitment to the principle of care for the individual guarantees that students are recognized and supported for who they are—and who they have the potential to become. What's more, the College develops graduates who have learned to think in complex ways, and to apply the rich heritage in human knowledge to tackle contemporary challenges with intelligence and empathy.

DONOR-CENTERED GIFT PLANNING

Donor-centered gift planning is a powerful way for individuals to give back to the College, while also carefully planning for their own futures. Gift planning promotes legacy gifts (also known as planned or deferred gifts) which are gifts constructed by donors to meet their personal planning needs for today and tomorrow, generally benefitting the College in the future. Legacy gifts usually take two forms, revocable and irrevocable. Revocable legacy gifts allow donors to make commitments now but reserve the right to alter their plans, while irrevocable legacy gifts are binding commitments that provide for the College in the future. Examples of revocable legacy gifts include naming the College the beneficiary of a will, living trust, or life insurance policy, and examples of irrevocable legacy gifts include charitable gift annuities, pooled income funds, and some charitable remainder trusts.

THE ROLE OF LEGACY GIFTS IN BUILDING ENDOWMENTS

The majority of legacy gifts are designated for endowments— organizational funds that are not wholly expendable on a current basis. These gifts provide permanent income for the College based upon a pre-determined spending rate.

In November 2008, Le Moyne received a truly transformative legacy gift of $50 million from the estate of Robert and Catherine McDevitt, the effects of which will be seen for generations to come. The McDevitts' gift was inspired by their deep belief in Jesuit education, and will benefit four areas of particular importance to them: physics, computer science, religious studies, and information processing. The McDevitts' generosity speaks volumes about their faith in Le Moyne, and the esteem in which they held Jesuit education.

Another recent legacy gift is the generous $1 million endowment from Francis and Marguerite Sanzone to establish the Sanzone Center for Catholic Studies and Theological Reflection. The center sponsors lectures, academic courses, and other events, drawing people from across campus and the greater Syracuse community. In conjunction with Le Moyne's Center for Continuing Education and the Roman Catholic Diocese of Syracuse, the Sanzone Center offers a certificate program in pastoral ministry, which helps prepare lay parish ministers for their duties. In addition, the center offers students the opportunity to engage in theological reflection on their volunteer service experience, whether through service trips abroad or local volunteer work.

Legacy gifts come from donors of varying means, many more modest than one would suspect. Le Moyne recently received an unrestricted $250,000 estate gift from Josephine Eagan who was a nursing student from 1951-1952. An exceptional student who transferred from Boston College, Josephine embraced her Jesuit education and as a result, her gift will be part of building a state-of-the-art science complex for the benefit of future generations of students.

Each of these gifts illustrates one of the important ways that Le Moyne uses endowments, to fund and pursue new programs that it could not otherwise offer due to limited financial resources.

Other important endowments in Le Moyne's history include the $5 million James Endowment, made by John and Marie "Pidge" James, both members of the class of 1966, to kick off the public portion of the College's Achieving New Heights campaign, and the $2.2 million Lanigan Endowment used to fund the Julia and Thomas Lanigan '60 Distinguished Visiting Chair in Science, Medicine, and Ethics at Le Moyne College. These gifts illustrate the second way that Le Moyne uses endowments, to help ensure the long-term future and viability of the College.

There are no more important gifts for donors who believe in our mission, to prepare young men and women to lead and serve their communities. Without these types of funds, Le Moyne would have to rely solely on tuition and current gifts, both of which can drop dramatically when the economy is uncertain. Properly designed, constructed, managed, and stewarded endowments strengthen the long-term well being of the College by assuring a base of support. Most importantly, though, they make both an immediate impact on the College and allow us to pursue our mission.

Le Moyne is committed to wisely managing its resources in the long term through thoughtful strategic planning and investing in programming, staff, and facilities, as well as by remaining true to its core values as a Catholic, Jesuit College. Our unique mission is our most valuable asset, and distinguishes us from other institutions of higher education. Legacy gifts and the endowments they fund are an integral part in sustaining and enhancing this mission.

Gift Planning Will Help Fund Institutional Priorities Today and Tomorrow

Le Moyne's highest priority will continue to be to educate young men and women in the Catholic and Jesuit tradition, preparing them for lives of leadership and service. Our graduates will be well versed in multiple areas, with a deep appreciation of the humanities, arts, and sciences. As citizens of the world, Le Moyne alumni will show reverence and appreciation for different cultures, and will work toward the promotion of social justice. Legacy gifts of the past help to support today's priorities, and legacy gifts set up today will support our priorities of tomorrow. Of equal importance, donors who set up legacy gifts double the amount of their annual support for Le Moyne because they are more engaged in our mission. Legacy donors make it possible for our graduates to reach their goals. That includes alumni like Gabriel Bol Deng '07, a native of Sudan who aspires to be a teacher and could not have attended Le Moyne without support from our scholarship endowment.

Wanting to give back to his home community in the same way, Gabriel recently spearheaded the effort to raise funds to construct a school in his native village, and recently broke ground on the project. With support from legacy gifts, Le Moyne will continue to strive to attract outstanding students and faculty, and to provide financial aid to ensure that deserving, talented individuals are not prevented from receiving a Le Moyne education because they cannot afford it.

Le Moyne Is Ready for a Robust Gift Planning Effort

Le Moyne has now been in existence for a sufficient time to begin to see the benefits of legacy gifts. The $50 million McDevitt estate gift is an extraordinary example of the power of gift planning. We have identified a wide range of alumni and friends who would use legacy gifts to express their passion for our mission. Some of these loyal individuals cannot make significant gifts during their lifetimes because they depend upon the income from these resources to meet their daily needs. However, when they die, they can part with the underlying principal through a legacy gift. Others have already supported Le Moyne in a significant and meaningful way and will use gift planning and legacy gifts as a capstone to their involvement. Le Moyne cannot afford to miss the opportunity to ask these individuals to support the College using legacy gifts.

Le Moyne Has Invested in a Formal Gift Planning Program

In order to maintain this incredible momentum, the College must invest in its fledgling gift planning program. It will enable the College to meet the goals established during the OneLeMoyne process. Those goals include proudly expressing the College's Jesuit heritage and exposing our students to a global curriculum, vibrant campus life, and the opportunity to be involved in civic projects. A robust gift planning program will allow the College not only to remain competitive within the field of higher education, but also to reach new levels of academic excellence and to enhance its reputation nationally and internationally.

Sample Internal Case for Donor-Centered Philanthropic Planning

GPD ACADEMY (FICTIONAL TEMPLATE)

STATEMENT OF PURPOSE, MISSION, AND HISTORY

Founded in 1898, GPD Academy (the "Academy") is an independent school located in the heart of Boston, and a leader in preparing students for higher education. The Academy integrates rigorous classroom studies with experiential learning opportunities—to prepare students for the rigors of top-flight colleges and universities and a lifetime of achievement. Under the able leadership of Head Master Christian James, the Academy has grown dramatically in the last 20 years, adding 300 additional students, 2 new buildings, and updated labs and athletic facilities. At the same time, the Academy has maintained small class sizes and added many nationally known faculty. The original funding for the Academy was provided by a gift under the will of Gavin P. Darcy, an immigrant who felt that too often education focused on books and not enough on experience. His vision for the school remains our focus today, with both academic and practical education required of every student.

WHAT IS DONOR-CENTERED PHILANTHROPIC PLANNING?

Philanthropic planning is a powerful and meaningful way for individuals to give to the Academy to ensure our long-term future, while also meeting personal planning objectives.

Donor-centered philanthropy is an emerging model for raising funds. Instead of asking what donors can do for the Academy, it asks what donors need to accomplish for themselves, their families, and their futures using a values-based approach. It seeks out what is really important to them in their lives. It then asks how the Academy and other charities they support can be integrated into their tax, estate, and financial planning to help meet these goals.

Legacy gifts (also called planned gifts, future gifts, or deferred gifts) are constructed in the present by donors, but usually do not benefit the Academy until some future date. These gifts frequently constitute core components in the philanthropic planning process, because they provide the mechanism for our donors to meet their personal planning goals while also supporting the Academy. Legacy gifts generally take two forms, revocable and irrevocable. Revocable legacy gifts allow donors to make commitments now but reserve the right to alter their plans up until death. The most common types of revocable legacy gifts include naming the Academy as the beneficiary of a will, living trust, life insurance policy, payable on death account, pension plan, or retirement account. Irrevocable legacy gifts are binding commitments now that provide for the Academy in the future. Most often they take the form of life-income gifts including charitable gift annuities, pooled income funds, and charitable remainder trusts.

The tools of donor-centered philanthropic planning provide donors with the ability to meet both their personal planning objectives and their philanthropic goals while passing their values to future generations, the most meaningful and lasting legacy of all.

The Important Roles of Endowments at the Academy

In order to maximize impact and long-term outcomes, the majority of legacy gifts are designated for endowments. Endowment funds are invested to provide future cash flow for the Academy. Some endowments provide the net-income earned by the fund each year, while others use a trustee-determined draw rate. The most famous endowment gift came from our founder Gavin P. Darcy. His estate gift of $400,000 provided that $200,000 should be used to create the school and an additional $200,000 should be used to endow its operations. The Academy recently received a gift of

$5 million from the estate of Bob and Jane Fellows, the effects of which will be seen for generations to come. The Fellows gift was inspired by their deep belief in experiential learning and will completely endow the hands-on learning component of our educational program. These gifts illustrate one of two important ways that the Academy uses endowments, to ensure its long-term future and viability. There are no more important gifts, as without these gifts the Academy would have to rely solely on tuition and current gifts, both of which can drop dramatically when the economy is uncertain.

In 1980, Yolanda Seri used a current gift to create the Seri Endowment for Writing, which paid to create our *Writer-In-Residence* Program. When she passed on last year, we received the proceeds of her retirement plan, worth more than $2 million, which were added to the endowment to ensure this program for the future. This type of gift illustrates the second use of endowments, to fund and pursue new programs that we could not otherwise offer due to limited financial resources. Without the Seri Endowment, Justine Bellini '89 would likely not have pursued a literary career and written her best-selling novel, *Our Own Worst Enemy*.

Properly designed, constructed, managed, and stewarded endowments strengthen the long-term well being of the Academy by assuring a base of support. More importantly, they provide the means for our donors to impact future generations of Academy students who will change the world.

WHY SHOULD THE ACADEMY COMMENCE A PHILANTHROPIC PLANNING PROGRAM NOW?

For the last 40 years, the Academy has received the majority of its gifts from donors who came of age during the Depression, World War II, and the period just after the war. Those donors had an intrinsic faith in our ability to utilize their gifts where the need was greatest, which stemmed from the time they were raised. They had witnessed the challenges faced by communities from difficult economic times and were investors in the social fabric required, particularly education, to give kids in Boston the type of education we offer.

This year the oldest of the Baby Boomers have reached retirement years. The Boomers, and the generations that follow, were raised in fundamentally different times. They do not trust charities like the generations that came before. They want to see the impact of their gifts and hope that their gifts will create long-term outcomes. They also want to be much more involved in their gifts than the prior generations. Most importantly, this new generation of donors, which Brian Sagrestano and Robert Wahlers refer to as the *New Philanthropists*, want to plan comprehensively. They want to integrate their philanthropy into their overall tax, estate, and financial planning so that they can pass their values, as well as their wealth, to the charities and family members they have grown with over their lifetimes. We need to adopt a philanthropic planning approach to appeal to these New Philanthropists.

WE ARE READY

The Board of Trustees, together with the President, recently completed a five-year strategic plan. To implement the plan, the Academy will need to increase current revenue as well as endowment. With clearly articulated immediate and long-term goals, we are prepared to share with prospects the impact they can have today and the outcomes they can create for tomorrow. We have a robust group of regular consistent donors of means, the type of people who are the most likely to consider philanthropic planning. The Academy is committed to a long-term approach, with endowment and gift policies that ensure confidentiality and that donor' wishes will be fulfilled. We have developed a stewardship program to share successes with donors and their families, illustrating the immediate impact and long-term outcomes created by their gifts. The President has committed resources to building a robust philanthropic program, designating Katherine Pitt, Vice President of Advancement, and Elizabeth Green, Director of Development, to lead our philanthropic planning effort.

Most importantly, we have a compelling mission, to help deserving kids from our communities to reach their full potential through classroom and experiential learning. A student like Barry Goldberg '74, who received a full scholarship to come here, but now provides scholarships to needy kids from his old neighborhood. Or a student like Debra Johnston '88, who later came back to run the writing center. GPD Academy alumni are changing Boston and the world, and future gifts will allow us to educate the next great generation of Academy alumni.

Typical Objections to Qualifying Visits

1. I am too busy right now to talk about Your Charity, I'll just send a check.

   Type of Objection: Lack of Time

   Suggested Response: Is there a better time in the coming weeks when I might call you again for a visit?

2. Can't you just send the materials?

   Type of Objection: Indifference

   Suggested Response: I promise not to take more than an hour of your time. It is helpful when I can expand upon the printed brochure and answer your questions.

3. I'm very committed to other charities right now.

   Type of Objection: Indifference/Personal Circumstances

   Suggested Response: I am pleased that you are so charitably minded. While now may not be the right time to make a gift to support our mission, I would still welcome the chance to meet with you and share a bit more about it.

4. My spouse makes the giving decisions.

   Type of Objection: Personal Circumstances/Indifference

   Suggested Response: Perhaps we could arrange a time for me to meet with you and your spouse together?

5. I'm unhappy with the education/services Your Charity is providing. OR Your Charity doesn't do enough for those it is supposed to serve.

   Type of Objection: Effectiveness

   Suggested Response: You are clearly passionate about our mission, but have concerns about how effective we are in achieving our goals. If you would agree to meet, I will bring some materials to illustrate how we approach the mission and would welcome your thoughts and feedback on how we can be more effective delivering on our mission.

6. I make an annual gift every year; I don't need to see you.

   Type of Objection: Lack of Time

   Suggested Response: Thank you for your annual gift. It makes a world of difference for Our Charity. I'd like to share with you the impact your gifts have had and share our future direction for your feedback and ideas.

7. I have several other large pledges that I'm paying off at this time.

   Type of Objection: Personal Circumstances

   Suggested Response: It is wonderful that you have been so generous to charities. The purpose of our meeting would not be to ask you for a gift but to share information about our mission and for us to learn more about what in our mission is of interest to you.

8. I need to conserve my assets for the future.

   Type of Objection: Personal Circumstances

   Suggested Response: I understand completely. When we work with individuals, we always want to be sure that your needs and the needs of your family are addressed before you consider the needs of Our Charity. The purpose of my visit is only to share information about our mission and learn more about what you might be interested in, I won't be asking you for a gift.

9. There are other charities I support who have a greater need than Your Charity.

   Type of Objection: Effectiveness

   Suggested Response: It is wonderful that you are supportive of other charities. Each charity has a unique and important mission deserving of your support. I'd love to hear more about the charities you support and why.

10. You have an endowment, why are you asking me for a gift?

    Type of Objection: Effectiveness

    Suggested Response: Endowments are just one piece of how we fund the operation of Our Charity. The funds are restricted, so we can only spend a set percentage of the value of the endowment each year to support our mission. The rest comes from other sources, including government grants, private foundations, and generous gifts from people like you.

11. I just sent in my gift for this year, so there is no reason to meet.

Type of Objection: Lack of Time/Effectiveness

Suggested Response: I can certainly understand if now is not a good time to meet. I am sure that you are quite busy. If you could spare a few minutes for a cup of coffee or the like, I'd welcome the chance just to introduce myself and tell you a little bit about how we are using your gift to achieve our mission.

12. You always ask for unrestricted money, which seems to go into a black hole—why should I give?

Type of Objection: Effectiveness

Suggested Response: We accept both restricted and unrestricted gifts. Unrestricted gifts give us the maximum flexibility to use the gift where the need is greatest. All unrestricted gifts to Our Charity are directed toward these programs (outline list of five programs getting your annual support). These are our core programs and vital to our mission (insert a story about a person who benefitted from one of these programs). If you would like to direct your annual gift to one of these core programs instead of making it unrestricted, you can certainly do so.

13. The salaries of top administrators are too high.

Type of Objection: Effectiveness/Indifference

Suggested Response: You are not the only person who has expressed this concern over the years. Why do you think the salaries are too high?

14. I have included Your Charity in my estate plans and don't want to part with the funds while I'm alive.

Type of Objection: Personal Circumstances

Suggested Response: How wonderful! We sincerely appreciate that you have remembered us in your estate plans. How about we meet for lunch and I can share some information on our legacy society, which is our way of thanking donors who have remembered us in their long-term plans?

15. I need my resources to provide for my own needs in retirement.

Type of Objection: Personal Circumstances

Suggested Response: We always say that you need to care for yourself and your family before supporting charities. Other donors who have expressed this concern have been surprised to learn about ways that they can provide for their retirement and still support our mission. Why don't we get together and I can share this information with you to see if it might be helpful?

16. I don't want to disinherit my kids by making a large gift.

   Type of Objection: Personal Circumstances

   Suggested Response: I can see that family is very important to you. Our Charity would never want you to disinherit your children to make a charitable gift to our mission. If there were a way to both provide an inheritance for your children and support our mission, would you be interested in learning more about it?

17. I am helping to pay my grandchildren's tuition, which takes up my free resources.

   Type of Objection: Personal Circumstances

   Suggested Response: How wonderful! An education is a fantastic gift. I've worked with a few individuals who were doing the same thing. We found a way to help them to pay for tuition while supporting our mission at the same time. Might that be of interest?

18. I provide support for my elderly mother.

   Type of Objection: Personal Circumstances

   Suggested Response: I hear that more that you would expect. There are more and more people supporting both parents and children at the same time. Because it is becoming so common, we worked with our professional advisors committee to come up with some solutions that allow you to support your mom while also providing for our future. Let's talk about it when we get together.

19. I'm afraid I'll outlive my assets, my family has a history of living past 100.

   Type of Objection: Personal Circumstances

   Suggested Response: How wonderful that your family is so long-lived (tell a story about your family also being long-lived or other donors who have lived to 104). Clearly you want to be prepared for a long life. I might have some charitable solutions that provide guaranteed income for the rest of your life, with the remainder benefitting Our Charity when you no longer need it. I'll bring some materials to our lunch.

20.   I'm in meetings all next week, then am out of town for two weeks after that.

Type of Objection: Scheduling Conflict/Lack of Time

Suggested Response: It sounds like this is a bad time for us to meet. Will things improve next month?

Sample Qualification Visit Preparation Worksheet

Prospect Name:

_____

Visit Location:

_____

Time:

_____

Date:

_____

Materials Sent:

_____

_____

Summary of Prior Moves with this Prospect:

_____

_____

_____

_____

Purpose of this Meeting:

_____

_____

_____

_____

At the end of this meeting, I will know:

_____

_____

_____

_____

_____

What outcomes do I desire?

_____

_____

_____

_____

_____

What questions will I ask?

_____

_____

_____

_____

_____

Materials/items to bring:

_____

_____

Likely objections and my responses:

_____

_____

Directions:

_____

_____

Qualification Visit Questions/Conversation Starters

GENERAL

Tell me more . . .
What makes you feel that way?
Did I understand you to say . . . ?
How can I help?

CAPACITY

1. Tell me about your career. What do you do? How long have you been with them? How has the industry changed since you started?
2. What was it like working for _____?
3. I understand that you started your own business. How did you get started?
4. Are these pictures of your children? Tell me about them. Where was this one taken? How old are they? Do you have any grandchildren?
5. You mentioned that you like to travel, where did you go this year? Who did you go with?
6. If I wanted to reach you during the winter, do you have an alternative address, or are you here year-round?
7. What are your interests outside of work? Do you have any hobbies?
8. Do you support other charities in addition to Our Charity?
9. If Our Charity were to demonstrate its commitment to an area that is important to you, would you consider increasing your giving to Our Charity?

10. Where does Our Charity fall on your list of charitable priorities?

11. Do you make gifts to other charitable organizations? What motivates those gifts?

12. Why would your friends choose to support Our Charity?

For Non-Donors:

13. Is there a reason you have not supported Our Charity in the past?

14. Would you consider supporting Our Charity in the future and what would have to happen for that to take place?

PROPENSITY

1. You have been a great supporter of Our Charity. What makes you write out a check every year? What about other charities?

2. How have your gifts to Our Charity made you and your family feel?

3. How did Our Charity help lead to your success?

4. What involvement with Our Charity gives you the most joy?

5. Describe your favorite moment(s) with Our Charity.

6. Have you been to visit Our Charity recently?

7. What do you think of the job the president and current board of trustees are doing?

8. How do you feel about the current direction of Our Charity?

9. Do you read our publications? What is your favorite part? What do you like the least?

10. If there was one thing you could change about Our Charity today, what would it be?

11. Tell me about your Our Charity experience.

12. How has your experience with Our Charity influenced who you are today?

13. Take Our Charity completely out of the picture, what is it that you really care about now in your life? What interests you? What are you involved in?

14. Bring Our Charity back into the picture, are there ways that you could envision Our Charity doing more to facilitate those interests?

15. If Our Charity had a program/event on your interest, would you want to participate? Would you be willing to plan or host such an event?

Philanthropic Planning Conversation Starters

APPRECIATED STOCK

1. Did you know that if you make a gift of appreciated stock instead of cash, you avoid the capital gain you would recognize on the sale? Even if you want to continue to hold the stock, you can donate it and then purchase new shares increasing your cost basis.
2. You mentioned that you are a vice president at Whirlpool. Will the pending merger with Maytag have any tax implication for your stock holdings?
3. (If a donor insists on making a gift today) I can't thank you enough for this tremendous commitment to Our Charity. Let's talk about how you want to direct your gift so that it accomplishes all you want to do for Our Charity. At the same time, let's also look at how we can maximize the tax benefits for you.

CLOSELY HELD BUSINESS INTERESTS/ PARTNERSHIPS/LIMITED LIABILITY COMPANIES

1. You mentioned that you are going to pass the business to your kids. Did you know there are some ways you can do that, that will actually save you money on the transaction by being charitable?
2. What does your business do? How is it structured? Is it difficult to get profits out due to tax concerns? Did you know there are some charitable solutions to help solve those problems?

ALTERNATIVE INVESTMENTS

1. Our Charity invests a fair portion of its endowment in alternative investments. If you were interested in donating a portion of your interest, I could share the information with our treasurer's office to see if it is something we could accept and hold in our portfolio until it matures.

QUALIFIED PLAN/IRA ASSETS

1. When most people consider a gift, they don't think about some of the assets in their portfolio that could help. Suppose, for example, you funded your gift now with $_____ in appreciated stock to take advantage of the matching gift program, and then you endowed it later by naming Our Charity as the beneficiary of your IRA? By giving the IRA to Our Charity instead of your kids, you avoid up to 60% tax due on the transfer to your children.

2. You mentioned before that you are single. Who have you named to benefit from your IRA or life insurance provided by your employer? Did you know you can name Our Charity and become a member of our legacy society?

LIFE INSURANCE

1. Now that you've retired, do you have any life insurance policies you no longer need?

REAL ESTATE

1. That's a great tan, where did you go? Do you own a place there?
2. Now that the kids are grown, will you be selling the house?
3. With vacation properties difficult to sell, we have seen an increase in interest in giving these properties to Our Charity. Do you own any properties that you no longer use that might be suitable gifts?

TANGIBLE PERSONAL PROPERTY

1. What a collection of art! Can you show me your favorites? In what pieces are you disappointed?
2. You've built up an amazing collection of Civil War items. Do your kids share your interest?

Sample Donor-Centered Gift Planning Marketing Plan

SUMMARY

The Office of Gift Planning is a central unit within the Institutional Advancement Division of GPD University (GPD), providing philanthropic planning services to central development, and all of the colleges, university centers, and programs that make up the University. It assists alumni, parents, and friends of the University in integrating their charitable intentions with their overall tax, estate, and financial planning. Our values-based, donor-centered approach ensures that goals are achieved both today and in the future.

PHILOSOPHY

Marketing gift planning for GPD encompasses all outreach efforts and communications in the arena of structured outright gifts, life-income gifts, and estate commitments to GPD. Marketing communications are intended to:

- Educate the entire GPD constituency about gift planning opportunities
- Identify prospects within the GPD constituency who may have a particular interest in gift planning
- Cultivate relationships with those who express an interest in gift planning
- Solicit identified prospects through various media
- Negotiate gifts through fulfillment materials

- Steward donors who have made endowment, life-income, and estate commitments to GPD

Our ultimate goal is to increase long-term financial resources for GPD by providing outstanding service to prospective donors, their advisors, and our GPD colleagues. Initiatives are strategically timed throughout the year, organized around donors' timing and significant University events. The plan is based on a moves management platform and includes customized marketing for each unit that makes up the University. The program is designed to maintain a steady stream of communication and achieve consistency in message through both content and visual identification, even while customizing for each unit. All marketing communication will encourage prospects to self-identify by presenting a compelling message and contact information or a private (sealable) reply mechanism.

EDUCATING AND QUALIFYING OUR BROAD CONSTITUENCY

A.   General education—Communications to broad University constituencies using gift planning messages to create awareness

   1. GPD *University Magazine*
      - *Purpose:* With a readership circulation of 40,000, these advertisements serve to raise awareness, generate interest, and compel action.
      - *Content:* Full-page, four-color ads positioned on the inside back cover or in the class notes section, featuring a donor/student profile to show impact and outcomes; use quick response (QR) codes to link readers back to the mobile web site for gift planning content
      - *Audience:* All alumni, friends, and students who receive the magazine
      - *Schedule:*

	Topic	Profile
Winter—DATE	Crafting Your Legacy—Wills	TBD
Spring—DATE	Increasing Retirement Income	TBD
Summer—DATE	Crafting Your Legacy—Retirement Plans	TBD
Fall—DATE	Increasing Retirement Income	TBD

- *Budget:* $0
- *Measure:* Number of self-replies and traffic at web site

2. Existing Alumni Office monthly e-mail newsletter (other newsletters TBD)—tip of the month
   - *Purpose:* Keep gift planning information in front of readers' minds
   - *Content:* Short segment each month, appropriate to the planning process, to drive traffic to the web site through a hot link
   - *Audience:* All alumni
   - *Schedule:* Monthly
   - *Budget:* $0
   - *Measure:* Traffic at web site

3. Web Site/Media:
   - *Purpose:* Provide an interactive on-line source of information
   - *Content:* Purchased from Virtual Giving and modified to our mission
   - *Audience:* All alumni, parents, and friends
   - *Schedule:* Complete updates to donor stories quarterly
   - *Budget:* $4,000 per year
   - *Measure:* Number of unique visitors per month; time on page; number of pages visited; most common downloads; most commonly visited pages

B. College-based education– Communication to College constituencies using gift planning messages to create awareness

   Each College should have a unique URL so that traffic from these communications can be traced back to these materials

1. Arts and Letters
   a. Magazine
      - *Purpose:* Raise awareness, generate interest, and compel action
      - *Content:* Donor-centered advertisements; profiles of students and faculty to show impact and outcomes tied to donor-centered gift planning opportunity (topics and students/faculty TBD)
      - *Audience:* Alumni
      - *Schedule:* February and September
      - *Budget:* $0

- *Measure:* Number of phone and e-mail responses; traffic at web site

   2. Architecture

     a. Magazine

- *Purpose:* Raise awareness, generate interest, and compel action
- *Content:* Donor-centered advertisements; profiles of students and faculty to show impact and outcomes tied to a donor-centered gift planning opportunity (topics and students/faculty TBD)
- *Audience:* Alumni
- *Schedule:* March and October
- *Budget:* $0
- *Measure:* Number of phone and e-mail responses; traffic at web site

C. Institutes, special programs, and alumni/parents/friends education—Communication to constituencies of particular University programs outside of the Colleges using gift planning messages to create awareness

   1. Athletics

     a. Newsletters

- *Purpose:* Raise awareness, generate interest, and compel action
- *Content:* Donor-centered advertisements, profiles of students and coaches to show impact and outcomes tied to a donor-centered gift planning opportunity and the successful student-athlete (topics and students/coaches TBD)
- *Audience:* Alumni and friends interested in athletics
- *Schedule:* Every other month
- *Budget:* $0
- *Measure:* Number of phone and e-mail responses; traffic at web site

   2. Library

     a. Newsletter

- *Purpose:* Raise awareness, generate interest, and compel action
- *Content:* Donor-centered advertisements; profiles of students and faculty to show impact and outcomes tied to a donor-centered gift planning opportunity and the benefits of the library collection (topics and students/faculty TBD)

- *Audience:* Alumni and friends
- *Schedule:* January, April, September, November
- *Budget:* $0
- *Measure:* Number of phone and e-mail responses; traffic at web site

D. Seminars—Outreach for Targeted Audiences

1. Parents' weekend
    - *Purpose:* Engage high-net-worth parents in discussion about gift planning
    - *Content:* Seminar on questions this donor group should be asking and discussing in their families prior to seeing their planning team (integrating philanthropic planning into their overall planning)
    - *Audience:* High-net-worth parents
    - *Schedule:* October 25
    - *Budget:* Estimated at $5,000
    - *Measure:* Number of attendees

2. Donor seminar for women's issues
    - *Purpose:* Engage women in discussion about gift planning
    - *Content:* Seminar on questions this demographic should be asking and discussing regarding estate planning and giving
    - *Audience:* Women who are mid-career or pre-retirement (age 40 to 60)
    - *Schedule:* April 11
    - *Budget:* Estimated at $5,000
    - *Measure:* Number of attendees

3. Donor seminars in conjunction with Colleges
    - *Purpose:* Educate prospects on impact of past gifts on students and faculty and how they came to be through the gift-planning process
    - *Content:* Lead with mission supplemented by how to meet personal planning objectives while supporting mission— Increasing income for retirement, unlocking the value of real estate, crafting a meaningful legacy, maximize the inheritance of heirs. Also consider hot legislative topics such as the IRA rollover. When possible, tie the topic into a faculty presentation about the College

- *Audience:* TBD by Colleges (but generally look to the identified gift planning prospects as the target audience)
  - Use volunteers to invite attendees—Recruit Society members from the featured College, and ask them to serve as hosts/hostesses on the seminar invitation. Get the volunteers to write personal notes on the invitation, or at a minimum to make some phone calls
  - Keep records of those who attend, and follow up with a personal note from the staff
- *Schedule:* TBD
- *Budget:* $0 (cost borne by Colleges)
- *Measure:* Number of attendees

4. College-based, prospect webinars/podcasts
   - *Purpose:* Educate prospects about personal planning opportunities with a gift planning slant without the need for a facility or for the prospect to leave his/her desk
   - *Content:* Elder care, coordinating your financial advice, investment issues in planning, selling a business, creating retirement income, and so on. A narrow topic is more likely to appeal to a specific area of interest to prospect. The topic need not appeal to everyone, just the audience segment the College wants to attract.
     - Use speaker names of national interest—The webinar format allows the speaker—as well as the prospect—to attend from a home or office location.
     - Publish the topics and schedule on the web site and in other College publications
   - *Audience:* TBD by the College for each webinar/podcast
     - Require donors to register (so that the College can follow up, and include those prospects in visits made to those cities)
     - Send follow-up information by e-mail (evaluation of seminar, next events, additional information)
   - *Schedule:* TBD
   - *Budget:* $0 (cost borne by Colleges)
   - *Measure:* Those who log-on; Attendance of 5 people with sincere interest and capacity is better than 25 without real interest

5. Reunion weekend educational program
   - *Purpose:* Educate reunion attendees on how to use charitable gifts to meet personal planning objectives
   - *Content:* Seminar on impact of legacy gifts and how they can be used to meet personal planning objectives—focus should be on fulfillment of mission
   - *Audience:* Reunion attendees
   - *Schedule:* Annual—June 14
   - *Budget:* TBD
   - *Measure:* Attendees

E. Professional Advisors
   1. Council
      - *Purpose:* Bring together up to 24 professional advisors closely affiliated with GPD's gift planning program to provide help for complex gifts, a referral network for top prospects, drafting for materials/steering committee for the Professional Advisors Network, and encourage gift planning generally
      - *Audience:* Advisors from each of the major professions
      - *Schedule:* Meet up to four times per year on campus to discuss tax law changes and other issues impacting charitable gift planning (February, June, September, November)
      - *Budget:* $1,000
      - *Measure:* Attendance at quarterly meetings and production of materials for Professional Advisors Network
   2. Professional Advisors Network
      - *Purpose:* Provide gift planning information to professional advisors with a connection to GPD to encourage them to:
        - Make gifts of their own
        - Encourage clients to do so (40 percent of all life-income gifts are recommended by advisors)
        - Serve as a referral source for prospects who need advisors
        - Serve as a resource to draw upon for state-specific questions
      - *Content:*
        - Notebook of materials to include:
          - General GPD information and giving opportunities
          - Donor, faculty, and student profiles

- Descriptions of personal planning objectives and tools available to help meet them
- Sample bequest language
- Technical information on gift and estate tax implications of gift types
- Contact information for Office of Gift Planning
- Information on accessing a social network of attorneys affiliated with GPD
  - *Audience:* All professional advisors in greater Philadelphia area and all GPD professional advisors nationally
  - *Schedule:* Update materials every July
  - *Measure:* Number of new members

F. University Community—Education programs designed for staff and volunteer leadership

1. Orientation
    - *Purpose:* Training for new calling officers as they are hired
    - *Content:* An introduction to marketing materials and the services offered by Gift Planning
    - *Audience:* All new calling officers
    - *Schedule:* Within one month of hire (one-on-one sessions with gift planner)
    - *Budget:* $0
    - *Measure:* Percentage of new gift officers trained

2. Donor-Centered Gift Planning Training
    - *Purpose:* Training to introduce new, donor-centered gift planning model
    - *Content:* Framework of donor-centered gift planning and how to effectively leverage resources of Office of Gift Planning
    - *Audience:* All calling officers at all levels, including president and senior management
    - *Schedule:* One-time training—September 21 (1.5 hours)
    - *Budget:* $0
    - *Measure:* Participation

3. Leadership gift and major gift officer training
    - *Purpose:* Training program to assist calling officers at the bottom and middle levels of the giving pyramid to identify prospects who are ready for the gift planning discussion

- *Content:* How to recognize gift planning opportunities and introduce the gift planning process into fundraising calls
- *Audience:* Annual fund and major gift officers
- *Schedule:* Five half-day sessions each year, repeated on an annual basis—First Monday of January, March, June, September, and November
- *Budget:* $10,000
- *Measure:* Percentage of gift officers trained

4. President, senior management, deans, and principal gift officer training (PRN Training)

   - *Purpose:* Training program for those working with the University's highest level prospects to understand the philanthropic planning process
   - *Content:* How to integrate prospects' philanthropic goals and objectives into their overall tax, estate, and financial planning
   - *Audience:* President, senior management, deans, and principal gift officers
   - *Schedule:* Two-hour training sessions once per calendar quarter, repeated on an annual basis—First Monday of January, March, September, and November
   - *Budget:* $8,000
   - *Measure:* Percentage of target audience trained

5. Board of Trustees training

   - *Purpose:* Training program for the board to educate trustees on how to introduce the philanthropic planning process
   - *Content:* How the long-term goals of the University lend themselves to the philanthropic planning discussion; review of case for philanthropic planning
   - *Audience:* Board of trustees
   - *Schedule:* One-hour training session once per calendar year, repeated on an annual basis—May Board Meeting
   - *Budget:* $2,000
   - *Measure:* Percentage of board members who join Society

6. Parents' Council training

   - *Purpose:* Training program for Parents Council on how to introduce the gift planning process

- *Content:* How the long-term goals of the University lend themselves to the gift planning discussion; review of case for legacy giving
- *Audience:* Parents' Council
- *Schedule:* One-hour training session once per calendar year, repeated on an annual basis—October Meeting
- *Budget:* $2,000
- *Measure:* Percentage of Parents' Council who join Society

PROSPECT IDENTIFICATION

A.   Audience Selection

- *Purpose:* Create the initial list of prospects most open to a philanthropic planning message
- *Method:* Review the database to find donors who have given:
  - 15 or more years
  - 10 of the last 15 years
  - 7 of the last 10 years
  - 5 of the last 7 years and
  - 3 of the last 5 years

Add to that list, to the extent that they are not already included, those who have made some gifts and are:

- Current or former Society members (or have informed us they have set up legacy gifts for GPD or another organization)
- Individuals who have expressed an interest in gift planning with GPD in the past by returning a reply card or other device
- Current and/or former board members
- Current and/or former staff members
- Long-term volunteers
- Tied to GPD long term through personal or family associations
- Strong in philosophical or religious belief in helping others or in giving back
- Others who are strongly tied to our mission in a meaningful way

Together, this group represents those who believe closely in GPD and will support us financially. They are the most open to a philanthropic planning message and providing long-term support.

Create the following rating system on the database:

Rating	Description
1	Known legacy gift donors
2	Prospects who have inquired about gift planning in the past but not captured in rating 1
3	Donors who have given for 15 or more years not captured in ratings 1 and 2
4	Donors who have given for 10 of the last 15 years not captured in ratings 1 to 3
5	Donors who have given for 7 of the last 10 years not captured in ratings 1 to 4
6	Donors who have given for 5 of the last 7 years not captured in ratings 1 to 5
7	Donors who have given for 3 of the last 5 years not captured in ratings 1 to 6
8	Current or former board members not captured in ratings 1 to 7
9	Long-term volunteers and those tied to GPD long term through personal or family associations but not captured in ratings 1 to 8
10	Current or former staff members with at least some giving history, but not captured in ratings 1 to 9
11	Donors and prospects previously rated 1 to 10, but who fall off the rating system when ratings are reviewed (typically every other year)
12	Donors who have turned down legacy gift asks, but really are saying "not now" (qualified prospects)
13	Do not solicit for future gifts (prospects that have been identified and qualified, but it is clear they will never make a legacy gift)

- *Schedule:* Complete by July 31
- *Budget:* $0
- *Measure:* Number of qualified prospects in pool

B.   Audience Segmentation

Begin the process of identifying donors in specific generational cohorts, target groups (married no children, single, women, those using "Miss", parents, grandparents) and those with a close affiliation from a University area other than a College (Libraries, Athletics) for messaging future communications.

- *Schedule:* Complete by December 31
- *Budget:* $0
- *Measure:* Number of prospects in each discreet group

C.   Prospect Survey

- *Purpose:* Encourage previously identified gift planning pool to express an interest in estate planning, allowing GPD to pursue them immediately

- *Content:* Electronic and print survey covering estate planning and questions typically asked in a first visit; provide Estate Information Organizer as the thank you for completing the survey (can also point them to the Estate Planning Wizard on the web site)
- *Audience:* All gift planning prospects ranked 2 through 12
- *Schedule:* Send to a modest group each month to allow staff to respond in a reasonable period of time, start September 1
- *Budget:* TBD (depends on number of identified prospects)
- *Measure:* 7 to 8 percent response rate

D. Tell Your Story Campaign
- *Purpose:* Encourage existing legacy gift and endowment donors to tell why they elected to make their gift; provides University with good stories to tell and identifies donors who are likely willing to make another gift to add to their existing gift; also serves a stewardship purpose
- *Content:* Simple mail and electronic request with form to fill in and return
- *Audience:* All gift planning prospects rated 1
- *Schedule:* Start July 1
- *Budget:* $2,500
- *Measure:* Number of responses (expect 5 percent response rate)

E. Telephone Calling Program
- *Purpose:* Identify prospective prospects from the gift planning pool who respond to a phone call, allowing GPD to pursue legacy gifts immediately
- *Content:* Phone calls to inquire about gift planning interest
- *Audience:* All gift planning prospects rated 2 through 12 who have not responded to a gift planning mailing in the last three years
- *Schedule:* Start January 1
- *Budget:* TBD (need proposals from vendors)
- *Measure:* Number of responses

CULTIVATION

A. Brochure program
1. General brochure
- *Purpose:* Leave-behind piece for calling officers

- *Content:* Four-color brochure on gift planning; delivers a comprehensive but generalized description of all gift planning options as well as motivation, impact, and outcomes
- *Audience:* Identified prospects for visits or who request information on multiple gift planning options
- *Schedule:* Complete by September 1
- *Budget:* $7,500 (depends on number printed)
- *Measure:* Number utilized

2. Society brochure/membership roster (two versions)
   - *Purpose:* Welcomes new members, thanks them, and explains the benefits of membership
   - *Content:* Printed brochure (reprinted annually); lists all members, provides information on the origins of the Society, member benefits, and its importance within the University; include sample language
   - *Audience:* New Society members
   - *Schedule:* Annually each fall
   - *Budget:* $1,000
   - *Measure:* None

3. PDF series (see Negotiation Section for negotiation purpose)
   - *Purpose:* Cultivate prospects who want to integrate their philanthropy into their overall tax, estate, and financial planning
   - *Content:* Donor-centered materials on financial planning topics that can be met by both charitable and non-charitable means including:
     - Crafting Your Legacy
     - Unlocking Value in Your Existing Assets
     - Using Your Real Estate Creatively
     - Increasing Your Retirement Income
     - Providing Income to Your Elderly Parents
     - Paying for College for Your Children or Grandchildren
     - Maximizing Your Children or Grandchildren's Inheritance
     - Creating a Family Vision and Multi-Generational Plan

   Branded for each College/unit to show impact and outcomes of the gifts
   - *Audience:* Responders to mailings, web site, advertisements, and other marketing

- *Schedule:* Completed by December 31
- *Budget:* TBD (at least $5,000 due to costs of content)
- *Measure:* Number utilized

B. Newsletter (see Stewardship section for more details on stewardship function)
- *Purpose:* Cultivate prospects who have requested gift planning information
- *Content:* Feature article with financial planning information (tied to giving when appropriate), tax updates, donor/faculty/student profiles, letters to the editor, letter from Director, travel schedule, list of new Society members since last edition, and Society calendar
- *Audience:* Prospects who have requested gift planning information in the last five years; existing Society members
- *Schedule:* Three editions per year (customized to Colleges if they wish to pay the cost) October, January, April; Both print and PDF versions
- *Budget:* $12,500
- *Measure:* Expected response rate of 0.5 percent

C. College-based Gift Planning Chairs—College affinity program with volunteer for each College
- *Purpose:* Encourage non-members to consider membership; steward existing members
- *Content:* Letters describing the volunteers' motivation to give and describing the programs impacted
- *Audience:* Gift planning prospects rated 1 through 12
- *Schedule:* Two letters per year timed to enhance the Annual Fund cycle—TBD
- *Budget:* Postage, will vary for each College
- *Measure:* Expected response rate of 1 percent

D. University Reply Cards/College Reply Cards
- *Purpose:* Reply mechanism designed to produce responses
- *Content:* Consistent language across the University matched to the fulfillment pieces created for gift planning purposes
- *Audience:* Entire population
- *Schedule:* For Gift Planning mailings-Complete by July 1; For all other College and University Cards—Share new language by April 30 for inclusion in materials for the coming fiscal year

- *Budget:* $500
- *Measure:* Number of gift planning responses on reply cards

SOLICITATIONS

A.   Postcard solicitation program
- *Purpose:* Solicit prospects to request information on gift planning or making a legacy gift
- *Content:* Five postcards per year, branded for each College/unit. The front of each card will have a student/faculty photo and a story about outcomes. The back of each card will tie that story to a gift planning opportunity and include a reply device or unique URL for responses
- *Audience:* Gift planning prospects rated 1 through 12, by College or unit
- *Schedule:*

	Topic
September	Increasing Retirement Income (split card)
November	Year-End Appreciated Stock and Other Assets
January	Beneficiary Designations—Retirement Plans (split card)
March	Increasing Retirement Income (split card)
May	Beneficiary Designations—Bequests (split card)

Split cards account for age differences, for example, the beneficiary designation cards can be split so that donors over age $70\frac{1}{2}$ get information on the IRA rollover instead of standard language on creating a meaningful estate legacy for GPD

- *Budget:* TBD based on vendor/internal cost; number to mail
- *Measure:* Expect 0.5 percent response rate

B.   E-mail follow up to post card program
- *Purpose:* Increase yield from postcard mailings
- *Content:* Reminder about postcard and hot link to web site with more information on the topic
- *Audience:* Same as postcard
- *Schedule:* Same as postcard
- *Budget:* $0
- *Measure:* Open and click through rates

C. Charitable IRA rollover solicitation program
- *Purpose:* Encourage outright gifts from IRAs allowed by IRA rollover
- *Content:* Postcard outlining how past IRA gifts have been used and encouraging future gifts, including information on technical aspects of the law; update front of web site with special link; send e-solicitation to those of appropriate age; phone calls from assigned calling officers to those who made IRA rollover gifts in the last two years
- *Audience:* Entire population age $70^1/_2$ or older
- *Schedule:* Mail by November 15
- *Budget:* $3,000
- *Measure:* Expect virtually no response

D. Proposal packages
- *Purpose:* Create a standard printed and electronic proposal package as a response device to each type of gift planning inquiry, so support team can assist with fulfillment and to ensure consistency of information and disclosures
- *Content:* Letter, description of gift type, corresponding disclosure statement, calculations page, and appropriate insert or brochure packaged in a branded Gift Planning folder or appropriate e-mail device
- *Audience:* All responders
- *Schedule:* Complete by July 1
- *Budget:* $0
- *Measure:* Completed gifts

E. Bequest stuffer program
- *Purpose:* Solicit donors who have already set up a life-income gift to consider an additional estate commitment
- *Content:* Buck slip with outcomes messaging and encouraging additional estate gifts
- *Audience:* Life-income gift donors, inserted with checks or advice notice
- *Schedule:* New version each fiscal year
- *Budget:* Estimated at $250
- *Measure:* Number of new estate intentions

F. Gift annuity addition program
- *Purpose:* Solicit donors who have already set up a gift annuity to consider an additional gift annuity

- *Content:* Letter once per year providing latest rate on a new gift annuity
- *Audience:* Gift annuity donors
- *Schedule:* Letters sent once each quarter, targeted to all gift annuitants who have passed a half birthday since the last quarter (January, April, July, October)
- *Budget:* Estimated at $400
- *Measure:* Number of new gift annuities

G. General Contact Information
- *Purpose:* Make it easy for prospects and donors to reach the Office of Gift Planning
- *Content:* Toll-free telephone number and general gift planning e-mail box such as giftplanning@GPD.edu
- *Audience:* Responders to all marketing
- *Schedule:* Completed by June 30
- *Budget:* $400 for the toll-free number
- *Measure:* Increased overall response rates

H. Acknowledgement Buck slip
- *Purpose:* Solicit existing donors to consider legacy opportunities
- *Content:* Buck slip with outcomes messaging and encouraging legacy gifts
- *Audience:* Those who receive receipts for current gifts
- *Schedule:* New version each fiscal year
- *Budget:* Estimated at $400
- *Measure:* Number of responses

STEWARDSHIP

A. Update membership criteria

Membership is currently offered to individuals who name GPD as a beneficiary of a will, living trust, life insurance policy, retirement plan, charitable remainder trust, charitable gift annuity, or pooled income fund. Broaden membership to include anyone who has set up a gift that matures in the future or lasts in perpetuity (an endowment), that is, a legacy gift.
- *Schedule:* Complete by July 31
- *Budget:* $0
- *Measure:* Number of new Society members

B.   Profile Society donors more broadly in University- and College-based publications

Donor profiles are the best way to steward donors while also encouraging others to consider similar gifts. Select a wide range of donors, young, middle age, older, and deceased. Highlight the impact and outcomes that their gifts achieved, and why those were important to the individual or family. Tie this to the personal history or motivation of the donor and students who benefitted or will benefit from these gifts.

- *Schedule:* Ongoing; start by September 30
- *Budget:* TBD

C.   Survey of Society members

- *Purpose:* Confirm existing members, gain insight into their gift intentions, ask if we can count gifts that qualify and we have not counted to date, and start a dialog for further cultivation and stewardship
- *Content:* Letter and survey asking for permission to use name and asking for details/confirmation of qualifying gift
- *Audience:* Endowment, life-income, and estate gift donors (legacy donors)
- *Schedule:* Complete by August 30
- *Budget:* Estimated at $400
- *Measure:* Confirm 80 percent of members

D.   Select a volunteer Society Chair for each society

- *Purpose:* Volunteer to sign letters and serve as an advocate/face of gift planning among the alumni
- *Content:* N/A
- *Audience:* Societies
- *Schedule:* As needed
- *Budget:* $0
- *Measure:* N/A

E.   College-based Gift planning chairs

- *Purpose:* Create a cadre of gift planning champions for each College to help spread the word, increase turnout, and assist with program growth/donor stewardship/event ideas
- *Content:* Send out thank you notes to new members in their specific College; annual letter to loyals from their college

- *Audience:* Society members and loyals
- *Schedule:* July 1
- *Budget:* $1,000

F.   Society brochure/membership roster (two versions) (see also Cultivation section for cultivation purpose)

- *Purpose:* Steward existing Society members
- *Content:* Lists all members, provides information on the origins of the Society, member benefits, and its importance within the University; needs to tell a great story for both Societies
- *Audience:* Existing Society members
- *Schedule:* Annual
- *Budget:* $500

G.   Benefits of Membership:

1. Donor recognition lists
    - *Purpose:* Honor existing Society members
    - *Content:* List of Society members in each College's donor recognition list, or a symbol next to each member indicating Society membership; should also include a brief explanation of what the Society is and how to become a member
    - *Audience:* Endowment, life-income, and estate gift donors (legacy donors)
    - *Schedule:* TBD
    - *Budget:* $0 (addition to existing publications at College level)

2. Dean's/President's letter
    - *Purpose:* Thank Society members for their ongoing support; inform members of addition of endowment donors to Society
    - *Content:* Letter from the Dean, updating Society members for the College on goings on, recent legacy gifts, impact of recent legacy gifts, and thanking for ongoing support
    - *Audience:* Society members affiliated with that specific College
    - *Schedule:* Complete by December 31
    - *Budget:* Estimated at $200

3. Newsletter (see also Cultivation section for cultivation purpose)
    - *Purpose:* Keep Society members engaged and informed about impact of outcome of gifts; provide educational materials on philanthropic planning

- *Content:* Feature article with financial planning information (tied to giving when appropriate), tax updates, donor/faculty/student profiles, letters to the editor, letter from David, travel schedule, list of new Society members since last edition, and Society calendar
- *Audience:* Prospects who have requested gift planning information in the last five years; existing Society members
- *Schedule:* Three editions per year (customized to Colleges if they wish to pay the cost) October, January, April; Both print and PDF versions
- *Budget:* $12,500
- *Measure:* Expected response rate of 0.5 percent

4. Birthday card program
   - *Purpose:* Steward members
   - *Content:* Custom birthday card with photo showing impact of a legacy gift, with caption to explain why it is photographed; branded for Society
   - *Audience:* Society members
   - *Schedule:* New version each fiscal year
   - *Budget:* $2,000

5. National Philanthropy Day/Thanksgiving Day/Holiday card program
   - *Purpose:* Steward members
   - *Content:* Custom holiday or Thanksgiving Day card with photo showing impact of a legacy gift, with caption to explain why it is photographed; Branded for Society
   - *Audience:* Society members
   - *Schedule:* New version each fiscal year; mail on November 1
   - *Budget:* $800

6. New Member Recognition Gift
   - *Purpose:* Public recognition of members
   - *Content:* Many options including: certificate of membership, pin, paperweight, mug, clock, picture frame, coasters, or something creative tied to GPD; Note that most charities have a giveaway that does not tie to their mission—if you can create something mission driven or tied to the name of the Society in a memorable and meaningful way, it will be

appreciated. You want something your donors can hang on the wall, display, or wear
- *Audience:* New Society members
- *Schedule:* October
- *Budget:* $2,000

7. Existing Member Recognition Gift
   - *Purpose:* Thank existing members for their on-going support each year
   - *Content:* Something useful that will spread the name of the Society—some options include: Note cards post-its, chocolates, wrist-bands, hats, pens, photo albums, and so on
   - *Audience:* Existing Society members
   - *Schedule:* April
   - *Budget:* $3,000

8. Events
   a. Reunion weekend reception
   - *Purpose:* Steward Society members
   - *Content:* Thank you speech from director, including highlights of outcomes created by legacy gifts
   - *Audience:* Society members
   - *Schedule:* Annual—June 14
   - *Budget:* $5,000

   b. Other University Events
   - *Purpose:* Steward and recognize Society members; Invite Society members to *all* University events for high-end donors, except annual fund recognition events (unless they have given at appropriate level for that year)
   - *Content:* No formal program; instead provide a small token of recognition, such as putting a special Society label/ribbon on the name tag; also may include free/valet parking; special reception area, and so on
   - *Audience:* Society members
   - *Schedule:* TBD
   - *Budget:* $200

   c. Society luncheon
   - *Purpose:* Steward Society members

- *Content:* Thank you speech from University president, including highlights of outcomes created by legacy gifts and success/impact of the program over time (luncheon should change locations each year to highlight legacy gifts at each of the Colleges over time); announce new members and deceased members
- *Audience:* Society members
- *Schedule:* Annual—April 19
- *Budget:* $12,500

Sample General Brochure— University of the Sciences

Ways of

GIFT PLANNING, LIKE SCIENCE, IS ALL ABOUT THE FUTURE.

When donors plan a gift to University of the Sciences, they have the greatest impact. They create a legacy and reach beyond their lifetimes to help shape thousands of futures. And they invest in our collective future because USciences produces leaders and innovators in the disciplines of tomorrow.

GIFT PLANNING EXPANDS WHAT IS POSSIBLE.

By funding scholarships, donors use gift planning to open doors of opportunity for students and connect them to the best education. By supporting faculty, facilities and academic programs, they sustain our greatest strengths, keeping USciences on the leading edge. By adding to endowment, they ensure the continued advancement of knowledge, improving lives for generations to come.

SUPPORTING OUR COMMUNITY IN PERPETUITY GIVES YOU MORE OPTIONS.

From gifts through Wills and IRAs to charitable trusts and gifts of appreciated assets, gift planning can help you meet personal financial goals and avoid tax burdens. It can leverage your assets' value and provide more security for your family. At the same time, you consider the bigger picture: the long-term needs of USciences, the ever-changing nature of health care and life sciences, and the sheer magnitude of discoveries yet to come. We invite you to become an indelible part of our extraordinary story — one that is nearly two centuries old and still unfolding.

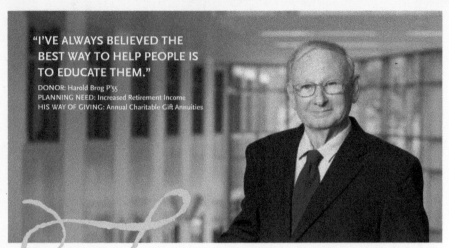

"I'VE ALWAYS BELIEVED THE BEST WAY TO HELP PEOPLE IS TO EDUCATE THEM."

DONOR: Harold Brog P'55
PLANNING NEED: Increased Retirement Income
HIS WAY OF GIVING: Annual Charitable Gift Annuities

FAMILY AND COMMUNITY ARE CORE ELEMENTS in the life story of **HAROLD BROG P'55**. For decades, he worked alongside his brother in a neighborhood pharmacy a few blocks from their childhood home in the Northern Liberties section of Philadelphia.

Since retiring, Harold has kept busy as a volunteer. He has continued a long-standing commitment to the local Friends Neighborhood Guild. He also drives an hour each way every Wednesday to train pharmacy students who provide care, alongside medical and dental students, to uninsured working families through Community Volunteers in Medicine.

When Harold decided to begin giving back to University of the Sciences, he chose to create the Brog Family Scholarship Fund, which he supports through **annual charitable gift annuities.** The annuities provide him with a dependable income, while the capital in the fund grows so it can one day defray tuition costs for several qualifying students each year.

"I ran into one of my classmates five or six years ago and got reacquainted with the University. I volunteered to get in touch with classmates for the 50th reunion and then I was elected to the Alumni Board," he explains. "I really like seeing what the University is doing and the growth period they are going through."

His scholarship fund connects the dots and makes bottom-line sense. "An annuity is an investment that stacks right up with my other investments and it makes me feel good. I hope the students whom I help get into research and discover something great. I've always believed the best way to help people is to educate them."

THE ROAD TO A BRIGHT FUTURE for MARIA AND MARVIN ZOBEL P'56 encompassed a love story tailor-made for Hollywood. They met in 1971 when she was modeling coats in Manhattan's Seventh Avenue Garment District. "This persistent man turned up several times to see me model the collection. I could have sworn Marvin was a buyer but it turned out he had just helped a friend set up the showroom," Maria recalls.

Perseverance paid off. The next year Maria and Marvin married and set off on a life filled with their share of adventure and entrepreneurship: raising a son and daughter; running and selling a textile business, followed by a home furnishings start-up; designing and building houses, including ones they called home; and finally retiring to active lives in Florida.

Along the way, Marvin reconnected with University of the Sciences, where he had followed in the academic footsteps of his father, a 1922 graduate. Never one to attend reunions, Marvin was quickly impressed by how far his alma mater had come. "When he saw the

University, after so many years, he was absolutely amazed at what had taken place on the campus," says Maria.

In concert with his wife, Marvin set up a **charitable remainder trust** to fund a future USciences scholarship in his father's memory. "Marvin had a vision of how he wanted things to be," Maria says of the trust, which continues to provide her with an annual income since Marvin's death in 2009. "He told me, 'You won't have to worry.' And he was right. It helps me live a comfortable life."

Above all, the trust is true to Marvin's philosophy. "Marvin had a very strong sense of people — of people bettering themselves, taking charge of their lives," Maria reflects. "Education was high up on his list. We both believed in learning something new each day. It feeds the spirit. That's why this gift means so much and why it will do so much good."

Legacy

REMARKABLE COMMITMENT MERITS SPECIAL RECOGNITION.

"MARVIN HAD A VERY STRONG SENSE OF PEOPLE — OF PEOPLE BETTERING THEMSELVES.... THAT'S WHY THIS GIFT MEANS SO MUCH AND WHY IT WILL DO SO MUCH GOOD."

DONORS: Maria Zobel and the late Marvin Zobel P'56
PLANNING NEED: Secure Income For My Wife
THEIR WAY OF GIVING: Charitable Remainder Trust

HAROLD BROG, MARIA ZOBEL AND SUZANNE MURPHY share two bonds: the permanent legacies they have crafted to benefit University of the Sciences and their membership in **The Remington Society.** Named for former dean, professor and alumnus Joseph Price Remington, among the first to support USciences through gift planning, the Society unites all donors who invest in our future through this discerning, most lasting approach to giving.

The impact of such generosity is profound. Contributions through Wills, charitable trusts and annuities, retirement plans and gifts to endowment have touched the lives of thousands of students. Members of The Remington Society are honored for their commitment to enable this proud tradition to continue.

THE _Remington_
REMINGTON SOCIETY
UNIVERSITY OF THE SCIENCES

"NAMING USCIENCES IN MY WILL ENSURES I'LL ALWAYS BE PART OF ITS FUTURE."

DONOR: Suzanne Murphy, Ph.D.
PLANNING NEED: A Significant Gift That I Can Change If I Need To
HER WAY OF GIVING: Bequest/Will

THE POWER OF GIFT PLANNING captured the imaginations of **SUZANNE MURPHY,** Dean of Misher College of Arts and Sciences, and her husband, Bob, years ago when the couple named several organizations as beneficiaries of their Wills. Topping Suzanne's list was University of the Sciences. "I have a strong devotion to this institution," she says. "Naming USciences in my Will ensures I'll always be part of its future."

Suzanne joined Misher College's full-time biology faculty in 1985, its second year, and still maintains a research laboratory. She and her colleagues have built Misher into a foundation of academic excellence at USciences. Now she wants her **bequest** to continue this work by supporting scholarships and a future Center for Undergraduate Research.

"These areas deserve investment," says Suzanne. "One student reminds me just why. Jack has worked in my lab since sophomore year. As the beneficiary of endowed research grants and scholarships, he has been extremely successful, presenting his work at regional and national scientific conferences. Although Jack ultimately plans to go on to medical school, he is passionate about his research and staying at USciences to complete his master's. The research students engage in can open many doors." Suzanne points to many alumni who launched careers because of the University's strong science focus combined with a diversified curriculum, early research opportunities and the University's ability to anticipate developments in health science markets.

Since naming USciences in her Will, Suzanne has enhanced her commitment to reflect changing family circumstances. "A pledge made through gift planning is not fixed. As life circumstances change, so can the pledge. We've been fortunate to be able to increase our bequest. As we get older, Bob and I are considering setting up annuities. The timing makes sense for us."

And it makes sense for a growing institution. "USciences as a whole — and Misher College in particular — has enormous potential, as do our students. USciences allows them to get on a track to success and decide which stop to get off. Planning a gift is very similar."

GIFT PLANNING SUPPORTS YOUR GOALS.

When you plan a gift to University of the Sciences, you invest in three important futures: those of our students, our institution and our society. At the same time, you can meet personal financial goals and craft an enduring legacy. Some ways of giving cost you nothing today. Here are four common goals we can help you meet.

CAN GIFT PLANNING HELP MY FAMILY MEET OTHER GOALS?

Gift planning can also offer many ways to address specific family circumstances, like providing for an elderly relative, or paying for your grandchildren's education, or even succession planning for your business. To learn more, please contact us at *giftplanning@usciences.edu;* fill out the reply card; or visit *www.giftplanning.usciences.edu* today to compare some of your options.

MY GOAL IS TO...
INCREASE MY RETIREMENT INCOME.

Whether you are still working or have retired, there are tax-advantaged ways to provide yourself with a secure retirement income **and** support those disciplines, opportunities and USciences programs that are most important to you and your family.

HERE ARE SOME WAYS:
Charitable Gift Annuity, Flexible Gift Annuity, Charitable Remainder Trust

MY GOAL IS TO...
MAXIMIZE MY FAMILY'S INHERITANCE.

If you are subject to gift and estate taxes, we can help you apply special giving techniques that will provide the greatest benefit to your family, while you invest in the futures of USciences and its students.

HERE ARE SOME WAYS:
Charitable Lead Trust, Wealth Replacement Charitable Remainder Trust

MY GOAL IS TO...
CONTINUE MY SUPPORT FOR USCIENCES AFTER I HAVE DIED.

By naming the University of the Sciences endowment as a beneficiary, you will create a legacy of support for USciences that will be there when it is most needed and will never go away.

HERE ARE SOME WAYS:
Naming USciences as a beneficiary of your:
Will/Living Trust, IRA, 401(k) or other Qualified Retirement Plan, Life Insurance Policy

MY GOAL IS TO...
INCREASE MY SUPPORT FOR USCIENCES NOW WITHOUT TAPPING MY CURRENT INCOME OR READY CASH.

Gifts of assets that have appreciated in value over time often provide more tax savings for you and your family than outright gifts of cash to USciences.

HERE ARE SOME WAYS:
Appreciated Securities (e.g., stock, mutual funds, bonds), Real Estate (e.g., homes, vacation homes, rental properties), Business Interests, Hedge Funds, REITs, Art and Collectables

USciences
University of the Sciences

600 SOUTH 43RD STREET, PHILADELPHIA, PA 19104
888.857.6264 | www.giftplanning.usciences.edu

52 Ways to Steward Legacy Donors

1. Anniversary card
2. Annual list showing all legacy donors, both living and deceased, highlighting how some gifts are making a difference today
3. Ask for advice about the charity/Society/particular program of interest
4. Ask how the donor wants to be stewarded, then deliver
5. Birthday card
6. Call from president/board chair/volunteer to say thank you
7. Chocolates embossed with Society logo
8. Coasters with your seal
9. Complimentary tickets to one of your events
10. Consistent philanthropist award (consecutive years giving)
11. Copies of press clippings
12. Deliver first gift annuity check
13. Designated parking for Society members with their name on it for special events
14. Drop by to just say "thanks"
15. Engraved clock
16. Flowers
17. Formal, handwritten, timely thank you from president/board chair/staff who will benefit from the gift
18. Help with holiday decorations
19. Invite to attend a board meeting
20. Invite to view program gift helped to fund
21. Lapel pin
22. Member of the month

23. Memorial gifts program
24. National Philanthropy Day card
25. Newsletter
26. Notes from those who get services from your charity and benefit from the gift (when appropriate)
27. Offer to pick them up for events
28. Paperweight with your charity's logo
29. Personal tour
30. Personalized Hershey kisses, M&Ms, or other candy
31. Personalized note cards or stationery for your charity
32. Photos from a recent event the donor attended
33. Picture frame with your charity's logo and a photo of the donor at your event
34. Plants
35. Poinsettia at the holidays
36. Pre- or post-concert reception to meet other Society members and musicians
37. Profile donor in your publications
38. Program updates showing the impact of a particular gift
39. Provide effective volunteer opportunities, appropriate to the generational cohort
40. Report showing how the gift is being used and its impact
41. Singing valentine or other singing thank you from a Barbershop Quartet
42. Tell your story campaign
43. Thank you lunch/dinner/cup of coffee
44. Thank you or stewardship luncheon
45. Tie tacks
46. Toll-free phone number
47. Tour of your facility, pointing out outcomes from legacy gifts
48. Tribute gifts program
49. Video weaving donor's personal story and philanthropy together with what their gift has or will accomplish
50. Visit in the hospital
51. Volunteer awards
52. Young philanthropist award

This list was compiled from Gift-PL listserv and Linked In on various dates from 2008 to 2011.[1]

Sample Society Brochure— University of the Sciences

One Gift
MANY
FUTURES

"SHAPING FUTURE LEADERS IS MY CALLING.
REMEMBERING UNIVERSITY OF THE SCIENCES
IN MY WILL IS A WONDERFUL WAY TO
INVEST IN LEADERSHIP FOR GENERATIONS
TO COME."

SUZANNE K. MURPHY, PHD, DEAN,
MISHER COLLEGE OF ARTS AND SCIENCES

THE
REMINGTON SOCIETY
UNIVERSITY OF THE SCIENCES

UNIVERSITY OF THE SCIENCES
600 SOUTH 43RD STREET, PHILADELPHIA, PA 19104
888.857.6264 | www.giftplanning.usciences.edu

THE
REMINGTON SOCIETY
UNIVERSITY OF THE SCIENCES

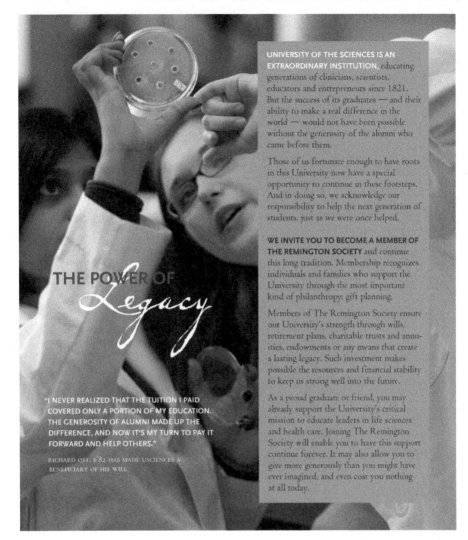

THE POWER OF *Legacy*

"I NEVER REALIZED THAT THE TUITION I PAID COVERED ONLY A PORTION OF MY EDUCATION. THE GENEROSITY OF ALUMNI MADE UP THE DIFFERENCE, AND NOW IT'S MY TURN TO PAY IT FORWARD AND HELP OTHERS."

RICHARD OST, P'82 HAS MADE USCIENCES A BENEFICIARY OF HIS WILL

UNIVERSITY OF THE SCIENCES IS AN EXTRAORDINARY INSTITUTION, educating generations of clinicians, scientists, educators and entrepreneurs since 1821. But the success of its graduates — and their ability to make a real difference in the world — would not have been possible without the generosity of the alumni who came before them.

Those of us fortunate enough to have roots in this University now have a special opportunity to continue in these footsteps. And in doing so, we acknowledge our responsibility to help the next generation of students, just as we were once helped.

WE INVITE YOU TO BECOME A MEMBER OF THE REMINGTON SOCIETY and continue this long tradition. Membership recognizes individuals and families who support the University through the most important kind of philanthropy: gift planning.

Members of The Remington Society ensure our University's strength through wills, retirement plans, charitable trusts and annuities, endowments or any means that create a lasting legacy. Such investment makes possible the resources and financial stability to keep us strong well into the future.

As a proud graduate or friend, you may already support the University's critical mission to educate leaders in life sciences and health care. Joining The Remington Society will enable you to have this support continue forever. It may also allow you to give more generously than you might have ever imagined, and even cost you nothing at all today.

A TRANSFORMATIVE *Vision*

IN 2010, University of the Sciences renamed its Benefactors Society in honor of a remarkable figure in its history, JOSEPH PRICE REMINGTON.

An alumnus, professor and dean here, Remington remains a trusted name in pharmaceutical science more than 125 years after publishing his gold-standard textbook, *Remington: The Science & Practice of Pharmacy*, now in its 22nd edition. In fact, since 1918, the American Pharmacists Association has named its highest prize the Remington Honor Medal.

Remington's influence is deeply felt on this campus. An early advocate of gift planning, he left the University a portion of his textbook's royalties. This gift continues to support University of the Sciences to this very day, and its impact, and the spirit in which it was made, still resonates with us, all these years later.

Remington's vision is an inspiration, encouraging each of us to follow in his footsteps and create our own legacy gift.

"MORE THAN 55 YEARS AFTER MY GRADUATION, I REMAIN GRATEFUL FOR THE MANY OPPORTUNITIES MY ALMA MATER GAVE ME. I WANT TO ENSURE THAT FUTURE GENERATIONS WILL GET THE SAME CHANCE TO SUCCEED THAT I DID."

HAROLD L. BROG, P'55 HAS FUNDED SEVERAL
CHARITABLE GIFT ANNUITIES TO BENEFIT USCIENCES.

TRADITION & *Impact*

THE REMINGTON SOCIETY pays tribute to individuals and families who have stood behind nearly two centuries of excellence.

When you become a member, you invest confidently in the future of this institution and its graduates. You create a permanent legacy for your family. You broaden the University's impact on the world. And you join a select group whose commitment to University of the Sciences stands apart.

Without the legacy gifts that came before, University of the Sciences would not be as vibrant as it is today. Our buildings and facilities, endowed chairs and named scholarships all reflect the foresight of individuals and families dedicated to keeping this institution strong.

The Remington Society connects its members to the life of the University and to our collective future. Your gift will help us address the challenges and opportunities of the coming decade, the next generation and our third century.

"I CHERISH MY MANY TIES TO UNIVERSITY OF THE SCIENCES AS AN ALUMNUS, ANNUAL DONOR AND TRUSTEE. PLANNING A GIFT TO BENEFIT MY ALMA MATER IS THE MOST LASTING CONNECTION OF ALL."

NICK MARASCO, P'96 HAS MADE USCIENCES
THE BENEFICIARY OF HIS LIFE INSURANCE POLICY
AND FUNDED A SCHOLARSHIP.

WAYS OF *Giving*

THROUGH GIFT PLANNING, you can create a legacy for University of the Sciences THAT COSTS YOU NOTHING TODAY. Even as you do so, you can tend to your own financial goals and address your family's long-term needs.

Gifts of a variety of assets, such as appreciated stock, mutual funds, real estate, business interests, retirement plans or life insurance policies can offer substantial tax savings. Other strategies can add to the security of your retirement years, or maximize your family's inheritance, all while supporting University of the Sciences across generations.

The most common vehicles for gift planning include:

- Wills
- Retirement Plans: IRAs, 401(k)s or 403(b)s
- Living Trusts
- Life Insurance Policies
- Charitable Gift Annuities
- Charitable Remainder Trusts
- Charitable Lead Trusts
- Real Estate with Retained Life Interests

If you have already included University of the Sciences in your estate plans, please let us know so we can welcome you to The Remington Society today.

TAKE THE NEXT STEP *Today*

PLANNING A GIFT IS A THOUGHTFUL, COLLABORATIVE PROCESS that must take into account both charitable intentions and personal financial goals.

First, you may want to use our interactive Legacy Planner at *www.giftplanning.usciences.edu* to compare your options. We also recommend involving your financial professional or estate attorney. When you are ready to take the next step, please contact:

Joseph S. Leive
Director of Major Gifts
215.596.8795
j.leive@usciences.edu

Establishing a legacy gift is one of the most important decisions you may ever make – for you, your family and your University.

On this campus, you may have taken your first steps toward a rewarding career and developed a passion for lifelong learning. By accepting this invitation to join The Remington Society, you will be able to GIVE BACK IN THE MOST PERMANENT WAY POSSIBLE to the university that made such a lasting difference in your life.

Sample Society Reply Card— University of the Sciences

YES! I'M INTERESTED
IN LEARNING MORE ABOUT THE REMINGTON SOCIETY.

_____
Name/Class Year

_____
Street Address

_____
City

_____
State, Zip Code

_____
Phone Number

_____
E-mail Address

_____
Date of Birth

☐ I have included University of the Sciences in my estate plans. Please send me a Remington Society welcome packet.

☐ I am considering adding University of the Sciences to my plans. Please contact me.

For additional information on The Remington Society, please contact Joseph S. Leive at 215.596.8795 or j.leive@usciences.edu You may also visit us online at www.giftplanning.usciences.edu

THE REMINGTON SOCIETY
UNIVERSITY OF THE SCIENCES

Sample Plan Timeline

Sample Plan Timeline : Year One

	July	August	September	October	November	December	January	February	March	April	May	June
Identifying & Segmenting Prospects												
Identifying Prospects					Audience Selection	GP Ratings on Database	Audience Segmentation					
Educating Prospects												
Ads				Magazine Ad						Magazine Ad		
E-Newsletters	GP Tip of Month- Alumni Newsletter	GP Tip of Month- Alumni Newsletter	GP Tip of Month- Alumni Newsletter	GP Tip of Month- Alumni Newsletter	GP Tip of Month- Alumni Newsletter	GP Tip of Month- Alumni Newsletter	GP Tip of Month- Alumni Newsletter	GP Tip of Month- Alumni Newsletter	GP Tip of Month- Alumni Newsletter	GP Tip of Month- Alumni Newsletter	GP Tip of Month- Alumni Newsletter	GP Tip of Month- Alumni Newsletter
Regional Events							Alumni Affinity Events	Alumni Affinity Events	Alumni Affinity Events			
Website						Update GP Website			Update GP Website			Update GP Website
New Staff Orientation	Staff Orientation	Staff Orientation	Staff Orientation	Staff Orientation	Staff Orientation	Staff Orientation	Staff Orientation	Staff Orientation	Staff Orientation	Staff Orientation	Staff Orientation	Staff Orientation
Intro Training							Intro Gift Planning Training					
Calling Officer Training	Calling Officer Training			Calling Officer Training			Calling Officer Training		Calling Officer Training		Calling Officer Training	
Tier One Prospect Training				Tier One Prospect Training			Tier One Prospect Training			Tier One Prospect Training		
Cultivating Prospects												
General Brochure								Draft	Design & Produce			
PDF series										Draft	Design	Produce
Reply Cards							Share new language			Share updated language		
Reply Envelopes							Share new language			Share updated Language		
Soliciting Prospects												
Postcards					Draft Jan.	Design Jan.	Print and Mail	Draft & Design March	Print and Mail	Draft & Design May	Print and Mail	
IRA Rollover			Draft	Design	Mail	Email Follow Up						
Proposal Packages							Draft	Design	Produce			
Contact Info							General Email	Permanent Phone Number				
Stewarding Donors												
Membership Criteria						Update						
Survey Members									Confirm membership and gift type			
Society Chairs							Select New Chairs					
Society Brochure						Draft	Design and Produce					
Donor Report						Develop and Implement						
President/Letter						Mail						
Birthday Cards	Mail	Mail	Mail	Mail	Mail	Mail	Mail	Mail	Mail	Mail	Mail	Mail

Activity					
National Phil. Day Cards			Select	Order	Award at Luncheon
New Member Gift					
Existing Member Gift			Select	Order	Give Out at Event
Reunion Luncheon	Schedule	Plan	Invite	RSVP	Host
Program Development					
Gift Acceptance Policies					
Gift Valuation Policies					
Gift Recognition Policies					
Gift Agreements					
Registration to do Business/Solicit					
Registration to Issue Gift Annuities					
Donor Interaction					
Tier One Visits					
Qualifying Visits–Tier Two					
Qualifying Visits -- Tiers Three and Four					
Cultivation Visits -- Tier Two					
Cultivation Visits -- Tiers Three and Four					
Solicitation Visits–Tier Two					
Solicitation Visits–Tiers Three and Four					
Stewardship Visits–Tier Two					
Stewardship Visits–Tiers Three and Four					
Solicitations/Proposals					
Quality Contacts					
Prospect Strategy Discussions					

Sample Plan Timeline : Year Two

Activity	July	August	September	October	November	December	January	February	March	April	May	June
Identifying & Segmenting Prospects												
Survey	Design Survey	Test Survey	Survey Those Rated 2-12	Survey Those Rated 2-12	Survey Those Rated 2-12	Survey Those Rated 2-12	Survey Those Rated 2-12	Survey Those Rated 2-12	Survey Those Rated 2-12	Survey Those Rated 2-12	Survey Those Rated 2-12	Survey Those Rated 2-12
Educating Prospects												
Ads				Magazine Ad			Magazine Ad			Magazine Ad		
E-Newsletters	GP Tip of Month- Alumni Newsletter	GP Tip of Month- Alumni Newsletter	GP Tip of Month- Alumni Newsletter	GP Tip of Month- Alumni Newsletter	GP Tip of Month- Alumni Newsletter	GP Tip of Month- Alumni Newsletter	GP Tip of Month- Alumni Newsletter	GP Tip of Month- Alumni Newsletter	GP Tip of Month- Alumni Newsletter	GP Tip of Month- Alumni Newsletter	GP Tip of Month- Alumni Newsletter	GP Tip of Month- Alumni Newsletter
Regional Events							Alumni Affinity Events	Alumni Affinity Events	Alumni Affinity Events			
Fam. Weekend Seminar	Schedule	Plan	Invite	RSVP	Host							
Reunion Seminar								Schedule	Plan	Invite	RSVP	Host
Website			Update GP Website			Update GP Website			Update GP Website			Update GP Website
New Staff Orientation	Staff Orientation	Staff Orientation	Staff Orientation	Staff Orientation	Staff Orientation	Staff Orientation	Staff Orientation	Staff Orientation	Staff Orientation	Staff Orientation	Staff Orientation	Staff Orientation
Calling Officer Training	Calling Officer Training			Calling Officer Training			Calling Officer Training		Calling Officer Training		Calling Officer Training	
Tier One Prospect Training	Tier One Prospect Training			Tier One Prospect Training			Tier One Prospect Training			Tier One Prospect Training		
Cultivating Prospects												
PDF Series	Update Content											
Reply Cards										Share updated language		
Reply Envelopes										Share updated language		
Soliciting Prospects												
Postcards		Draft & Design September	Print and Mail September	Email Follow Up September; Draft & Design November	Print & Mail November	Email Follow Up November; Draft & Design January	Print and Mail January	Email Follow Up January	Draft & Design April	Print and Mail April	Email Follow Up April	
IRA Rollover	Update Content		Draft	Design	Mail	Email Follow Up						
Proposal Packages	Update Content											
Stewarding Donors												
Society Chairs	Select New Chairs											
Society Brochure		Draft	Design and Produce									
Donor Report		Include Society members in donor report										
President Letter	Refresh Letter											
Newsletter	Mail	Draft & Design	Print & Mail	Mail	Mail	Draft & Design	Print & Mail	Mail	Mail	Draft & Design	Print & Mail	Mail
Birthday Cards	Mail	Mail	Mail	Mail	Mail	Mail	Mail	Mail	Mail	Mail	Mail	Mail
National Phil. Day Cards				Draft & Design	Print & Mail							
New Member Gift	Mail to New Members Who Do Not Attend									Select	Order	Award at Luncheon

	Schedule	Plan	Select / Invite	Order / RSVP	Give Out at Event / Host
Existing Member Gift					
Reunion Luncheon					
Program Development					
Gift Acceptance Policies					
Gift Valuation Policies					
Gift Recognition Policies					
Gift Agreements					
Registration to do Business/Solicit					
Registration to issue Gift Annuities					
Donor Interaction					
Tier One Visits					
Qualifying Visits–Tier Two					
Qualifying Visits–Tiers Three and Four					
Cultivation Visits –Tier Two					
Cultivation Visits –Tiers Three and Four					
Solicitation Visits–Tier Two					
Solicitation Visits–Tiers Three and Four					
Stewardship Visits–Tier Two					
Stewardship Visits–Tiers Three and Four					
Solicitations/Proposals					
Quality Contacts					
Prospect Strategy Discussions					

Sample Plan Timeline : Year Three

	July	August	September	October	November	December	January	February	March	April	May	June
Identifying & Segmenting Prospects												
Survey		Survey Those Rated 2-12	Survey Those Rated 2-12	Survey Those Rated 2-12	Survey Those Rated 2-12	Survey Those Rated 2-12	Survey Those Rated 2-12	Survey Those Rated 2-12	Survey Those Rated 2-12	Survey Those Rated 2-12	Survey Those Rated 2-12	Survey Those Rated 2-12
Telephone Calling	Review Vendors	Select Vendor	Start Calling	Calling	Calling		Calling	Calling	Calling			
Tell Your Story	Plan	Mail	Telephone Follow Up	Telephone Follow Up	Telephone Follow Up							
Educating Prospects												
Ads				Magazine Ad			Magazine Ad			Magazine Ad		
E-Newsletters	GP Tip of Month- Alumni Newsletter	GP Tip of Month- Alumni Newsletter	GP Tip of Month- Alumni Newsletter	GP Tip of Month- Alumni Newsletter	GP Tip of Month- Alumni Newsletter	GP Tip of Month- Alumni Newsletter	GP Tip of Month- Alumni Newsletter	GP Tip of Month- Alumni Newsletter	GP Tip of Month- Alumni Newsletter	GP Tip of Month- Alumni Newsletter	GP Tip of Month- Alumni Newsletter	GP Tip of Month- Alumni Newsletter
Regional Events							Alumni Affinity Events	Alumni Affinity Events	Alumni Affinity Events			
Fam. Weekend Seminar	Schedule	Plan	Invite	RSVP	Host							
Reunion Seminar								Schedule	Plan	Invite	RSVP	Host
Prof. Advisors Council	Formulate	Invite	Meeting		Meeting			Meeting		Meeting		
Prof. Advisors Network			Formulate	Draft Materials	Draft Materials	Print Materials	Launch					
Website			Update GP Website			Update GP Website			Update GP Website			Update GP Website
New Staff Orientation	Staff Orientation	Staff Orientation	Staff Orientation	Staff Orientation	Staff Orientation	Staff Orientation	Staff Orientation	Staff Orientation	Staff Orientation	Staff Orientation	Staff Orientation	Staff Orientation
Calling Officer Training	Calling Officer Training			Calling Officer Training			Calling Officer Training		Calling Officer Training		Calling Officer Training	
Tier One Prospect Training	Tier One Prospect Training			Tier One Prospect Training			Tier One Prospect Training			Tier One Prospect Training		
Cultivating Prospects												
PDF Series	Update Content											
Gift Plannign Chairs	Formulate	Solicit Volunteers	Solicit Volunteers	Compose Letters	Approval for Drafts	Approval for Drafts	Send Letters		Compose Letters	Approval for Drafts	Send Letters	
Reply Cards										Share updated language		
Reply Envelopes										Share updated language		
Soliciting Prospects												
Postcards		Draft & Design September	Print and Mail September	Email Follow Up September; Draft November	Print & Mail November	Email Follow Up November; Draft January	Print and Mail January	Email Follow Up January	Draft & Design April	Print and Mail April	Email Follow Up April	
IRA Rollover	Update Content		Draft	Design	Mail	Email Follow Up						
Proposal Packages	Update Content											
Bequest Buck Slip	Draft	Design	Print and Add to Checks			Add to Checks			Add to Checks			Add to Checks
Receipt Buck Slip	Draft	Design	Print and Add to Checks			Add to Checks			Add to Checks			Add to Checks
CGA Addition Letter	Draft	Mail		Draft	Mail		Draft	Mail		Draft	Mail	

Task												
Stewarding Donors												
Society Chairs	Select New Chairs											
Society Brochure	Draft	Design and Produce										
Donor Report	Include Society members in donor report											
President Letter	Refresh Letter											
Newsletter	Draft & Design	Print & Mail				Draft & Design	Print & Mail			Draft & Design	Print & Mail	
Birthday Cards		Mail					Mail				Mail	
National Phil. Day Cards						Draft & Design	Print & Mail					
New Member Gift	Mail to New Members Who Do Not Attend							Select	Order			Award at Luncheon
Existing Member Gift								Select	Order			
Reunion Luncheon							Schedule	Plan	Invite	RSVP	Host	Give Out at Event
Program Development												
Gift Acceptance Policies												
Gift Valuation Policies												
Gift Recognition Policies												
Gift Agreements												
Registration to do Business/Solicit												
Registration to Issue Gift Annuities												
Donor Interaction												
Tier One Visits												
Qualifying Visits–Tier Two												
Qualifying Visits – Tiers Three and Four												
Cultivation Visits – Tier Two												
Cultivation Visits – Tiers Three and Four												
Solicitation Visits – Tier Two												
Solicitation Visits – Tiers Three and Four												
Stewardship Visits – Tier Two												
Stewardship Visits – Tiers Three and Four												
Solicitations/Proposals												
Quality Contacts												
Prospect Strategy Discussions												

Activities Measures Reports

			Philanthropic	Office
	Fundraiser	**Gift Planner**	**Planner**	**Totals**

Monthly Prospect Activity Report

Month:

	Fundraiser	Gift Planner	Philanthropic Planner	Office Totals
TIER ONE				
Philanthropic Planning Visits				
This Month	1	2	3	6
Year-to-Date	0	0	0	0
TIERS TWO, THREE AND FOUR				
Qualifying Visits				
This Month	7	9	3	19
Year-to-Date	0	0	0	0
Cultivation Visits				
This Month	7	9	3	19
Year-to-Date	0	0	0	0
Solicitation Visits				
This Month	7	9	3	19
Year-to-Date	0	0	0	0
Stewardship Visits				
This Month	7	9	3	19
Year-to-Date	0	0	0	0
Solicitations/Proposals				
This Month	0	5	2	7
Year-to-Date	5	45	3	53
Quality Contacts				
This Month	11	64	122	197
Year-to-Date	68	629	138	835
Prospect Strategy Discussions				
With Front-Line Fundraisers				
This Month	2	5	4	11
Year-to-Date	19	41	12	72

Monthly Fundraiser Activity Report

Month:

	Fundraiser	Gift Planner	Philanthropic Planner	Office Totals
Prospect Strategy Discussions With Front-Line Fundraisers				
This Month	2	5	4	11
Year-to-Date	19	41	12	72
By Fundraiser this Month				
Fundraiser 4	1	2	1	
Fundraiser 5	1	1	0	
Fundraiser 6	1	1	0	
Fundraiser 7	2	1	0	
Fundraiser 8	3	1	0	
Fundraiser 9	2	1	0	
Fundraiser 2	1	1	0	
Fundraiser 1	2	1	0	
Fundraiser 3	3	1	0	

Legacy Society	Current Month	Year-to-Date	Campaign-to-Date
New Members	3	3	4
Qualifying Asks	36	80	80
Fundraiser 4	2	4	4
Gift Planner 2	1	5	5
Fundraiser 5	0	6	6
Fundraiser 6	4	7	7
Fundraiser 7	4	4	4
Fundraiser 8	8	9	9
Fundraiser 9	1	2	2
Fundraiser 10	0	5	5
Fundraiser 2	7	10	10
Fundraiser 1	5	6	6
Gift Planner 1	2	18	18
Fundraiser 3	2	4	4

Sample Gift Acceptance Policy XYZ Charity

XYZ Charity (the "Charity"), a not-for-profit organization organized in the State of New York, encourages the solicitation and acceptance of gifts to further and fulfill its mission of (*insert your mission statement here*).

I. PURPOSE OF POLICIES

This statement articulates the policies of the Board of Directors (the "Board") of the Charity concerning the acceptance of charitable gifts and provides guidance to prospective donors and their advisors when making gifts to the Charity. The Advancement Committee of the Board will adopt appropriate procedures to implement these policies.

II. RESPONSIBILITY TO DONORS

A. *Commitment to a Donor-Centered, Philanthropic Planning Approach:* The Charity, its staff, and volunteer representatives shall endeavor to assist donors in accomplishing their philanthropic objectives in a donor-centered way. In many circumstances, this may involve the donor's professional advisors, as charitable support is often integrated with a donor's overall tax, estate, and financial planning.

B. *Confidentiality:* Information concerning all transactions between a donor and the Charity shall be held by the Charity in confidence, and may be disclosed only with the permission of the donor or the donor's designee.

C. *Anonymity:* The Charity shall respect the wishes of any donor offering anonymous support and will implement reasonable procedures to safeguard such donor's identity.

D. *Ethical Standards:* The charity is committed to the highest ethical standards. The Charity, its staff, and volunteer representatives shall adhere to both the *Model Standards of Practice for the Charitable Gift Planner*, as adopted by the Partnership for Philanthropic Planning ("PPP"), and the *Code of Ethical Principles and Standards* as adopted by the Association of Fundraising Professionals ("AFP"). The Charity will not participate in gift discussions if there is a question as to the title/ownership of the asset or the donor's competency to transfer an asset.

III. LEGAL CONSIDERATIONS

A. *Compliance:* The Charity shall comply with all local, state, and federal laws and regulations concerning all charitable gifts it encourages, solicits, or accepts. All required disclosures, registrations, and procedures shall be made and/or followed in a thorough and timely manner.

B. *Endorsement of providers:* The Charity shall not endorse legal, tax, or financial advisors to prospective donors.

C. *Finder's fees and commissions:* The Charity shall not pay fees to any person as consideration for directing a gift by a donor to the Charity.

D. *Legal, tax, and financial advice:* The Charity shall inform prospective donors that it does not provide, legal, tax, or financial advice, and shall encourage prospective donors to discuss all charitable gift planning decisions with their own advisors before entering into any commitments to make gifts to the Charity.

E. *Preparation of legal documents:* The Charity shall not prepare legal documents for execution by donors, except forms to create charitable gift annuities. The Charity may provide model language, such as sample bequest language, gift agreements, or charitable remainder trusts, but shall strongly encourage prospective donors to have this language reviewed by their own counsel.

F. *Payment of fees:* It will be the responsibility of the donor to secure an appraisal (where required) and to pay for the advice of independent legal, financial, or other professional advisers as needed for all gifts made to the Charity.

G.   *Service as executor or living trust trustee:* Unless approved in advance by the Vice President of Finance, the Charity will not agree to serve as executor of a decedent's estate or as trustee of a living trust or other trust intended to serve as a person's primary estate planning document.

H.   *Trusteeship:* The Charity may serve as trustee of trusts to maintain its gift annuity reserve accounts, as required by relevant state insurance law, in connection with the Charity's gift annuity program. The Charity may serve as trustee of charitable remainder trusts, provided that 100 percent of the remainder interest in the trust is irrevocably dedicated to the Charity, and the charitable remainder trust meets the minimum standards set forth in the Gift Acceptance Procedures. The Charity may serve as a trustee of trusts only in circumstances in which its investment authority as trustee is unrestricted. The Charity will not serve as co-trustee of a charitable trust.

   1.   *Use of counsel:* The Charity shall seek the advice of legal counsel in matters relating to the acceptance of gifts when appropriate. Review by counsel is recommended for gifts involving: closely held stock transfers that are subject to restrictions; gifts involving contracts, such as bargain sales; reformation of charitable trusts; and transactions involving potential conflicts of interest.

IV. Gift Acceptance

   A.   *Implementation:* Gift acceptance, as outlined in these policies, is delegated by the Board to the Vice President of Advancement (the "Vice President"). The Vice President is authorized to accept all gifts permitted by this policy.

   B.   *Approval of exceptions:* Acceptance of gifts outside the scope of this policy requires the unanimous, written approval of the Gift Acceptance Committee (the "GAC"). The Vice President shall report all gifts accepted as exceptions to the policy to the Advancement Committee of the Board at its next regular meeting.

   C.   *Gift acceptance committee:* The GAC shall be made up of the Chair of the Advancement Committee of the Board, the Vice President, and the Vice President of Finance.

D. *Gift acceptance procedures:* The Board delegates to the GAC the responsibility of approving gift acceptance procedures to implement these policies.

E. *Gift acceptance alternatives:* In the event the GAC rejects a gift, the Charity will attempt to assist the donor in finding a suitable third-party charity to accept the gift and share the proceeds, less costs, with the Charity.

F. *Gift agreements:* The Charity generally uses non-binding statements of intent to document gift commitments. The GAC shall create and maintain samples for use by staff and volunteer leadership. All statements of intent shall include a short profile of the donor, the donor's commitment and timeframe for payments, the Charity's commitment (including restrictions), how the completed gift will be managed, alternative use and saving language, stewardship, and donor recognition.

1. *Unrestricted commitments within a fiscal year:* The Charity does not require statements of intent for unrestricted gift commitments within the current fiscal year.

2. *Unrestricted commitments covering more than one fiscal year:* If the unrestricted commitment shall cover more than one fiscal year, a simple letter or card documenting the gift amount and payment schedule may be substituted for a formal statement of intent.

3. *Commitments subject to restrictions:* The Charity requires an executed statement of intent for all commitments subject to restrictions, including restricted endowment gifts.

4. *Commitments over $1,000,000:* The Charity requires an executed, binding gift agreement (pledge) for all commitments over $1,000,000, unless waived in writing by the Vice President.

V. GIFT RESTRICTIONS

A. *Unrestricted gifts:* To provide the Charity with maximum flexibility in the pursuit of its mission, donors shall always be encouraged to consider unrestricted gifts or gifts restricted to budgeted priorities of the Charity.

B. *Budgeted programs or facilities:* The Charity may accept gifts restricted to specific budgeted programs and purposes.

C. *Other restrictions on gifts:* The Charity may accept gifts restricted to non-budgeted programs and purposes only upon the prior, written approval of the Vice President. The Charity reserves the right to decline gifts which are too restrictive in purpose, too difficult to administer, or for purposes outside of its mission.

D. *Unrestricted future gifts:* As donors making large future gifts generally intend for these gifts to benefit the long-term future of the Charity, all future gifts (bequests, retirement plan and life insurance designations, etc.) with a value over $25,000 shall be added to the Board Designated Unrestricted Endowment.

VI. TYPES OF PROPERTY

These assets may be considered for acceptance by the Charity, subject to the following criteria:

A. *Cash:* Acceptable in any negotiable form, including currency, check, and credit card gifts.

B. *Securities:*

1. *Publicly traded securities:* Stocks, bonds, and mutual funds traded on an exchange or other publicly reported market are acceptable.

2. *Closely held securities and business interests:* Debt and equity positions in non-publicly traded businesses, hedge funds, real estate investment trusts (REITs), interests in limited liability companies, and partnerships may only be accepted upon prior written approval of the GAC after review in accordance with the gift acceptance procedures.

3. *Options and other rights in securities:* Warrants, stock options, and stock appreciation rights may only be accepted upon prior written approval of the GAC.

C. *Life insurance:* The Charity will accept a gift of life insurance provided that the policy has a positive cash surrender value and the Charity has been named both beneficiary and irrevocable owner of the policy.

D. *Real property:* Personal and commercial real property, real estate interests/derivatives, and remainder interests in property (gifts subject to a retained life estate) may only be accepted upon prior written approval of the GAC after review in accordance with the Gift Acceptance Procedures, including appropriate environmental screenings. The Charity does not accept debt-encumbered real property, real property subject to a mortgage or lien, or time share interests. For gifts subject to a retained life estate, the donor or primary life beneficiary shall be responsible for all expenses other than capital expenditures during the life tenancy, including but not limited to maintenance, real estate taxes, assessments, and insurance.

E. *Tangible personal property:* Jewelry, books, works of art, collections, equipment, and other property which may be touched, may only be accepted after review in accordance with the Gift Acceptance Procedures.

F. *Other property:* Property not otherwise described in this section, whether real or personal, of any description (including but not limited to mortgages, notes, contract rights, copyrights, patents, trademarks, mineral rights, oil and gas interests and royalties) may be only be accepted upon prior written approval of the GAC.

VII. STRUCTURED CURRENT GIFTS

A. *Bargain sales:* Transactions wherein the Charity pays less than full value for an asset and issues a gift receipt for the difference may only be accepted upon prior written approval of the GAC after review in accordance with the Gift Acceptance Procedures.

B. *Charitable lead trusts:* The Charity may accept a designation as income beneficiary of a charitable lead trust. The Charity will not serve as trustee of a charitable lead trust.

C. *IRA charitable rollover:* The Charity may accept all gifts directly transferred from an IRA, as permitted under the Pension Protection Act of 2006 and subsequent extensions.

D. *Matching gifts:* The Charity will accept all matching gifts, subject to the terms and conditions of Section VI.

E. *Other structured current gifts:* The Charity may only accept other structured current gifts with prior written approval of the GAC after review in accordance with the Gift Acceptance Procedures.

VIII. FUTURE GIFTS

A. Future Gifts Subject to a Payment Interest

  1. *Charitable gift annuities:* The Charity offers immediate payment, deferred payment, commuted payment, and flexible payment charitable gift annuities, provided:

       i. Minimum funding amount: $10,000

       ii. Maximum funding amount: 25 percent of total gift annuity pool [if pool is unrestricted]; 10 percent of total gift annuity pool [if pool is restricted]

       iii. Minimum age(s): None (All proposals for donors with an average age under 60 shall include an option with a hedge against inflation)

       iv. Maximum number of lives: Two

       v. Ultimate beneficiary: The Charity for 100 percent, irrevocably

       vi. Payout rate: American Council on Gift Annuities recommended rates (All proposals shall include offer of 100 percent, 90 percent, and 80 percent of the ACGA recommended rate)

       vii. Payment schedule: Monthly, quarterly, semi-annual, or annual

       viii. Funding assets: Prior written approval of the GAC is required for assets other than cash or publicly traded securities

  2. *Charitable remainder trusts when the charity serves as trustee:* The Charity will serve as trustee of charitable remainder trusts, provided:

       i. Minimum funding amount: $100,000

       ii. Maximum funding amount: None

       iii. Minimum age(s): None

       iv. Maximum number of lives: None

       v. Ultimate beneficiary: The Charity for 100 percent, irrevocably

       vi. Payout rate: Per gift acceptance procedures (generally 5 to 7 percent)

       vii. Minimum charitable remainder: 25 percent of the funding amount (using the income tax charitable deduction methodology)

       viii. Payment schedule: Monthly, quarterly, semi-annually, or annually

ix. Funding assets: Prior written approval of the GAC is required for assets other than cash or publicly traded securities, although a broader array of assets will be approved for a charitable remainder trust than a charitable gift annuity

x. Costs charged to the trust: Investment management, administration, legal counsel, and tax return preparation

3. *Charitable remainder trusts when the charity does not serve as trustee:* The Charity will accept designation as charitable beneficiary of charitable remainder trusts that do not name the Charity as trustee. Donors who create externally managed and trusteed trusts will be asked to provide the Charity with a copy of the trust document and annual investment reports for record-keeping purposes.

4. *Pooled income funds:* The Charity offers a pooled income fund provided

   i. Minimum funding amount: $10,000
   ii. Maximum funding amount: None
   iii. Minimum age(s): None
   iv. Maximum number of lives: Two
   v. Ultimate beneficiary: The Charity for 100 percent, irrevocably
   vi. Payout: Net income (capital gains treated as income)
   vii. Payment schedule: Quarterly
   viii. Funding assets: Prior written approval of the GAC is required for assets other than cash or publicly traded securities.
   ix. Costs charged to the pool: Investment management, administration, legal counsel, and tax return preparation

B. Future Gifts Not Subject to a Payment Interest

1. *Gifts by will or living trust:* Donors and supporters of the Charity will be encouraged to designate the Charity as a beneficiary of their wills or living trusts.

2. *Retirement plan, life insurance, and other beneficiary designations:* Donors and supporters of the Charity will be encouraged to designate the Charity as beneficiary or contingent beneficiary of their retirement plans, life insurance policies, and other accounts on which they can name a beneficiary.

IX. DONOR RECOGNITION

A. *General:* The Board, upon recommendation of the GAC and the Advancement Committee, establishes criteria for recognizing, honoring and stewarding donors.

B. *Buildings:* Except in the case of naming opportunities that appear on a schedule approved by the Board, the advancement staff of the Charity shall make no commitments to donors concerning the naming of buildings or facilities without the approval of the Board upon recommendation of the GAC.

X. REPORTING AND VALUATION STANDARDS

A. *Gift Reporting and Counting:* For outright gifts, the Charity shall follow the Council for Advancement and Support of Education (CASE) *Reporting Standards and Management Guidelines for Educational Institutions*, Fourth Edition, 2009. For future gifts, the Charity shall follow the *PPP Guidelines for Reporting and Counting Charitable Gifts*, Second Edition, 2009. All exceptions to these standards shall be made by the GAC.

B. *Gift Valuation:* The Charity shall follow the *PPP Valuation Standards for Charitable Planned Gifts*. All exceptions to these standards shall be made by the GAC.

XI. PERIODIC REVIEW

A. *Regular Review:* The GAC shall review these policies in even-numbered years to ensure that they continue to accurately describe the policies of the Charity with respect to acceptance of charitable gifts, and shall propose to the full Board for ratification those revisions that the GAC shall determine to be necessary or appropriate.

B. *Special Review:* The GAC shall initiate a supplemental review of these policies upon the enactment or promulgation of legislation or regulatory rules affecting fundraising and gift acceptance by the Charity, or prior to the start of a formal fundraising campaign. All proposed changes shall be shared with the full Board for ratification.

O

Gift Counting and Reporting Policy Summary

_____ (hereinafter "Our Charity") has adopted the Council for Advancement and Support of Education gift counting standards for counting outright gifts and the Partnership for Philanthropic Planning (PPP) gift counting standards for counting future gifts. For complete details, please refer to the Our Charity Gift Acceptance Policy, http://www.pppnet.org/pdf/NCPG-counting-guidelines-(rev-2008).pdf, and the *CASE Reporting Standards and Management Guidelines, 4th Edition.*

Gift counting and reporting applies to all gifts generally and for fundraising campaigns. Recognition or crediting does not stem from any of the factors of counting and reporting, although Our Charity generally uses its gift counting amount as the basis for gift recognition. In some cases, however, Our Charity will recognize a gift for an amount other than the counting amount. For example, if John and Susan Jones, husband and wife, each give Our Charity $500,000, we may recognize them both as $1,000,000 donors because their joint giving totals this amount. Similarly, Our Charity gives a donor "soft credit" for recognition purposes when a corporate matching gift is received as a result of the donor making his or her own contribution. Because gift recognition is fundamentally different than gift counting and reporting, it is covered in Section IX of Our Charity's Gift Acceptance Policy.

I. GIFT COUNTING AND REPORTING

The CASE Reporting Standards suggest that charities report two numbers for their fundraising results. The first number is the total of outrights gifts and pledges received, reported at face value. The second number is the total of irrevocable deferred commitments, reported at face and present value, using the IRS income tax charitable deduction as a proxy for a true present value calculation. Revocable deferred commitments are not reported.

Our Charity recognizes that these standards substantially under report the value of both irrevocable and revocable deferred commitments, thereby making them less attractive to prospective donors, even though they are potentially the largest gifts many prospects can make. These standards also make it difficult, when reviewing a gift report, particularly during a campaign, to determine which funds are available now, which funds will not be accessible until the future, and which funds may not be received at all. Finally, such standards create an incentive for gift officers to solicit outright gifts when a future gift may better serve both the donor and Our Charity. With this in mind, Our Charity has adopted the PPP gift counting standards for both irrevocable and revocable deferred commitments, or what Our Charity calls future gifts.

Under its gift acceptance policy, Our Charity adheres to the following gift reporting standards:

Three Separate Reporting Numbers

1. Category A—Outright gifts: The total of outright gifts and pledges received, reported at face value.
2. Category B—Irrevocable deferred gifts: The total of irrevocable deferred commitments, which will be received at an undetermined time in the future, reported at face value.
3. Category C—Revocable gifts: The total of revocable deferred commitments, which may be received at an undetermined time in the future, reported at estimated current value.

When to report gifts: Outright gifts are reported only when assets are transferred irrevocably to Our Charity or a gift intention is executed. Deferred irrevocable gifts should be reported only when assets are transferred to the gift instrument. Revocable commitments should be reported when the gift instrument is executed and sufficient documentation is received by Our Charity.

What to report: All gifts, pledges, and commitments falling into categories covered by these standards may be reported. However, in keeping with the spirit of these standards, it is never appropriate to add all three categories together and report only one number when announcing gift results.

II. CATEGORY A: OUTRIGHT GIFTS

1. Definition: Gifts that are usable or will become usable for institutional purposes including:
   a. Cash
   b. Marketable securities
   c. Other current gifts of non-cash assets
   d. Irrevocable pledges collectible during the reporting period (five years or the campaign period, whichever is greater)
   e. The gift portion of bargain sales
   f. Lead trust distributions received during the reporting period (five years or the campaign period, whichever is greater)
   g. Cash value of life insurance owned by Our Charity (net of policy loans)
   h. Realized life insurance or retirement plan benefits in excess of the amounts previously counted
   i. Realized bequests in excess of the amounts previously counted
2. Statement of Intent: Statements of Intent are counted upon receipt of the written intention, provided the intention is in accord with these guidelines.
   a. Intentions to make outright gifts: Such intentions should be written and should commit to a specific dollar amount that will be paid according to a fixed time schedule. The payment period, regardless of when the intention is made, should not exceed five years. Therefore, an intention received even on the last day of a campaign is counted in campaign totals and may be paid over a five-year period.
   b. Oral statements of intent: Oral intentions should not be reported in giving or campaign totals. On the rare occasion when an exception is warranted, Our Charity should write to the individual making an oral pledge to document the commitment, place a copy of the confirmation in the donor's file and gain specific, written approval from the Gift Acceptance Committee.

3. Guidelines for Reporting Specific Types of Assets
    a. Cash: Report cash at full value as of the date received by Our Charity.
    b. Marketable securities: Marketable securities should be counted according to the IRS standards then in effect for gifts of this type. The current standard values a gift of marketable securities at the average of the high and low quoted selling prices on the gift date (the date the donor relinquished dominion and control of the assets in favor of Our Charity). If there were not any actual trades on the gift date, the fair-market value can be computed using the weighted average of the mean of the high and low trading prices on a date before and a date after the gift date, if those dates are a reasonable number of days before and after the actual gift date. If there were no actual trades in a reasonable number of days before and after the gift date, then the fair-market value is computed based on the average of the bid and the ask price on the gift date. Exactly when dominion and control has been relinquished by a donor depends on the method of delivery of the securities to Our Charity. These reporting standards do not address the multitude of tax rules regarding the delivery of securities by the donor to Our Charity.
    c. Closely held stock:
        i. Gifts of closely held stock exceeding $10,000 in value should be reported at the fair-market value placed on them by a qualified independent appraiser as required by the IRS for valuing gifts of non-publicly traded stock. Gifts of $10,000 or less may be valued at the per-share cash purchase price of the closest transaction. Normally, this transaction will be the redemption of the stock by the corporation.
        ii. If no redemption is consummated during the reporting period, a gift of closely held stock may be credited to gift or campaign totals at the value determined by a qualified independent appraiser. For a gift of $10,000 or less, when no redemption has occurred during the reporting period, an independent CPA who maintains the books for a closely held corporation is deemed to be qualified to value the stock of the corporation.

d. Gifts of property:

   i. Gifts of real and personal property that qualify for a charitable deduction should be counted at their full fair-market value. Gifts in-kind, such as equipment and software, shall be counted at their fair-market value.

   ii. Caution should be exercised to ensure that only gifts that are convertible to cash or that are of actual direct value to Our Charity are counted. Mega gifts of software and hardware may require special care. These types of gifts can be especially complex, and Our Charity should exercise extreme caution in counting these gifts in gift totals. Gifts with fair market value exceeding $5,000 should be counted at the value placed on them by a qualified independent appraiser as required by the IRS for valuing non-cash charitable contributions. Gifts of $5,000 and under may be reported at the value declared by the donor or placed on them by a qualified expert.

e. Non-governmental grants and contracts: Grant income from private, non-governmental sources should be reported; contract revenue should be excluded. The difference between a private grant and contract should be judged on the basis of the intention of the awarding agency and the legal obligation incurred by Our Charity in accepting the award. A grant is bestowed voluntarily, without expectation of any tangible compensation. It is donative in nature. A contract carries an explicit quid pro quo relationship between the source and Our Charity.

f. Realized testamentary gifts: All realized bequests should be counted at full value in gift totals, insofar as the amount received exceeds commitments counted previously. If a revocable testamentary commitment made during a current counting period and counted in Category C matures during the same counting period, it should be removed from Category C and included as an outright gift in Category A.

g. Realized retirement plan assets: All realized gifts of retirement plan assets should be counted at full face value in gift totals to the extent the gift was not counted previously.

4. Gifts in Contemplation of a Campaign: From time to time, Our Charity will engage in comprehensive and targeted fundraising

campaigns. It is often the case that certain prospects, to meet their own personal planning objectives or to help Our Charity launch the initiative, will make gifts before the official start date of the campaign, in contemplation of the fundraising effort. In such cases, the Gift Acceptance Committee shall make a recommendation of all gifts which should be counted and reported in the campaign, even though such gifts were received prior to the official start date of the campaign.

III. CATEGORY B: IRREVOCABLE DEFERRED GIFTS

1. Definition: Gifts committed during the reporting period, but likely usable by Our Charity only at some point after the end of the period, including:
   a. Split interest gifts such as charitable gift annuities, pooled income funds and charitable remainder trusts in which the beneficiary designation is irrevocable
   b. Gifts of a remainder interest in a personal residence or farm with a retained life estate
   c. Death benefit of paid up life insurance in which Our Charity is both owner and beneficiary
   d. Irrevocable testamentary pledges or contract to make a will
   e. Lead trust distributions to be made after the reporting period
2. Charitable Remainder Trusts, Pooled Income Funds, and Gift Annuities: Gifts made to establish charitable remainder trusts for which the remainder is not subject to change or revocation, pooled income fund gifts, and gifts to fund charitable gift annuities should be counted at face value. When additions are made to gifts that have been counted previously, the additions can be counted at face value. Counting deferred gifts at face value meets several critical needs. First, in a donor-centered environment, the donor is getting gift credit for the amount of assets actually transferred to fund a life-income gift. While these assets may be worth less to the charity due to the income interest retained by the donor, the donor likely feels like he/she has made a gift of the face value amount. Second, by counting such gifts at face value, it creates an incentive for the fundraisers

to use a donor-centered approach in their donor work. If the fund-raiser were to only receive credit for the net present value of a gift, the fundraiser might push a donor to an alternative gift option that gave the fundraiser more credit, but did not meet the needs of the donor. By counting at face value, the interests of the donor remain paramount.

3. Remainder Interest in a Personal Residence or Farm with Retained Life Estate: A gift of a remainder interest in a personal residence or farm should be counted at the face value of the remainder interest.

4. Charitable Lead Trusts: Charitable lead trusts are gifts in trust that pay an income to the charity over a period of time. These payments should be counted in Category A for amounts received during the campaign period (or during the next five-year period if not in a campaign). The remainder of the payments to be received by Our Charity should be counted in Category B.

IV. Category C: Revocable Deferred Gifts

1. Definition: Gifts solicited and committed during the reporting pe-riod, but for which the donor retains the right to change the com-mitment and/or beneficiary including:
   a. Estate provisions, either from a will or a living trust.
   b. Charitable remainder trusts in which the donor retains the right to change the beneficiary designation. When additions are made to gifts that have been counted previously, the additions can be counted in the current reporting period.
   c. IRAs or other retirement plan assets in which Our Charity's in-terest remains revocable by the donor.
   d. Life insurance in which the donor retains ownership (face value less any policy loans) and in which Our Charity is owner but premiums remain due.
   e. Other revocable pledges

2. Uncertainty of Revocable Commitments: It is difficult to put spe-cific numbers on certain revocable commitments when the ultimate maturation value is uncertain, or if it is uncertain that the gift will mature to Our Charity at all. Examples include Our Charity being

named the beneficiary of a trust to which another person retains access to principal; or a contingent bequest that relies upon another person pre-deceasing the donor in order for any funds to come to Our Charity. The numbers reported in Category C should be best estimates and reflect both a conservative and realistic understanding of each donor's circumstances. If the commitment is difficult to value or will likely be nominal, it should be counted in Category C at $1. If the gift matures at a date in the future, the full value can then be counted in Category A.

3. Estate Provisions: To include estate provisions in giving totals, the following requirements must be satisfied:

    a. The commitment should specify an amount to be distributed to Our Charity or, if a percentage of the estate or a trust, specify a credible estimate of the value of the estate at the time the commitment is made. If a credible estimate is not possible, then Our Charity shall use a rolling five-year average of all bequests received. Until a five-year average can be calculated, an estimated value of $50,000 shall be utilized. (Note that for the top 100 planned giving programs in the United States, the average bequest is approximately $240,000 according to a study by *Changing our World*, completed in 2008.)

    b. Have verification of the commitment through one of the following forms:

        i. A letter or agreement from the donor or donor's advisor affirming the commitment

        ii. Copy of will

        iii. Notification form provided by Our Charity, signed by donor or advisor

        iv. Charitable/Deferred pledge agreement. A deferred pledge agreement is a legally binding document that places an obligation on the estate of the issuer to transfer a certain amount to Our Charity. Under such an agreement, the executor of the donor's estate is held legally responsible for payment of the specified amount from the estate.

    c. Our Charity will carefully investigate the actual circumstances underlying the estate and be conservative in counting such commitments toward gift totals. If any circumstances should make it unlikely that the amount pledged by bequest will actually be realized by Our Charity, then the commitment should be further adjusted according to specific circumstances, or reported at $1.

4. Retirement Plan Assets:

  a. Our Charity may be named as the beneficiary of retirement plan assets. A testamentary pledge of retirement plan assets shall be included in gift totals if the following requirements have been satisfied:

    i. There must be a means to establish a credible estimate of the value of the retirement plan account at the time the commitment is made. If a credible estimate is not possible, then Our Charity shall use a rolling five-year average of all bequests received. Until a five-year average can be calculated, an estimated value of $50,000 shall be utilized.

    ii. Have verification of the commitment in the form of a letter from the donor or the donor's advisor affirming the commitment.

    iii. Our Charity will carefully investigate the actual circumstances underlying the plan and be conservative in counting such commitments toward gift totals. If any circumstances should make it unlikely that the amount pledged will actually be realized by Our Charity, then the commitment should be further adjusted according to specific circumstances, or reported at $1.

V. Gifts That May Be Counted in More Than One Category, Depending on the Circumstances

1. Life Insurance: To include commitments of life insurance in gift totals, the following requirements must be satisfied

  a. Ownership:

    i. Our Charity should be made the owner and irrevocable beneficiary of gifts of all new policies, paid-up policies, and existing policies that are not fully paid up.

    ii. If Our Charity is the beneficiary only and not the owner of a policy, gift credit will be given but only in Category C, in the same way as credit is given to any other revocable gift commitment.

   iii. The remainder of these guidelines assume that Our Charity is the owner of the policy.

 b. Paid-up life insurance policies: Counted at face value in Category B.

 c. Existing policies/not fully paid up: A life insurance policy that is not fully paid up on the date of contribution should be counted at face value only in Category C.

 d. New policies: Face amount of these policies should be counted in Category C.

 e. Realized death benefits: The insurance company's settlement amount for an insurance policy whose death benefit is realized during the campaign period, whether the policy is owned by Our Charity or not, should be counted in gift totals, less amounts previously counted in former campaigns.

2. Wholly Charitable Trusts Administered by Others:

 a. A wholly charitable trust is one that is held for the irrevocable benefit of Our Charity, where the principal is invested and the income is distributed to us. All interests in income and principal are irrevocably dedicated to charitable purposes (as opposed to a charitable remainder or lead trust). While it is similar in that sense to an endowment fund, it is created as a freestanding entity.

 b. The fair-market value of the assets, or a portion of the assets, of such a trust administered by an outside fiduciary should be counted in Category A, in the gifts and pledges section of gift totals, for the year in which the trust is established, provided that Our Charity has an irrevocable right to all or a predetermined portion of the income of the trust. If the trustee retains or is awarded the right to designate or alter the income beneficiary, only the income should be reported and then only as it is distributed.

 c. In cases where less than the entire income of the trust is to be distributed Our Charity, the amount to be reported is the income to be distributed to Our Charity over the total income (or the stated percentage to be distributed, if the trust terms spell this out as a percentage) multiplied by the value of the trust assets. The income of the trust, thereafter, is reported as a gift.

    d. Community and private foundations: Gifts to community foundations, the income from which is irrevocably designated, in whole or in part, to Our Charity, and private foundations established solely to benefit Our Charity or where Our Charity is to receive a specified percentage of the annual income each year, are two examples of wholly charitable trusts administered by others. (Gift credit will generally be given to the foundation, although the original donors or their families should certainly be kept apprised of the distributions if at all possible and given recognition credit.)

    e. Donor-advised funds: Donor-advised funds are IRS-approved public charities generally managed by investment companies and community foundations that serve as conduits for gifts. The donor's contribution is made to the fund. The donor reserves the right to suggest which charities should receive the annual income. Gifts from DAFs will be counted like any other gift as received. If Our Charity is entitled to receive a certain percentage of the annual distributions of a DAF, it may count the value of that percentage as if it were an irrevocable trust administered by others.

VI. Gifts That Change Character During a Counting or Campaign Period

1. All campaigns face the dilemma of reporting commitments that change character during the campaign period. A commitment should, at the end of the campaign period, be reported only once and should reflect the final (or most recent) form of the commitment.

2. It is possible for a donor to establish an irrevocable deferred gift or a revocable gift commitment that would be reported in Categories B or C, and then for that gift to mature within the same campaign. In such cases, the cumulative campaign report will recognize the gift only in Category A, and any previous interim report of the gift in Categories B or C is deleted. The annual report would note this change as well.

    a. Example: A donor creates a charitable remainder trust but retains the right to change the remainder beneficiary. That commitment would appear in Category C. If, later in the campaign period, the donor made the remainder beneficiary irrevocable, the commitment would shift in the cumulative campaign report to Category B and be removed from Category C. The annual report would note the shift as well.

b. Example: Our Charity is named as the payment beneficiary of a 20-year charitable lead trust paying $10,000 per year ($200,000 in total) in the first year of a seven-year comprehensive campaign. The annual report in year one will note $10,000 (the amount actually received that year) in Category A and $190,000 in Category B. The cumulative comprehensive campaign report (covering all seven years) will report $70,000 in Category A (the amount committed and to be received during the campaign period) and $130,000 in Category B. In years two through seven, the annual report will again count a $10,000 cash gift with a note that this commitment had previously been reported in Category B. There would be no further reporting in the annual report for the Category B portion of the gift, since there had been no new commitment in year two.

Gift Reports By Tender Type

Gifts by Tender Type: Five Year

Asset Tender Types	FY07	FY08	FY09	FY10	FY11	Five Year Total	Possible Gift Structure Types Associated With These Tenders (do not show on report)
Category A: Outright Gifts (reported at face value)							
Cash							Will/Living Trust Proceeds
Marketable Securities							Life Insurance Proceeds
Artwork and Collectibles							Retirement Plan Proceeds (IRA, 401(k), 403(b), etc.)
Real Estate							Commericial Annuity Proceeds
Other Gifts-in-Kind							Perpetual Trust Proceeds – Income
Hedge Fund Interests							Perpetual Trust Proceeds – Principal
Venture Capital Funds							Revocable PIF Proceeds
Closely Held Stock/Business Interests							Revocable CGA Proceeds
							Revocable CRT Proceeds
Total Category A	$ -	$ -	$ -	$ -	$ -	$ -	IRA Rollover Proceeds
							Outright
Category B: Irrevocable Future Gifts (reported at face value)							
Irrevocable Future Tender TBD							Irrevocable Bequest/Living Trust Designation
Cash							Irrevocable Life Insurance Beneficiary Designation
Marketable Securities							Irrevocable Retirement Plan Designation
Artwork and Collectibles							Charitable Gift Annuity – Immediate Payment (CGA)
Real Estate							Charitable Gift Annuity – Deferred Payment (DCGA)
Other Gifts-in-Kind							Charitable Gift Annuity – Flexible Payment (FCGA)

Hedge Fund Interests
Venture Capital Funds
Closely Held Stock/Business Interests

Charitable Gift Annuity – Commuted Payment (CPGA)
Pooled Income Fund (PIF)
Charitable Remainder Unitrust (CRUT)
Charitable Remainder Annuity Trust (CRAT)
Net-Income Charitable Remainder Trust (NICRUT)
Net-Income with Makeup Charitable Remainder Trust (NIMCRUT)
Flip Charitable Remainder Trust (Flip CRT)

Total Category B $ - $ - $ - $ - $ - $ -

Category C: Revocable Future Gifts (reported at face value)

Revocable Future Tender TBD
Cash
Marketable Securities
Artwork and Collectibles
Real Estate
Other Gifts-in-Kind
Hedge Fund Interests
Venture Capital Funds
Closely Held Stock/Business Interests

Bequest Designation/Living Trust Beneficiary Designation
Life Insurance Beneficiary Designation
Revocable Retirement Plan Designation
Commericial Annuity Beneficiary Designation
Perpetual Trusts – Income
Perpetual Trusts – Principal
Revocable Charitable Gift Annuities
Revocable Pooled Income Fund
Revocable Charitable Remainder Trust

Total Category C $ - $ - $ - $ - $ - $ -

Gifts by Tender Type: Detail

TT Name	Prospect Manager	Secondary Manager	Designation (Purpose/Fund)	Gift Structure	Date of Gift	Amount	Possible Gift Structure Types Associated With These Tender Types
Category A: Outright Gifts (reported at face value)							Will/Living Trust Proceeds
Cash							Life Insurance Proceeds
Flintstone, Wilma	Fundraiser 1	Gift Planner 2	New College House	Life Insurance Proceeds	9/10/2010	$ 250,000	Retirement Plan Proceeds (IRA, 401(k), 403(b), etc.)
Prinzi, Ricardo	Gift Planner 1		Unrestricted	Retirement Plan Proceeds	8/14/2010	$ 10,000	Commercial Annuity Proceeds
							Perpetual Trust Proceeds – Income
Marketable Securities							Perpetual Trust Proceeds – Principal
Smith, John	Fundraiser 2	Gift Planner 1	Financial Aid	Will/Living Trust Proceeds	7/21/2010	$ 43,128	Revocable PIF Proceeds
Artwork and Collectibles							Revocable CGA Proceeds
Verde, Maria	Fundraiser 1	Gift Planner 1	Unrestricted	Outright	7/3/2010	$ 2,500,000	Revocable CRT Proceeds
Real Estate							IRA Rollover Proceeds
Jetson, George	Fundraiser 3	Gift Planner 1	Scholarship Endowment	Outright	11/14/2010	$ 400,000	Outright
Other Gifts-in-Kind							
Hedge Fund Interests							
Shipley, David	Fundraiser 2		Unrestricted	Hedge Fund Interest	12/14/2010	$ 850,000	
Venture Capital Funds							
Closely Held Stock/ Business Interests							
Total Category A						$ 4,053,128	

Category B: Irrevocable Future Gifts (reported at face value)

Irrevocable Future Tender TBD

Cash

Marketable Securities
Artwork and Collectibles

Real Estate

Other Gifts-in-Kind

Hedge Fund Interests

Venture Capital Funds
Closely Held Stock/Business Interests

Irrevocable Bequest/Living Trust
    Designation
Irrevocable Life Insurance Beneficiary
    Designation
Irrevocable Retirement Plan Designation
Charitable Gift Annuity – Immediate
    Payment (CGA)
Charitable Gift Annuity – Deferred
    Payment (DCGA)
Charitable Gift Annuity – Flexible
    Payment (FCGA)
Charitable Gift Annuity – Commuted
    Payment (CPCGA)
Pooled Income Fund (PIF)
Charitable Remainder Unitrust (CRUT)
Charitable Remainder Annuity Trust
    (CRAT)
Net-Income Charitable Remainder Trust
    (NICRUT)
Net-Income with Makeup Charitable
    Remainder Trust (NIMCRUT)
Flip Charitable Remainder Trust (Flip
    CRT)

Total Category B

$ -

(continued)

Gifts by Tender Type: Detail (continued)

TT Name	Prospect Manager	Secondary Manager	Designation (Purpose/Fund)	Gift Structure	Date of Gift	Amount	Possible Gift Structure Types Associated With These Tender Types
Category C: Revocable Future Gifts (reported at face value)							
Revocable Future Tender TBD							Bequest Designation/Living Trust
							Beneficiary Designation
Cash							Life Insurance Beneficiary Designation
Marketable Securities							Revocable Retirement Plan Designation
Artwork and Collectibles							Commericial Annuity Beneficiary
							Designation
Real Estate							Perpetual Trusts – Income
Other Gifts-in-Kind							Perpetual Trusts – Principal
Hedge Fund Interests							Revocable Charitable Gift Annuities
Venture Capital Funds							Revocable Pooled Income Fund
Closely Held Stock/Business Interests							Revocable Charitable Remainder Trust
Total Category C						$ -	

Gift Reports By Gift Structure

Gifts Reports By Gift Structure: Five Year

Gift Structure Types	FY07	#	FY08	#	FY09	#	FY10	#	FY11	#	Five Year Total	#	Possible Tender Types Associated With These Gift Structures (do not show on report)
Category A: Outright Gifts (reported at face value)											$ -		
Will/Living Trust Proceeds									$ 43,128	1	$ 43,128	1	Cash
Life Insurance Proceeds									$ 250,000	1	$ 250,000	1	Marketable Securities
Retirement Plan Proceeds (IRA, 401(k), 403(b), etc.)									$ 10,000	1	$ 10,000	1	Artwork and Collectibles
Commericial Annuity Proceeds											$ -		Real Estate
Perpetual Trust Proceeds – Income											$ -		Other Gifts-in-Kind
Perpetual Trust Proceeds – Principal											$ -		Hedge Fund Interests
Revocable PIF Proceeds											$ -		Venture Capital Funds
Revocable CGA Proceeds											$ -		Closely Held Stock/Business
Revocable CRT Proceeds											$ -		Interests
IRA Rollover Proceeds											$ -		
Outright									$ 3,750,000	3	$ 3,750,000		
Total Category A	$ -		$ -		$ -		$ -		$ 4,053,128	6	$ 4,053,128		

Category B: Irrevocable Future Gifts (reported at face value)

Irrevocable Bequest/Living Trust Designation

Irrevocable Life Insurance Beneficiary Designation

Irrevocable Retirement Plan Designation

Charitable Gift Annuity – Immediate Payment (CGA)

Charitable Gift Annuity – Deferred Payment (DCGA)

Charitable Gift Annuity – Flexible Payment (FCGA)

Possible Tender Types:

Irrevocable Future Tender TBD

Cash

Marketable Securities

Artwork and Collectibles

Real Estate

Other Gifts-in-Kind

Hedge Fund Interests
Venture Capital Funds
Closely Held Stock/Business Interests

Charitable Gift Annuity – Commuted Payment (CPCGA)
Pooled Income Fund (PIF)
Charitable Remainder Unitrust (CRUT)
Charitable Remainder Annuity Trust (CRAT)
Net-Income Charitable Remainder Trust (NICRUT)
Net-Income with Makeup Charitable Remainder Trust (NIMCRUT)
Flip Charitable Remainder Trust (Flip CRT)

Total Category B $ - $ - $ - $ - $ -

Category C: Revocable Future Gifts (reported at face value)

Revocable Future Tender TBD
Cash
Marketable Securities
Artwork and Collectibles
Real Estate
Other Gifts-in-Kind
Hedge Fund Interests
Venture Capital Funds
Closely Held Stock/Business Interests

Bequest Designation/Living Trust Beneficiary Designation
Life Insurance Beneficiary Designation
Revocable Retirement Plan Designation
Commericial Annuity Beneficiary Designation
Perpetual Trusts – Income
Perpetual Trusts – Principal
Revocable Charitable Gift Annuities
Revocable Pooled Income Fund
Revocable Charitable Remainder Trust

Total Category C $ - $ - $ - $ - $ -

Gifts Reports By Gift Structure: Detail

Gift Structure Name	Prospect Manager	Secondary Manager	Designation (Purpose/Fund)	Tender Type	Date of Gift	Amount	Possible Tender Types Associated With These Gift Structures
Category A: Outright Gifts (reported at face value)							Cash
Will/Living Trust Proceeds							Marketable Securities
Smith, John	Fundraiser 1	Gift Planner 1	Financial Aid	Marketable Securities	7/21/2010	$ 43,128	Artwork and Collectibles
Life Insurance Proceeds							Real Estate
Flintstone, Wilma	Fundraiser 2	Gift Planner 2	New Building	Cash	9/10/2010	$ 250,000	Other Gifts-in-Kind
Retirement Plan Proceeds (IRA, 401(k), 403(b), etc.)							Hedge Fund Interests
Prinzi, Ricardo	Gift Planner 1		Unrestricted	Cash	8/14/2010	$ 10,000	Venture Capital Funds
Commericial Annuity Proceeds							Closely Held Stock/
							Business Interests
Perpetual Trust Proceeds – Income							
Perpetual Trust Proceeds – Principal							
Revocable PIF Proceeds							
Revocable CGA Proceeds							
Revocable CRT Proceeds							
IRA Rollover Proceeds							
Outright							
Jetson, George	Fundraiser 3	Gift Planner 1	Scholarship Endowment	Real Estate	11/14/2010	$ 400,000	
Shore, David	Fundraiser 1		Unrestricted	Hedge Fund Interest	12/14/2010	$ 850,000	
Verde, Maria	Fundraiser 2	Gift Planner 1	Unrestricted	Artwork and Collectibles	7/3/2010	$ 2,500,000	
Total Category A						**$ 4,053,128**	

Category B: Irrevocable Future Gifts (reported at face value)

Irrevocable Bequest/Living Trust Designation
Irrevocable Life Insurance Beneficiary Designation
Irrevocable Retirement Plan Designation
Charitable Gift Annuity – Immediate Payment (CGA)
Charitable Gift Annuity – Deferred Payment (DCGA)
Charitable Gift Annuity – Flexible Payment (FCGA)
Charitable Gift Annuity – Commuted Payment (CPCGA)
Pooled Income Fund (PIF)
Charitable Remainder Unitrust (CRUT)

Charitable Remainder Annuity Trust (CRAT)
Net-Income Charitable Remainder Trust (NICRUT)
Net-Income with Makeup Charitable Remainder Trust (NIMCRUT)
Flip Charitable Remainder Trust (Flip CRT)

Total Category B

Irrevocable Future Tender TBD
Cash
Marketable Securities
Artwork and Collectibles
Real Estate
Other Gifts-in-Kind
Hedge Fund Interests
Venture Capital Funds
Closely Held Stock/Business Interests

$ -

Category C: Revocable Future Gifts (reported at face value)

Bequest Designation/Living Trust Beneficiary Designation
Life Insurance Beneficiary Designation
Revocable Retirement Plan Designation
Commericial Annuity Beneficiary Designation
Perpetual Trusts – Income
Perpetual Trusts – Principal
Revocable Charitable Gift Annuities
Revocable Pooled Income Fund
Revocable Charitable Remainder Trust

Total Category C

Revocable Future Tender TBD
Cash
Marketable Securities
Artwork and Collectibles
Real Estate
Other Gifts-in-Kind
Hedge Fund Interests
Venture Capital Funds
Closely Held Stock/Business Interests

$ -

Sample Gift Agreement

AGREEMENT TO ESTABLISH THE (NAME OF ENDOWED FUND) AT THE (NAME OF CHARITY)

For the last century, the Name of Charity ("Charity") has thrived in large part due to the philanthropic support of alumni and friends. Many donors have made gifts providing immediate funding to an area of interest. Others have planned for the long-term future through gifts to the Charity's endowment. In order to ensure that donors' gifts are used for the intended purpose, to allow the Charity to plan effectively, and to comply with accounting and auditing requirements, the Charity and its donors execute legally binding gift agreements for commitments of more than $25,000.

The Charity gratefully acknowledges the generosity of [name(s) of donor(s)] ("Donor") who through this Agreement establish the [name of endowed fund] ("Fund"), at the Charity. [Insert language about the donor and his/her motivation for making the gift. For example . . . The Donor has been a longstanding supporter of our mission. Over the years, he has made significant investments in the School of Education because he believes in the unique way that our Charity approaches the education of teachers. Through this scholarship fund, he intends that our Charity will continue to pursue cutting-edge teaching methods and continue to educate up-and-coming teachers on how to implement them.] In order to protect the interests of both the Donor and the Charity, we agree as follows:

1. ***Donor's Commitment:*** The Donor is making a charitable gift of $(amount written numerically) to the Charity, in the form of cash or readily marketable securities ("stocks"), according to the following schedule:

   (January 1, 2008)   ($payment amount written numerically)
   (January 1, 2009)   ($payment amount written numerically)
   (January 1, 2010)   ($payment amount written numerically)
   (January 1, 2011)   ($payment amount written numerically)
   (January 1, 2012)   ($payment amount written numerically)

   Gifts of stock will be valued according to Internal Revenue Service guidelines in effect at the time the stock is transferred to the Charity. Currently, these guidelines value the stock at the average of the high and low trades on the date of transfer to the Charity. As the Charity is relying upon this gift for its planning purposes, the Donor acknowledges that this gift shall be a legally binding obligation of himself and that this Agreement will be governed by New York law.

2. ***Charity's Commitment:*** In recognition of this generous commitment, the Charity will create an endowed fund to be known as the (name of endowed fund). The purpose of the Fund is to provide financial support to (description of endowed fund).

3. ***Management of the Completed Gift:*** The Charity will invest the gift in the (name of endowed fund), which it may pool and manage with its other endowed funds in accordance with regular Charity investment and management policies. Net income from the Fund, as determined by application of the Charity's spending rule policy, as it may be amended from time to time, may be used for any purpose in support of the (name of endowed fund).

4. ***Planning for the Future:***
   a. Endowment gifts are designed to last for all time. However, it is impossible to anticipate how changing circumstances in the future may impact the Charity's ability to comply with all of the provisions of this Agreement. Accordingly, in the event future developments make it impracticable for the Charity to carry out the specific terms of this Agreement, the president of the Charity

shall have the discretion to direct the use of the Fund for a purpose as close as possible to the Donor's original intent.

b. If at any time following approval of a naming, circumstances change substantially so that the continued use of that name may compromise the public trust, the president of the Charity shall have the discretion to remove or rename the Fund.

5. *Recognition:*

a. The Donor will be referred to as (name(s) of donor(s)) in connection with this gift. This contribution may be publicized in donor recognition vehicles produced by the Charity or other entities, including print, spoken broadcast, and/or electronic media; and

b. The Charity will recognize the gift with an appropriate public announcement unless directed otherwise by the Donor.

DONOR

By: _____
    (Name of Donor)

Date:

Title:

THE TRUSTEES OF THE CHARITY

By: _____
    (Name of Authorized Signator)

Date:

Title:

Bibliography

Advisory Board. *What No One Else Can Do: Trustees' Vital Role in Health Care Philanthropy*. Washington, DC (2007).

Bhagat, Vinay, Pam Loeb, and Mark Rovner. *The Next Generation of American Giving: A Study on the Multichannel Preferences and Charitable Habits of Generation Y, Generation X, Baby Boomers, and Matures*. Convio, Edge Research and Sea Change Strategies, March 2010.

Brown, Ronald A. "Practical Ideas for Discussing Family, Wealth and Philanthropy," *Planned Giving Today*, August 2011.

Burg, Bob. *Endless Referal*. New York: McGraw-Hill Companies (1999).

Burk, Penelope. *Donor Centered Fundraising*. US ed. Canada: Burk & Associates (2003).

Burnett, Ken, and George Smith. *Relationship Fundraising*. London: White Lion Unlimited (1992).

Burnett, Ken. *Friendship for Life: Relationship Fundraising in Practice*. London: White Lion Unlimited (1996).

Caldwell, Sam. "Navigating Rough Seas: Why Planned Giving is Moving to the Forefront of Fundraising in This Challenging Economy," Keynote Presentation for Planned Giving Day, Partnership for Philanthropic Planning of Greater Philadelphia, October 26, 2011.

Campbell & Company. Bequest Donors: Demographics and Motivations of Potential and Actual Donors. Indiana. (2007).

Cannon, JD, Garry Curtis, and Marc Lee, CFRE. Registration to Solicit Webinar, Affinity Registration Services, http://www.affinityseminars.com/pgs/seminars/seminar090924.html.

Card, Matt. "Bank of America Merrill Lynch Announces Findings from the 2010 Study of High Net Worth Philanthropy", November 9, 2010. www.philanthropy.iupui.edu/news/2010/11/pr-BankofAmericaStudy.aspx.

Carnegie, Dale. *How to Win Friends And Influence People*. New York: Pocket (1981).

Center on Philanthropy at Indiana University, The 2010 Bank of America Merrill Lynch Study of High Net Worth Philanthropy, Indianapolis, Indiana, November 2010.

Collier, Charles W. *Wealth in Families* (2nd Ed.). Boston: Harvard University (2006).

Covey, Stephen. *Seven Habits of Highly Effective People* (1st Ed.), Free Press (1990).

Cullinan, Tom. "Charitable Bequests." USA: *Planned Giving Today*, 2003.

DeWitt, Brydon M. *The Nonprofit Development Companion*. Hoboken: John Wiley & Sons (2011).

Diefendorf, Monroe M., and Robert S. Madden. *Three Dimensional Wealth*. Locust Valley: 3 Dimensional Wealth (2005).

Dove, Kent E., Alan M. Spears, and Thomas W. Herbert. *Conducting a Successful Major Gifts and Planned Giving Program*. San Francisco: Jossey-Bass (2002).

Esperti, Robert A., Renno L. Peterson, and Jeffrey L. Knapp. *Giving: Philanthropy For Everyone*. Denver: Quantum LLC (2003).

Feldmann, Derrick and Grossnickle, Ted, *Millennial Donors Report 2011*. Johnson Grossnickle and Associates and Achieve (2011), www.millennialdonors.com.

Fidelity Charitable Gift Fund. *Entrepreneurs & Philanthropy: Investing in the Future*. November 2010, page 7, http://www.fidelity.com/inside-fidelity/individual-investing/cgf-entrepreneurs-study.

File, Prince. *The Seven Faces of Philanthropy*. San Francisco: Jossey-Bass (1994).

Fredericks, Laura. *The Ask*. San Francisco: Jossey-Bass (2010).

Franklin, Benjamin. *The Autobiography of Benjamin Franklin*. New York: Russell & Perrin (1939).

Freedman, Phyllis, "Confessions of an Aging Baby Boomer", *Planned Giving Blogger*, July 27, 2011. www.smart-giving.com/plannedgivingblogger.

Freedman, Phyllis, "Sobering Insight for the New Year", *Planned Giving Blogger* January 6, 2011. www.smart-giving.com/plannedgivingblogger.

Fritz, Joanne, New 990 Makes Nonprofit Fundraising Registration Unavoidable, About .Com. http://nonprofit.about.com/od/fundraisingbasics/a/frregistration990.htm?p=1

Gary, Tracy. *Inspired Philanthropy*. 3rd ed . San Francisco: Jossey-Bass (2008).

Gaudiani, Claire. *The Greater Good: How Philanthropy Drives the American Economy and Can Save Capitalism*. New York: Henry Holt and Company, (2003).

Giving USA Foundation (2011). Giving USA 2011: The Annual Report on Philanthropy for the Year 2010. Chicago: Giving USA Foundation.

Gladwell, Malcolm. *The Tipping Point*. Boston: Little, Brown (2002).

Hamilton, Walter. "Many Baby Boomers Don't Plan to Leave Their Children an Inheritance", *Los Angeles Times*, September 5, 2011.

Hill, Catey. "Things Baby Boomers Won't Say", *Smart Money*, November 10, 2011.

Hughes, James E., Jr., *Family Wealth, Keeping It In the Family*, Revised Edition. Princeton: Bloomberg Press (2004).

Johnson, Kevin. *The Power of Legacy and Planned Gifts*. San Francisco: Jossey-Bass (2010).

Katya Andresen, "Extreme Website Makeover: From Ick to Slick,", January 2011, www.fundraising123.org/article/extreme-website-makeover-ick-slick.

Kennedy, Marilyn Moats, "The Extras Xers Want." *Across the Board*, June 1998.

Kinder, George. *The Seven Stages of Money Maturity*. New York: Delacorte (1999).

Lawson, Douglas M. *Volunteering: One Hundred and One Ways You Can Improve The World And Your Life*. San Diego: ALTI (1998).

Lloyd, Robert J. Remember to Say "Thank You". Tidings.org. February 2004.

Loehr, Anne, "How to Speak so Gen X Will Listen," *The Gen Y Code Blog*, December 7, 2010. http://anneloehr.wordpress.com.

Logan, Timothy D., ACFRE, and Dr. James O. Preston. Phoning it In: Prospecting for Planned Gift Leads by Phone, National Conference on Philanthropic Planning, October 14-17 2009.

Maister, David H., Charles H. Green, and Robert M. Galford. *The Trusted Advisor*. New York: FREE (2000).

Mannheim, Karl. *Essays on the Sociology of Knowledge*. London, Routledge (1928).

Meredith, Geoffrey E., Charles D. Schewe, Ph. D. with Janice Karlovich. *Defining Markets, Defining Moments: America's 7 Generational Cohorts, Their Shared Experiences, and Why Businesses Should Care*. New York: Hungry Minds, Inc. (2007).

Mikaelian, Viken, "Seven Proven Steps to Drive Traffic to Your Planned Giving Website, Inbox and Phone," White Paper, 2011.

"Millennials, A Portrait of Generation Next", Pew Research Center, February 2010, page 2. www.pewresearch.org/millennials.

Miree, Kathryn W. *Professional Advisors' Guide to Planned Giving*. 2006 ed . Chicago: CCH INCORPORATED, 2006.

Navarro, Joe, and Marvin Karlins. *What Every Body Is Saying*. New York: HarperCollins (2008).

Nichols, Judith. *Pinpointing Affluence*. Chicago: Precept (1994).

Nierenberg, Andrea R. *Million Dollar Networking*. Herndon: Capital (2005).

Nierenberg, Andrea R. *Savvy Networking*. Herndon: Capital (2007).

Northern Trust. *Wealth in America 2008: Findings from a Survey of Millionaire Households*. Chicago (2008).

Odendahl, Teresa. *Charity Begins at Home: Generosity and Self-Interest Among the Philanthropic Elite*. New York: Basic Books (1990).

O'Leary, Susan. Effective Stewardship and Donor Relations, Charity America. http://charityamerica.com/BackPI.cfm?lft=81&rht=80.

Osborne, Karen. *Creating a Culture of Philanthropy Resulting in Increased Major Giving*. Mt. Kisco, NY: The Osborne Group, Inc. (2005).

Panas, Jerold. *Mega Gifts: Who Gives Them, Who Gets Them*. Medfield: Emerson & Church (2006).

Partnership for Philanthropic Planning. Executive Summary: Guidelines for Reporting and Counting Charitable Gifts. http://www.pppnet.org/pdf/executive-summary2.pdf.

Partnership for Philanthropic Planning. *Planned Giving in the United States 2000: A Survey of Donors*. Indianapolis: Partnership for Philanthropic Planning (2001) www.pppnet.org/resource/donors-survey.html.

Partnership for Philanthropic Planning. Valuation Standards for Charitable Planned Gifts. http://www.pppnet.org/pdf/2009_valuation_standards.pdf.

Prince, Russ Alan, and Karen Maru File. *The Seven Faces of Philanthropy: A New Approach to Cultivating Major Donors*. San Francisco: Jossey-Bass Publishers (1994).

Rosen, Micheal J., and H. F. Lenfest. *Donor-Centered Planned Gift Marketing*. Hoboken: John Wiley & Sons (2011).

Rosenkrantz, Linda. *Telegram!* New York: Henry Holt (2003).

Ross, Walter. *Crusade.* New York: Arbor House (1987).

Rosso, Henry A. *Achieving Excellence in Fundraising*. San Francisco: Jossey-Bass (1991).

Ryder, Norman B. The Cohort as a Concept in the Study of Social Change, reprinted in the *American Sociological Review*, 1965.

Salamon, Julie. *Rambam's Ladder*. New York: Workman (1979).

Sanborn, Mark, and John C. Maxwell. *The Fred Factor*. New York: Waterbrook (2004).

Sargeant, Adrian and Jen Shang. "Identification, Death and Bequest Giving", Report. Association of Fundraising Professionals, September 2008.

Schultz, JD, LLM, Kristen, "Is Your Charity Using Social Media Yet? Why You Can't Afford to Wait", *Crescendo Notes*, Fall 2011.

Schuman and Scott, "Generations and Collective Memories," *American Sociological Review*, 1989, vol. 54.

Schwartz, David J. *The Magic of Thinking Big*. New York: Cornerstone Library (1965).

Seymour, Harold J. *Designs for Fund-Raising*. Rockville: Fund Raising Institute (1988).

Smith, George. *Asking Properly: The Art of Creative Fundraising*. London: White Lion Unlimited (1996).

Spaulding, Tommy. *It's Not Just Who You Know*. New York: Broadway (2010).

Spectrem Group. *Charitable Giving and the Ultra High Net Worth Household: Reaching the Wealthy Donor*. Spectrem Group, 2002.

Stanley, Thomas J., and William D. Danko. *The MIllionaire Next Door*. Marietta: Longstreet (1996).

Stapinski, Helene. Y Not Love? *American Demographics*, February 1999, page 63.

Stelter, Larry and J. Ann Selzer. *Discovering the Secret Giver: Groundbreaking Research on the Behavior of Bequest Givers in America*. The Stelter Company and Selzer & Company, Inc. 2008.

Stern, Gary J. *Marketing Workbook for Nonprofit Organizations, Volume I: Develop the Plan* St. Paul: Wilder Foundation (1990).

Sturtevant, William T. *The Artful Journey: Cultivating and Soliciting the Major Gift*. Chicago: Institutions Press (2004).

"The Future of Charitable Gift Planning: A Report of the NCPG Strategic Directions Taskforce", Journal of Gift planning, Partnership for Philanthropic Planning, Indianapolis, Indiana (2007). http://www.pppnet.org/pdf/NCPGJv11n2s3.pdf.

Tubbs, Stewart L. *A Systems Approach to Small Group Interaction*. 7th ed . New York: McGraw-Hill Companies (1978).

Walton, R. Christopher. The Psychology of Major Gifts, *Fundraising Management* 1999.

Webster's II New College Dictionary. Boston: Houghton Mifflin Company (2001).

Wheeler-Newman, David, IRS Updates Rules for Donors and Grantmakers, http://www.pgdc.com/pgdc/irs-updates-rules-donors-and-grantmakers.

Widmer, Candace, and Susan Houchin. *The Art of Trusteeship*. San Francisco: Jossey-Bass, (2000).

Young, Dorothy. *Touring With Houdini*. Neptune: Penrod (2001).

Zeeb, Rodney C., JD, CWC, and Ryan Zeeb, CWC. *The Elements of Heritage Planning*. Portland, OR: The Heritage Institute, 2010.

Notes

CHAPTER 1

1. *Webster's II New College Dictionary*. Boston: Houghton Mifflin Company. (2001).
2. Franklin, Benjamin, *The Autobiography of Benjamin Franklin*. New York: Russell & Perrin (1939).
3. Partnership for Philanthropic Planning, December 2, 2011, http://www.pppnet .org
4. "The Future of Charitable Gift Planning: A Report of the NCPG Strategic Directions Taskforce", *Journal of Gift Planning,* Partnership for Philanthropic Planning, Indianapolis, IN (2007) http://www.pppnet.org/pdf/NCPGJv11n2s3.pdf.

CHAPTER 2

1. Freedman, Phyllis, "Sobering Insight for the New Year", *Planned Giving Blogger,* January 6, 2011, www.smart-giving.com/plannedgivingblogger.
2. There is a significant difference in this analysis than the May 2008 study by the Center on Philanthropy at Indiana University (CPIU) titled "Generational Differences in Charitable Giving and in Motivations for Giving." The CPIU study investigated whether there were different motivations for charitable giving among generational cohorts, particularly after controlling for income, marital status, race, education, region, religious attendance, and age of youngest child. This analysis focuses on how the different shared values of each generational cohort suggest that charities should approach that cohort about charitable giving opportunities.
3. Meredith, Geoffrey E., Charles D. Schewe, Ph.D. with Janice Karlovich, *Defining Markets, Defining Moments: America's 7 Generational Cohorts, Their Shared Experiences, and Why Businesses Should Care,* Hungry Minds, Inc., 2007, page17.
4. Mannheim, Karl. *Essays on the Sociology of Knowledge*. London: Routledge (1928).

5. Ryder, Norman B., The Cohort as a Concept in the Study of Social Change, reprinted in the *American Sociological Review,* 1965, p. 843-861.

6. Generations and Collective Memories, Schuman and Scott, *American Sociological Review,* 1989, vol. 54, pages 359—381.

7. Meredith, Geoffrey E., Charles D. Schewe, Ph.D. with Janice Karlovich. *Defining Markets, Defining Moments: America's 7 Generational Cohorts, Their Shared Experiences, and Why Businesses Should Care.* New York: Hungry Minds, Inc. (2007) pages 31-33.

8. Ibid, page 62.

9. Ibid, page 58.

10. Ibid, page 69.

11. Ibid, page 86.

12. Ibid, page 94.

13. Ibid, pages 37-38; 104-109.

14. Ibid, pages 104, 111.

15. Ibid, page 38, 136-137.

16. Ibid, page 138.

17. Ibid, page 149.

18. Burk, Penelope. *Donor Centered Fundraising.* Chicago: Cygnus Applied Research, Inc. (2003) pages 31-33.

19. Hamilton, Walter. Many Baby Boomers Don't Plan to Leave Their Children an Inheritance, *Los Angeles Times,* September 5, 2011.

20. Hill, Catey, "Things Baby Boomers Won't Say", *Smart Money,* November 10, 2011.

21. Ibid.

22. "Millennials, A Portrait of Generation Next", Pew Research Center, February 2010, page 2, www.pewresearch.org/millennials.

23. Meredith, Geoffrey E., Charles D. Schewe, Ph.D. with Janice Karlovich. *Defining Markets, Defining Moments: America's 7 Generational Cohorts, Their Shared Experiences, and Why Businesses Should Care.* New York: Hungry Minds, Inc. (2007) page 157.

24. Ibid, pages 38, 161-163.

25. Ibid, page 165.

26. Ibid, pages 166-167.

27. Ibid, page 170.

28. Ibid, pages 180-183.

29. Ibid, page 187.

30. Ibid, page 185.

31. Ibid, page 38.

32. Ibid, page 193.

33. Ibid, page 189.

34. Ibid, page 196.

35. Kennedy, Marilyn Moats. "The Extras Xers Want." *Across the Board,* June 1998, page 51.

36. Loehr, Anne, How to Speak so Gen X Will Listen, *The Gen Y Code Blog,* December 7, 2010, http://anneloehr.wordpress.com.

37. Meredith, Geoffrey E., Charles D. Schewe, Ph.D. with Janice Karlovich. *Defining Markets, Defining Moments: America's 7 Generational Cohorts, Their Shared Experiences, and Why Businesses Should Care.* New York: Hungry Minds, Inc. (2007) page 213.

38. Ibid, page 209.

39. "Millennials, A Portrait of Generation Next", Pew Research Center, February 2010, page 2, www.pewresearch.org/millennials.

40. Ibid, page 71.

41. Meredith, Geoffrey E., Charles D. Schewe, Ph.D. with Janice Karlovich, *Defining Markets, Defining Moments: America's 7 Generational Cohorts, Their Shared Experiences, and Why Businesses Should Care.* New York: Hungry Minds, Inc. (2007) pages 214-215.

42. "Millennials, A Portrait of Generation Next", Pew Research Center, February 2010, page 1, www.pewresearch.org/millennials.

43. Meredith, Geoffrey E., Charles D. Schewe, Ph.D. with Janice Karlovich. *Defining Markets, Defining Moments: America's 7 Generational Cohorts, Their Shared Experiences, and Why Businesses Should Care.* New York: Hungry Minds, Inc. (2007) page 217.

44. Helene Stapinski. Y Not Love? *American Demographics,* February 1999, page 63.

45. Feldmann, Derrick and Grossnickle, Ted, *Millennial Donors Report 2011,* Johnson Grossnickle and Associates and Achieve, 2011, www.millennialdonors.com, page 10.

46. Ibid, page 15.

47. Freedman, Phyllis. Confessions of an Aging Baby Boomer. *Planned Giving Blogger,* July 27, 2011, www.smart-giving.com/plannedgivingblogger.

CHAPTER 3

1. Caldwell, Sam. "Navigating Rough Seas: Why Planned Giving is Moving to the Forefront of Fundraising in This Challenging Economy" Keynote Presentation for Planned Giving Day, Partnership for Philanthropic Planning of Greater Philadelphia, October 26, 2011.

CHAPTER 4

1. Stern, Gary J. *Marketing Workbook for Nonprofit Organizations, Volume I: Develop the Plan.* St. Paul: Wilder Foundation (1990), page 32.

2. Osborne, Karen. *Creating a Culture of Philanthropy Resulting in Increased Major Giving.* Mt. Kisco: The Osborne Group, Inc. (2005).

3. Nierenberg, Andrea R. *Million Dollar Networking.* Herndon: Capital Books, Inc. (2005).

4. Campbell & Company. *Bequest Donors: Demographics and Motivations of Potential and Actual Donors.* Indiana (2007).
5. Giving USA Foundation. *Giving USA 2011: The Annual Report on Philanthropy for the Year 2010.* Chicago: Giving USA Foundation (2011), page 50.
6. The Advisory Board. *What No One Else Can Do: Trustees' Vital Role in Health Care Philanthropy.* Washington, DC (2007), page 3.
7. Northern Trust. *Wealth in America 2008: Findings from a Survey of Millionaire Households.* Chicago (2008).
8. Tarnside Consulting. Curve of Involvement. Cumbria, UK (2005).

CHAPTER 5

1. Partnership for Philanthropic Planning, September 2, 2011, http://www.pppnet .org/pdf/NCPGJv11n2s3.pdf, page 6.
2. The Stelter Company, September 22, 2011, www.stelter.com/pdfs/SecretGiver .pdf.
3. Partnership for Philanthropic Planning, September 2, 2011, www.pppnet.org.
4. Advisors in Philanthropy, September 12, 2011, http://www.advisorsinphilan- thropy.org.
5. Spectrem Group. *Financial Planning Among America's Wealthy.* Spectrem Group (2001).
6. Spectrem Group. *Trends and Opportunities in the Affluent Market.* Spectrem Group (2002).
7. Partnership for Philanthropic Planning, September 12, 2011, http://www .pppnet.org/ethics/model_standards.html.
8. Association of Fundraising Professionals, September 12, 2011, http://www .afpnet.org/files/ContentDocuments/CodeOfEthicsLong.pdf

CHAPTER 6

1. Card, Matt, "Bank of America Merrill Lynch Announces Findings from the 2010 Study of High Net Worth Philanthropy", November 9, 2010, www.philanthropy .iupui.edu/news/2010/11/pr-BankofAmericaStudy.aspx.
2. Dove, Kent E., Alan M. Spears, and Thomas W. Herbert. *Conducting a Suc- cessful Major Gifts and Planned Giving Program.* San Francisco: Jossey-Bass (2002).
3. Spectrem Group. *Charitable Giving and the Ultra High Net Worth Household: Reach- ing the Wealthy Donor.,* Spectrem Group (2002).
4. Ibid.
5. Ibid.
6. Center on Philanthropy at Indiana University. *The 2010 Bank of America Merrill Lynch Study of High Net Worth Philanthropy,* Indianapolis, Indiana, November 2010, page 39.

7. Spectrem Group. *Charitable Giving and the Ultra High Net Worth Household: Reaching the Wealthy Donor.* Spectrem Group (2002).

8. Ibid.

9. Center on Philanthropy at Indiana Universit., *The 2010 Bank of America Merrill Lynch Study of High Net Worth Philanthropy,* Indianapolis, Indiana, November 2010, page 7.

10. Odendahl, Teresa. *Charity Begins at Home: Generosity and Self-Interest Among the Philanthropic Elite.* New York: Basic Books (1990).

11. Prince, Russ Alan, and Karen Maru File. *The Seven Faces of Philanthropy: A New Approach to Cultivating Major Donors.* San Francisco: Jossey-Bass Publishers (1994).

12. Tubbs, Stewart L. *A System Approach to Small Group Interaction (Seventh Ed.).* New York: McGraw Hill (2001) page 106-107.

13. Salamon, Julie. *Rambam's Ladder.* New York: Workman Publishing (2003).

14. Diefendorf, Monroe M., Jr. and Robert Sterling Madden, *3 Dimensional Wealth,* 3 Dimensional Wealth Publishing, 2005, page 63.

15. Center on Philanthropy at Indiana University. *The 2010 Bank of America Merrill Lynch Study of High Net Worth Philanthropy.* Indianapolis, Indiana, November 2010, page 47.

16. Ibid, page 48.

17. Ibid, pages 25-26, 33-34.

18. Ibid, page 40.

19. Fidelity Charitable Gift Fund, *Entrepreneurs & Philanthropy: Investing in the Future,* November 2010, page 7. http://www.fidelity.com/inside-fidelity/individual-investing/cgf-entrepreneurs-study.

20. Ibid.

21. Ibid.

22. Center on Philanthropy at Indiana University. *The 2010 Bank of America Merrill Lynch Study of High Net Worth Philanthropy,* Indianapolis. Indiana, November 2010, pages 70-71.

23. Ibid, page 72.

24. Ibid, page 69.

25. Ibid, pages 49-51.

26. Ibid, pages 16-18.

27. Ibid, page 18.

28. Hughes, James E. Jr. *Family Wealth, Keeping It In the Family, Revised Edition.* Princeton: Bloomberg Press (2004).

29. Collier, Charles W. *Wealth in Families (2nd Ed.).* Boston: Harvard University (2006).

30. Brown, Ronald A. "Practical Ideas for Discussing Family, Wealth and Philanthropy." *Planned Giving Today,* August 2011.

31. Gary, Tracy. *Inspired Philanthropy: Your Step by Step Guide to Creating a Giving Plan and Leaving a Legacy (Third Ed.).* San Francisco: Jossey-Bass (2008).

32. Zeeb, Rodney C., JD, CWC, and Ryan Zeeb, CWC. *The Elements of Heritage Planning.* The Heritage Institute (2010).

33. Covey, Stephen. *Seven Habits of Highly Effective People (1st Ed.)*. New York: Free Press (1990).

34. Tubbs, Stewart L. *A System Approach to Small Group Interaction (Seventh Ed.)*. New York: McGraw Hill (2001) page 218-219.

35. Ibid, page 219.

CHAPTER 7

1. Sturtevant, William T. *The Artful Journey: Cultivating and Soliciting the Major Gift*. Chicago: Institutions Press (2004).

2. Walton, R. Christopher. "The Psychology of Major Gifts." *Fundraising Management*, 1999.

CHAPTER 8

1. Partnership for Philanthropic Planning, November 21, 2011, www.pppnet.org.

2. Convio, Inc., November 19, 2011. www.convio.com/nextgen.

3. The Stelter Company, September 22, 2011, www.stelter.com/pdfs/SecretGiver .pdf.

4. Partnership for Philanthropic Planning, September 2, 2011, http://www.pppnet .org/pdf/NCPGJv11n2s3.pdf, page 6.

5. Johnson Grassnickle and Associates and Achieve, November 19, 2011, www.mil-lennialdonors.com.

6. Association of Fundraising Professionals, November 17, 2011, www.afpnet.org/ audiences/reportsresearchdetail.cfm?itemnumber=4455.

CHAPTER 9

1. Sargeant, Adrian, and Jen Shang. "Identification, Death and Bequest Giving", Report. Association of Fundraising Professionals, September 2008, pages 34-42.

2. Ibid, pages 34-35.

3. Ibid, pages 35-39.

4. Ibid, page 42.

5. To see the complete LEAVE A LEGACY® campaign, visit: www.pppnet.org/ council_resources/lal-campaign-materials.html

6. Sargeant and Shang. "Identification, Death and Bequest Giving", page 43.

7. Burk, Penelope. *Donor Centered Fundraising* (Cygnus Applied Research, Inc., 2003), pages 31-33.

8. Sargeant and Shang, "Identification, Death and Bequest Giving", page 44.

9. Ibid, page 45.

10. Rosen, Michael. *Donor-Centered Planned Gift Marketing*. Hoboken: John Wiley & Sons (2011), pages 127-128.

11. Ibid, page 124, quoting Larry Stelter, president, The Stelter Company.
12. Andresen, Katya. "Extreme Website Makeover: From Ick to Slick", January 2011, www.fundraising123.org/article/extreme-website-makeover-ick-slick.
13. Mikaelian, Viken. "Seven Proven Steps to Drive Traffic to Your Planned Giving Website, Inbox and Phone," White Paper, 2011.
14. Schultz, Kristen, JD, LLM. "Is Your Charity Using Social Media Yet? Why You Can't Afford to Wait." *Crescendo Notes*, Fall 2011.
15. Ibid.

Chapter 10

1. Caldwell, Sam. *Navigating Rough Seas: Why Planned Giving is Moving to the Forefront of Fundraising in This Challenging Economy,* Keynote Presentation for Planned Giving Day, Partnership for Philanthropic Planning of Greater Philadelphia, October 26, 2011.

Chapter 11

1. Partnership for Philanthropic Planning. *Planned Giving in the United States 2000: A Survey of Donors.* Indianapolis: Partnership for Philanthropic Planning, 2001, www.pppnet.org/resource/donors-survey.html.
2. Rosen, Michael J. *Donor-Centered Planned Gift Marketing.* Hoboken: John Wiley and Sons (2011), pages 199-200.
3. Caldwell, Sam. *Navigating Rough Seas: Why Planned Giving is Moving to the Forefront of Fundraising in this Challenging Economy.* Partnership for Philanthropic Planning of Greater Philadelphia, October 26, 2011.
4. Ibid.
5. Logan, Timothy D., ACFRE, and Dr. James O. Preston. *Phoning it In: Prospecting for Planned Gift Leads by Phone,* National Conference on Philanthropic Planning. October 14-17, 2009.

Chapter 12

1. Burk, Penelope. *Donor Centered Fundraising.* Chicago: Cygnus Applied Research, Inc. (2003), page 31.
2. Ibid, page 36.
3. Sturtevant, William T. *The Artful Journey: Cultivating and Soliciting the Major Gift.* Chicago: Institutions Press (2004), page 194.
4. Burk, Penelope. *Donor Centered Fundraising.* Chicago: Cygnus Applied Research, Inc. (2003), page 111.
5. Panas, Jerold. *Mega Gifts: Who Gives Them, Who Gets Them.* Medfield: Emerson & Church (2006).
6. Webster's II New College Dictionary., Boston: Houghton Mifflin Company (2001).

a

7. Rosso, Henry A. and Associates. *Achieving Excellence in Fund Raising.* San Francisco: Jossey-Bass Publishers (1991).
8. O'Leary, Susan. *Effective Stewardship and Donor Relations.* Charity America, http://charityamerica.com/BackPI.cfm?lft=81&rht=80.
9. Lloyd, Robert J. *Remember to Say "Thank You".* Tidings.org. February 2004.
10. Rosenkrantz, Linda. *Telegram!.* New York: Henry Holt & Co. (2003).

CHAPTER 13

1. Rosso, Henry A. and Associates. *Achieving Excellence in Fund Raising.* San Francisco: Jossey-Bass Publishers (1991), page 145.
2. Sturtevant, William T. *The Artful Journey: Cultivating and Soliciting the Major Gift.* Chicago: Institutions Press (2004), page 207.

CHAPTER 14

1. Executive Summary: Guidelines for Reporting and Counting Charitable Gifts, Partnership for Philanthropic Planning, http://www.pppnet.org/pdf/executive-summary2.pdf, page 4.
2. Ibid.
3. Valuation Standards for Charitable Planned Gifts, Partnership for Philanthropic Planning, http://www.pppnet.org/pdf/2009_valuation_standards.pdf
4. Valuation Standards for Charitable Planned Gifts, Partnership for Philanthropic Planning, http://www.pppnet.org/pdf/2009_valuation_standards.pdf, pages 2-3.
5. Higher Education Price Index, The Common Fund, http://www.commonfund.org/CommonfundInstitute/HEPI/Pages/default.aspx
6. Valuation Standards for Charitable Planned Gifts, Partnership for Philanthropic Planning, http://www.pppnet.org/pdf/2009_valuation_standards.pdf, page 17.
7. For the formulas for other types of gifts, visit http://www.pppnet.org/pdf/2009_valuation_standards.pdf.

CHAPTER 15

1. Cannon, Gary Curtis and Marc Lee, Affinity Fundraising Seminars, November 9, 2011, http://www.affinityseminars.com/pgs/seminars/seminar090924.html.
2. Fritz, Joanne, *New 990 Makes Nonprofit Fundraising Registration Unavoidable,* About.Com, November 11, 2011, http://nonprofit.about.com/od/fundraising-basics/a/frregistration990.htm?p=1.
3. The authors do not endorse particular providers; this list is included for the convenience of the reader without guarantees about their work product.
4. The authors do not endorse particular providers; this list is included for the convenience of the reader without guarantees about their work product.

5. The authors do not endorse particular providers; this list is included for the convenience of the reader without guarantees about their work product.
6. Wheeler-Newman, David, *IRS Updates Rules for Donors and Grantmakers,* November 11, 2011, http://www.pgdc.com/pgdc/irs-updates-rules-donors-and-grantmakers

EPILOGUE

1. Young, Dorothy. *Touring With Houdini.* Neptune: Penrod (2001).
2. Schwartz, David J. *The Magic of Thinking Big.* New York: Cornerstone Library (1965).

APPENDIX I

1. With thanks to the many charities that submitted their ideas through LinkedIn and Gift-Pl.

About the Authors

BRIAN M. SAGRESTANO, JD, CFRE

Brian is the president and founder of Gift Planning Development, LLC, a full-service gift planning consulting firm. He provides gift planning services to a wide range of charitable clients from national organizations focused on high-end philanthropic planning to local charities seeking to start new gift planning programs using his Gift Planning Essentials and Planned Giving In a Box® programs. Some of his clients include the University of Notre Dame, Temple University, Create a Jewish Legacy, Harmony Foundation, Children's Hospital of Philadelphia, and Delaware Art Museum. Prior to starting GPD, he spent 12 years as a charitable gift planner, directing the gift planning programs for the University of Pennsylvania, Middlebury College, and Meridian Health Affiliated Foundations.

Brian is a nationally sought-after speaker on gift planning topics and has presented at the National Conference on Philanthropic Planning, the National Conference on Planned Giving, the Association of Fundraising Professionals (AFP) International Conference, the American Council on Gift Annuities Conference, and the Crescendo Practical Planned Giving Conference, as well as at many local and regional conferences around the country. He has taught thousands of fundraisers, professional advisors, board members, and philanthropists how to use a donor-centered approach to integrate philanthropic goals with tax, estate, and financial planning.

Brian is a past board member of the Partnership for Philanthropic Planning (PPP), the Gift Planning Council of New Jersey and PPP of Greater Philadelphia, as well as a past member of the editorial board of the *Journal of Gift Planning*. Brian has been a contributor to *Planned Giving*

Today, Planned Giving Mentor, Plannedgiving.com, and *Planned Giving Tomor-row* and been cited in numerous publications, including *CASE Currents* and the *Chronicle of Philanthropy,* among others.

An honors graduate of both Cornell University and Notre Dame Law School, Brian lives with his wife and children in New Hartford, New York, the scenic gateway to the Adirondack Mountains. In his off hours, Brian sings with the Mohawk Valley Chapter of the Barbershop Harmony Society, an internationally ranked barbershop chorus, as well as his local church choir. He also likes to spend time outdoors, hiking, canoeing, kayaking, and skiing in the Adirondack Park.

To learn more about GPD or to share your thoughts with Brian, visit www.giftplanningdevelopment.com or e-mail brian@giftplanningdevelopment.com.

ROBERT E. WAHLERS, MS, CFRE

Robert is the senior director of development and gift planning for Meridian Health Affiliated Foundations where he oversees the gift planning program for the six hospitals in the Meridian Health System and the development program for Jersey Shore University Medical Center and K. Hovnanian Children's Hospital. Over his more than 20-year career, Robert has worked as a professional advisor in the financial and estate planning field and in the nonprofit sector with the Boy Scouts of America, the American Cancer Society, Virtua Foundation, and now Meridian Health. Robert learned early on the value of developing relationships with professional advisors and honed those skills while with the American Cancer Society where he saw how philanthropic planning can be an asset for both the donor and the charity. A speaker to audiences of 5 to 5,000, Robert has presented at such conferences as the National Conference on Philanthropic Planning, the National Conference on Planned Giving, the Association of Fundraising Professionals (AFP) International Conference, the Boy Scouts of America All Hands Conference, and the American Cancer Society Distinguished Gifts Conference as well as several regional and local conferences.

Robert is an honors graduate with a Master of Science degree in Human Development & Leadership with a concentration in Nonprofit Management from Murray State University and a Bachelor of Arts degree in Psychology from Muhlenberg College. He has been published in *Planned*

Giving Today and has been cited in the *Nonprofit Times* and *Advancing Philanthropy*, among others. Robert serves on the faculty at Columbia University in their Masters of Fundraising Management Program.

He is a national board member with the Partnership for Philanthropic Planning (PPP) and is active on several Association of Fundraising Professional Committees and serves as the Chairman of the Education Advisory Committee for the AFP International Conference. Robert served on the boards of the Gift Planning Council of New Jersey and the Association of Fundraising Professionals—New Jersey Chapter, including a two year term as president in 2008–2009. Robert is also active as a 32nd degree York Rite and Scottish Rite Mason and Shriner.

When not working, Robert spends time with his wife and two children at their home at the Jersey Shore or on the Inner Banks of North Carolina. He also enjoys racing wooden sailboats as part of the Barnegat Bay Yacht Racing Association and maintains a studio for illustration and oil painting.

Index